BEYOND TATTOO

Art Direction by Samuel Ratcliffe.

Text by Johannes van Castrum
©Johannes van Castrum 2013

Published in 2013 by Graffito Books Ltd, 32 Great Sutton Street, London EC1V 0NB, UK
www.graffbooks.co.uk
© Graffito Books Ltd, 2013.
ISBN 978-09560284-7-1
All rights reserved. No part of this publication may be reproduced, in any form whatsoever, without prior written permission from the Publisher.

The information in this book is true and complete to the best of our knowledge. All recommendations are made without any guarantee on the part of the author or publisher, who also disclaim any liability incurred with the use of this data, or specific details. This publication has been prepared solely by the Publisher and is not approved or licensed by any other entity. We recognize that some words or terms are the property of the trademark holder. We use them for identification purposes only. This is not an official publication.

All images in this book have been reproduced with the knowledge and the prior consent of the artists concerned, and no responsibility is accepted by Publisher, Printer or Producer for any infringement of copyright, or otherwise, arising from the contents of this publication. Every effort has been made to ensure that credits accurately comply with the information supplied.

British Library cataloguing-in-publication data:
A catalogue record of this book is available at the British Library.

Printed in China.

BEYOND TATTOO

Allan Graves

GRAFFITO

CONTENTS

Introduction
Alted ~ 8
Ariel 7 ~ 12
Armourd Soul ~ 16
Barthez ~ 20
Burlton ~ 24
Campise ~ 28
Castaño ~ 32
Clarke ~ 36
Collins ~ 40
Conlon ~ 44
Davis ~ 50
de Sabe ~ 54
Difa ~ 60
du Congo ~ 66
El Carlo ~ 72
Enfruns ~ 78
Gaffron ~ 82
Ganji ~ 86
Giant ~ 92
Graves ~ 98
João ~ 104
Jondix ~ 108

Jørgensen ～ 112

Kezam ～ 116

Kyle ～ 120

Monga ～ 126

Montez ～ 132

Olive ～ 136

Reinke ～ 140

Rico ～ 144

Robinson ～ 148

Rotor ～ 152

Sento ～ 158

Serra ～ 164

Sinnes ～ 168

Smith ～ 172

Tonelli ～ 178

Turyanskiy ～ 182

Uncle Allan ～ 188

Von Lucky ～ 192

Walkin ～ 196

Xico ～ 200

Appendix

A note on title style in *Beyond Tattoo*

In the artist listings that follow we indicate, below the artist's name:

Originally from / Now working in.

Where the artist is still working in their state or country of origin, we will just list one location.

For the USA we use the abbreviations for US states, so for instance, CA for California, NM for New Mexico, OH for Ohio and so on.

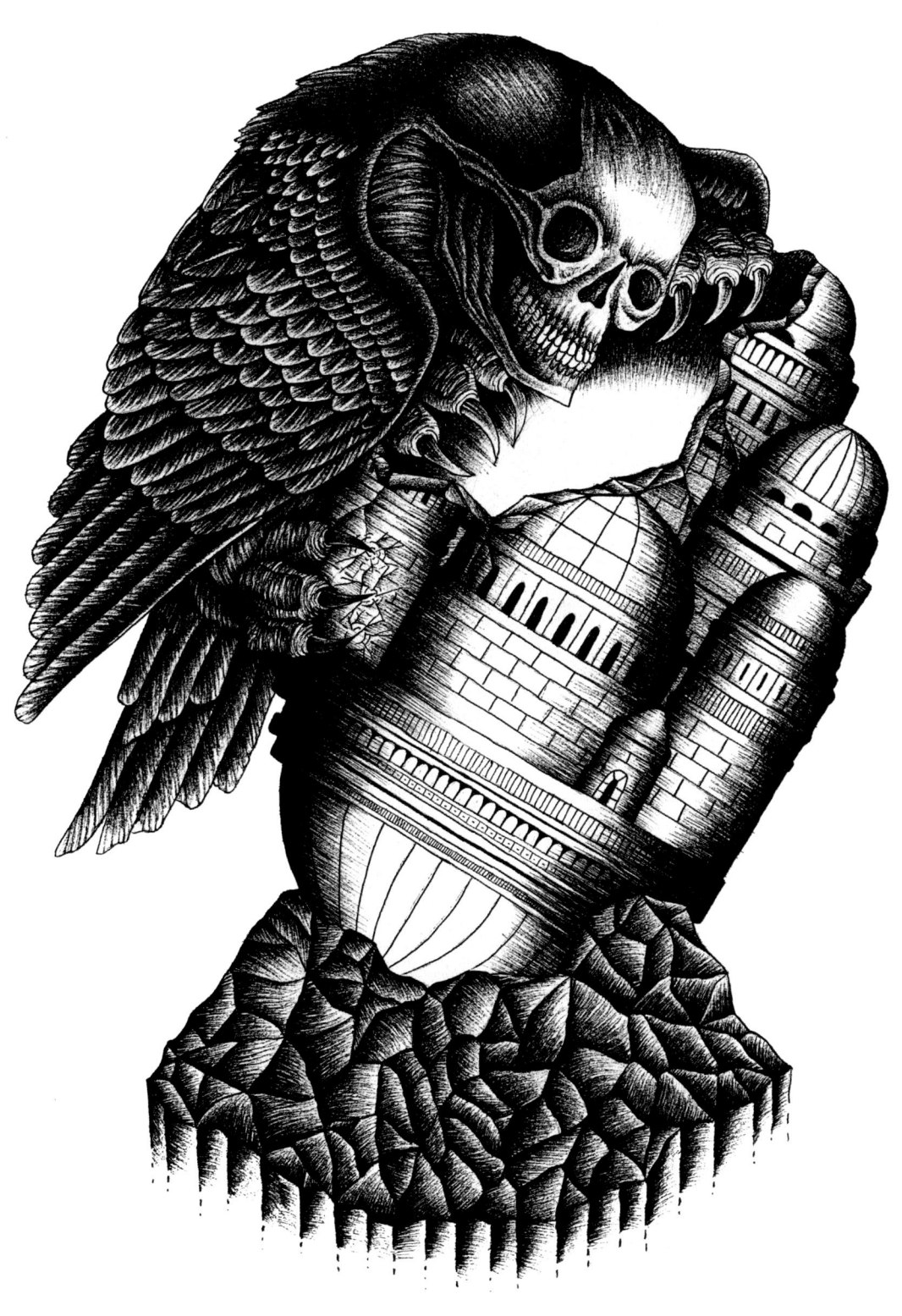

ABOVE: *The Crow and the Church*.
Pen and ink on paper. By El Carlo.

INTRODUCTION

The ancient and intriguing art of tattoo finds itself today at a pinnacle of global popularity. A custom once practiced by tribespeople across the world and then popularised by Western sailors on voyages of exploration is now the subject of books, magazines, websites, blogs and, recently, reality and documentary television shows. Due to the popularity of such shows as *L.A. Ink* and *Miami Ink,* tattooists such as Kat Von D are now household names. Numerous magazines are published worldwide every week showcasing thousands of practioners of the art. Add to that list the massive presence of tattoo on the Internet and tattooing is available to almost everyone.

The public's seemingly insatiable apetite for celebrity culture has also fueled the popularity of the art. As a tattooist myself, I can testify to the immense impact someone of the renown of David Beckham has on tattooing when his latest piece is revealed in the media. Tattoo shops will immediately be contacted by people wanting to emulate their favourite star's inked artwork.

When tattooing started to become popular at the start of the 20th Century with members of the armed forces and more generally the working classes (I say this with respect), most of the designs were single-image pieces depicting similar themes. They featured military imagery, fair maidens and buxom wenches, or love tokens such as the iconic pierced heart, entwined with a scroll with a sweetheart's name. Mum and Dad would often feature, probably to limit the potential disapproval to the tattoo!

Things continued along their traditional path until the mid-'70s, when tattooing spawned a group of artists, predominantly, but not exclusively, from North America's West Coast. Leo Zulueta, Bob Roberts, Mike Malone, Greg Irons and Jack Rudy were to cut a swathe through existing ideas of what constituted the art of tattoo. They were smashing some of the barriers that, it's fair to say, were holding back the art of tattooing. At the head of this 'tattoo bulldozer' was Don Ed Hardy. Don, latterly better known for his iconic clothing designs, was then a visionary who saw the potential tattoo had as an art and how much more could be achieved through the medium. Through his publishing arm he issued the ground-breaking *Tattoo Time* series of journals along with various other art and tattoo related publications. As a result the interest in tattoos grew with more and more clients seeking designs which steered away from the stereotypical images of old-time flash. With this interest came new challenges, which tattooists had to meet.

Simultaneously with tattoo's growing popularity, tattoo equipment became more readily available and the ancient techniques of tattooing became a little less secret. The Internet became a major source of information and inspiration. A host of new artists entered the trade, many bringing an art-school education and fresh ideas. Artists working in different media were entering the world of tattoo and in turn their influence got many tattooists turning their hand to art.

It is the brilliant results of this crossover that *Beyond Tattoo* documents and celebrates: tattooists creating remarkable works away from needle and ink on human skin. As revealed within, it is a global phenomenon and the works within use all manner of media, from pencil to ink on paper, acrylics to oils on board and canvas, digital artworks to screenprints.

The incredible creativity within will, I am sure, be of great interest to tattooed fans, tattooed people and tattoo artists themselves. It goes beyond that however. This is an art form which, as many prestigious galleries around the world are realising, will in addition be fascinating to anyone wishing to be across one of the most inspiring aspects of the contemporary art scene.

Lal Hardy, London.

ALTED

SPAIN / LONDON, UK.

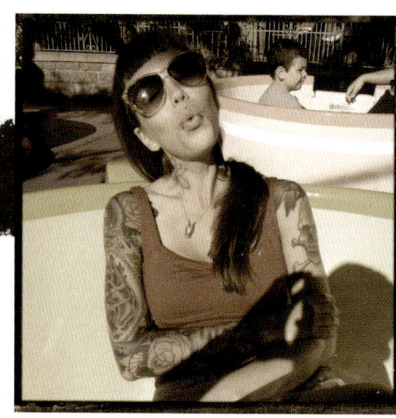

"When I was 15 a friend of my sister's who was a London-based piercer, saw my drawing and suggested I give tattooing a go. I thought he was kidding, but went ahead and loved it. The moment I turned 16 I moved to London and chased down an apprenticeship," says Inma of her beginnings as a tattoo artist. She eventually found her start at a shop in Camden but "none of it was easy. Everyone has their own way of working and I had to learn a lot through trial and error; when I found what worked for me I also found my confidence." A year into tattooing she decided to broaden her skills and took a mixed media course at Westminster University but, whilst she met some great people there, it didn't impact her art much. Tattooing has influenced her painting and drawing far more "and for the better; now I mainly use pencil colours and markers: it's a lot more immediate, no second chances as in oil painting. I find that anything I paint now would also make a great tattoo, as I'm far more aware of contrasts and outlines." Today Inma works at the renowned London tattoo studio, The Family Business. Most of the artworks she creates are for her clients, although "I also spend a lot of time at the drawing table, making art for my own pleasure." When she needs inspiration it's "anything that catches my eye; if I don't know where to start, then I'll go to classic art or art nouveau for inspiration."

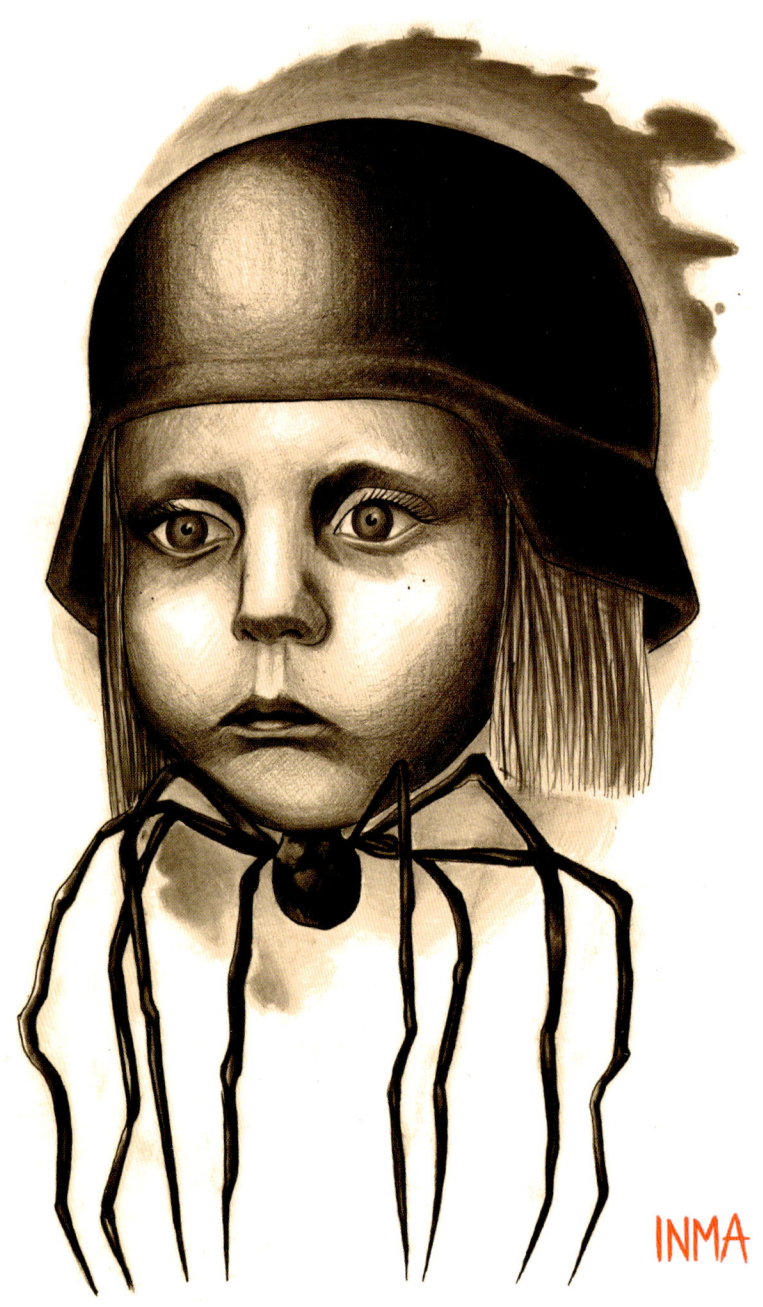

RIGHT: *Spider*. Graphite on paper.
FAR RIGHT: *Gypsy*. Graphite on paper.
OVERLEAF: *Unplugged*. Pen and ink, markers and graphite on paper.

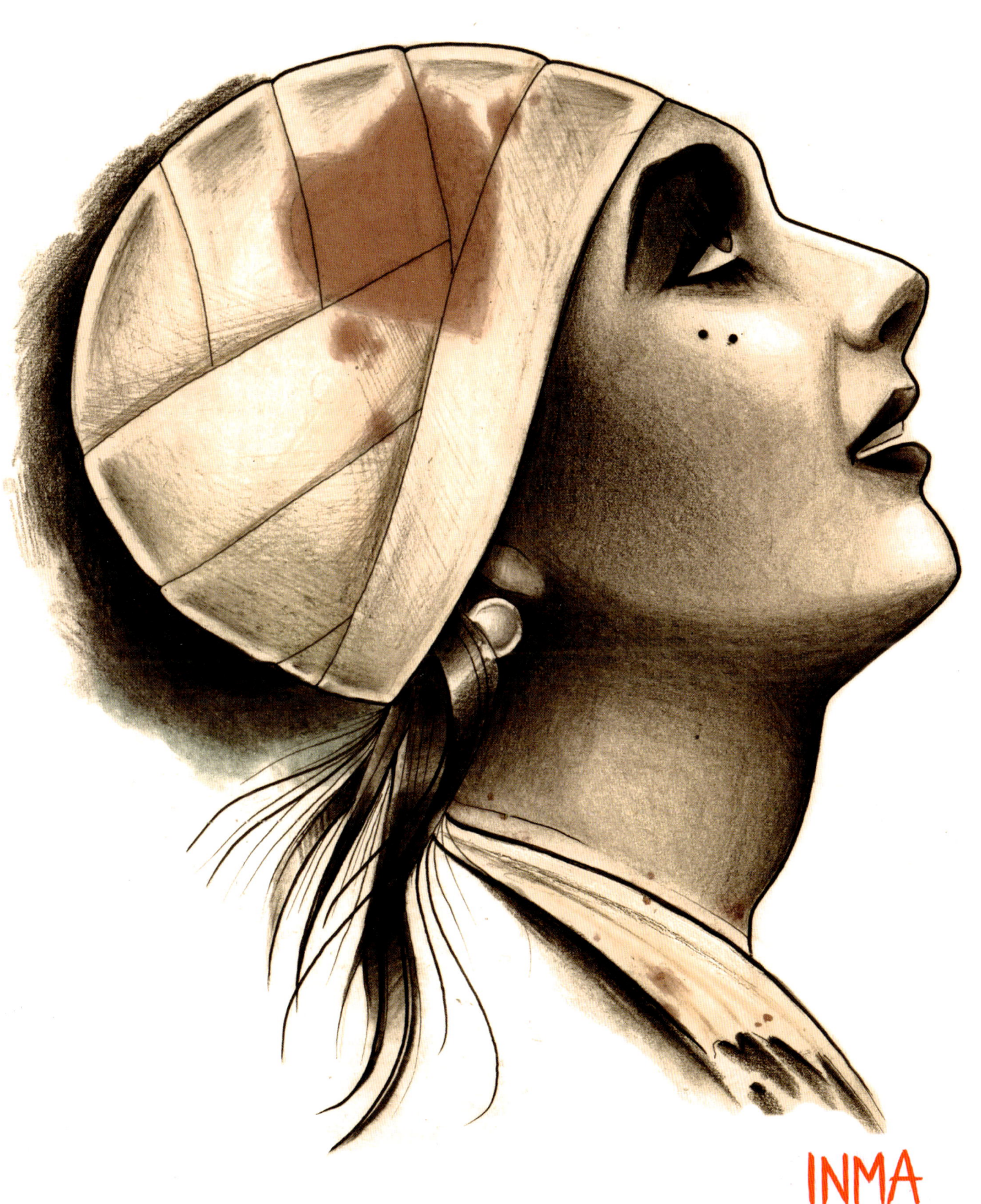

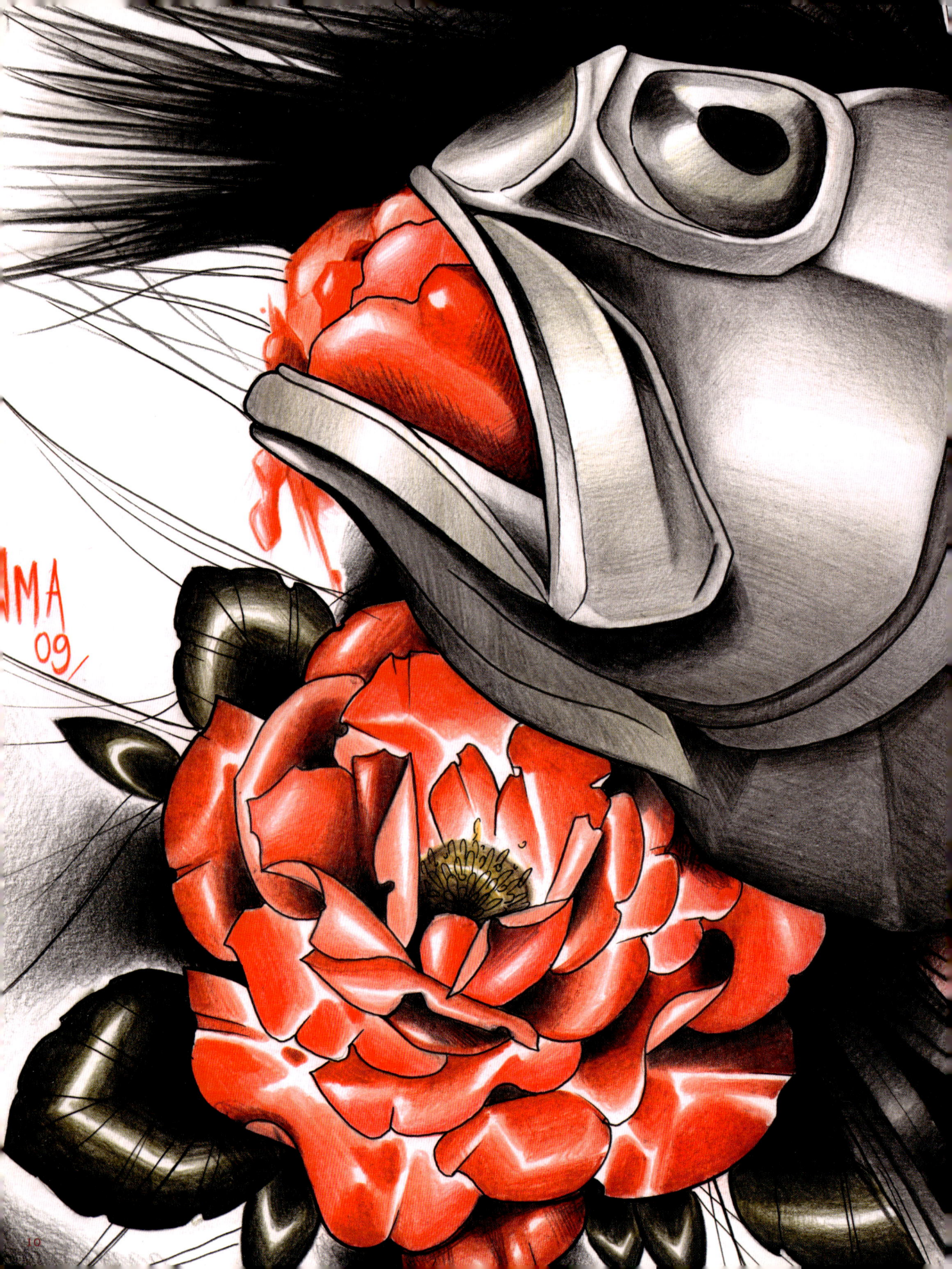

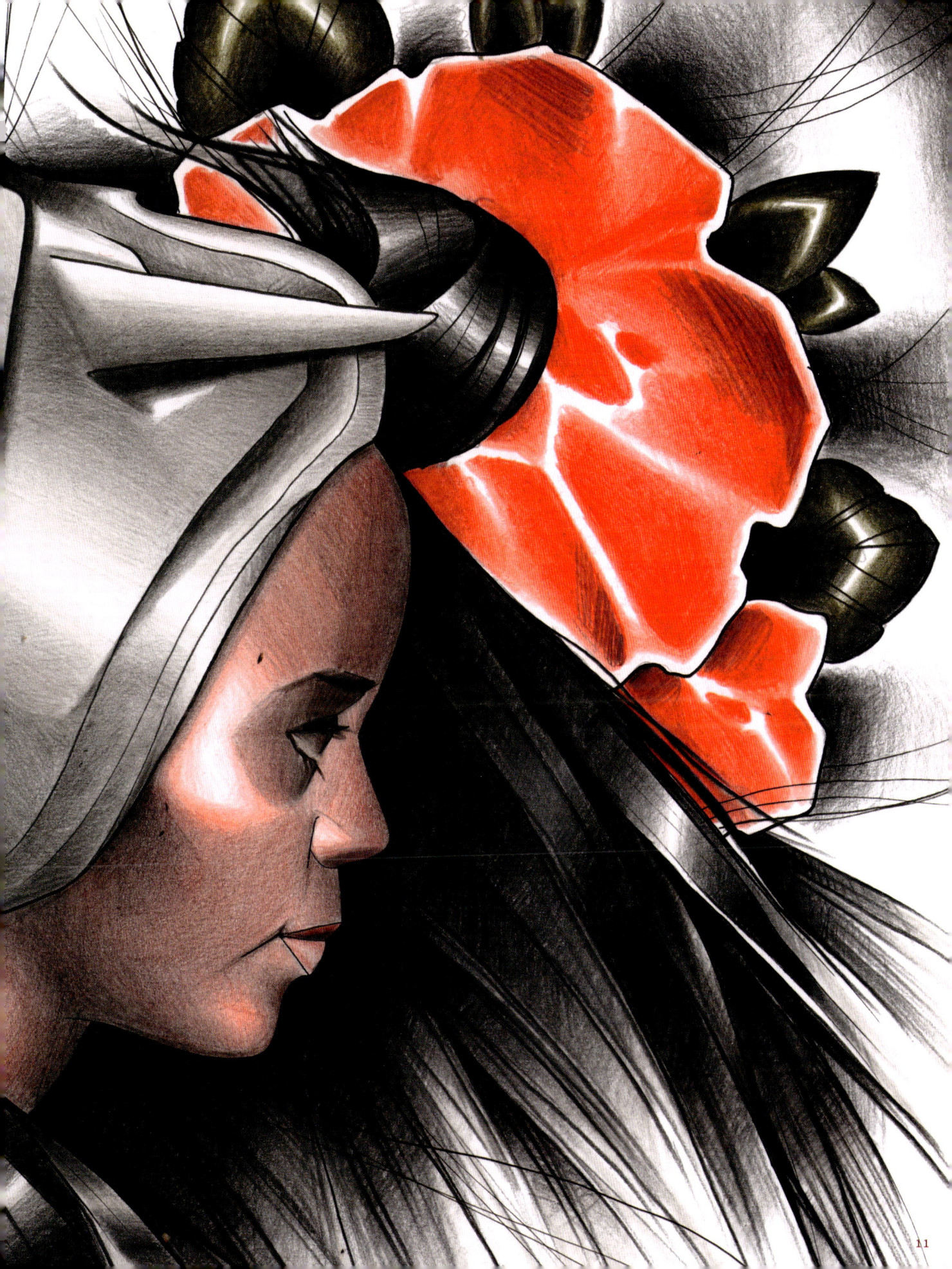

ARIEL 7

ARGENTINA / MADRID, SPAIN.

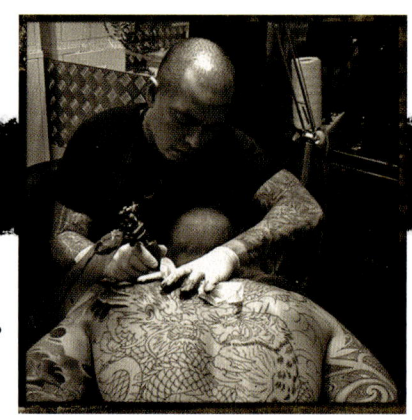

"It was an incredible experience the first time I drew on someone's body" says Barcelona-based Ariel. He had always been keen on drawing and it seemed a natural progression after school to turn tattooist. His apprenticeship was "Mostly designs for guys who had just come out of prison. There was lots of demand, so I began to perfect my technique." After a few years Ariel opened his own studio – "The early days of that were really tough, but then business seemed to flow." A period of travel followed, to Miami and California, before Ariel returned to Spain and joined the Tattoo Magic shop in Madrid. Amongst his influences Ariel cites Tim Lehi, Chris Trevino, Aaron Cain and Timothy Hoyer. His art is entirely based on the traditions of tattoo, in effect larger versions of his flash in coloured inks. Ariel travels extensively. "It's still important to exchange ideas, see other tattooists' work, so I try to get to all the main conventions: Milan, Rome, Stockholm, Berlin and London at least!" Of the scene he says "In the past five years it has exploded; in the next five I think it will get even bigger."

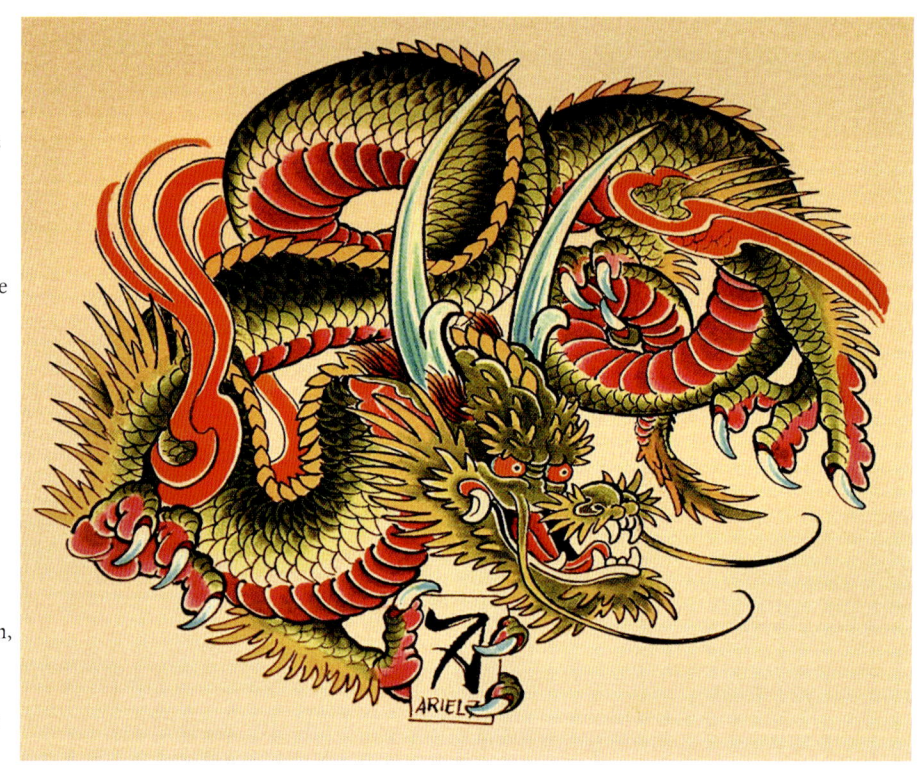

ABOVE: *Dragon I*. Pen, ink and watercolour.
RIGHT: *Chrysanthemum cobra*. Pen, ink and watercolour.

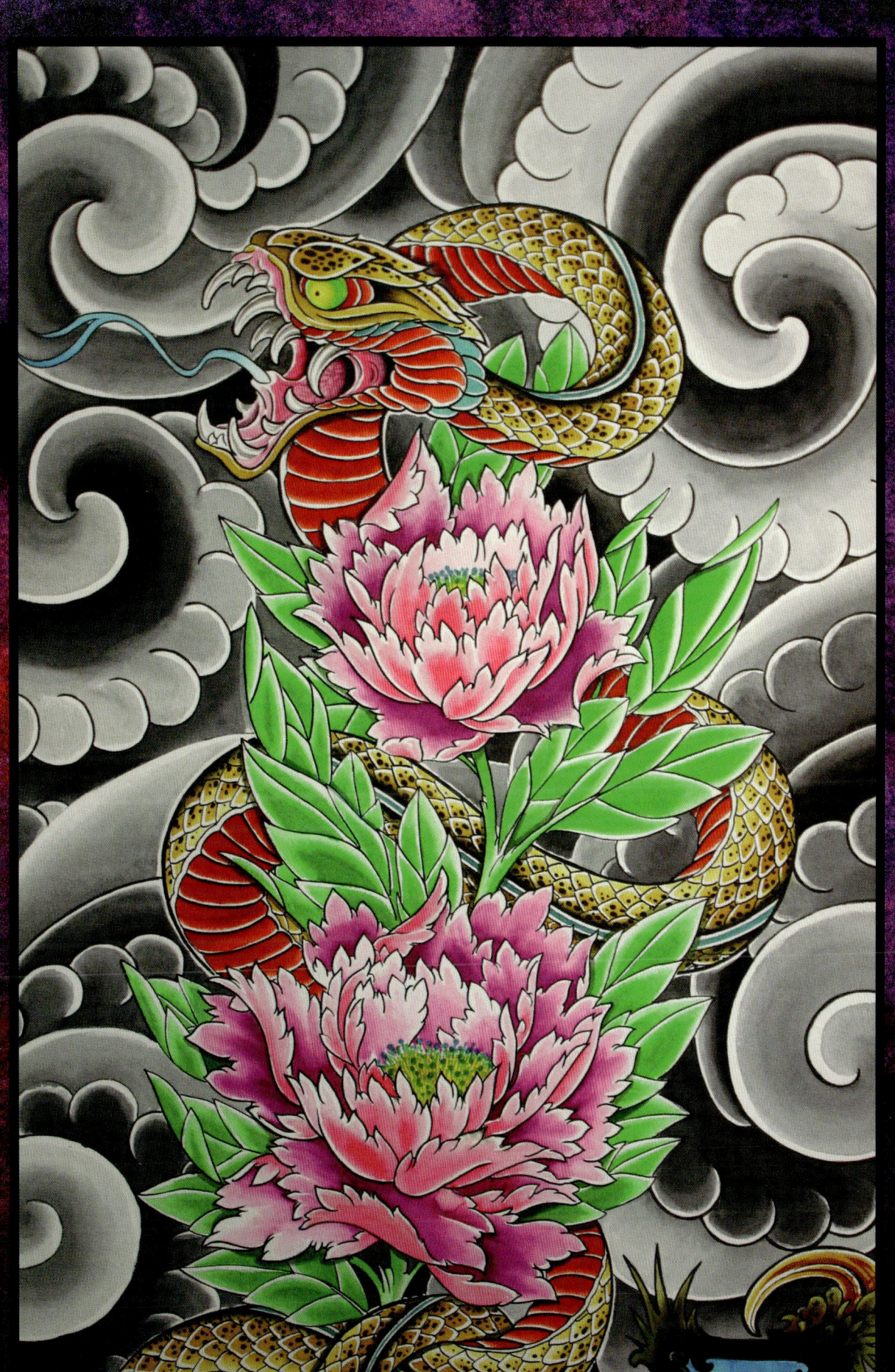

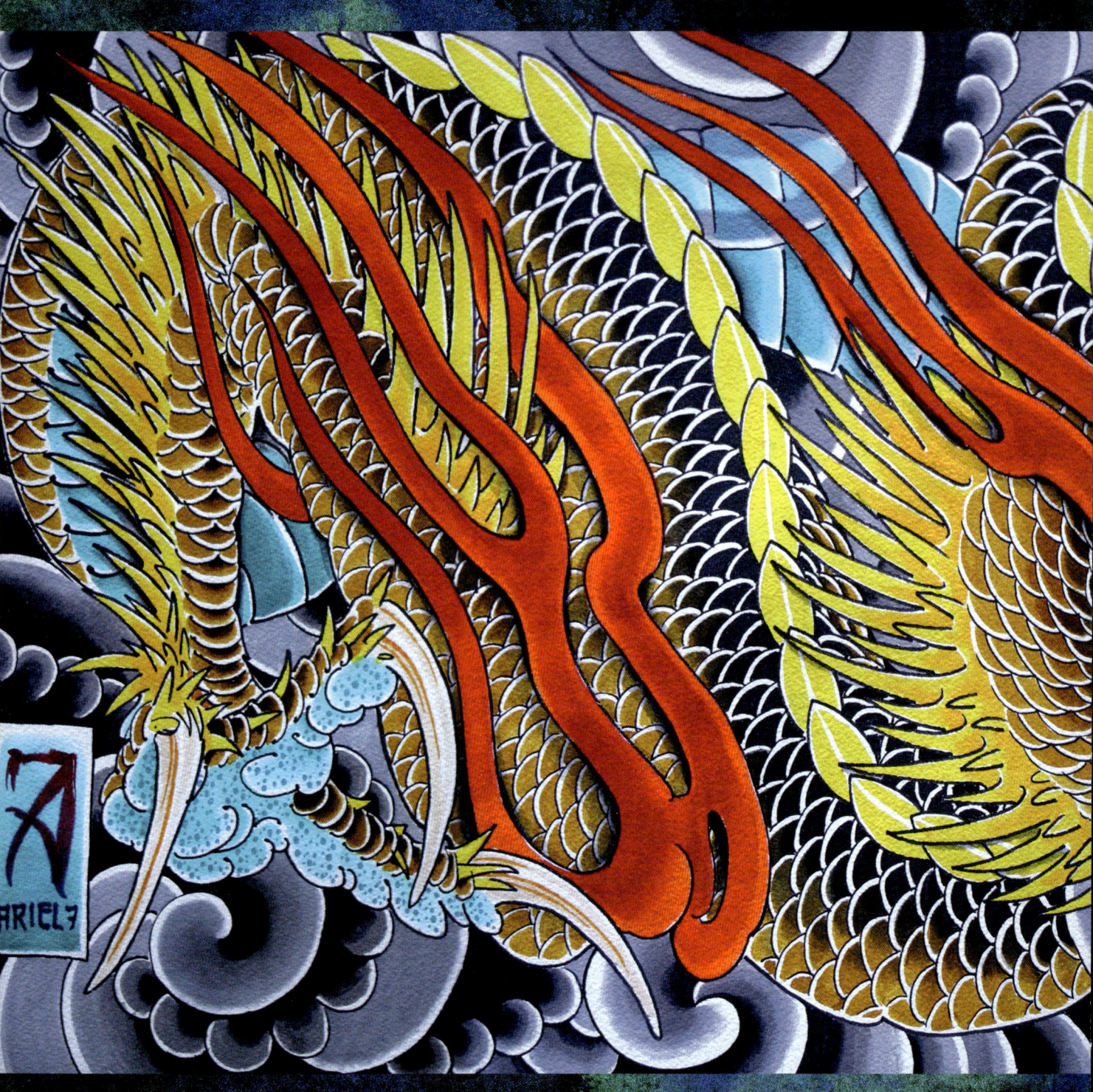

ABOVE: *Dragon II*. Pen, ink and watercolour.

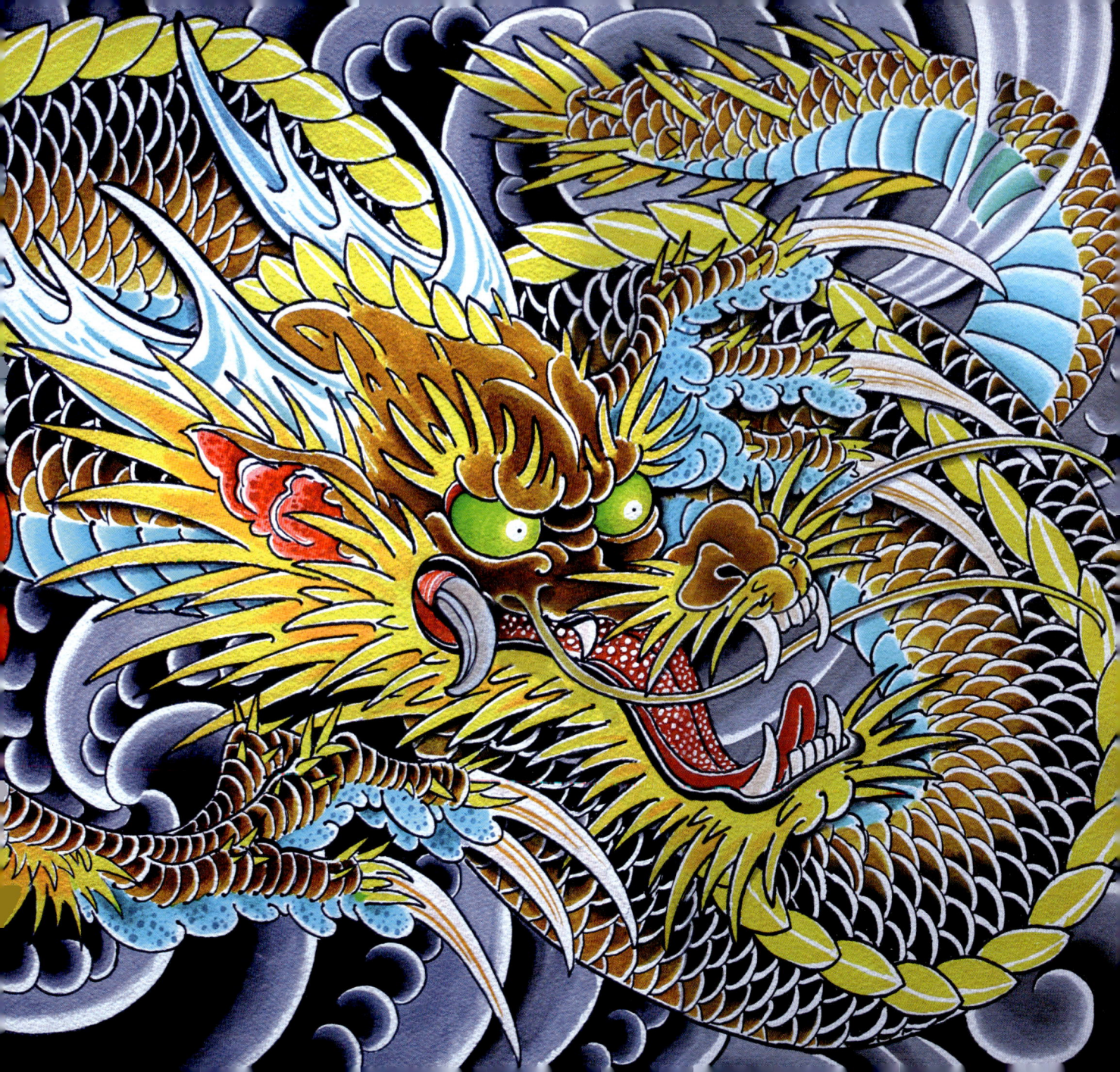

ARMOURED SOUL

BARCELONA / TORONTO, CANADA.

After studying art, fashion and illustration in Barcelona and on the Canary Islands, Susie became apprenticed to her boyfriend and then married him: "It's been eight years now with my partner in crime, all in the same shop." It was tough at the beginning – "it always is if you take it seriously" – but now it's something she loves, particularly as the shop also has a gallery space: "For the art it's great – you can really showcase what you're doing to your clients with total freedom, without all the hassle and pressure of another gallery."

For Susie, tattoo and painting have become interlinked – "The tattoo helps the painting and viceversa, blending, colours….well pretty much everything." She is constantly experimenting with new techniques and particularly likes painting on wood; "But in the end all painting comes from the gut."

Susie loves the horror scene: "I much prefer horror expos and festivals to tattoo conventions…..the vibe is much freakier but also more relaxed…I am a lot happier with that crowd." Horror is a huge influence, from movies, to music and comics, "especially the '80s flicks with their saturated colours; those are a real weakness." It's critical to never stop learning she says; "I still pick up a lot from the guest artists who come to work at our shop, like David Alexander, Gunnar Foley, Eneko and Sento. Clients are also becoming more discriminating and research their artists much more carefully. Anyone can buy a tattoo kit and scratch at a friends' skin, but the good artists are as rare as they've always been…. you've got to seek them out!"

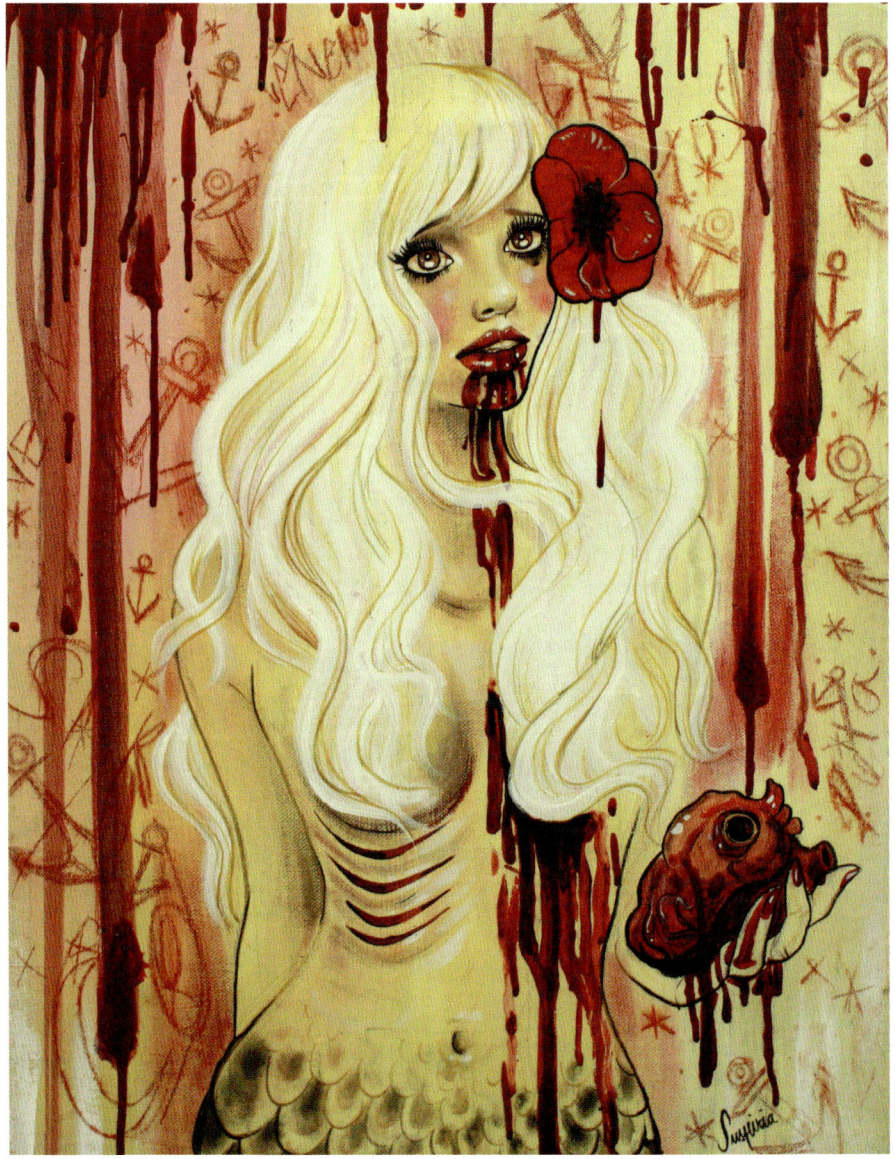

ABOVE: *Bleeding Heart*. Acrylic on canvas.
RIGHT: *Madonna Of The Dead*. Acrylic on canvas.

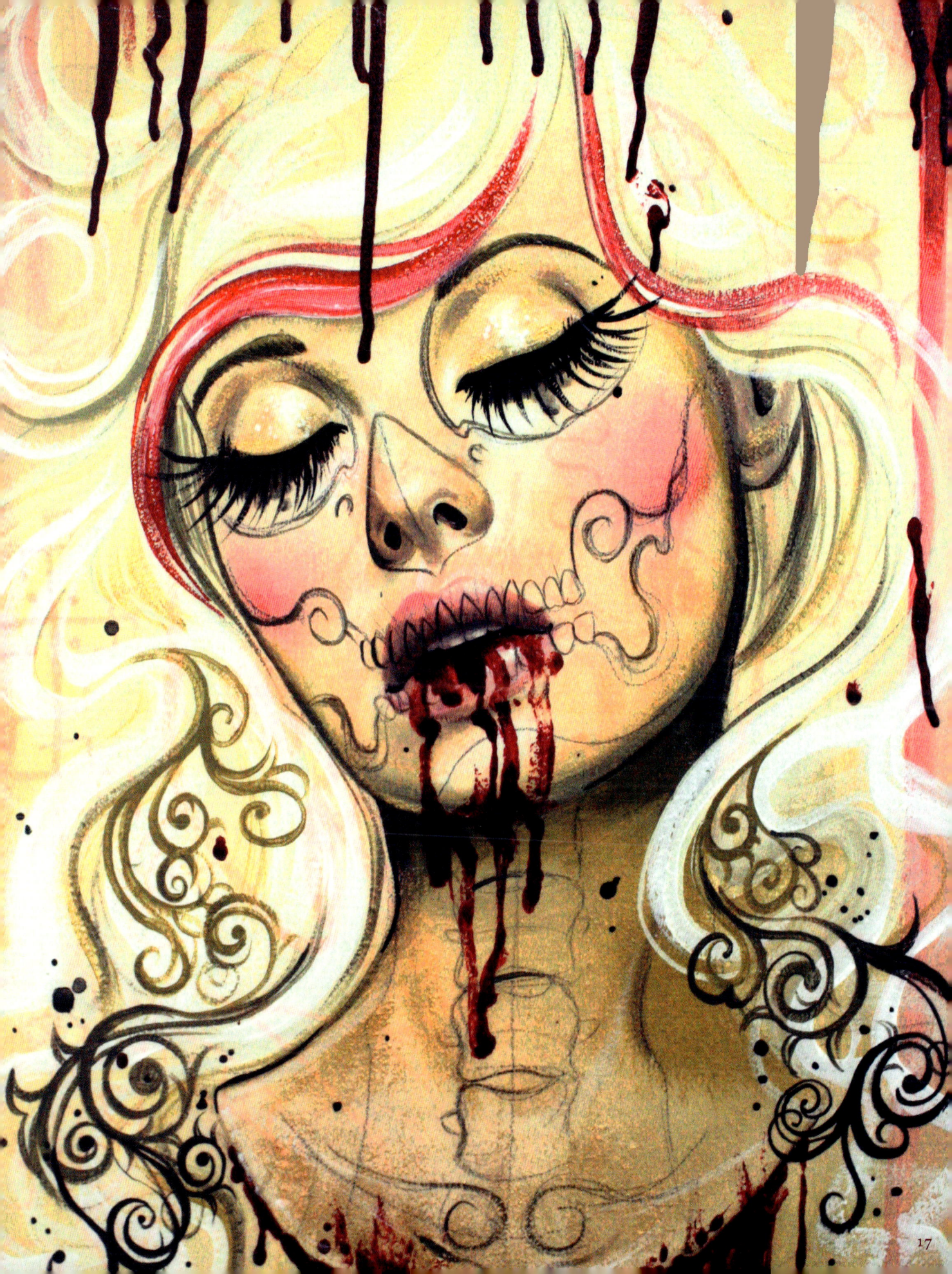

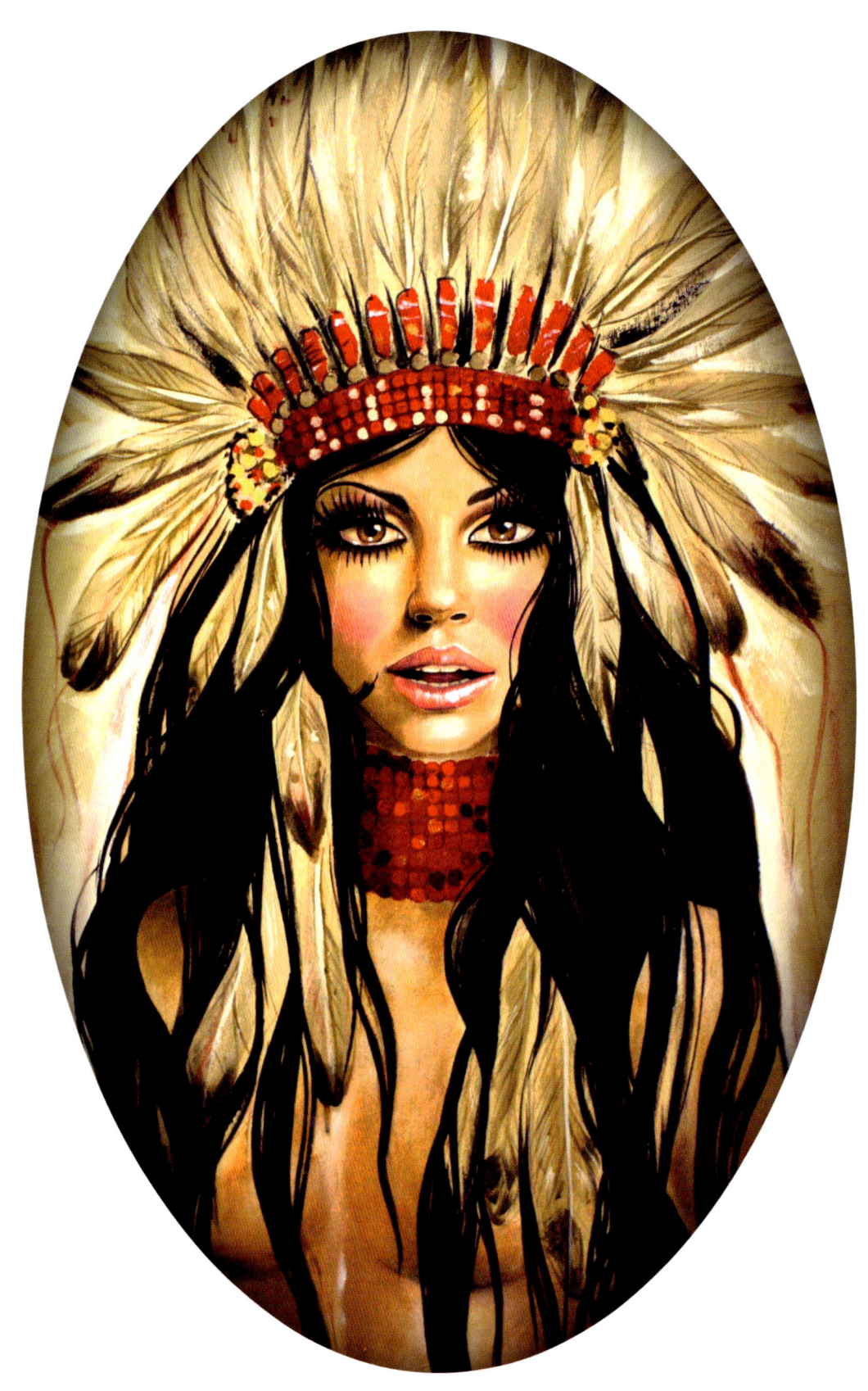

ABOVE: *Sioux*. Acrylic on canvas.
RIGHT: *Maliciosa*. Acrylic on canvas.

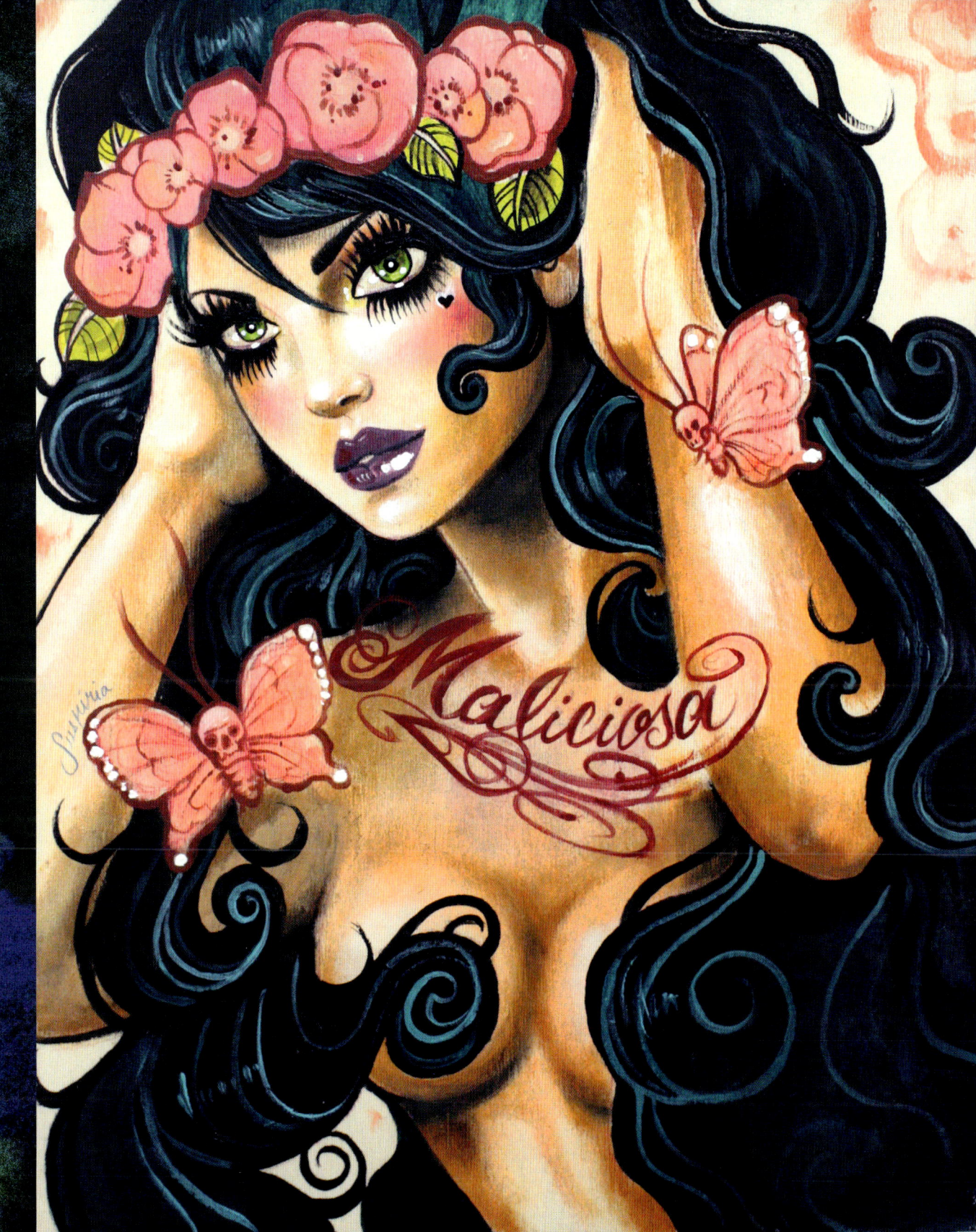

BARTHEZ

PAZARDJIK, BULGARIA.

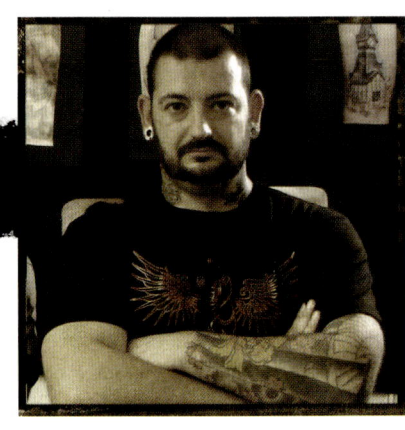

Born and growing up in Bulgaria, Barthez remembers the effects of the fall of Communism around 1995. The heady atmosphere of those days, when he was a student in fine art and sculpture in Sofia, he thinks is what determined his course as a tattooist: "We wanted to do whatever had been considered rebellious - from listening to hard rock, to painting graffiti and street art on walls; tattooing our bodies was just an extension of that." With a group of friends they established a tattoo studio, which was tough at first given that they had no experience of electric tattooing and had to fashion a machine using motors from a walkman and leads from an old electric guitar. They had no model to follow, although occasionally a friend's father would bring over tattoo magazines published in the West. In 2005 Barthez moved to Madrid and then tattooed in many cities in Europe (London, Glasgow, Prague and Stockholm included) before returning to Bulgaria and opening his own tattoo shop. Barthez sees his art as one with his tattooing: "I employ the same techniques to art I might show in a gallery to my tattoos, I am a tattooist first and foremost." His influences are many, but particularly horror movies: "You'll find a lot of references to those in my work." Barthez is hugely positive about the tattoo scene; whereas some artists are disappointed that it has expanded as much as it has. He sees the fact that it's easier to set up as allowing a new bunch of young tattooists to express "some fantastic new ideas; almost everyday I see amazing new designs or techniques."

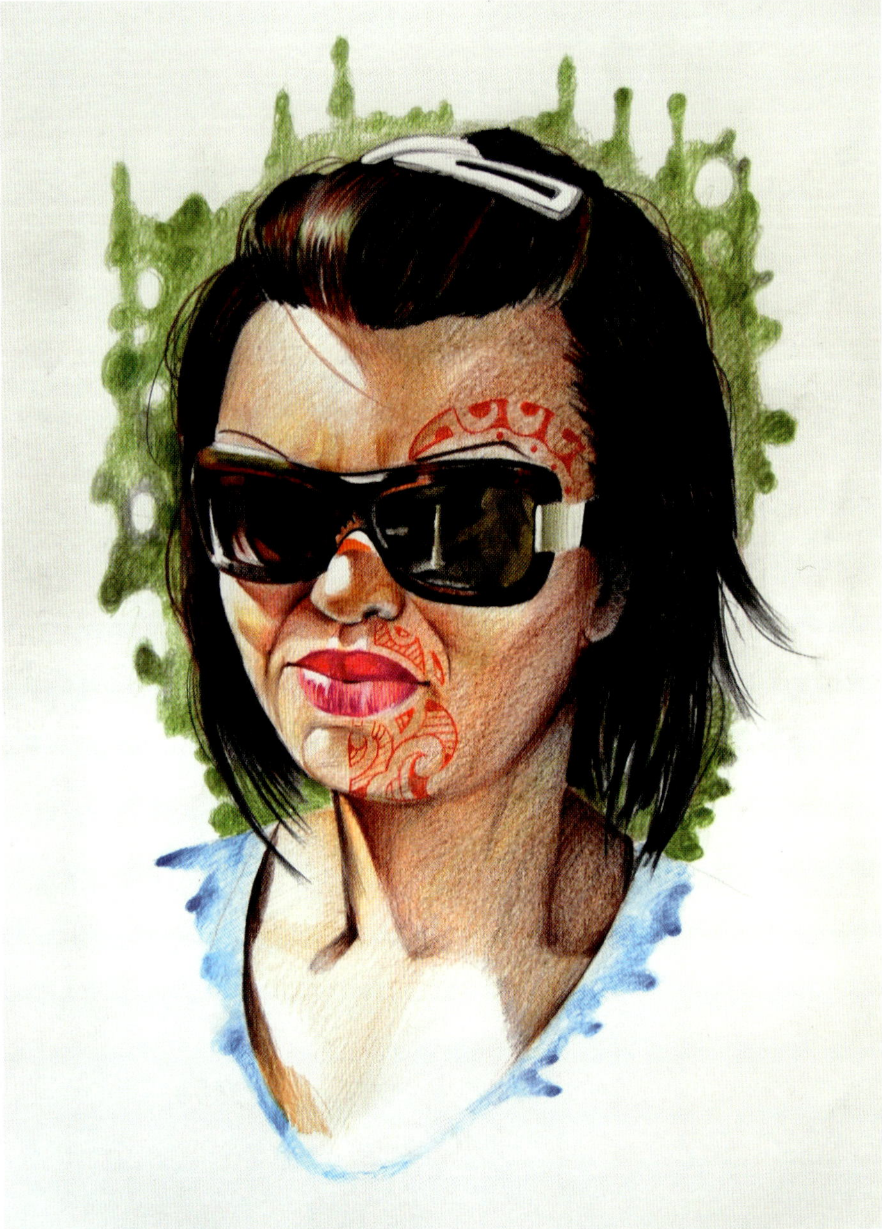

ABOVE: *Girl In Shades*. Coloured pencils and watercolour.
RIGHT: *Seer*. Pencil and watercolour wash.

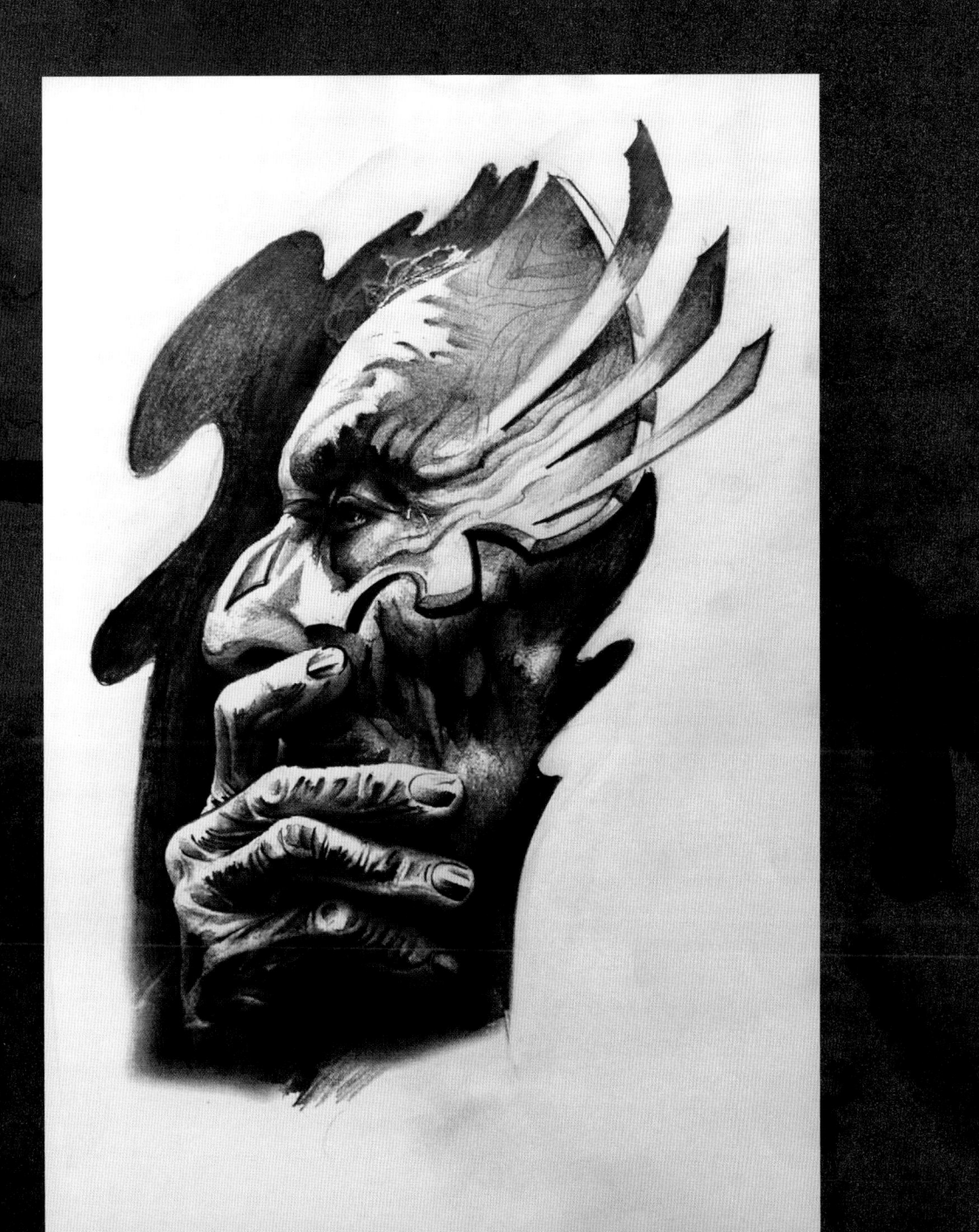

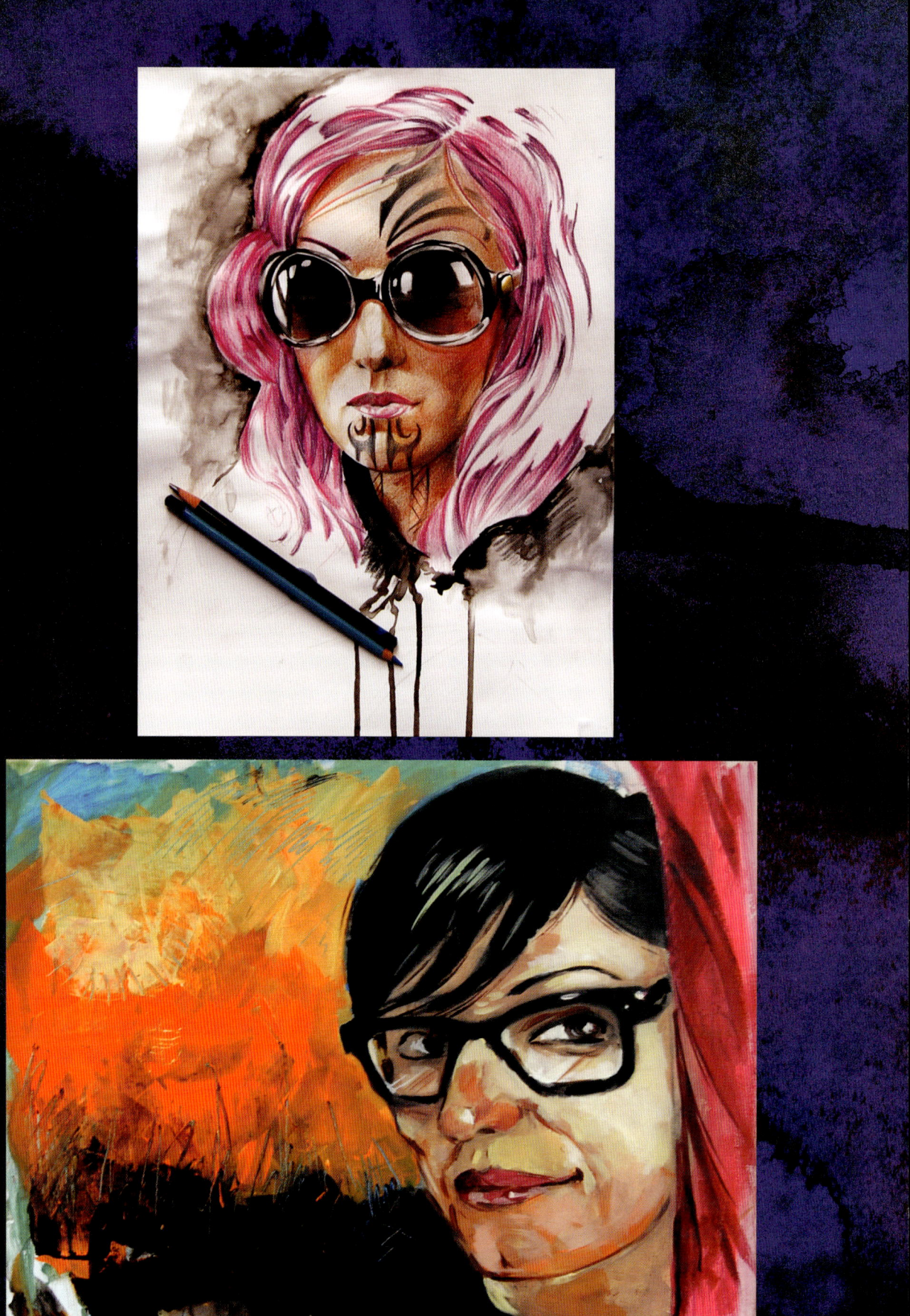

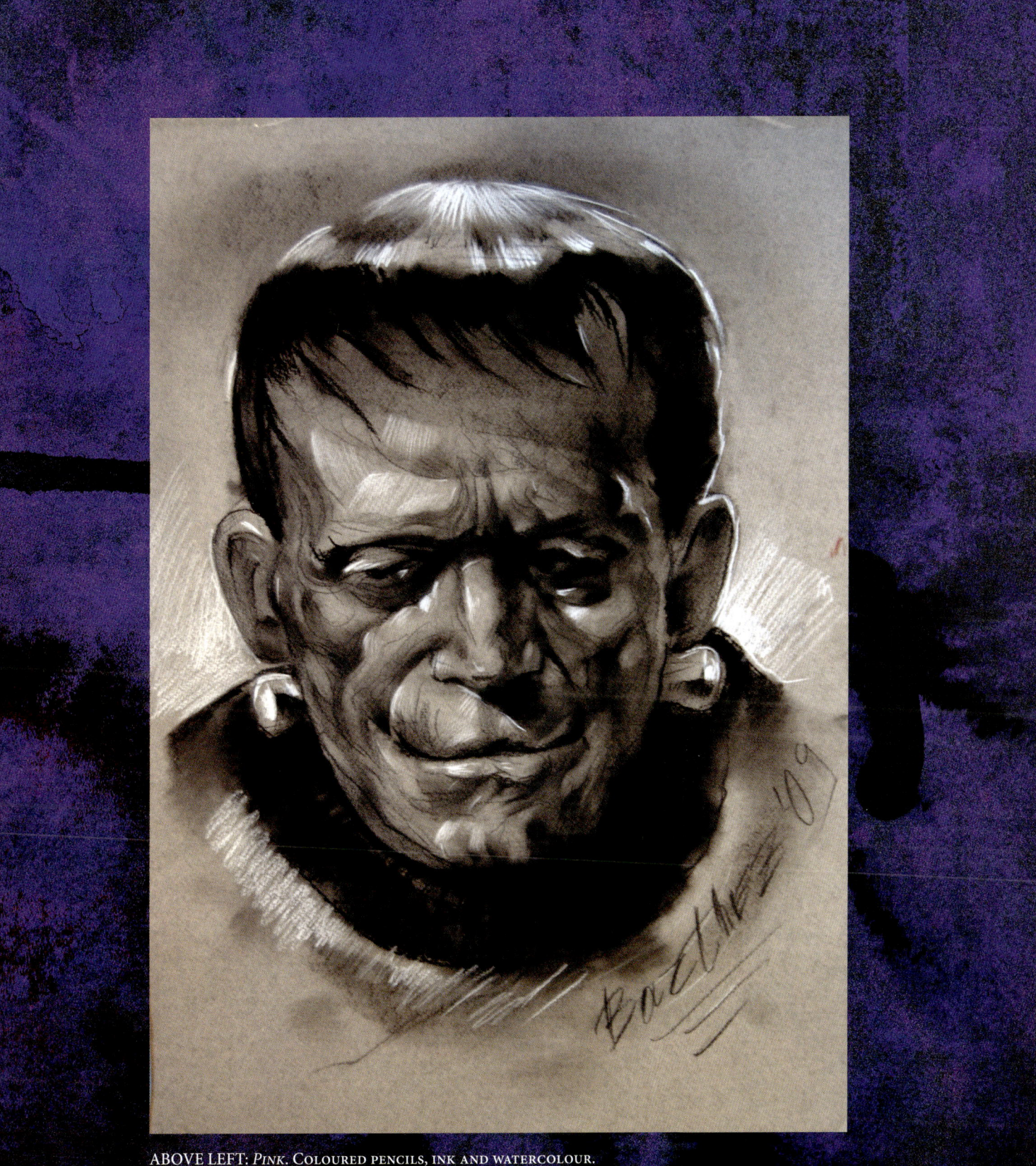

ABOVE LEFT: *Pink*. Coloured pencils, ink and watercolour.
LEFT: *Someone's Watching You*. Acrylic on canvas.
ABOVE: *Frankenstein's Thinking*. Pen and ink, pastels and

BURLTON

WHITBY, ONTARIO, CANADA.

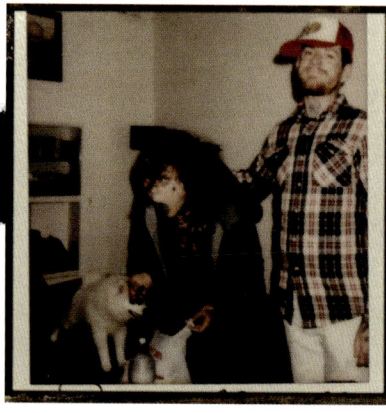

"Tattooing was the only career I found where I didn't want to kill myself after a full day's work, so I made the best of it and now it's the only thing I know," says Steven Burlton. He grew up in Ontario, and like for most tattooists, the start was tough. "No one in my family had any sort of artistic background and so I was pretty much alone with my interest in painting. I am pretty much self-taught, apart from high school art classes. Early on I got into life drawing classes and that was really useful. I keep going back to re-learn stuff I already know!" He's influenced by dead as well as living tattooists "and sculptors and painters. If I had to name a few it would be Joseph Noel Paton, Dave Cummings and Dean Parkin in New Zealand; he's doing some great work right now." Music is big inspiration, and Steven sees it as part of the aesthetic he's pushing. "Black, speed, grind, death and doom..there's always a soundtrack to which I can draw and tattoo." He also cites movies, particularly *Bram Stoker's Dracula*: "That's a great source of visual and audio reference." Steven is big on references. "I reference the shit out of everything, good and bad, as a way of knowing what *not* to do. I tend to go slowly with a new image. If I'm not happy with what I've drawn half way through, I might put it away until I don't hate it, or start on something else." He likes to stay loose, spending half the year in Australia, the rest pretty much on the road. 'The scene has changed dramatically in the past five years. With the Internet, nothing is sacred and everything is too accessible. It's now so common to have tattoos by big names; the walk-ins have pretty much gone, with most shops being by appointment. Hopefully the massive wave of pop culture having its way with our trade will be over soon."

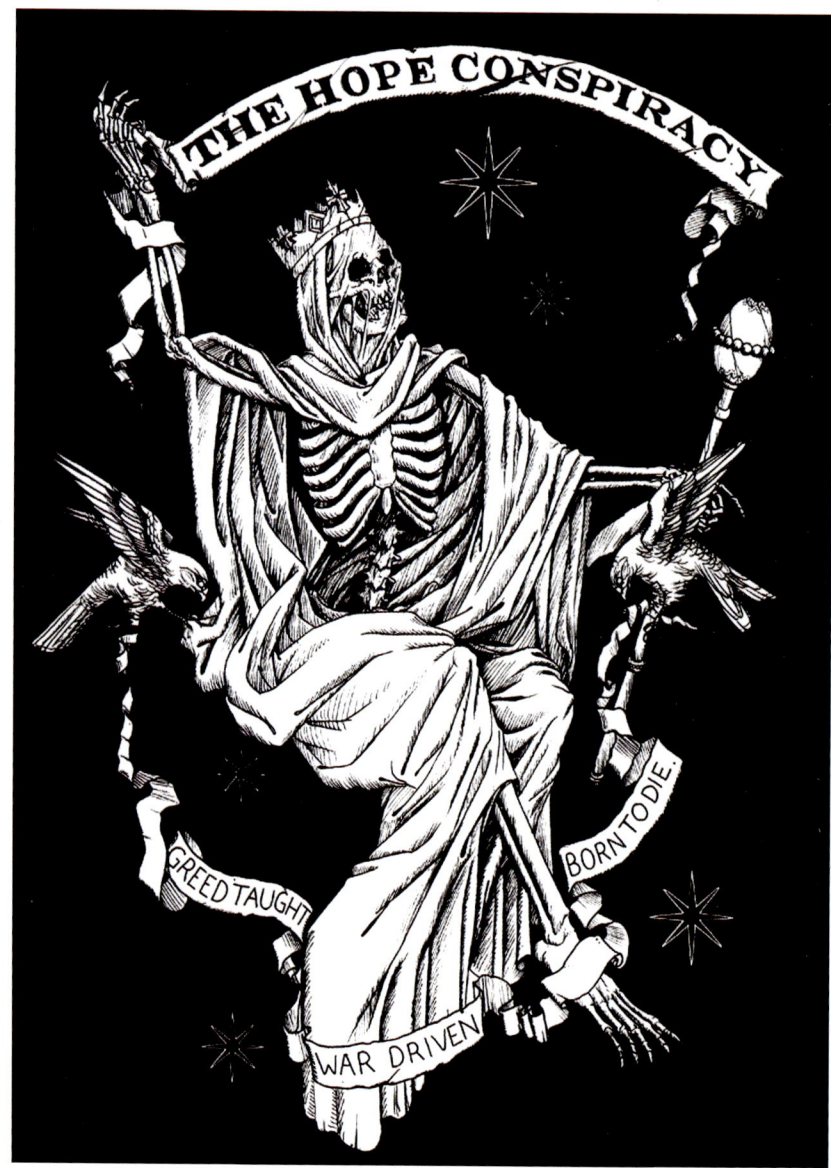

ABOVE: *The Hope Conspiracy*. Pen and ink.
RIGHT: *Hooded Skull*. Pen, ink and watercolour.

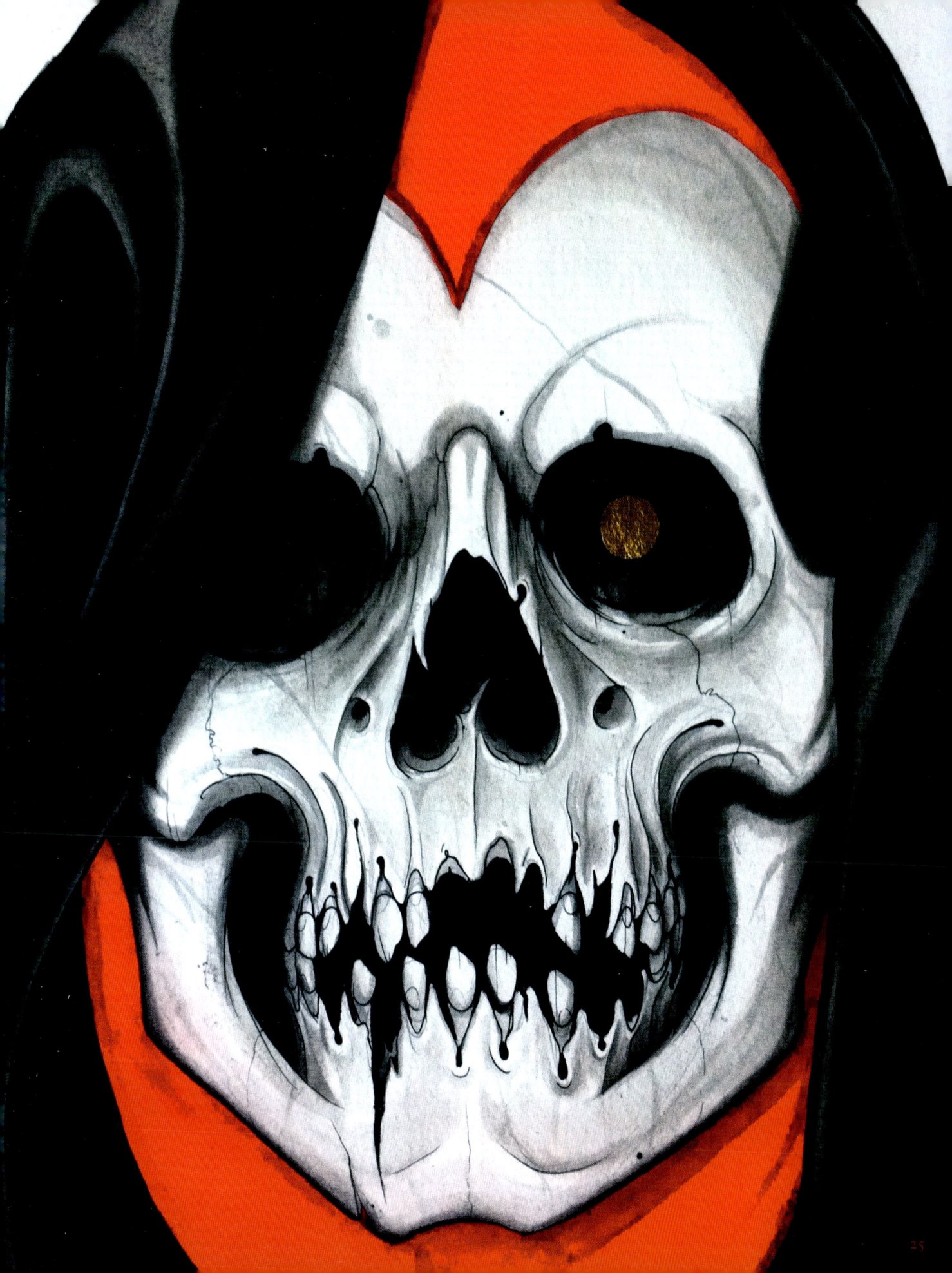

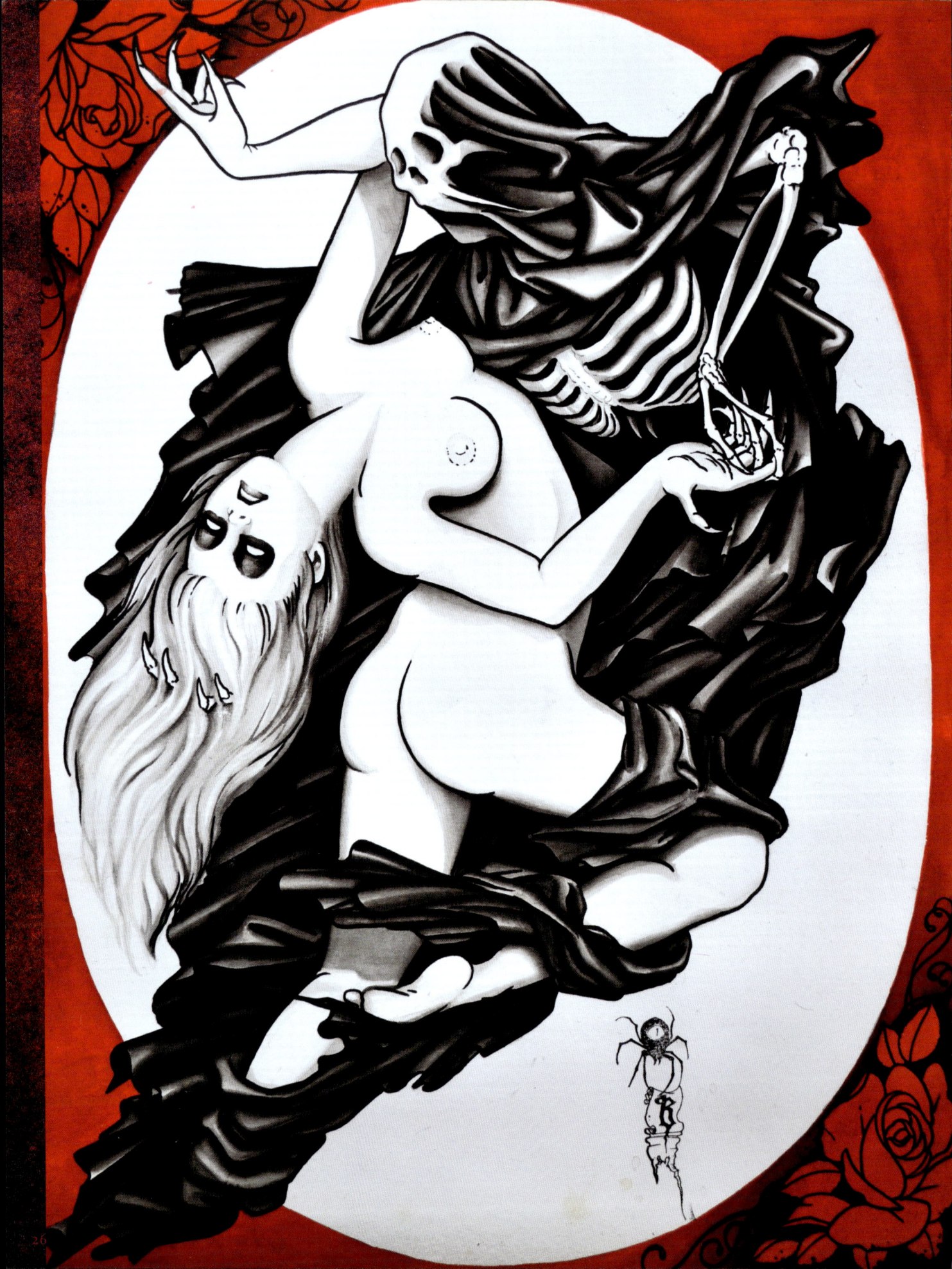

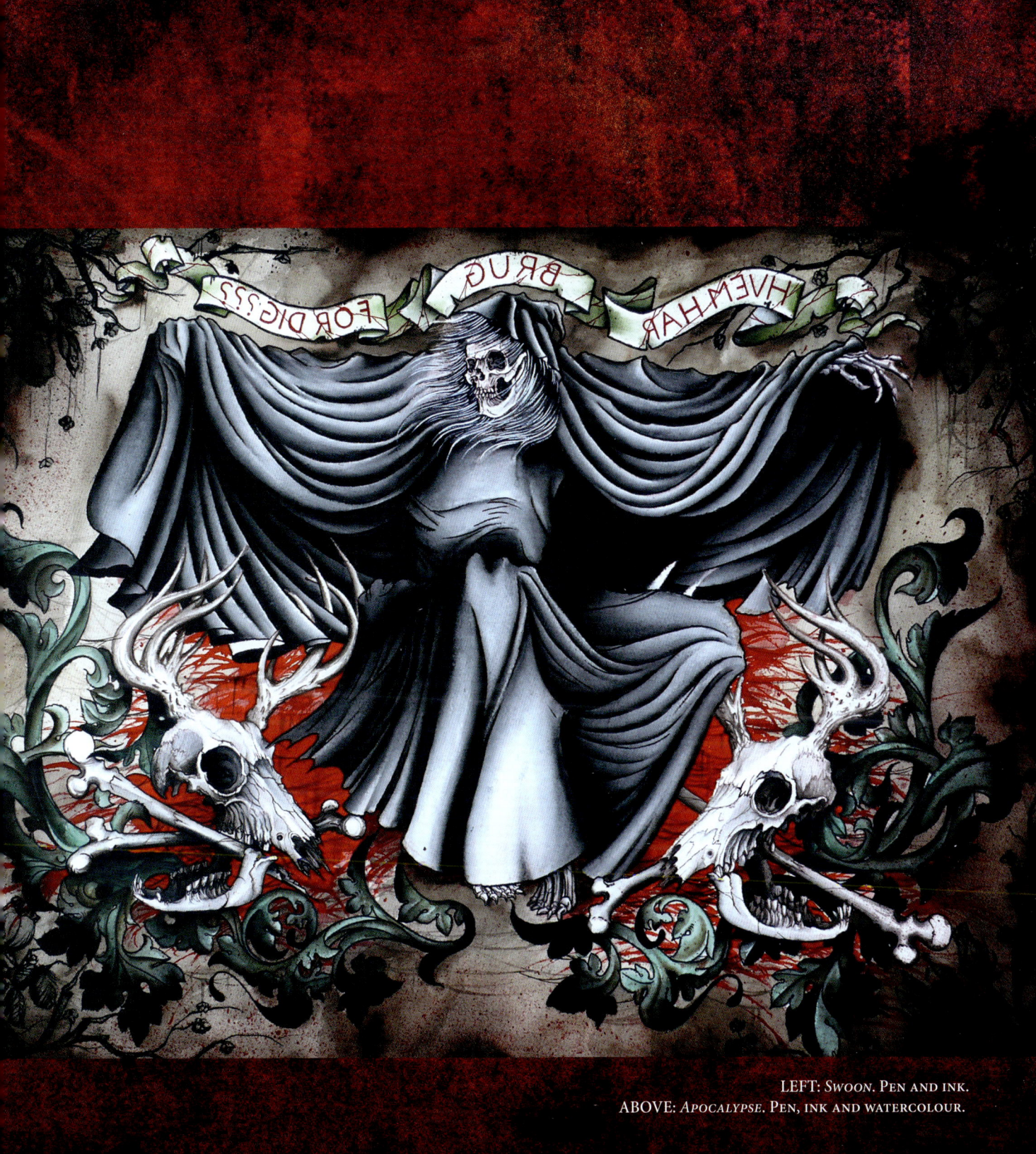

LEFT: *Swoon*. Pen and ink.
ABOVE: *Apocalypse*. Pen, ink and watercolour.

CAMPISE

BERKELEY CA, USA.

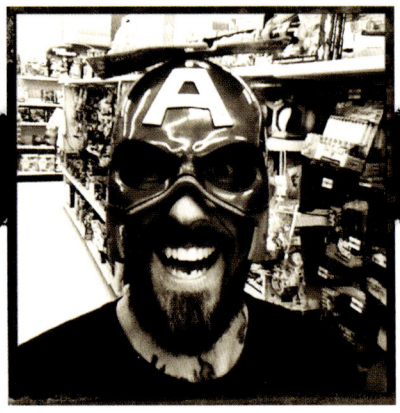

"When I first started tattooing in 1993 it was at once terrifying and exciting" says Berkeley-based George, "Tattooing was infinitely harder to get into in those days, but at times it could be dangerous.....not much before this, if you went into a shop and asked too many questions about the technical aspects of tattooing, you could end up getting beaten up and having your hands broken." George says that learning the actual process was the hardest thing he's ever done; "even after twenty years it continues to be challenging when it comes to design composition. But then it was a looooong, slowww process, with no Internet, few books; the only thing that kept me going was being young, enthusiastic and incredibly naive."

With no formal art education, "just a healthy dose of humiliation", George is entirely self-taught. He worked first at Davis Tattoo Company (in Davis, CA) for a summer, then at Erno Tattoo, on Fillmore in San Francisco, before opening up his own shop – War Horse Tattoo – in Berkeley, CA. His clients are "everyone: firemen/women, contractors, doctors, lawyers, soldiers, musicians, artists, scientists, professors, mothers, fathers, grandfathers, and more." He shows his art in group shows such as Year of the Tiger/ Year of the Dragon and Samuel O'Reilly's Zombie Show, and has been published extensively in books as well as magazines including *Sin N Ink*, *Tattoo Magazine*, *Tattoo Energy*, *Tattoo Life*, *Skin 2* and *International Tattoo Art*. Inspiration comes from co-workers past and present – "but I don't want to mention who, in case I forget somebody", movies and conceptual art from the movies, books and "anything which has a strong visual or emotional impact." As for the future, "the rise of social media will continue to have a major impact: it's great to see work from all over the world and that has raised the bar; on the negative side geographically-specific styles are disappearing and that's a shame."

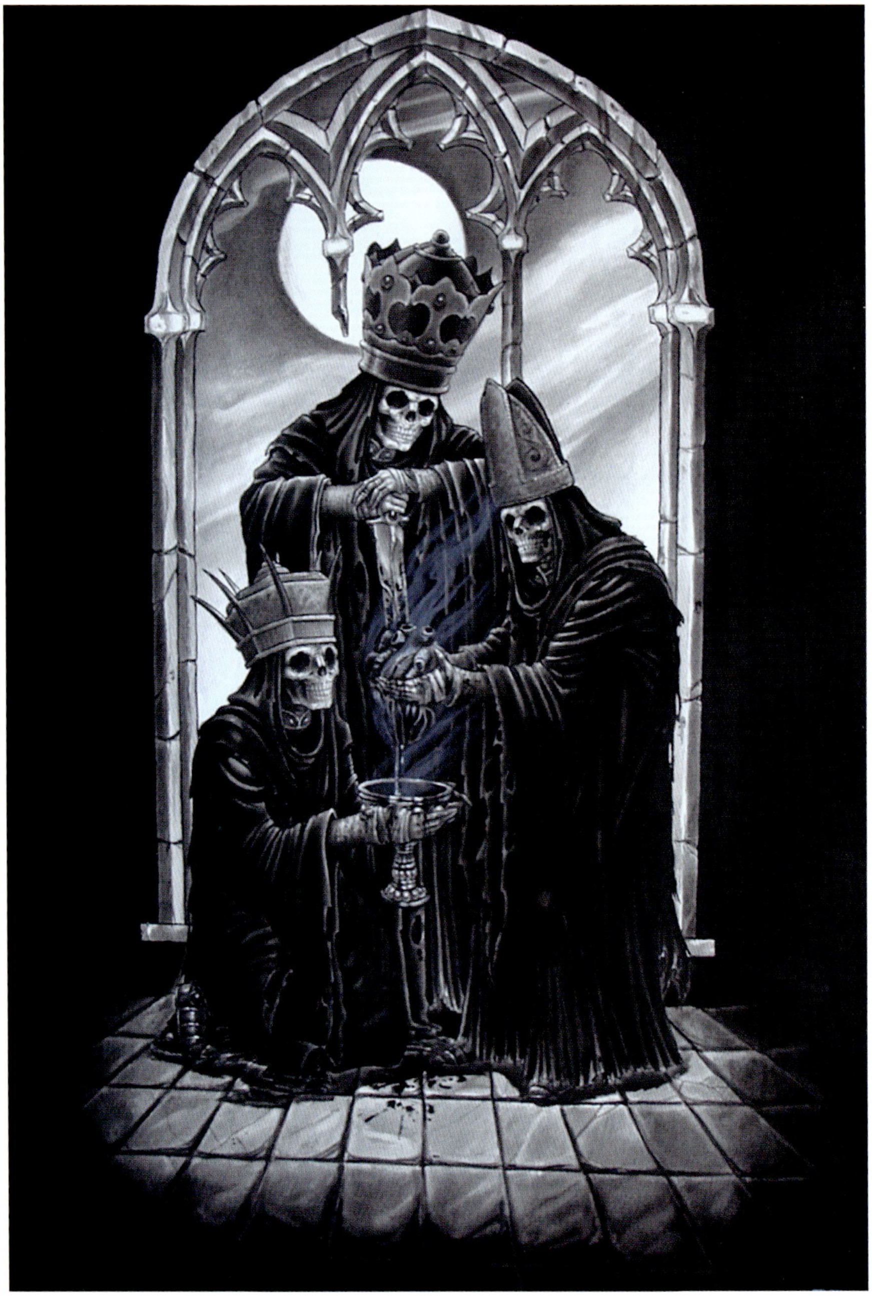

ABOVE: *Three Kings*. Pen and ink.
RIGHT: *Kasai*. Pen, ink and watercolour.

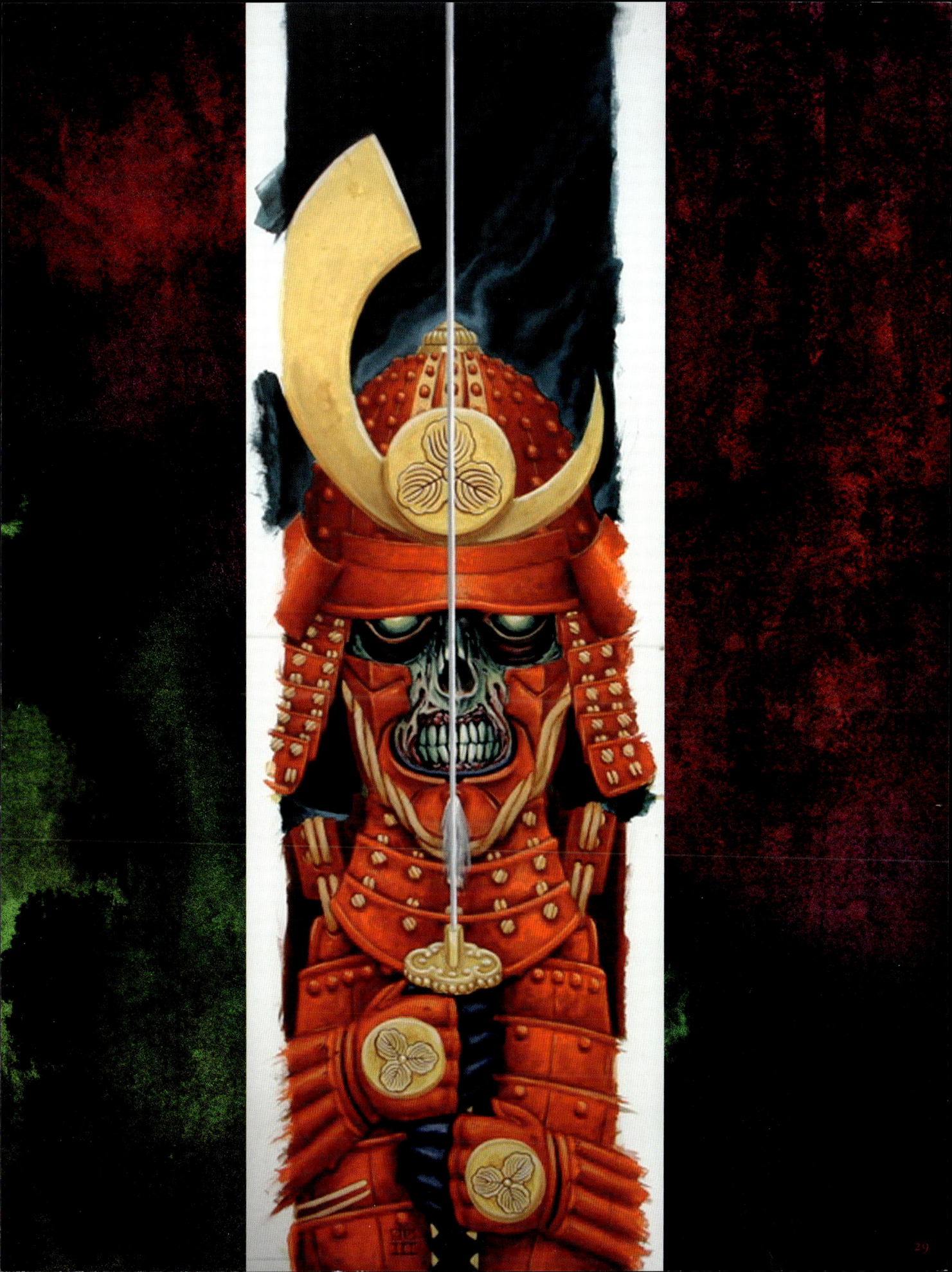

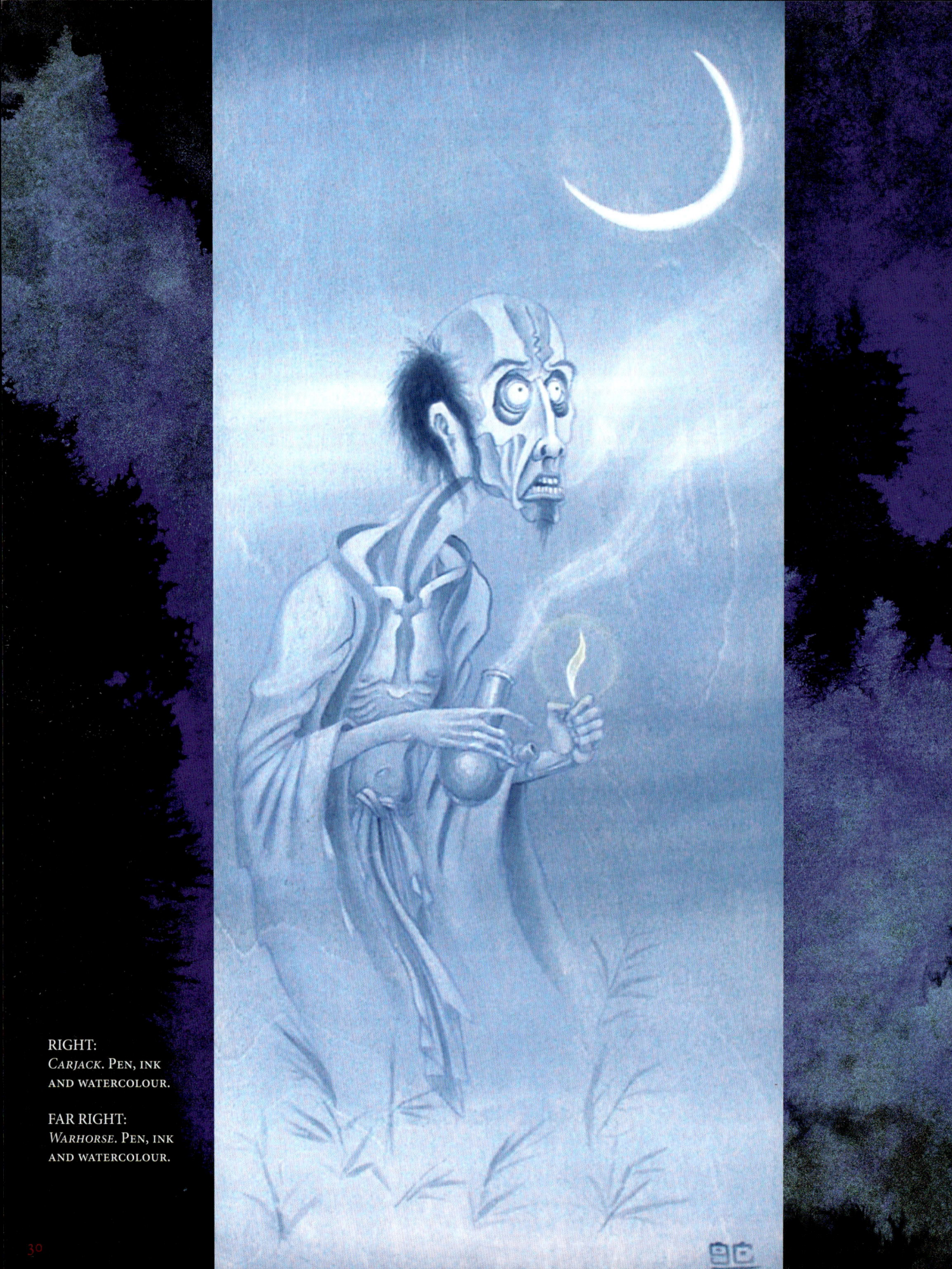

RIGHT:
Carjack. Pen, ink and watercolour.

FAR RIGHT:
Warhorse. Pen, ink and watercolour.

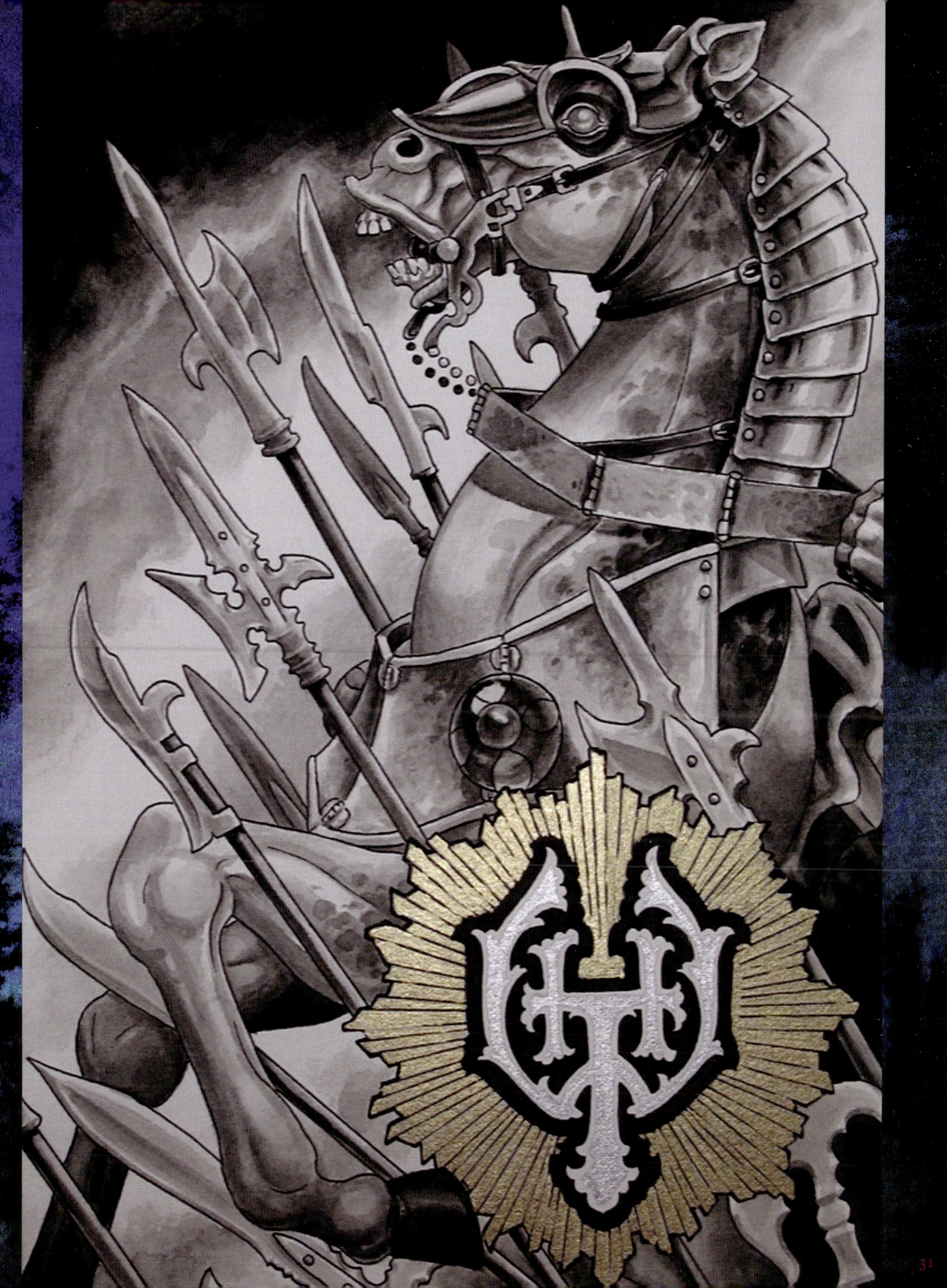

CASTAÑO

BARCELONA, SPAIN.

Owner of the famed Barcelona Electric tattoo studio, Javi can't remember when he started drawing, "It's just something I always did." He started by tattooing some friends "in a garage full of cockroaches in Barcelona in 1996." In those days there were very few tattoo shops in the city, but Javi managed to get an apprenticeship in 1997. Twelve years later he opened his own shop.

Javi's experience of tattooing has, he says, hugely influenced his art: "It has really changed the way I draw, although I still keep in touch with influences other than tattoo, like Joaquim Patinir, Rubens, Dali, Mark Riddick, Joe Petagno and Robert Crumb." The influence doesn't work the other way however: "When I tattoo I am in a different mode and I like tattoos to look like tattoos, not like paintings!" He now has a very strong client base who trust him to do a great design and give him the freedom to decide on their behalf…"well nearly always; I do occasional have to be held back a little!"

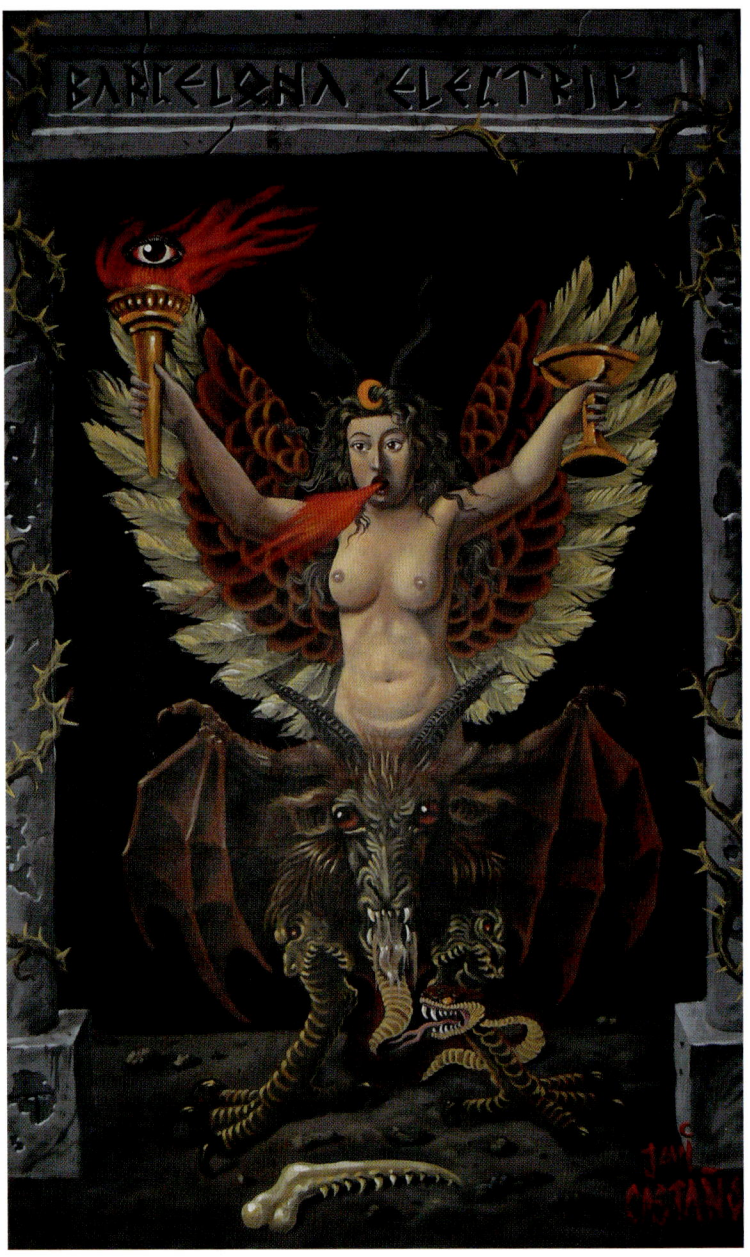

ABOVE: BARCELONA ELECTRIC BANNER FOR TATTOO CONVENTION.
RIGHT: *THE TEMPTATIONS OF SAINT ANTHONY (SELF PORTRAIT)*. OIL ON CANVAS.

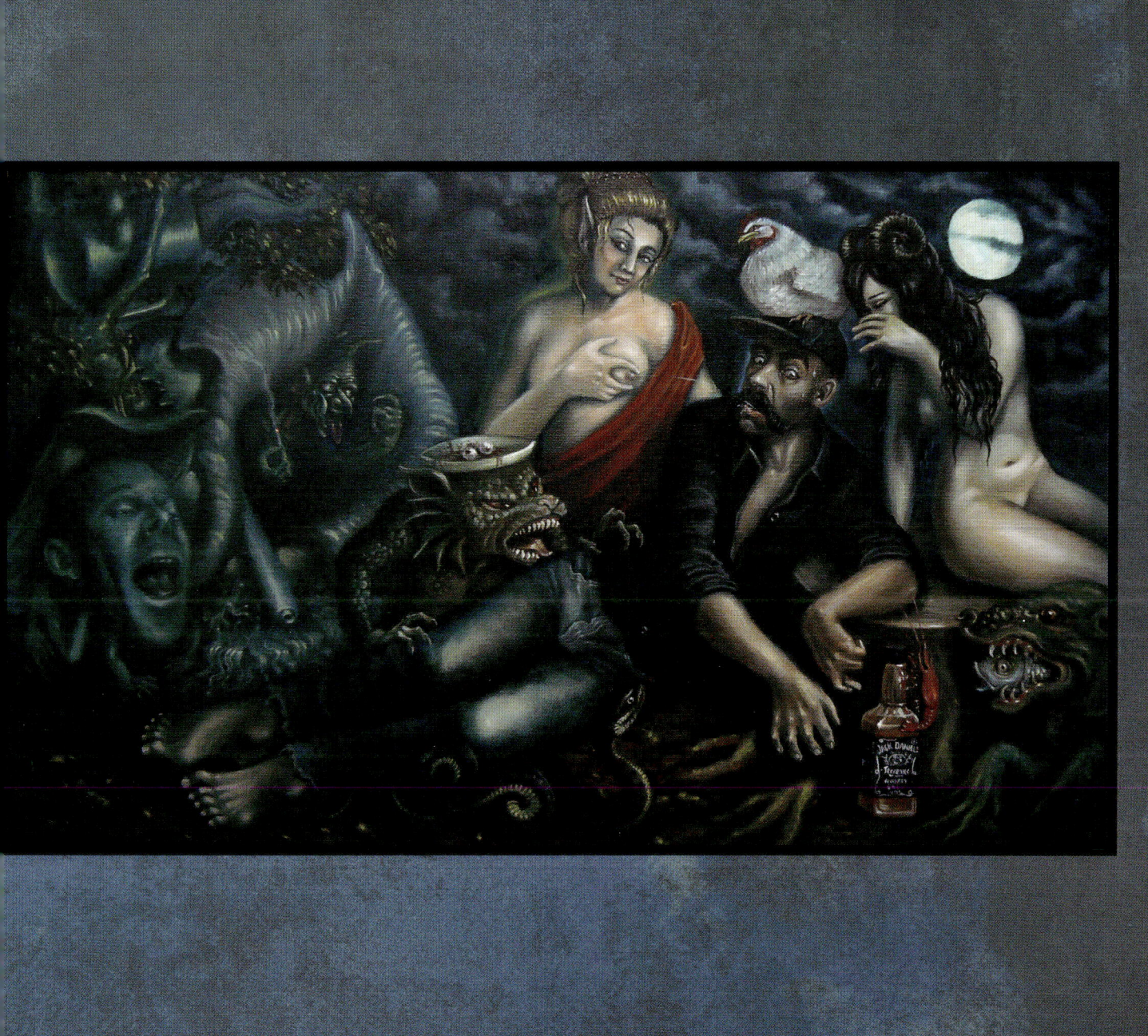

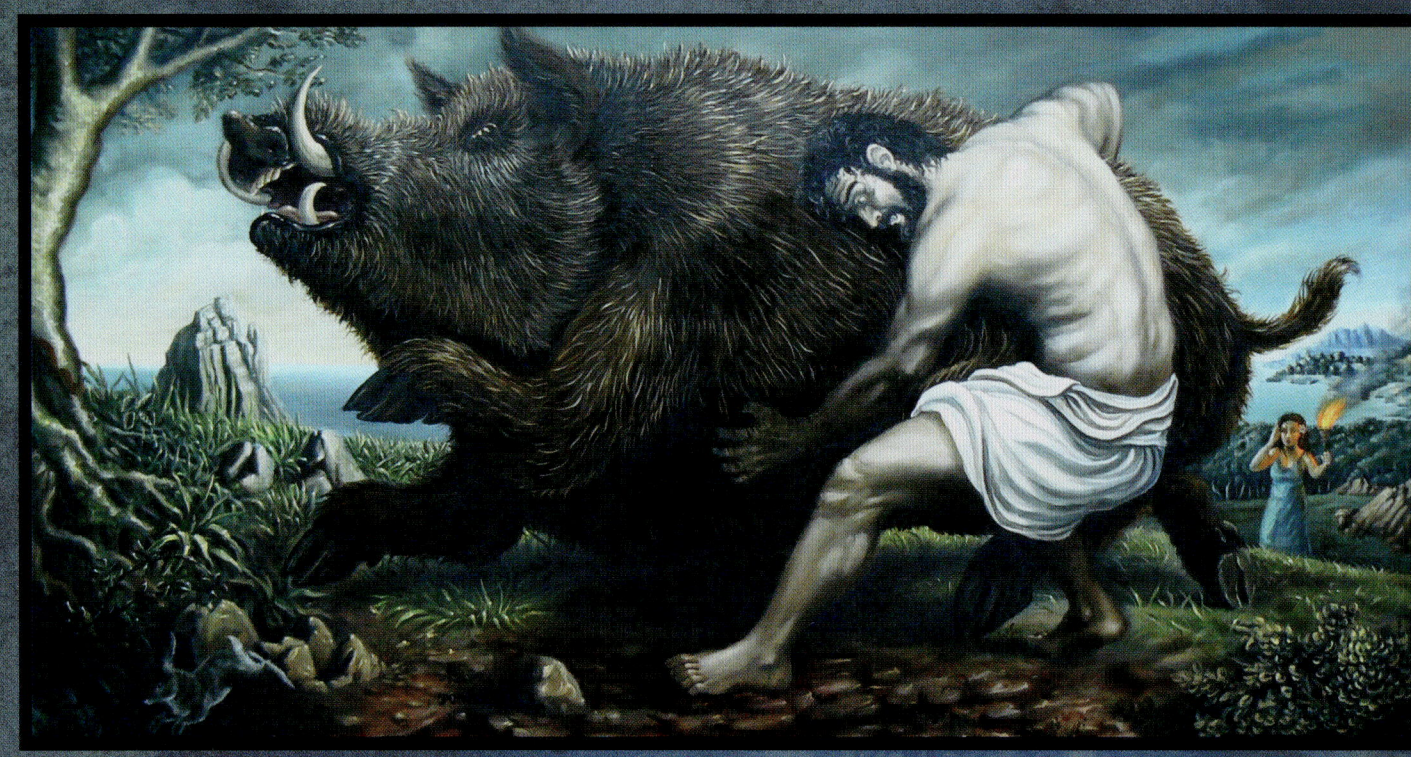

ABOVE: *Hercules Y El Jabali Del Monte Erimanto (Hercules and the Wild Boar of Mount Erimanto)*. Oil on canvas.
RIGHT: *Anfitrite (Amphitrite, wife of Poseidon)*. Acrylic on canvas.

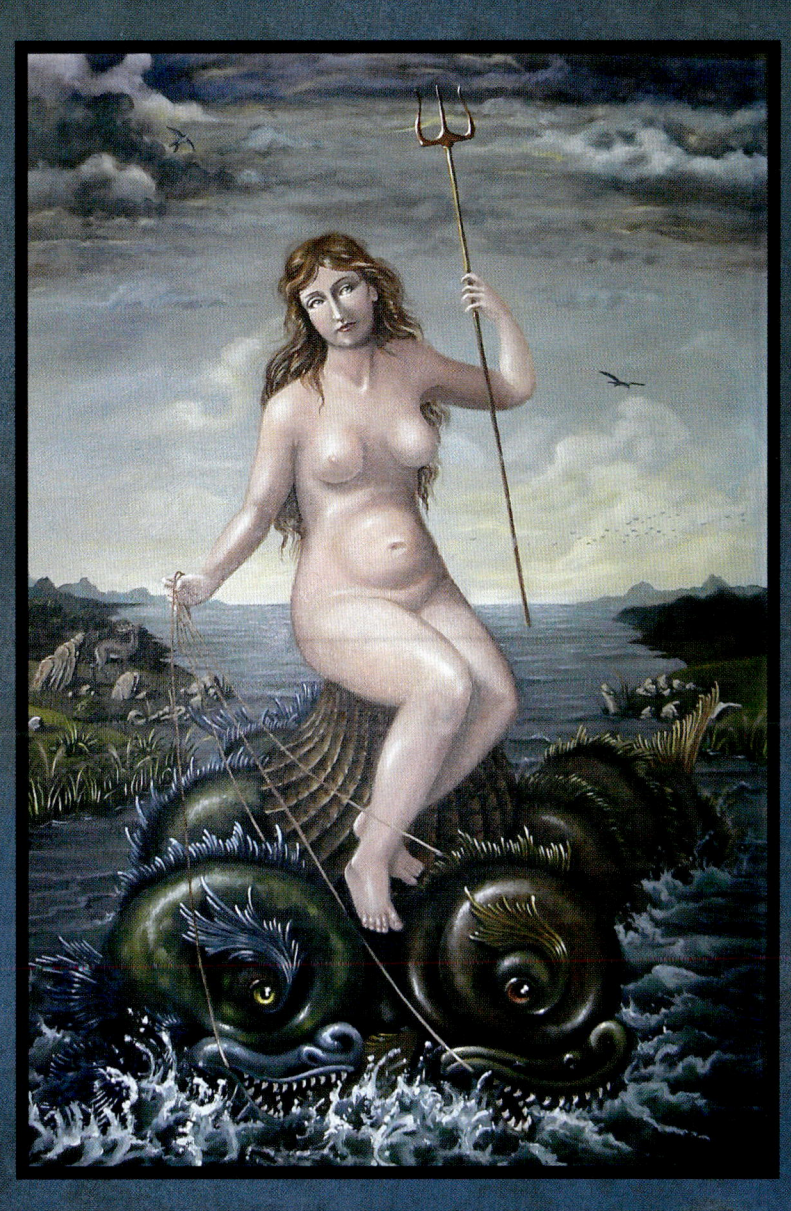

CLARKE

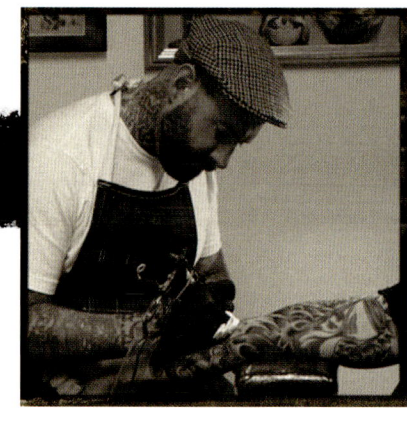

LIVERPOOL, UK.

In the lates '80s and early '90s most of Richie's friends were in bands and he did the artwork. He started getting tattooed aged 18 and then went to New York (in those days tattooing there was still illegal), sat in watching Mike McCabe in his underground studio and "that was it." His start on the scene was really, really tough: "The guy who used to do my tattoos found out that I was trying to learn, doing some artwork with a local biker guy. He told me never to come back to his shop again; I was outcast by everyone connected to him. It was two years before I was able to open my own shop, Forever True." Richie sees his work very much as a trade: "I am really just like a barber with a faithful client list. I keep it tight, and manage to travel the world doing guest spots and conventions; I also get many tattooists coming to guest at Forever True." His influences are "the greats – Owen Jensen, Bob Wicks, George Burchett, Dock King and Norman Collins." His artworks are completely permeated by the techniques of tattoo; "I use good old fashioned watercolour on board or paper. The paintings I do are really just vintage tattoo flash." The scene he says has changed dramatically over the last ten years: "It's a totally different industry now. It's gone from being a trade to a fine art; the tattooers and people getting tattooed are a different breed these days and want a totally different product and experience from getting tattooed. It will never be the way it used to be, but, hey, nothing will."

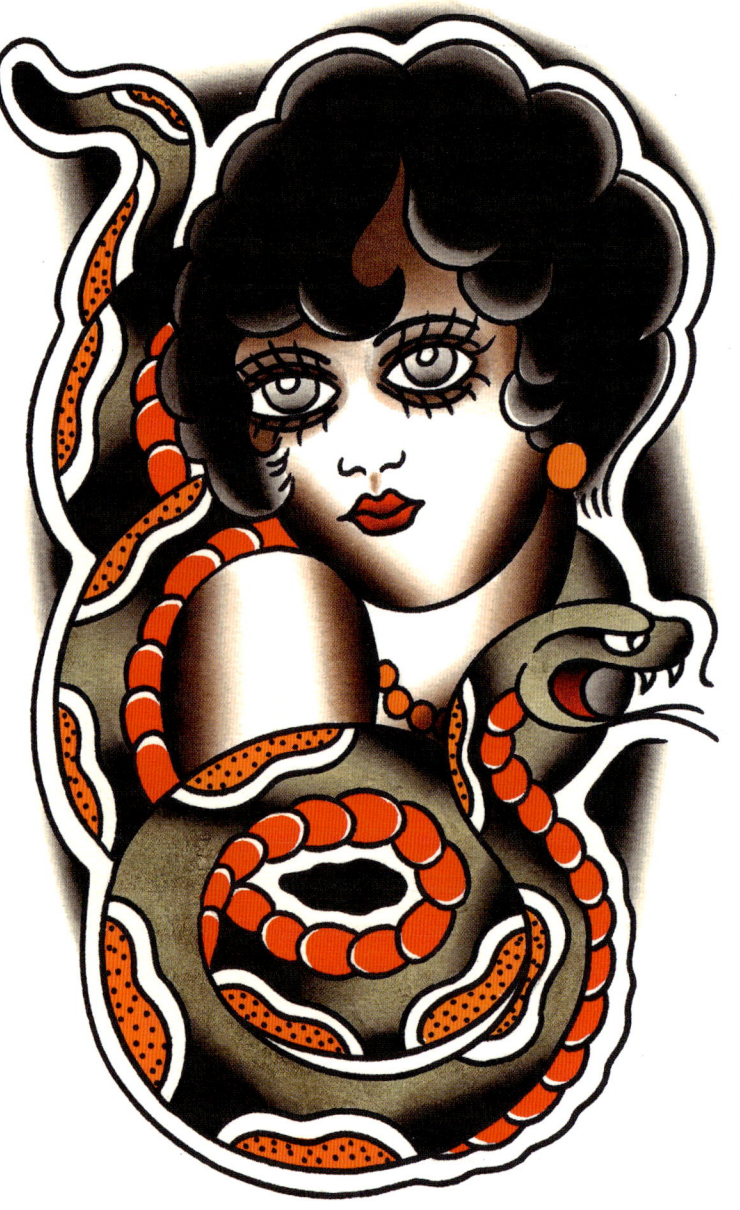

ABOVE: *Snake Woman*. Pen, ink and markers.
RIGHT: *Ship and Anchor*. Pen, ink and markers.

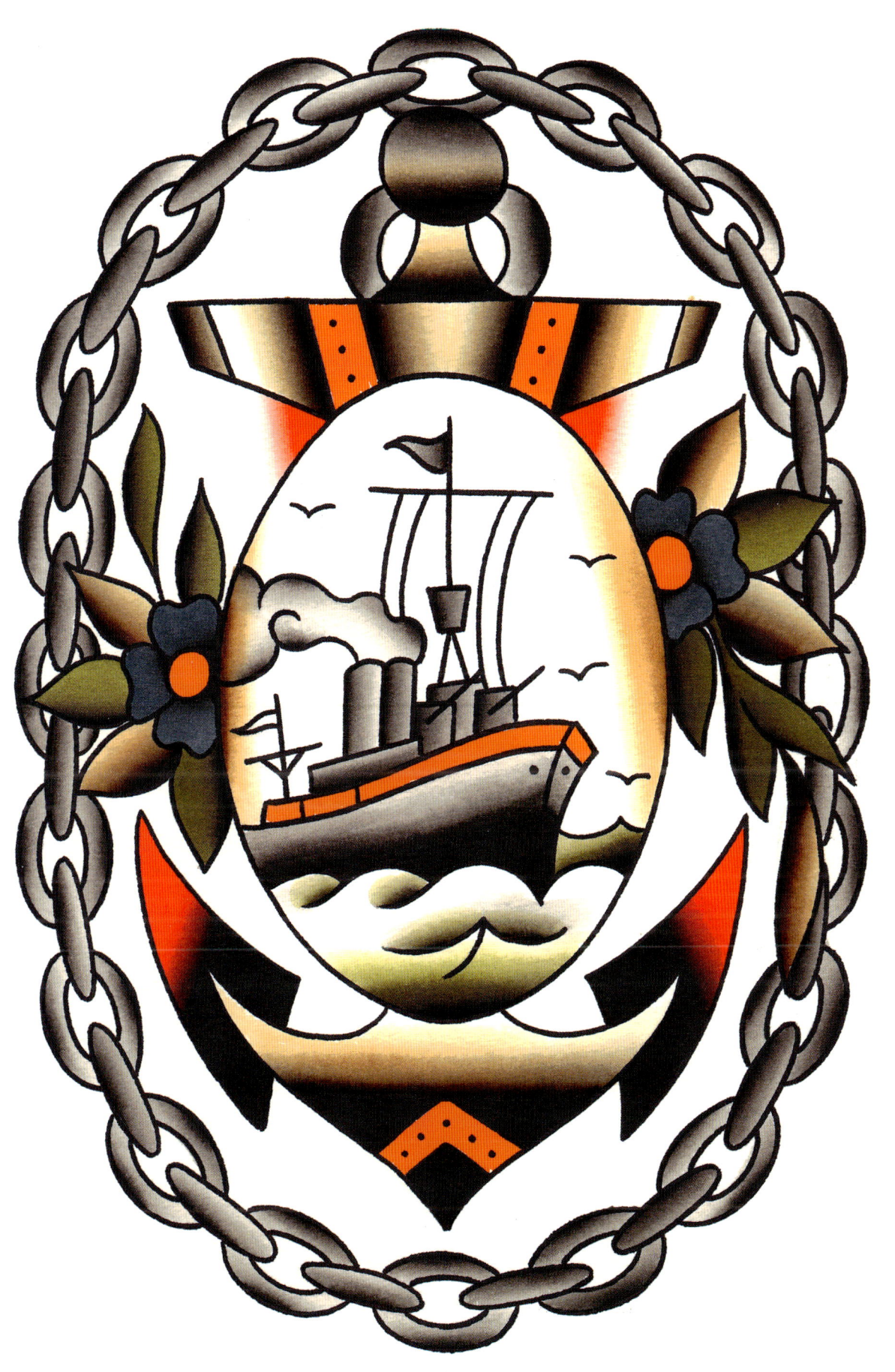

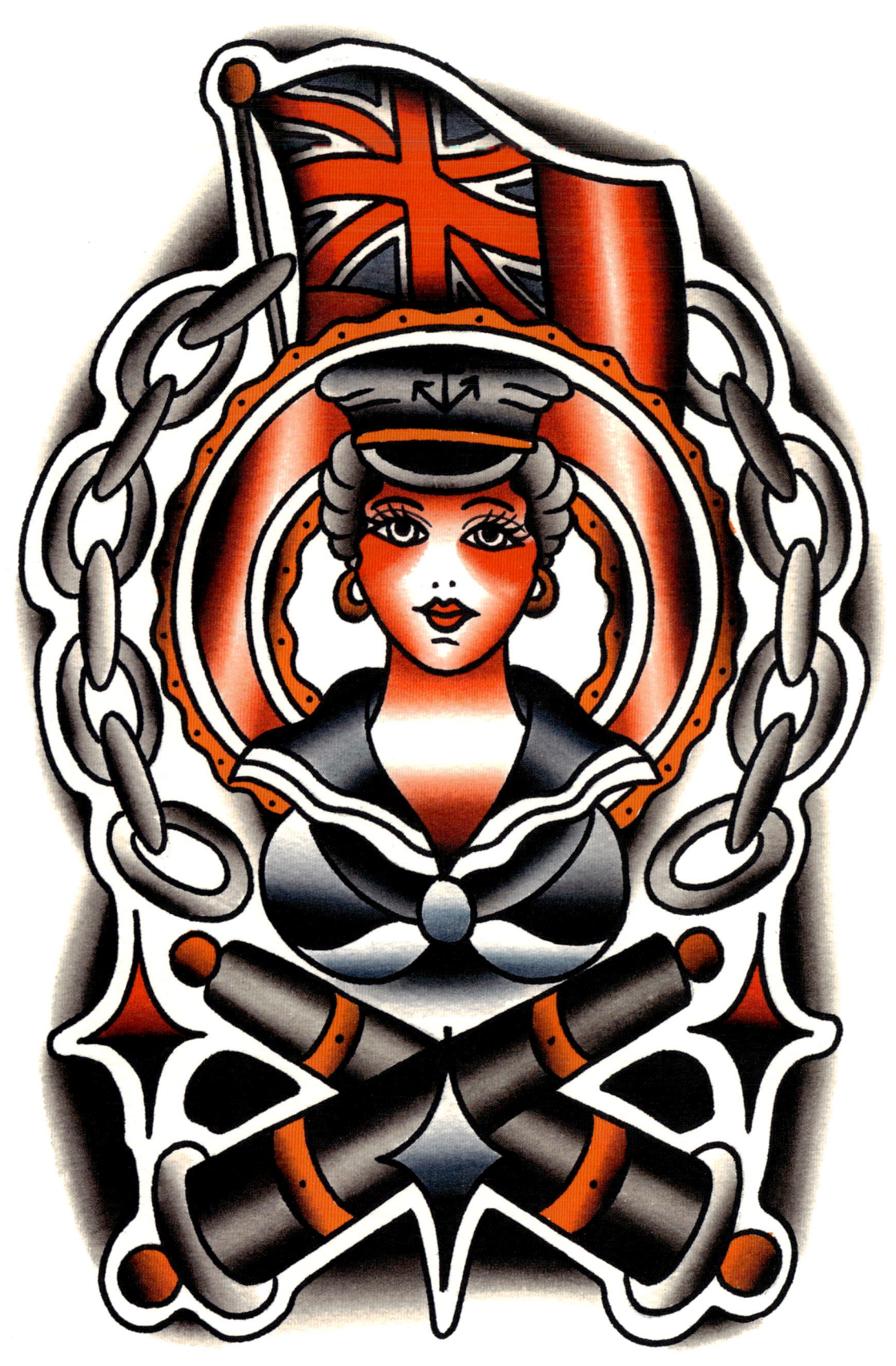

ABOVE: *Senior Service*. Pen, ink and markers.
RIGHT: *Chief and Sioux*. Pen, ink and markers.

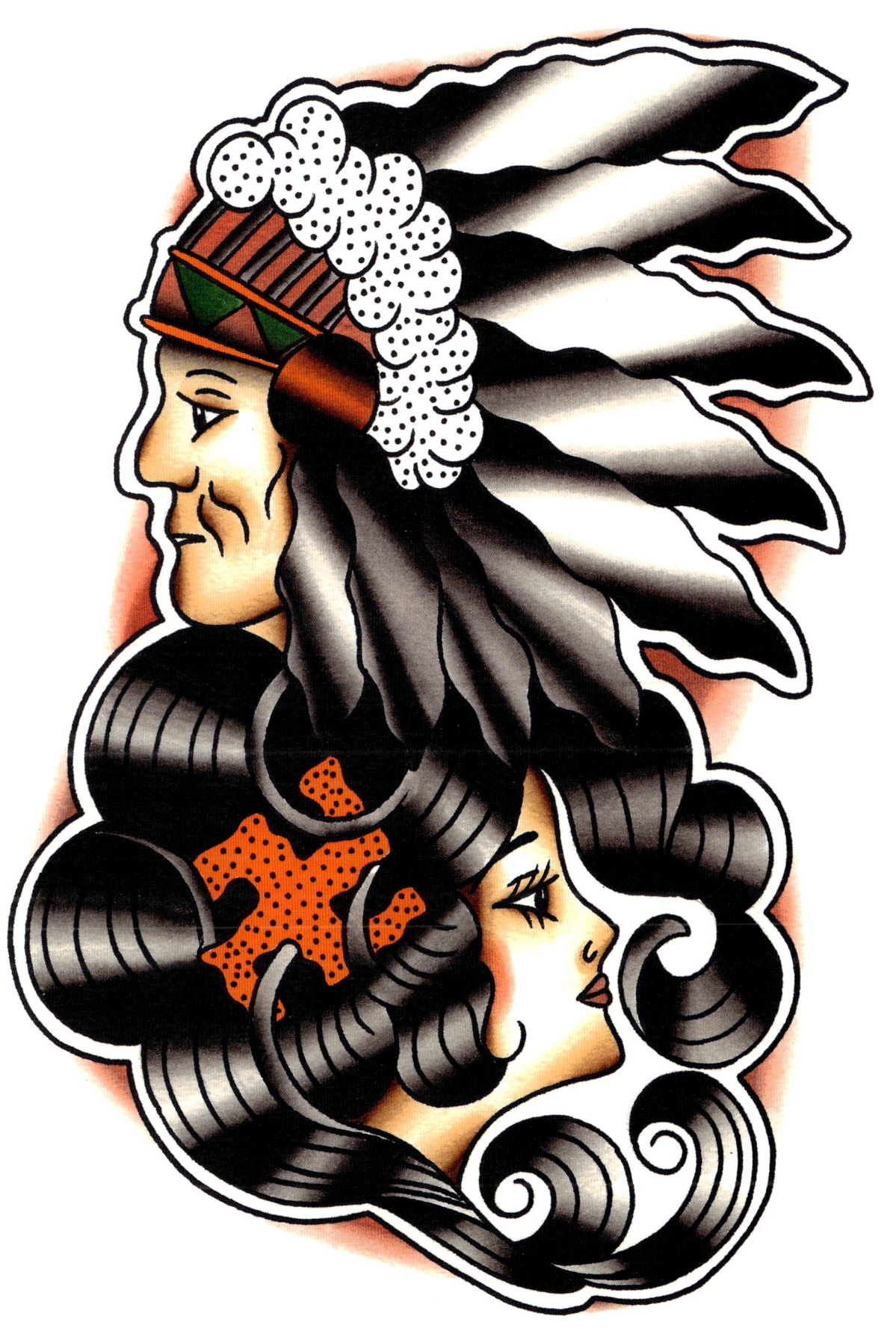

COLLINS

LONDON, UK.

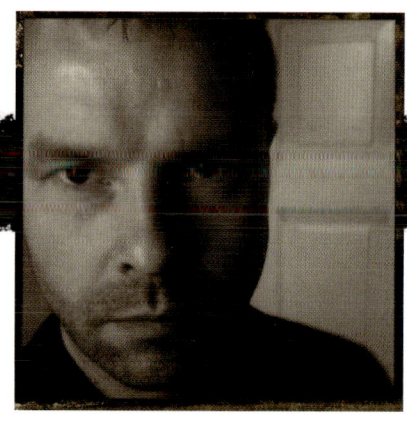

Adam Collins tripped into tattooing quite easily: "I had designed a few tattoos for some friends who got them done by Bug in Camden in the late '80s; they looked pretty good so I had some done myself. I then simply added the word 'tattooist' to my name (becoming instantly more popular) and had no trouble finding people happy to let a complete novice tattoo them from scratch. The toughest thing was stopping springs snapping on my first machines." He started out tattooing in Deptford, east London in '92, then had a shop in Waterloo with Andy Bone before landing on his feet at New Wave Tattoo in Muswell Hill "with the legendary Lal Hardy. I'm still there now." Today he is "not so much influenced as inspired to do my own thing, which is much more difficult." Before then it was Christopher Nevinson, H.R. Giger, propaganda posters from the Second World War and "the scribblings of toddlers." His work has been extensively featured, including on the covers of four tattoo magazines, in *Total Tattoo* and *Tattoo Master* as well as in *The Sun* newspaper's Bizarre column. In 2009 he won first prize in the black and grey category at the London Tattoo Convention, for Alicia's Alien backpiece; "most of my clients now trust me to get on with it once they have told me their ideas...I happily don't seem to attract 'fashion ink' victims."

Adam creates his art for pleasure, working with a Wacom Bamboo tablet for the initial design and then acrylics; "I don't count it as work – throwing away four days' worth of effort and concentration out the window as my eyes bleed at three in the morning because it doesn't look right and I can't step away....now that is not 'work'!" Tattoo obviously influences his painting, but it's also "a good source of cynicism....the end result of my brush work is a long way from a tattoo flash design." In addition to tattoo, he also draws inspiration from Orson Wells movies, shadows, train journeys, Victorian asylums, solitude, Tom Russell, Slayer..."to name a few." Of the scene in general he says "It's going straight to Hell. Tattooing has become a fashion. People who would have crossed the street at the sight of a tattoo shop now bore the flash of the walls with their reasons for getting inked. The media mosquitos are polishing the shine out of this folk art with reality shows. It's barrell-scraping boredom, but this fashion train, which has no meaning will, like all others, eventually derail." He adds, "but I still love tattooing and all its power and glory and remain faithful in my quiet corner of Muswell Hill."

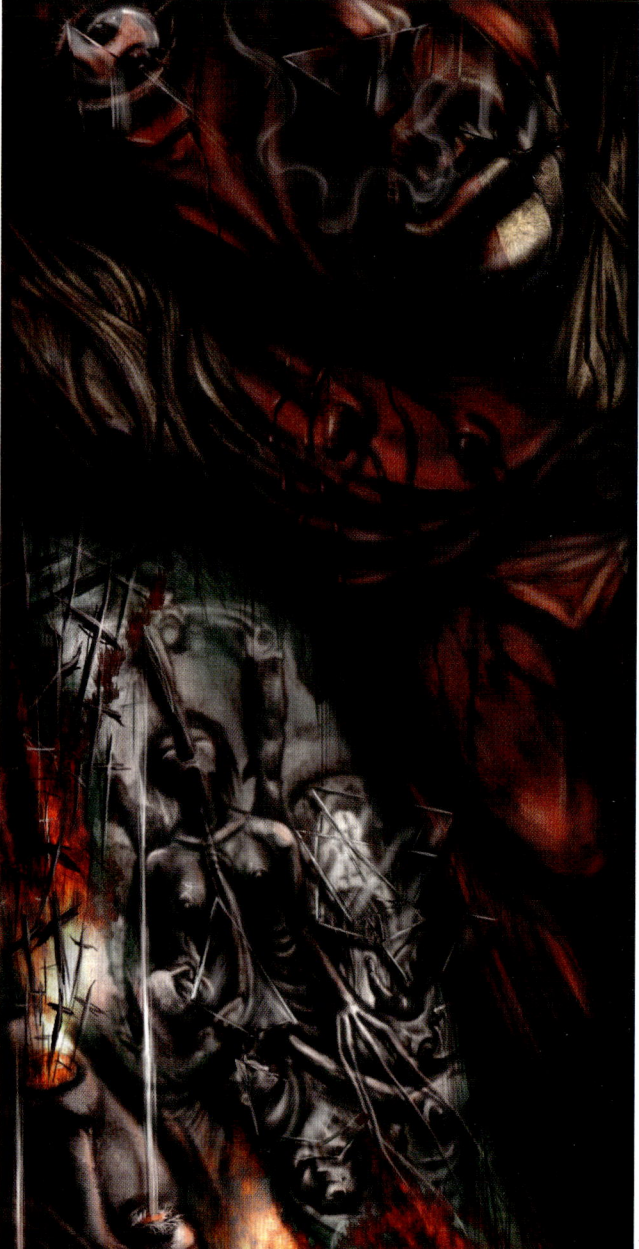

ABOVE: *Lynching*. Acrylic on canvas.
RIGHT: *Fear*. Acrylic on canvas.

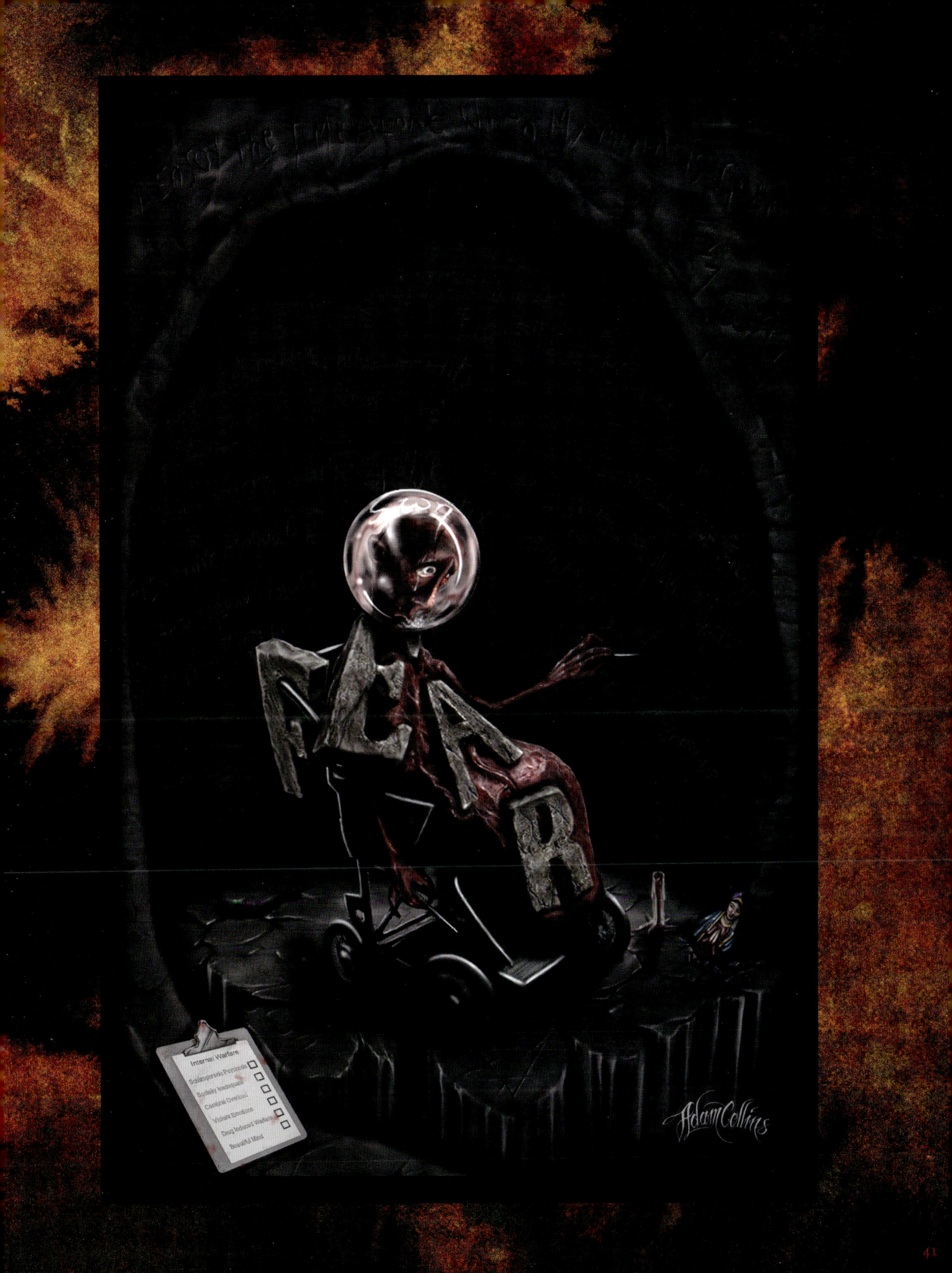

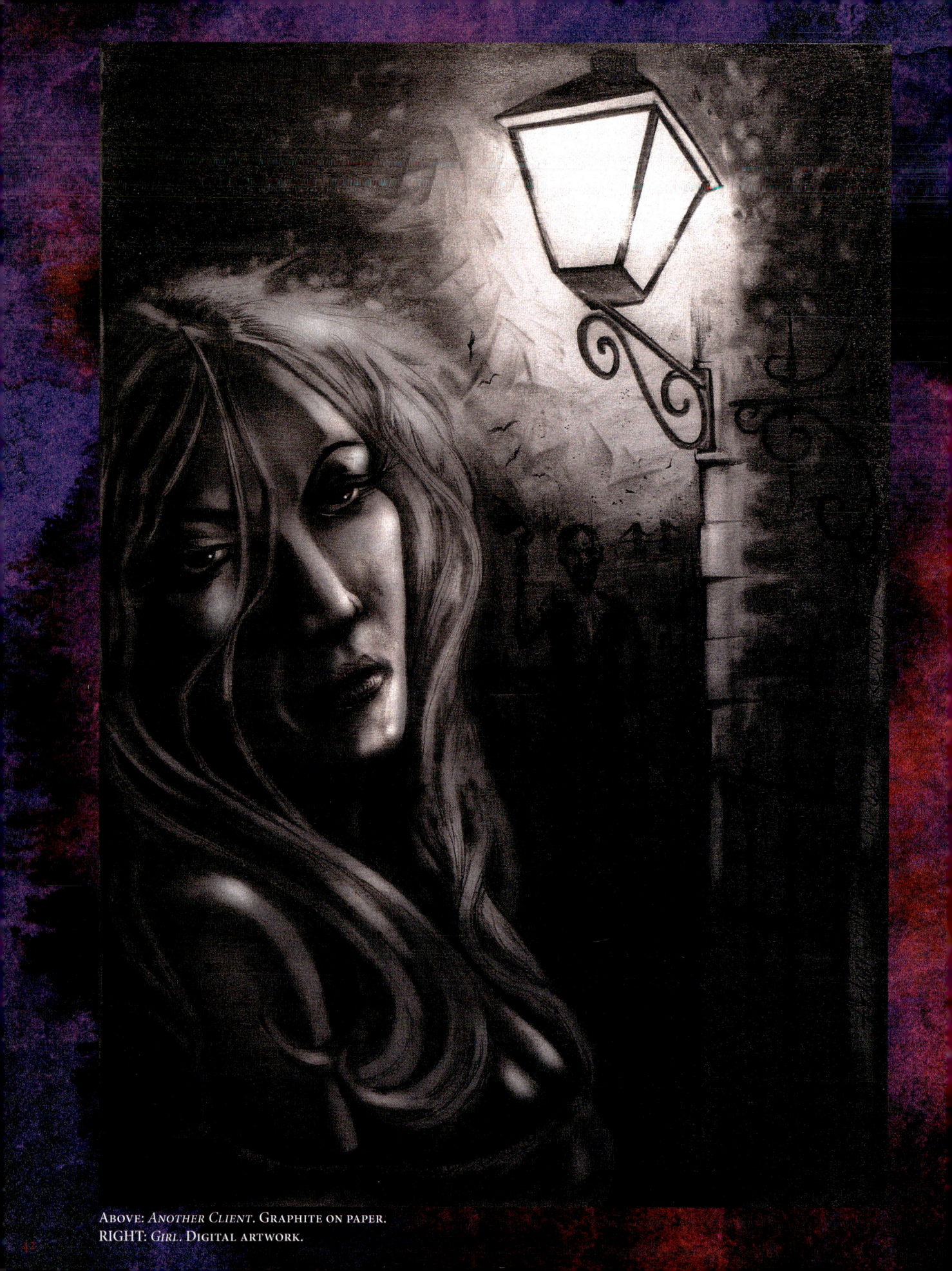

ABOVE: *Another Client*. Graphite on paper.
RIGHT: *Girl*. Digital artwork.

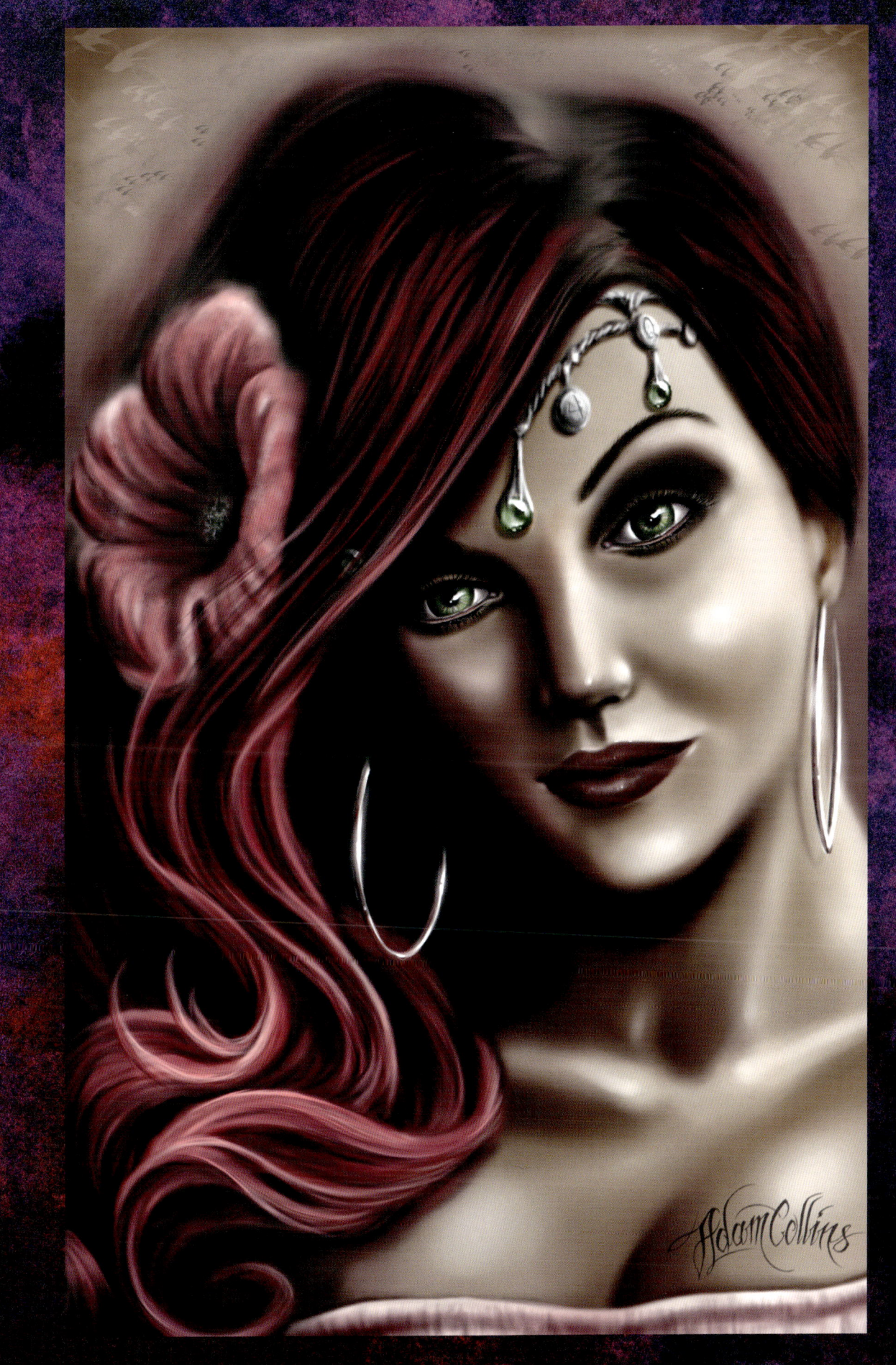

CONLON

CA / NEW YORK, USA.

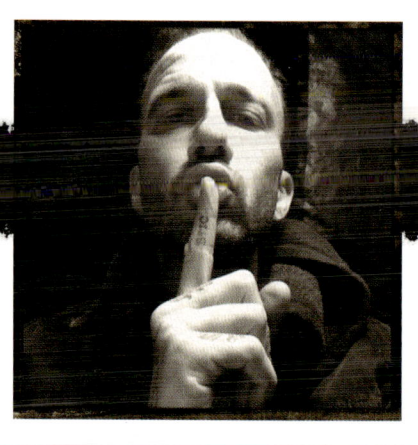

"It's all Popeye's fault," says Patrick Colon, "seeing those inked anchors on his arms as a kid is what got me into tattoo." He started at Erno Tattoo in San Francisco – "it was a bit nerve-wracking at first, but my co-workers helped me hugely and I tried not to bite off more than I could chew." Today, twenty-one years later, he is on the East Coast, working at East Side Ink, in Alphabet City N.Y.C. and at Graceland in Brooklyn. Patrick trained at the School of the Museum of Fine Art, Boston and then at Academy of Art College, San Francisco.

He sees a useful interaction between his fine art and tattooing: "My tattooing helps my painting and illustration art; people come to me with a lot of wacky ideas and it's fun to try and give them life; the fine art also helps my tattooing." When talking of influences it's "the numerous artists I have met over the years and also the great new crop of talent currently emerging….and also, in no particular order, comic books, old masters, museums, video games, books, history, photography…you name it." Most of the art he creates is illustrative work – figures, animals and scenery – and is done to commission; "Folks come to me when they need custom drawing done." He is mindful however of the traditions of tattoo: "I think you can push some of the laws of tattooing, but only so much; the techniques that the masters of skin art have developed, over many, many decades, also have to be borne in mind." Patrick has exhibited extensively, usually in gallery group shows, and has also been featured in myriad magazines; "I'm particularly fond of *Tattoo Life*," he says.

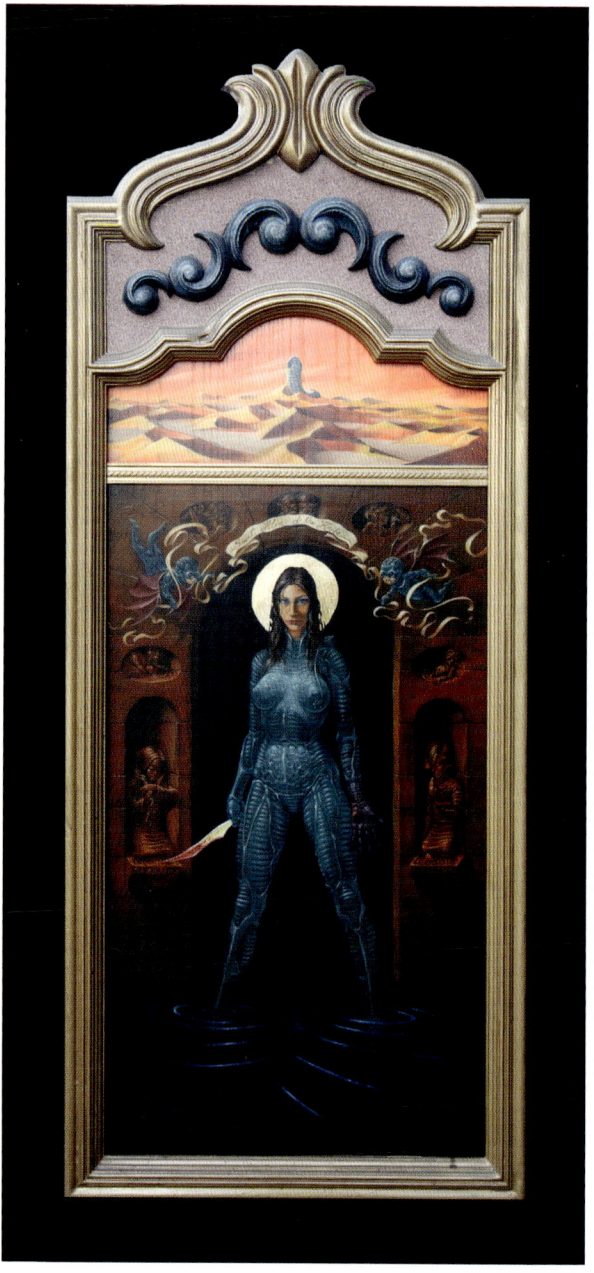

ABOVE: *Saint Alia of the Knife*. Oil on wood.
RIGHT: *Siren*. Pastels and pencil on paper.

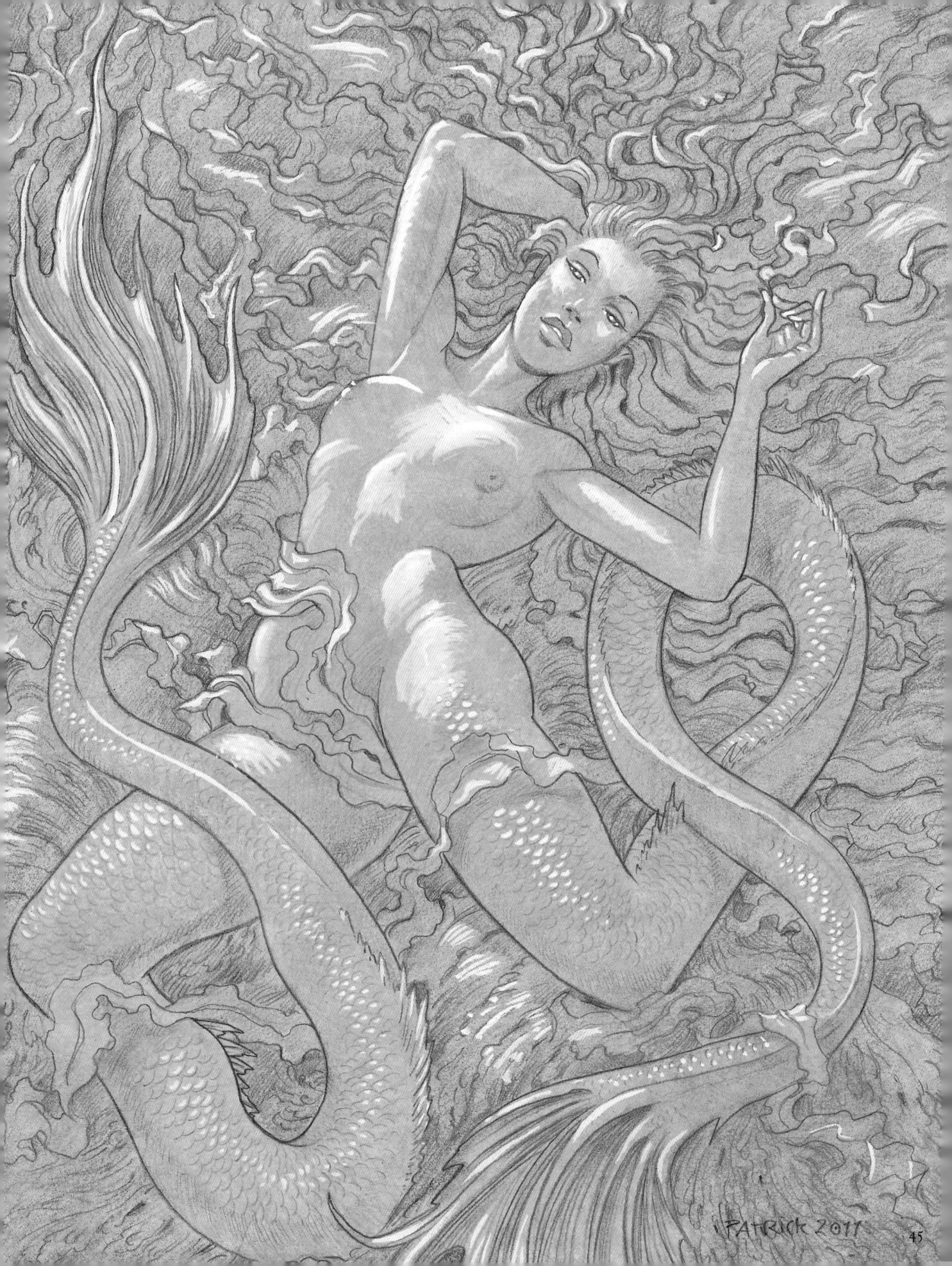

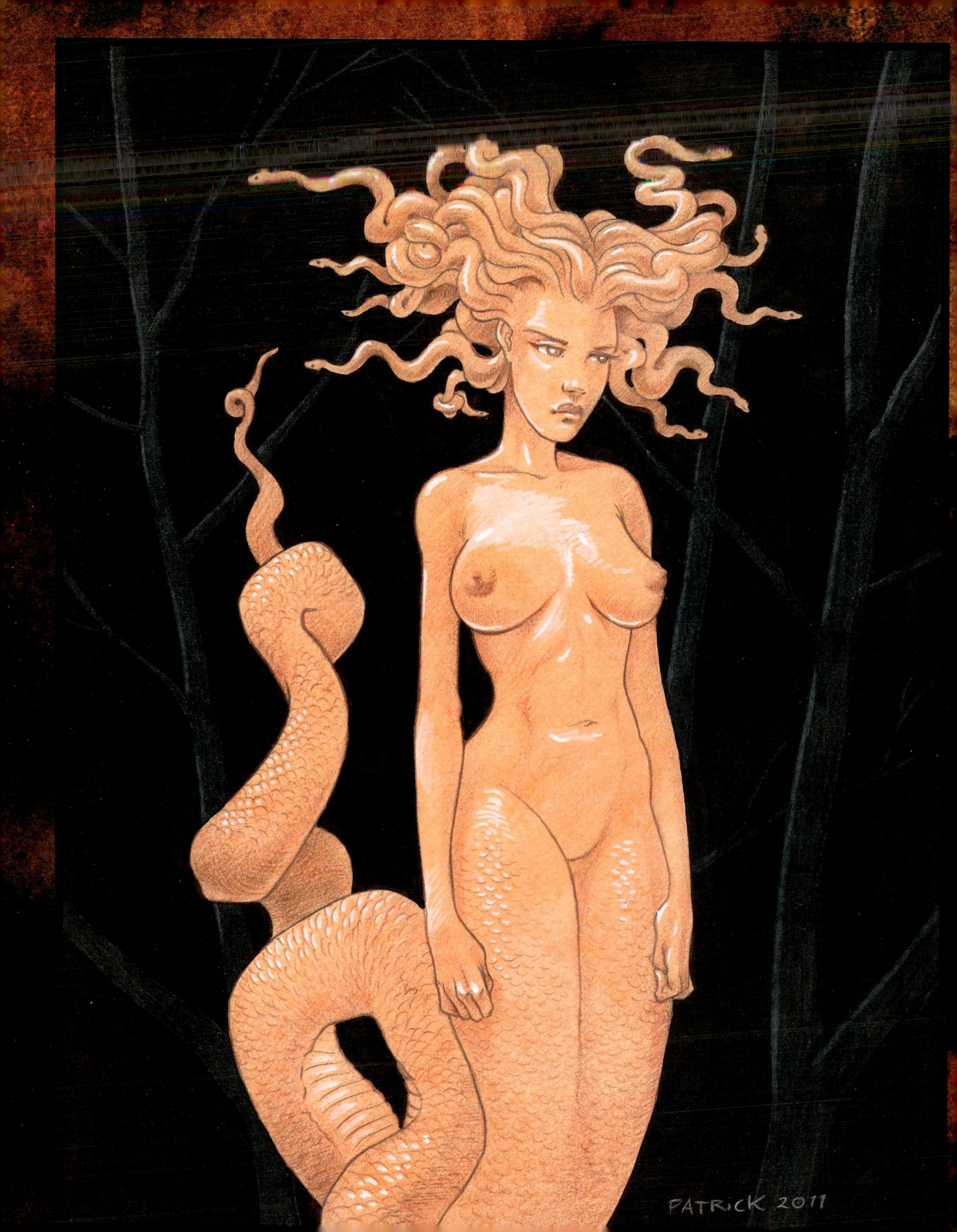

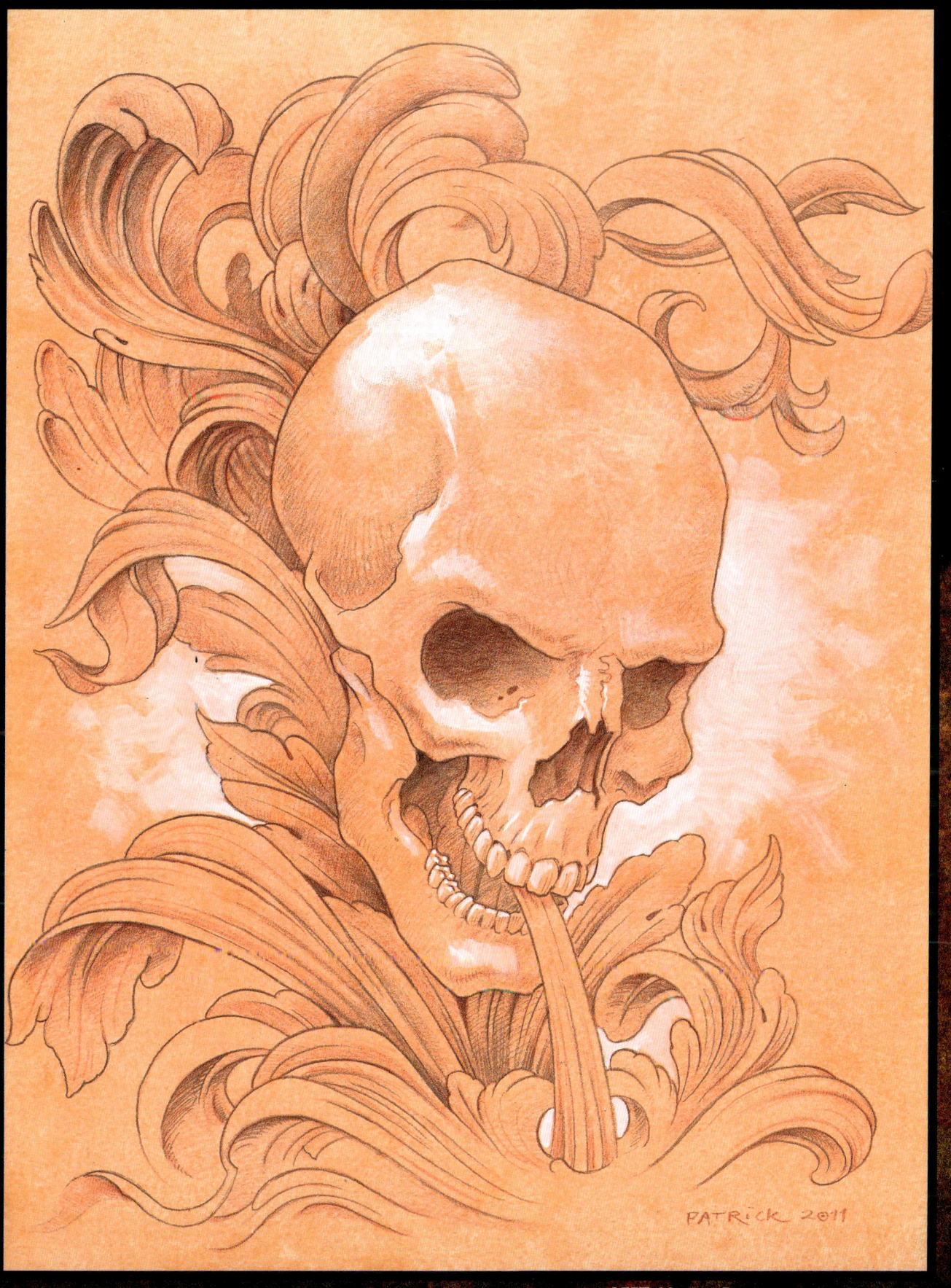

LEFT: *Medusa*. Pastels and pencil on paper.
ABOVE: *Skull*. Pastels and pencil on paper.
OVERLEAF: *Cavalry Charge (The Monster)*. Oil on canvas.

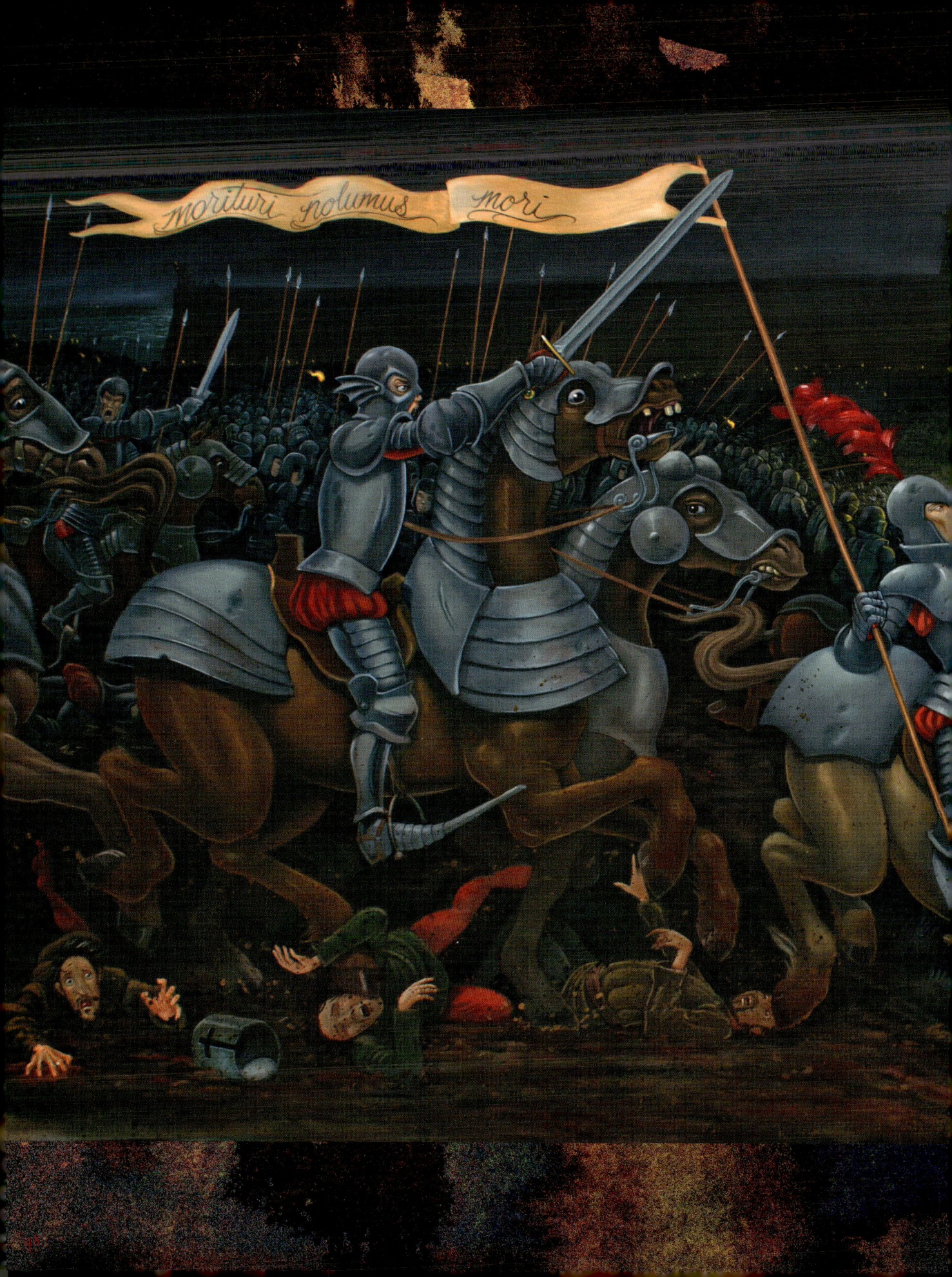

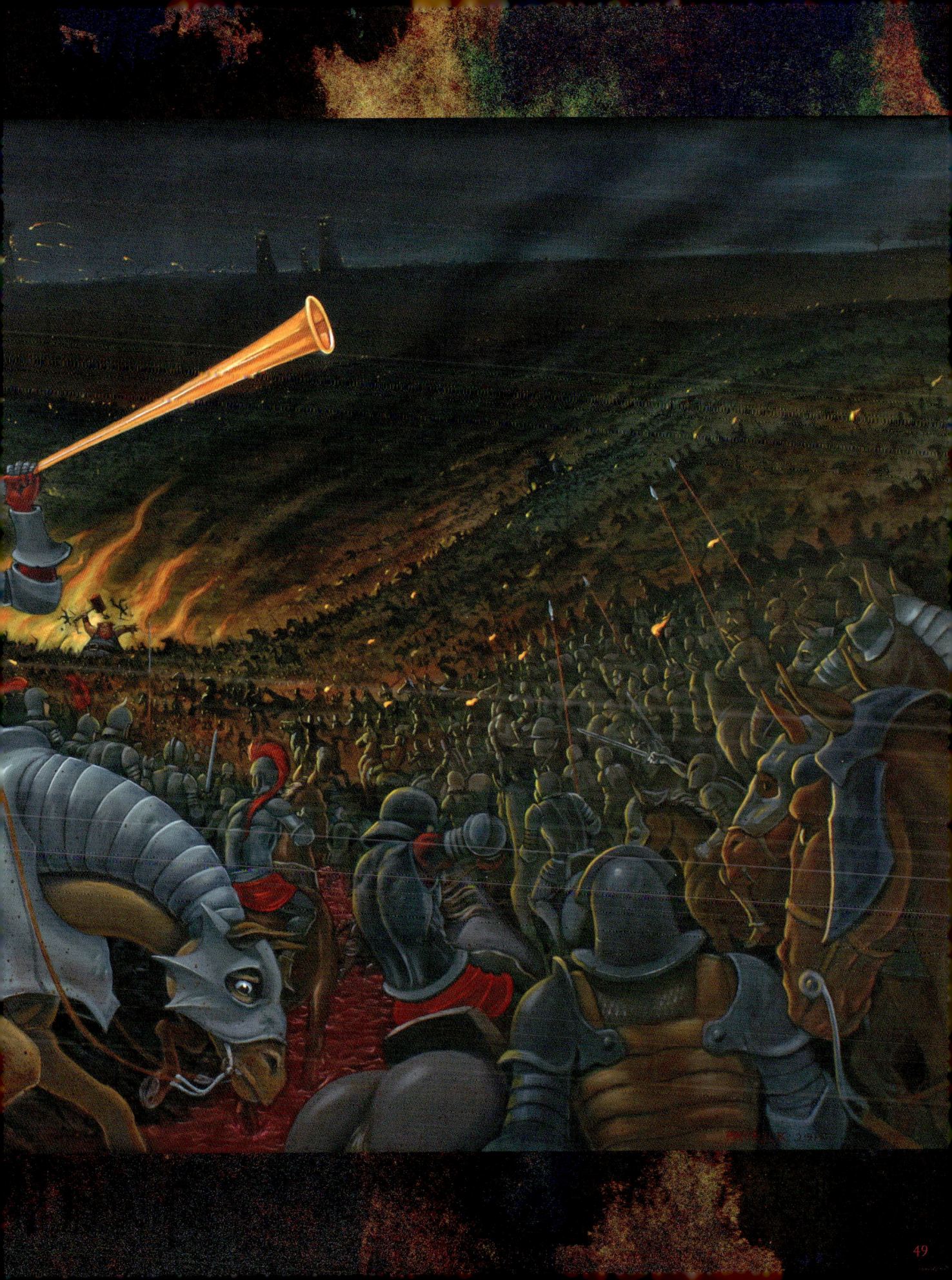

DAVIS

OH / SAN FRANCISCO, USA.

Mike Davis, a completely self-taught artist, whose first job was painting theatrical scenery, says the spark that got him tattooing was seeing the work of his subsequent mentor, Dana Brunson, and later of Bernie Luther. "Apprenticeships in those days were really hard to come by, so I started on my own. Information (no Internet) was really hard to come buy, and also knowing which equipment to buy. However, with a little help and a lot of encouragement from Dana I was soon tattooing out of my house." That was over twenty years ago, in Cincinnati, Ohio. He then moved to San Francisco, got a job in a tattoo shop and "really kicked into gear," before opening Everlasting Tattoo in 1992. Tattooing and drawing every day has hugely helped Mike develop as an artist. "Those drawing skills are the basis of what I do with the painting, although I like to keep a distinction between the two; my tattooing and art come from different traditions and feature different subject matters." When it comes to his art, it is old Dutch and Flemish masters who are his biggest influence. "I guess it's pretty obvious when you look at my paintings that I really love that old European art, particularly the work of Jan van Eyck and Pieter Bruegel. I try and get the same look and finish. I work in as traditional a fashion as possible: oil on canvas or wood panel." Occasionally however his interest in military history (the US Civil War and World War II in particular) also makes its way into his work. Mike paints first and foremost for himself. He does however also undertake commissions. He has been widely exhibited in the US and Europe and is represented by several galleries. His work also appears frequently in *Juxtapoz* and *Hey* and has been featured in numerous books.

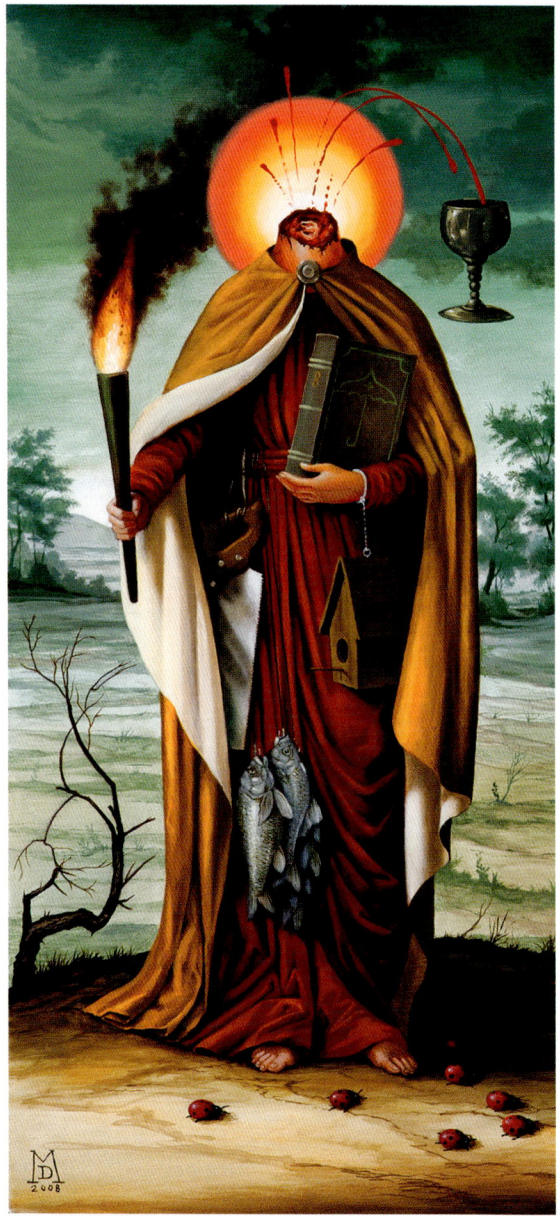

ABOVE: *We Meat Again*. Oil on canvas.
RIGHT: *A Mutual Agreement*. Oil on wood panel.

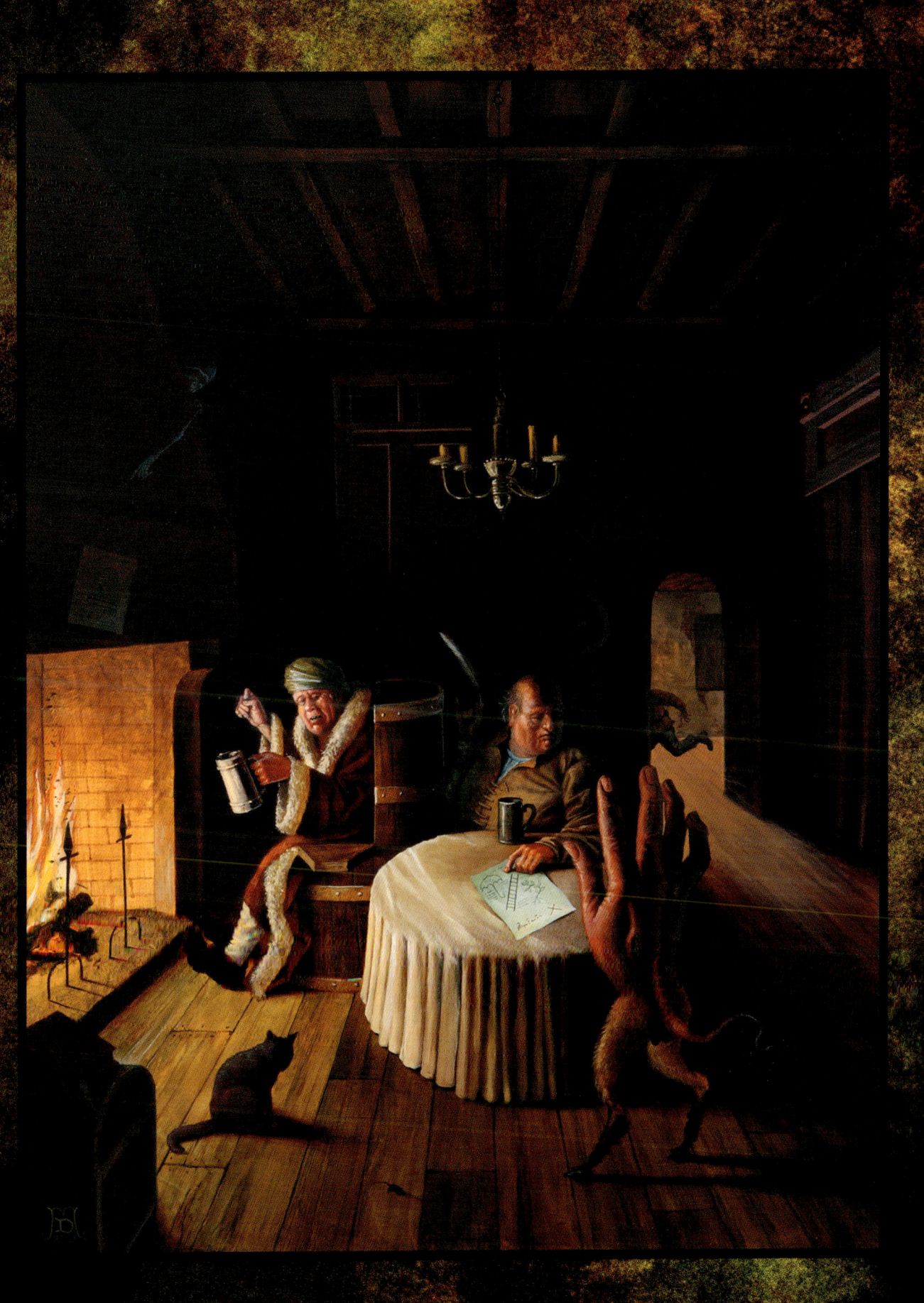

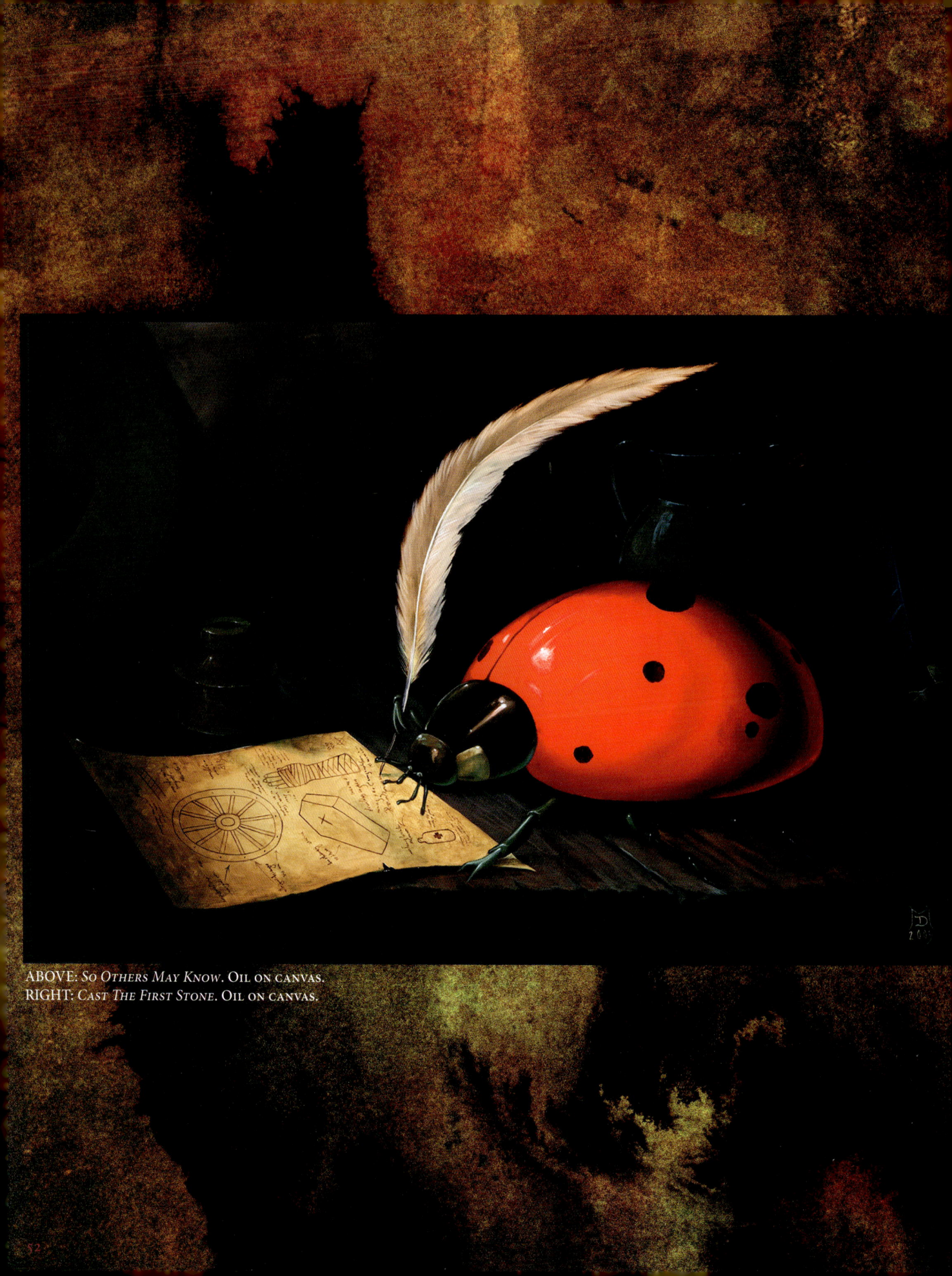

ABOVE: *So Others May Know*. Oil on canvas.
RIGHT: *Cast The First Stone*. Oil on canvas.

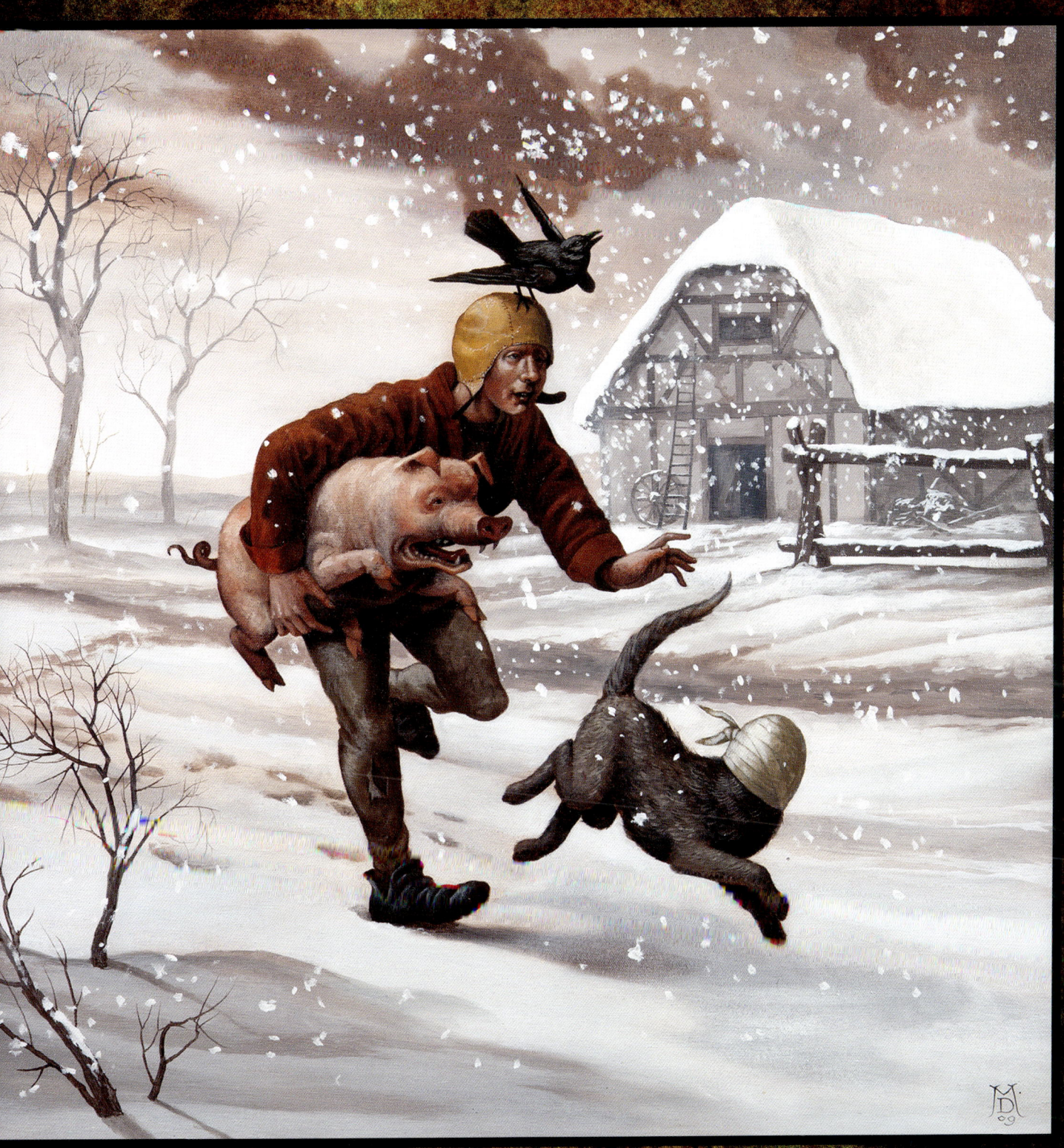

DE SABE

ITALY / LONDON, UK.

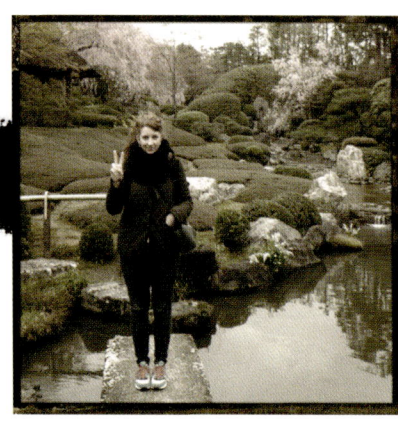

"I just couldn't see myself having a 'proper' job..." says Claudia... "what I knew was that I loved drawing, some serious challenges and tattoos, so it felt natural that I should follow the latter course." At the start everything was tough; Claudia even made her own needles. "I didn't know quite what to do at first, but I do remember the thrill of seeing the ink staying under the skin." She started in her living room, then joined a shop where, she says, "I was literally 'The Bitch'. I was working for no money and was given no knowledge. When I realised I would learn fuck all there, I left." Today she works at Jolie Rouge in London and tattoo is "all I do. I can't imagine spending a day not tattooing. Even when I paint traditional themes, I am doing it within the traditions of tattoo." Claudia is largely self taught, other than some art at school in Italy, which was largely focussed on architecture. She says she tries not to get directly influenced by other artists, but rather looks for inspiration. Amongst painter/tattooists she admires Regino Gonzales, Andre Malcolm, Steve Boltz, Horiyoshi III, Daniel Albrigo and Alexander Grim. More generally she is "a fan of everything old. I love the pre-Raphaelites, the arts and crafts movement, art deco, art nouveau, '80s graffiti, Miss Van, Modez, Canova and the whole momento mori thing...and not forgetting those many brilliant Japanese artists like Ukiyoe, Kuniyoshi, Hokusai and Kyosai. Claudia paints for pleasure. "Every day I respond to a commission when I tattoo. When I paint it's a case of what I like, when I like." Her work has been featured in many publications, including *Tattoo Life* and *Total Tattoo*. She has also exhibited at London Miles Gallery, Galleria Cavour in Padua and at tattoo conventions in London, Florence, Paris and Milan. Of the scene in general she says: "It has lost a lot of its magic. I believe the trade should retain some aspects of secrecy, so I don't discuss my techniques. A lot of people are also getting into tattooing because they think its cool, rather than for the love of the trade. It's become too easy to start. I just hope that the pleasure of meeting with some of those great down-to-earth artists won't disappear...that's all I can hope for!"

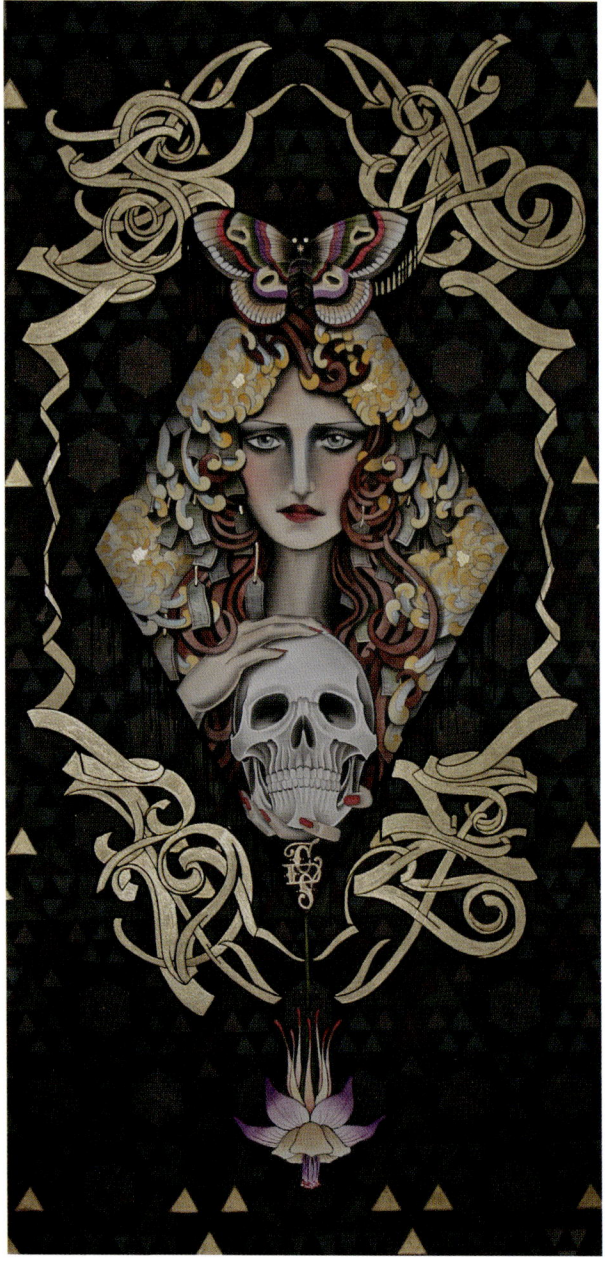

ABOVE: *Girl With The Fuschia*. Acrylic and pastels on board.
RIGHT: *Girl With Scarf*. Pen, ink and wash on paper.

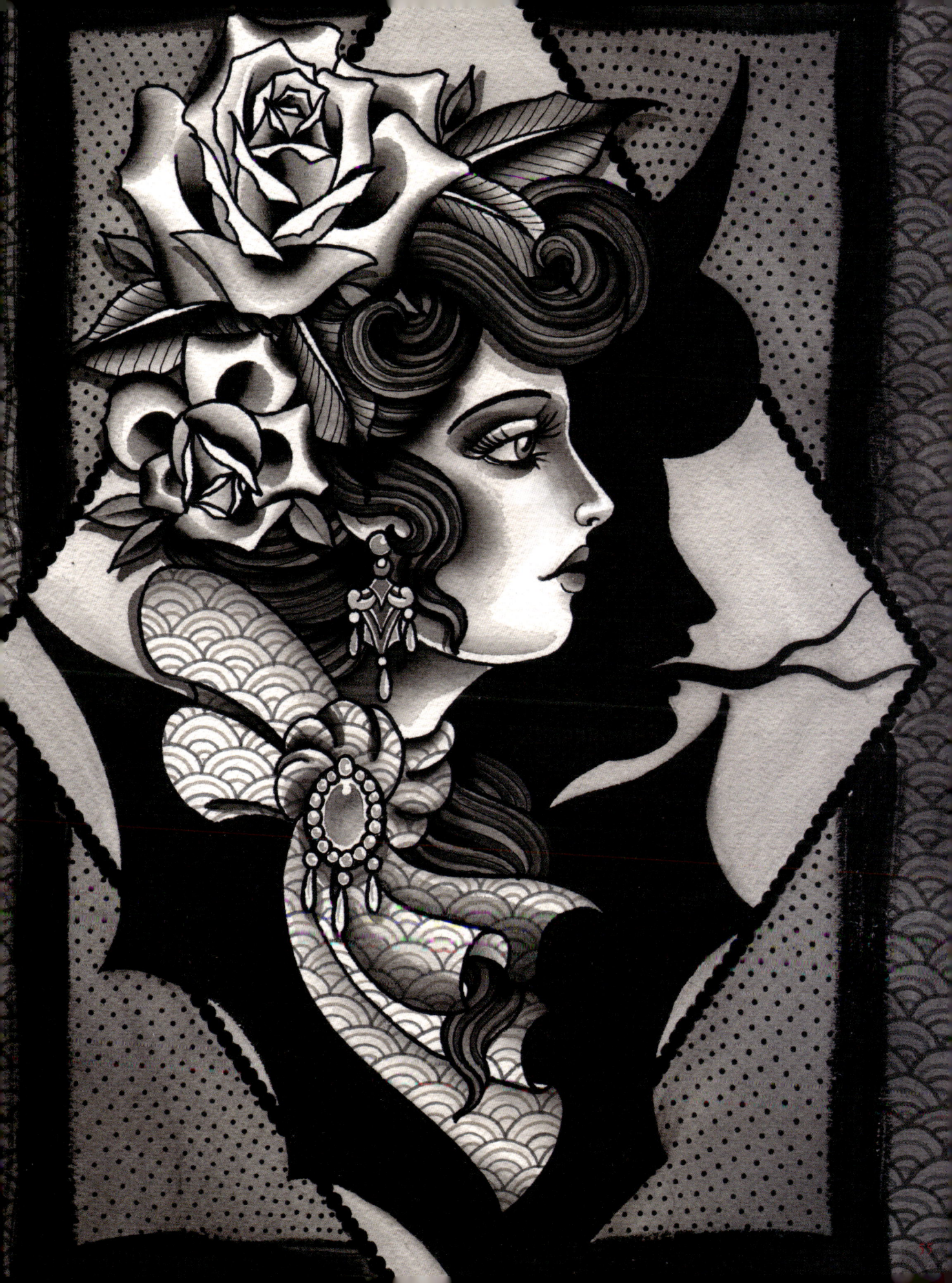

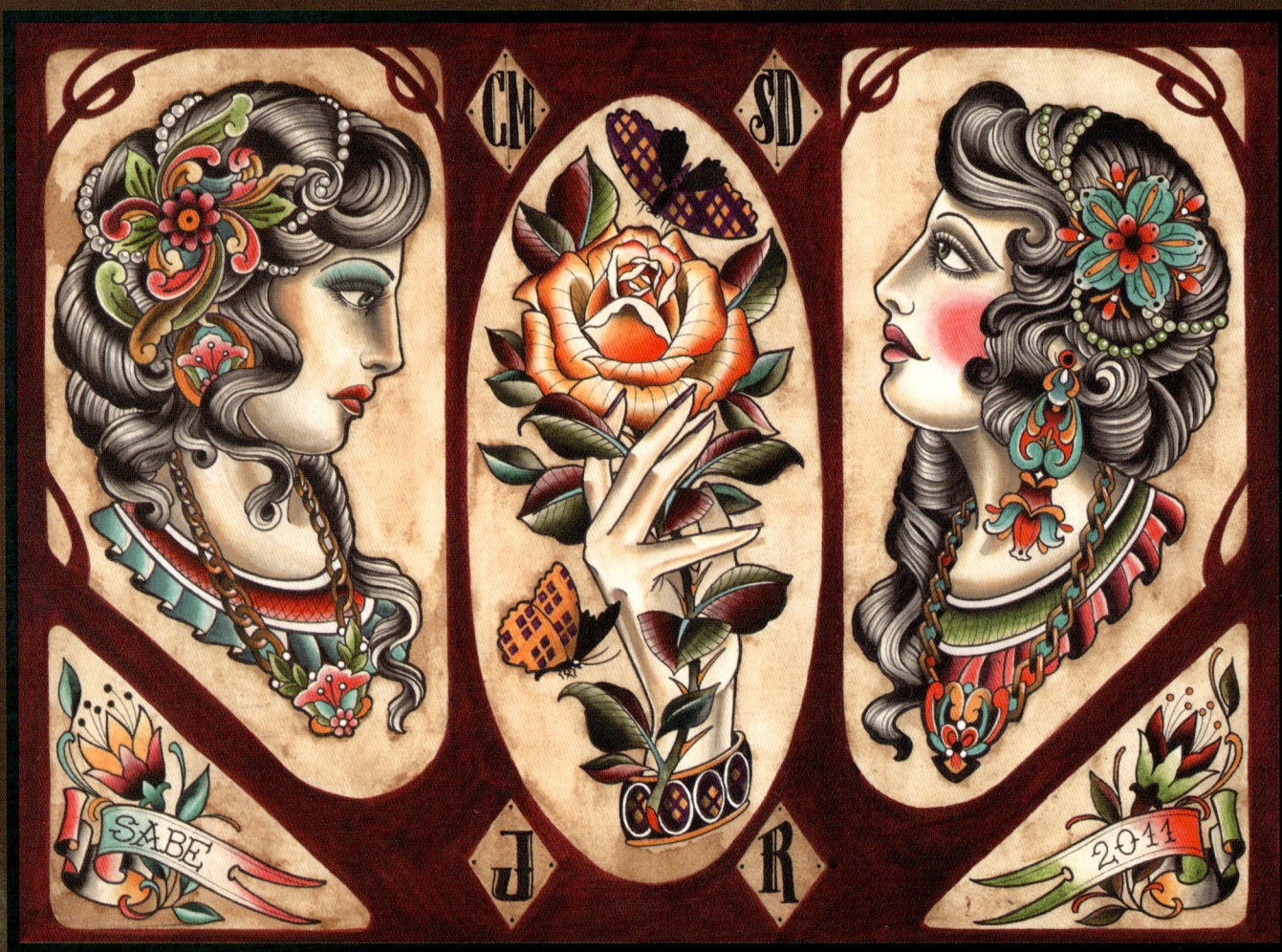

ABOVE: *Gypsy Girls*. Pen, ink and watercolour.
RIGHT: *Burlesque Dancer*. Pen, ink and watercolour.
OVERLEAF: *Love Ya*. Pen, ink and watercolour.

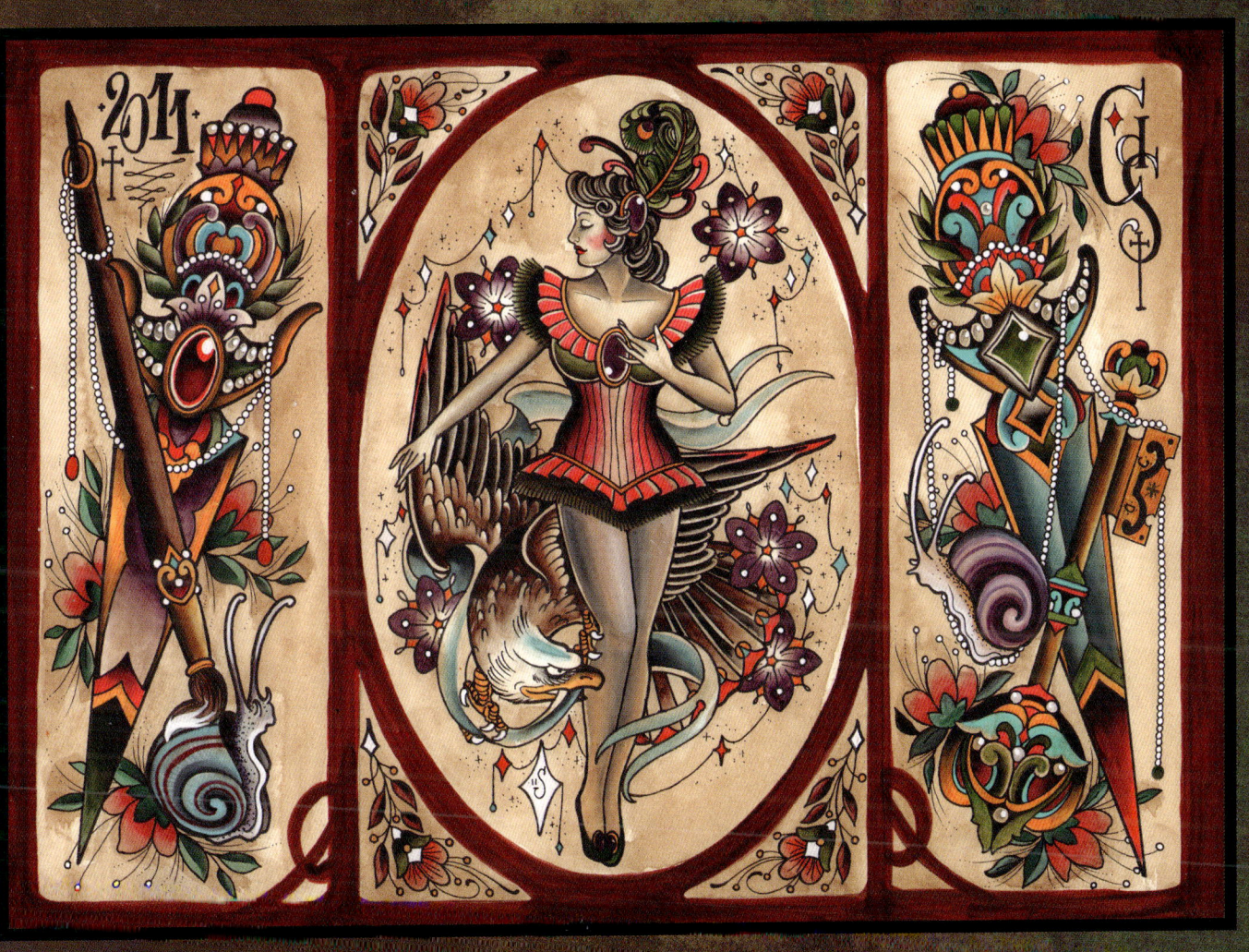

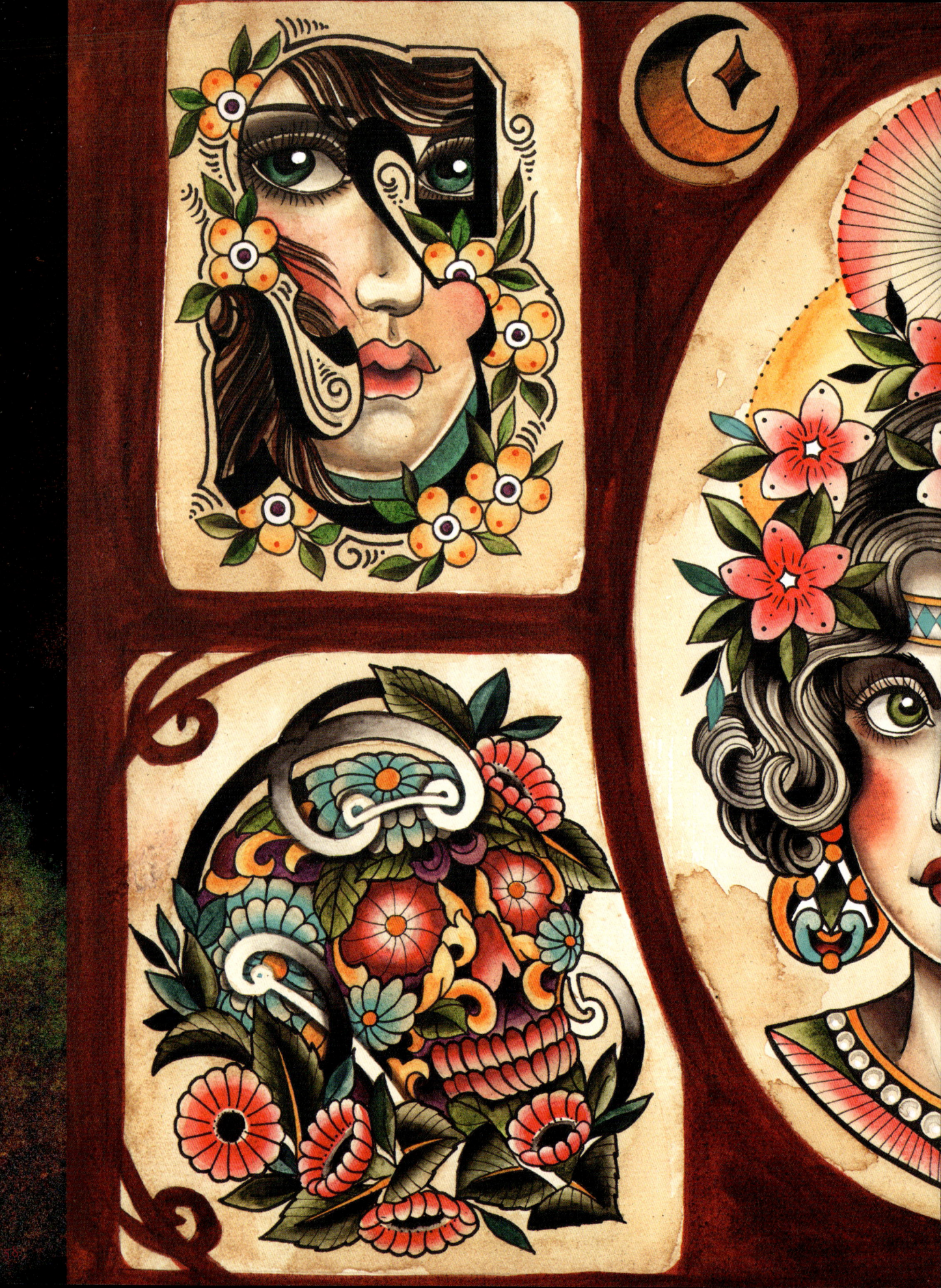

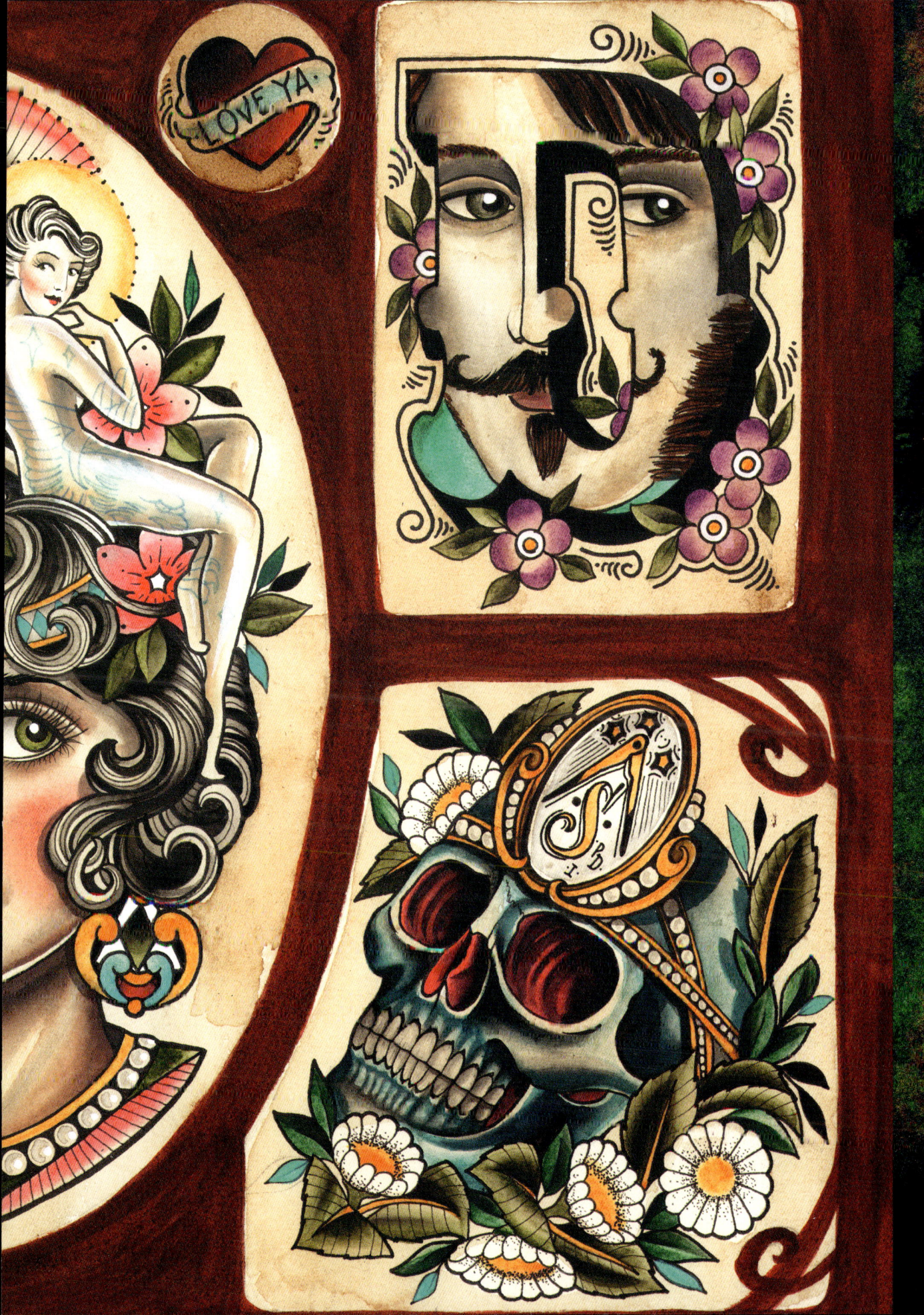

DIFA

LONDON, UK.

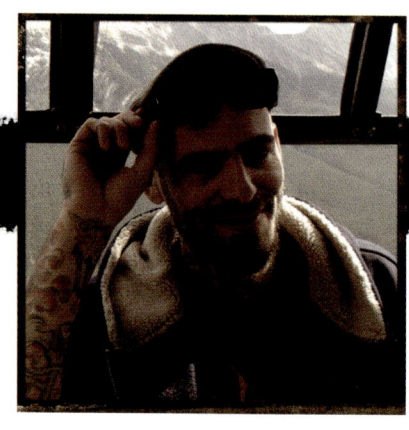

"For some reason I was into tattoos from a really young age. Even at the age of eight I used to draw tattoo designs for my swimming instructor, hoping he'd actually get them done (no luck). Then I started getting tattooed myself, hung out with a few artists and began to try and learn." Those were the days when you really had to know people to get hold of any kit and apprenticeships were really hard to come by. Matt pestered the guys who tattooed him, drew "like a loon", and got thrown out of many shops before he was introduced "to the mighty Jason Saga (RIP), who taught me the art." That was 14 years ago. Matt first tattooed at a stall in London's Camden Market, then worked at Tribalize with Andy Bone, before starting his own shop, Jolie Rouge, in 2005. He is largely self taught: "I got as far as starting an art A-level, but then got caught up in life until I had to draw for a living aged 22." He paints mostly for fun, as a release from the endless commissions at the shop. "The painting and the tattooing merge into one. When I paint I am always thinking 'could I tattoo this?', and my painting I'm sure benefits from my understanding of the human body, a result of drawing on them all day....my clients tell me a lot that they come to me because they like the way I draw boobs!" Asked to name artists who have influenced him Matt says: "Mostly comic and game concept artists – Joe Chiodo, Jim Murray, Simon Bisley, James Ryman and so many more – I could go on forever." His inspiration? "Anyone who knows me knows the first thing has to be Star Wars !! But also computer games and other nerdy films." Of the scene he says "In the last five years tattooing has evolved into a monster. In the future it will either devour the world or itself!"

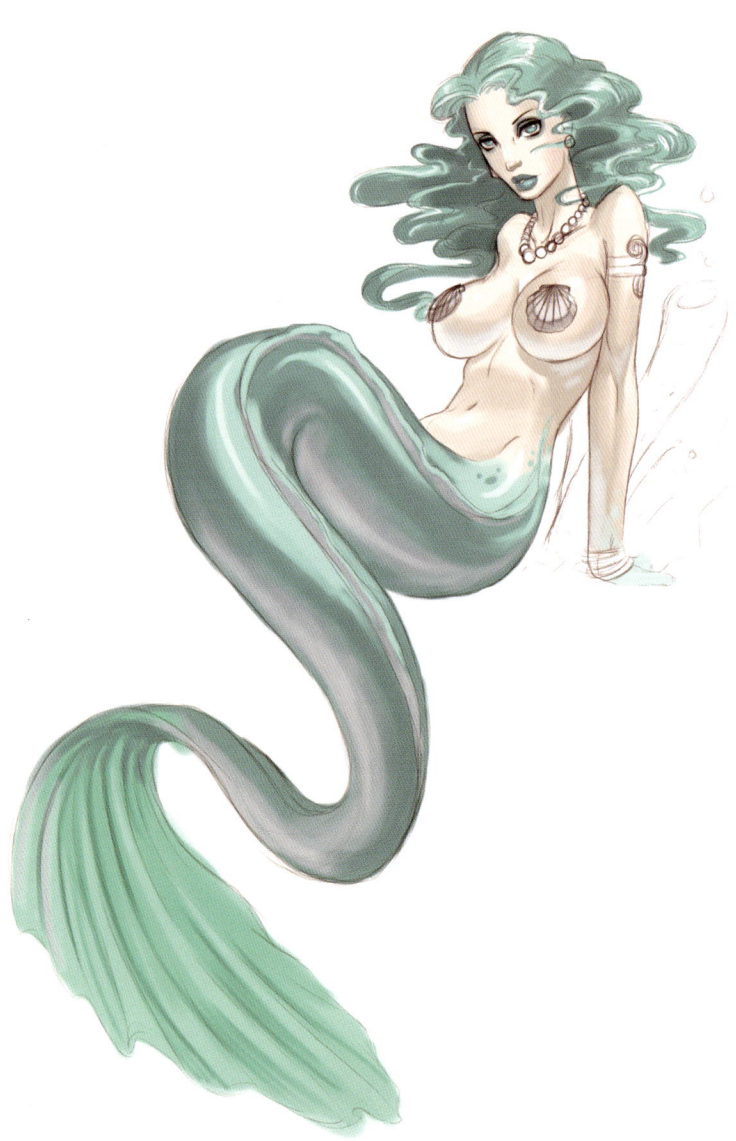

ABOVE: *Untitled*. Pen, ink and watercolour.
RIGHT: *Memories*. Digital artwork.

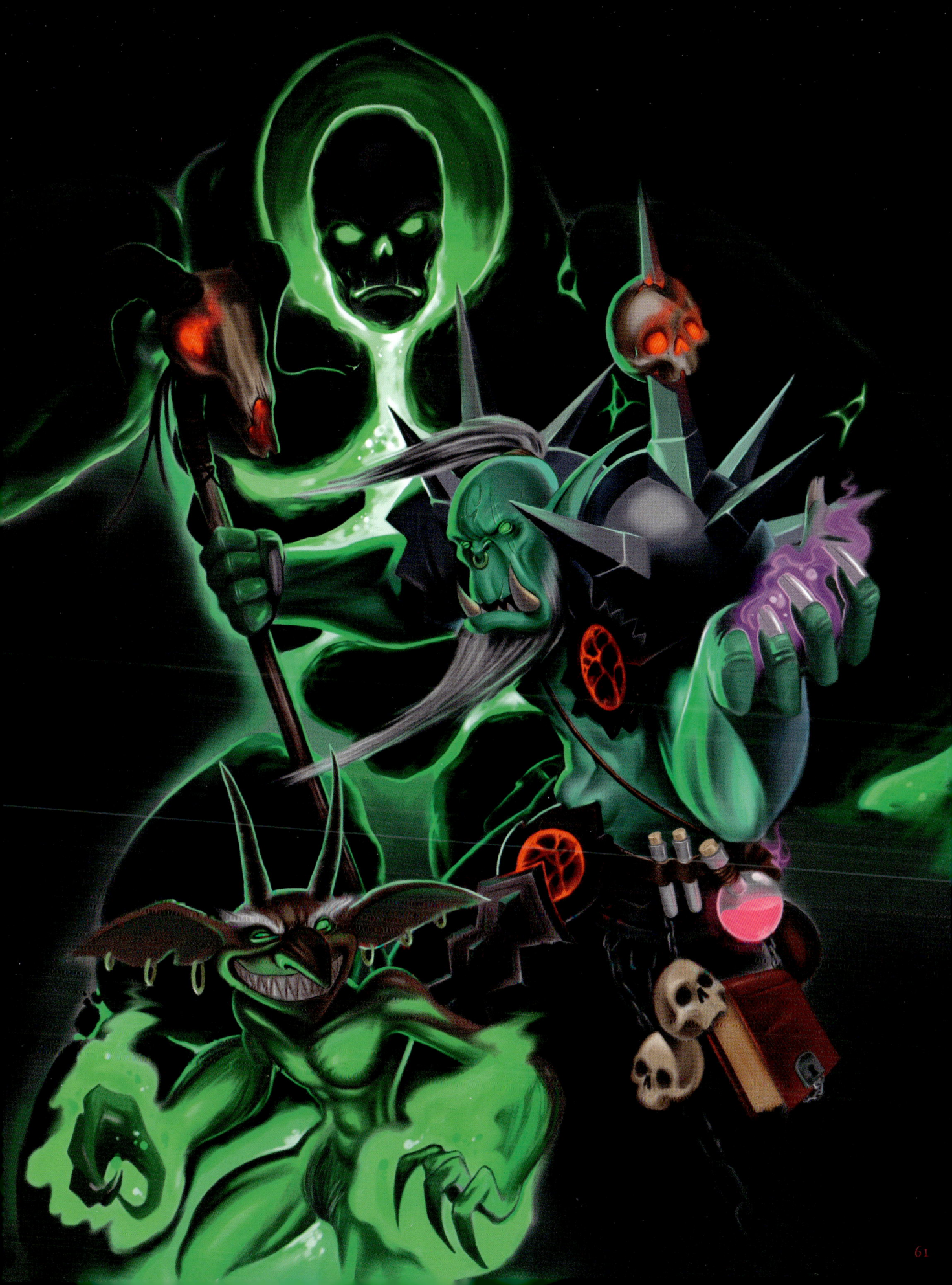

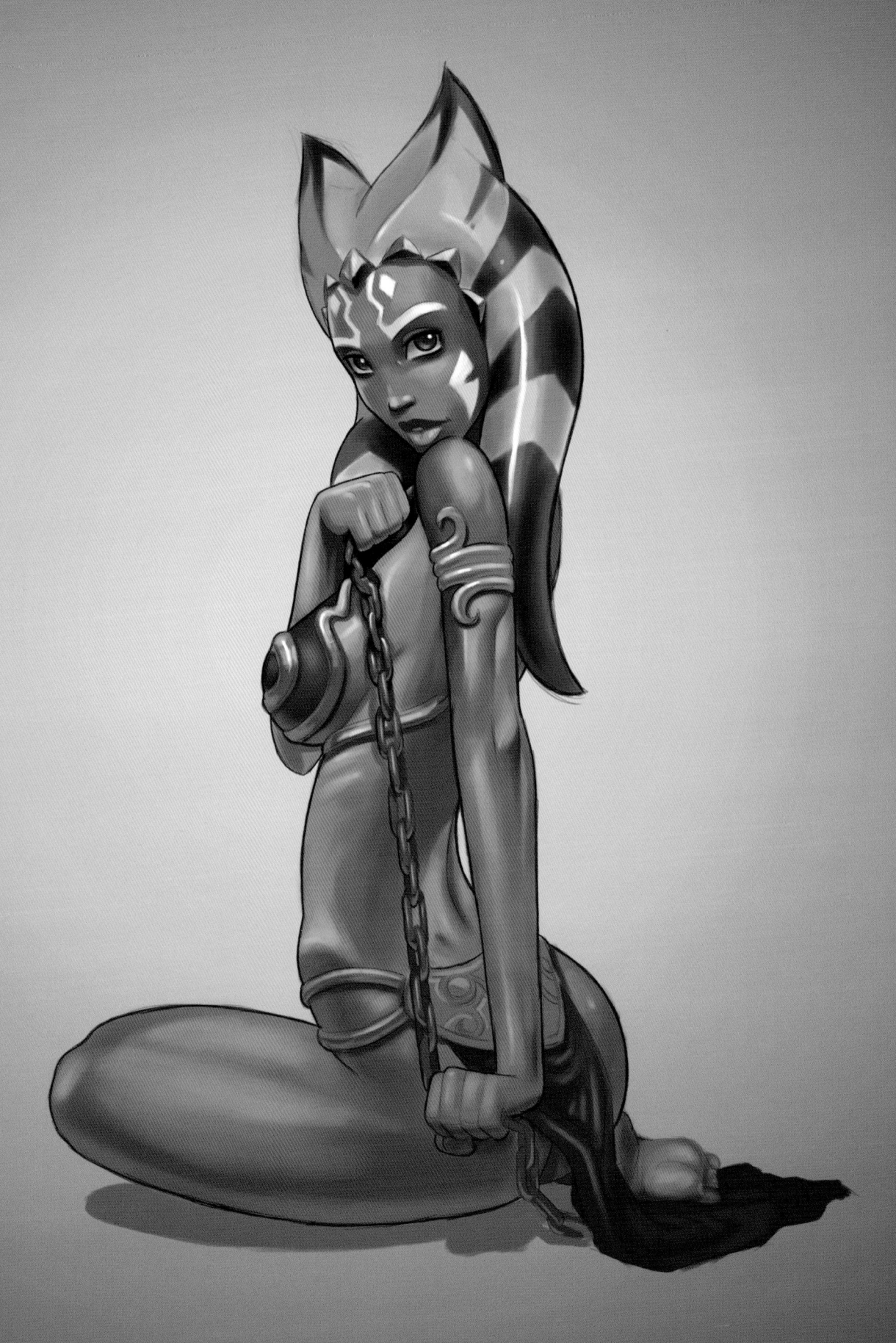

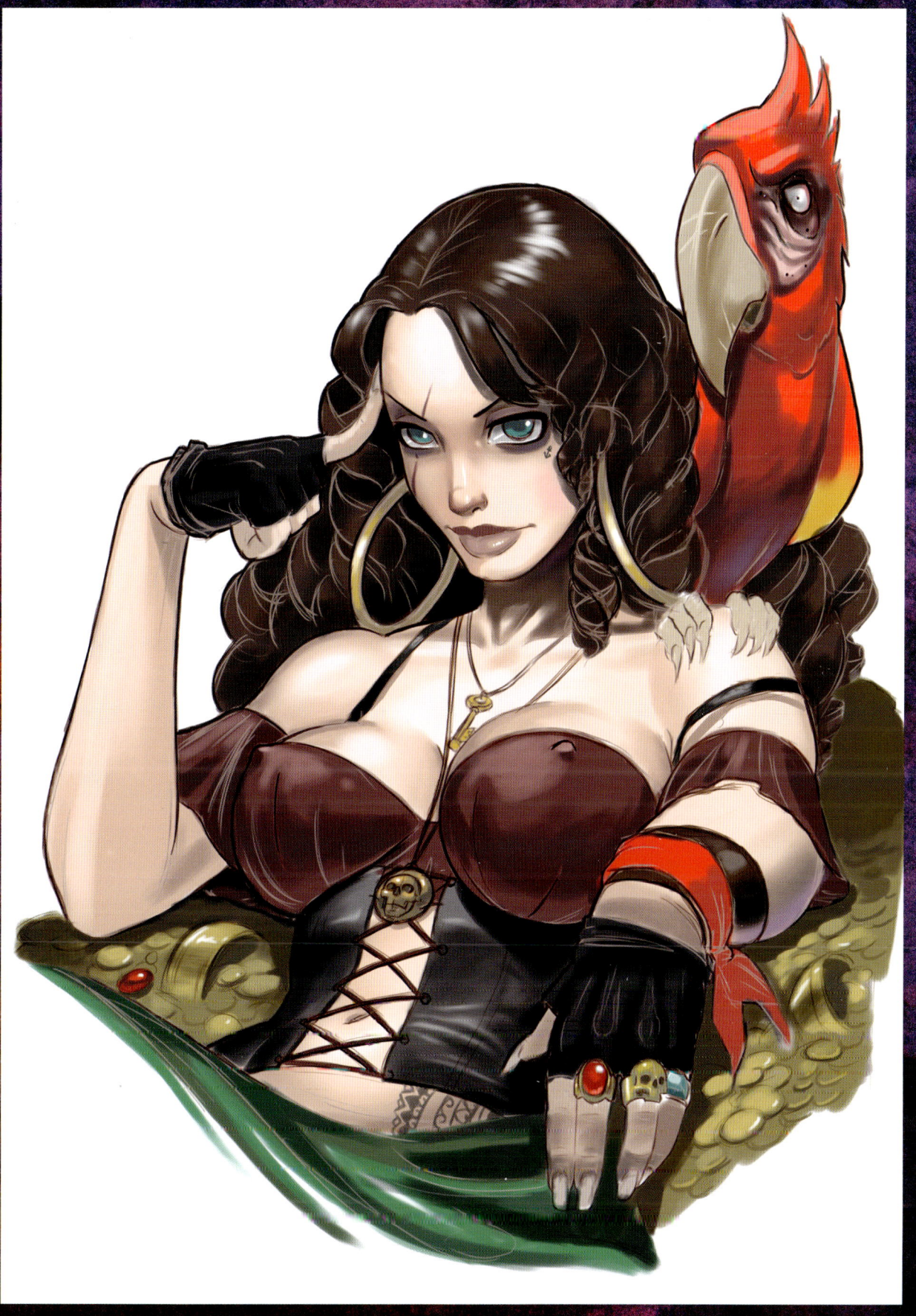

LEFT: *Untitled.* Pen, ink and digital.
ABOVE: *Untitled.* Pen, ink and digital.

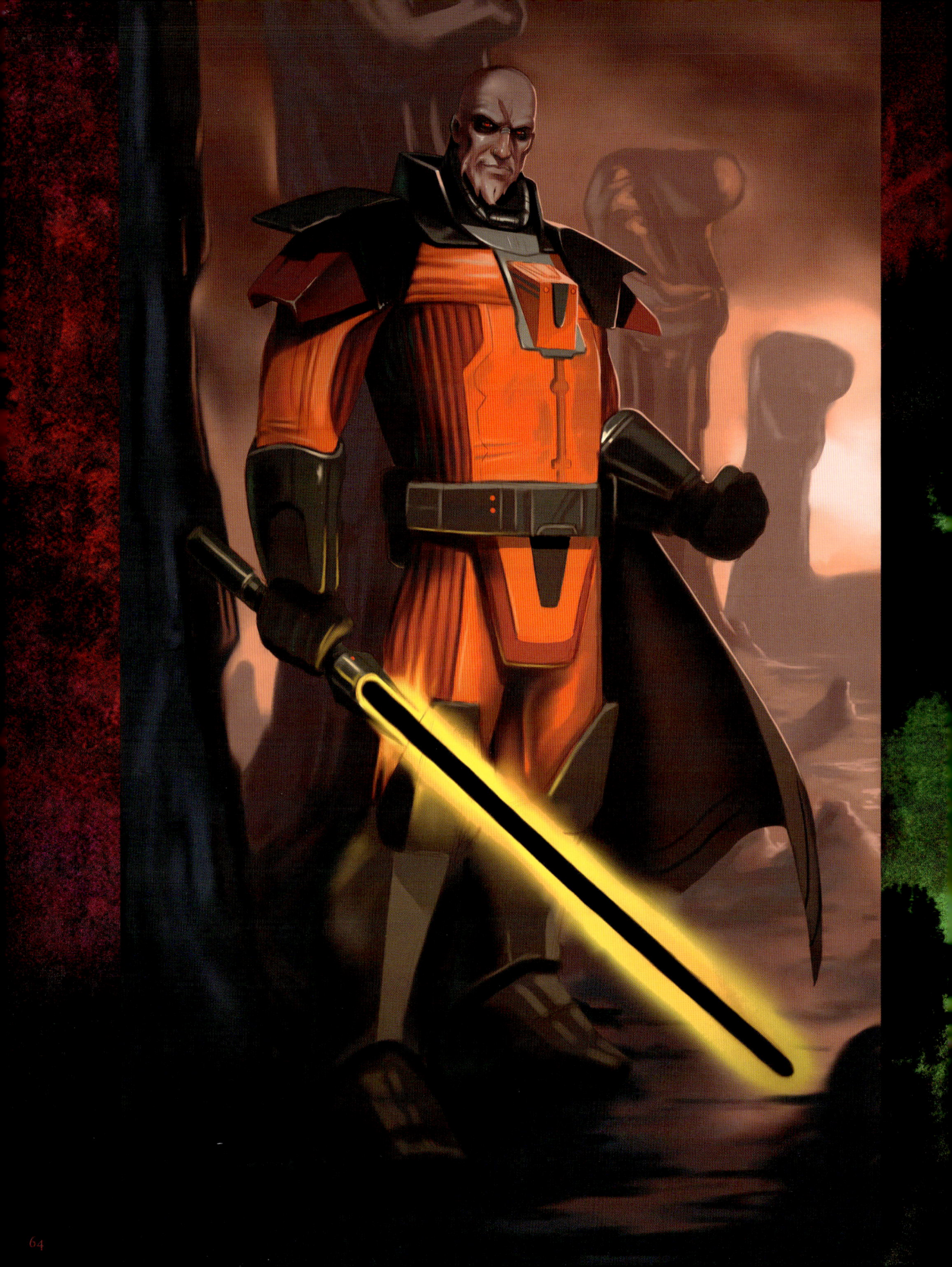

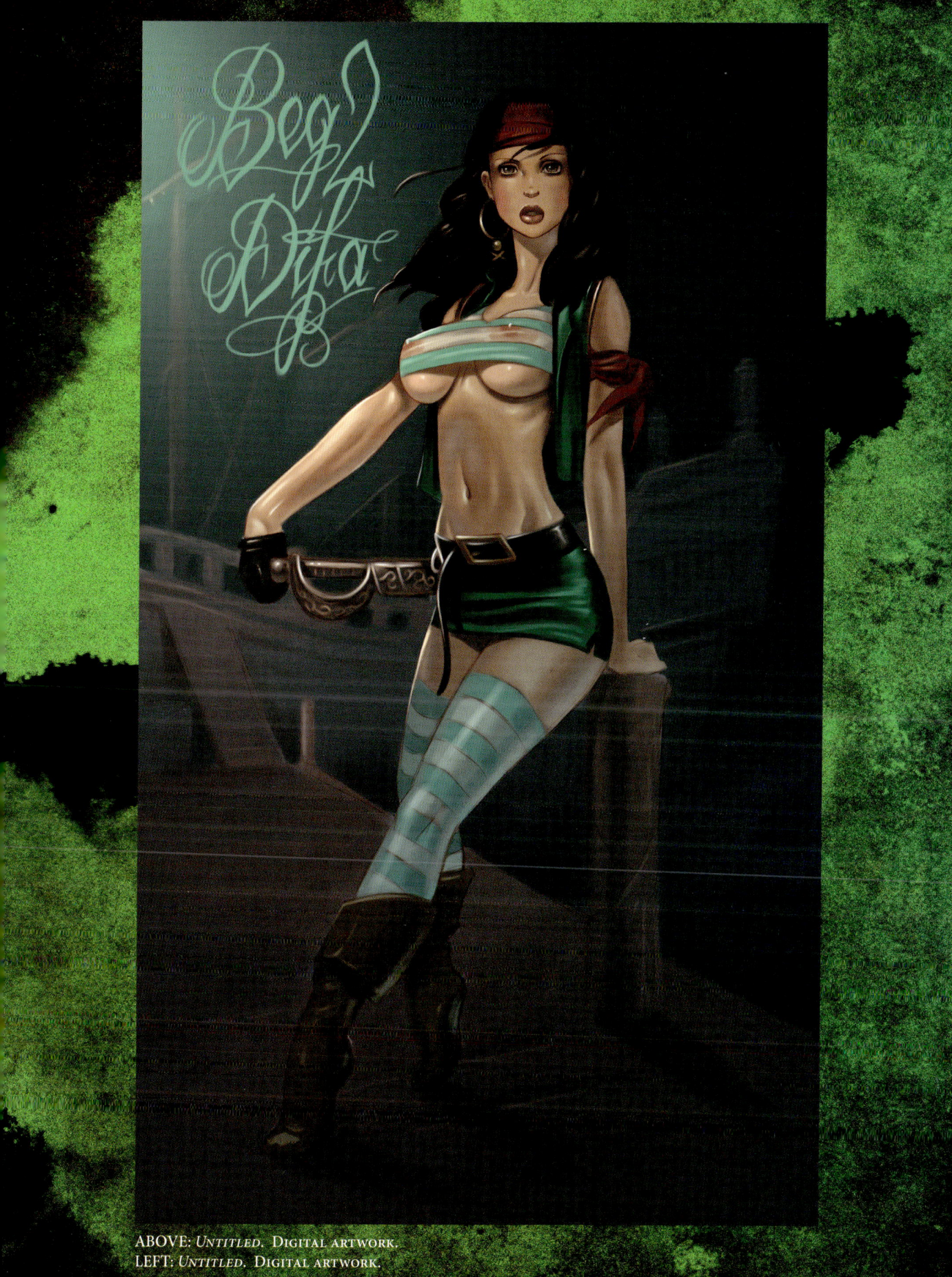

ABOVE: *Untitled*. Digital artwork.
LEFT: *Untitled*. Digital artwork.

DU CONGO

ANTWERP, BELGIUM.

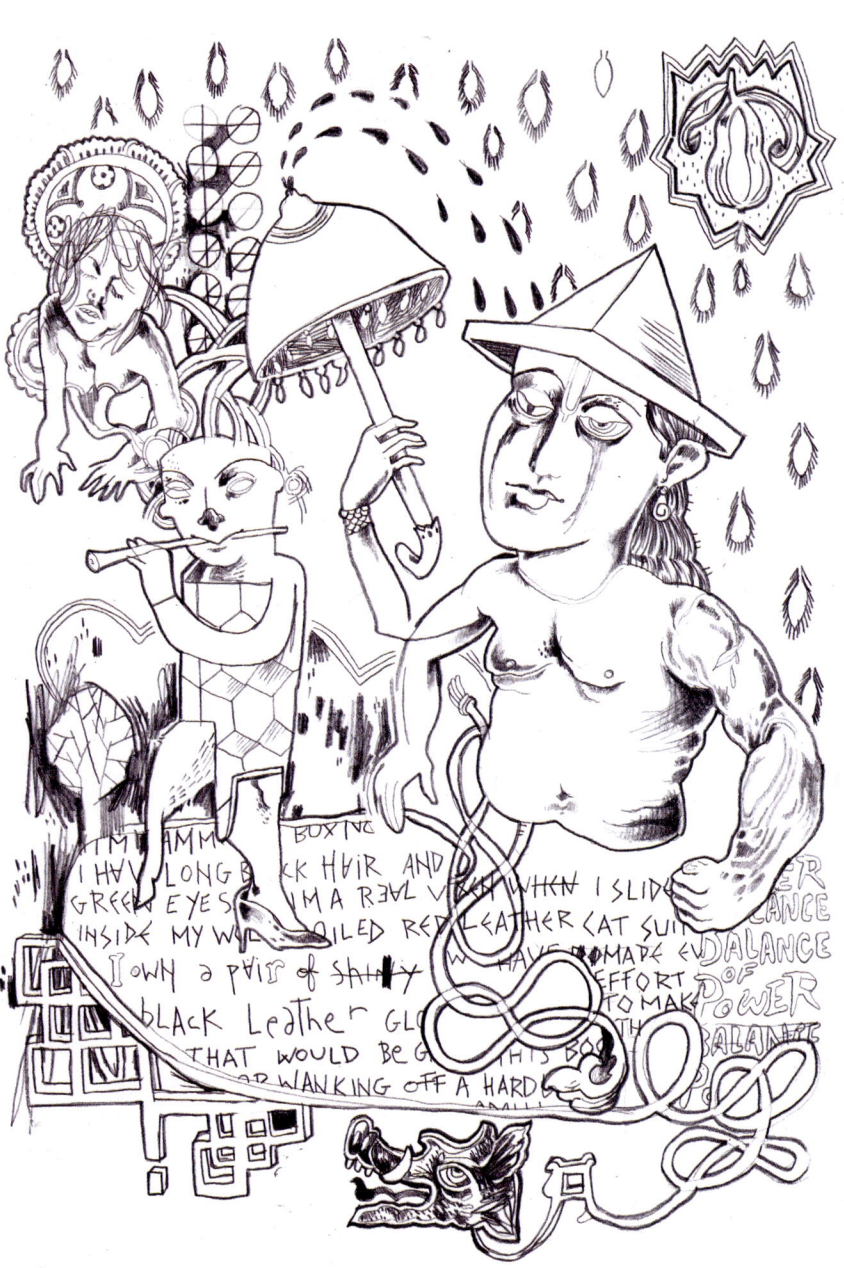

Piet du Congo studied fine art at the Academie des Beaux Arts in Brussels for ten years and treid to launch his career; "I had a mass of drawings from my time at art school, tried to find exhibitions to show my work only to find that I had stored stuff up for nothing." This was also the time he got a few tattoos and Piet realised that "tattooing could be an interesting way to get back to drawing." He started at home and then Yann Black introduced him to Jef Kostek (who had just opened the Boucherie Moderne in Brussels) and Piet began working there a couple of days a week. He then began travelling, tattooing in Paris, Berlin and Prague, before opening his own shop "in the wild Belgian countryside."

Piet's art is partially influenced by tattoo: "Old school tattoo I find inspiring with its themes of animals, weapons, women and flower ornamentals", but says that it's more that his drawing work influences his tattooing. Other sources of inspiration include the work of Grosz, Basquiat, Kostek and Rauschenberg and more generally, medieval art, bad painting, art brut, anatomy, engravings "and my friend Satan." As for his own work Piet says "The technical feat in art doesn't interest me. I like the fact that when people see my art they think they can do it themselves. When a piece is too technical it looses its radical aspect...having a dirty side in a tattoo avoids the pitfall of the 'fashion' tattoo....I deliberately add mistakes and randomness." As for his clients he says, "They are only beautiful women, coming to sublimate their bodies."

ABOVE: *Tribute to Radhadesh*. Pencil on paper.
RIGHT: *Taxi Girl*. Ink and fluorescent marker on paper.

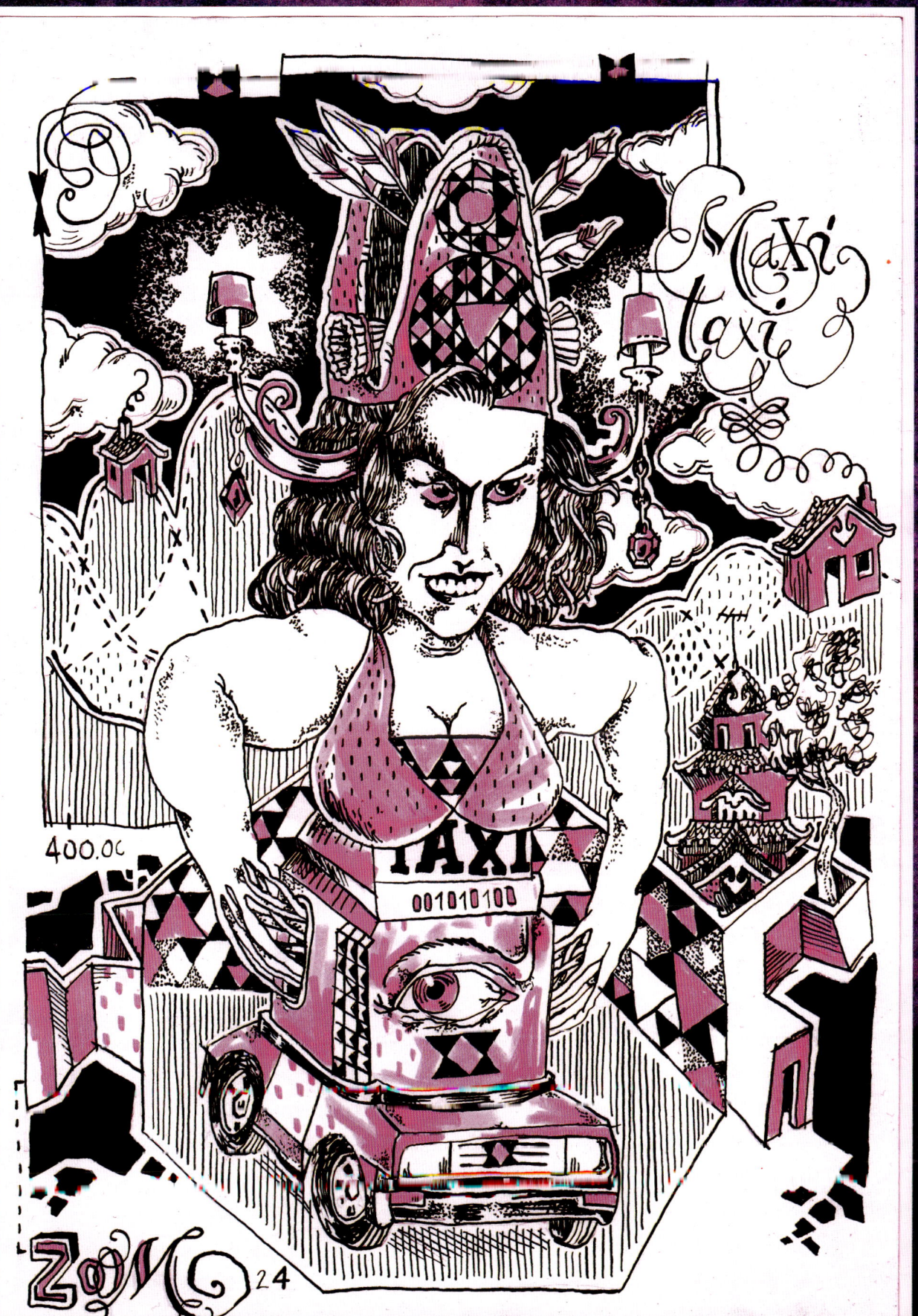

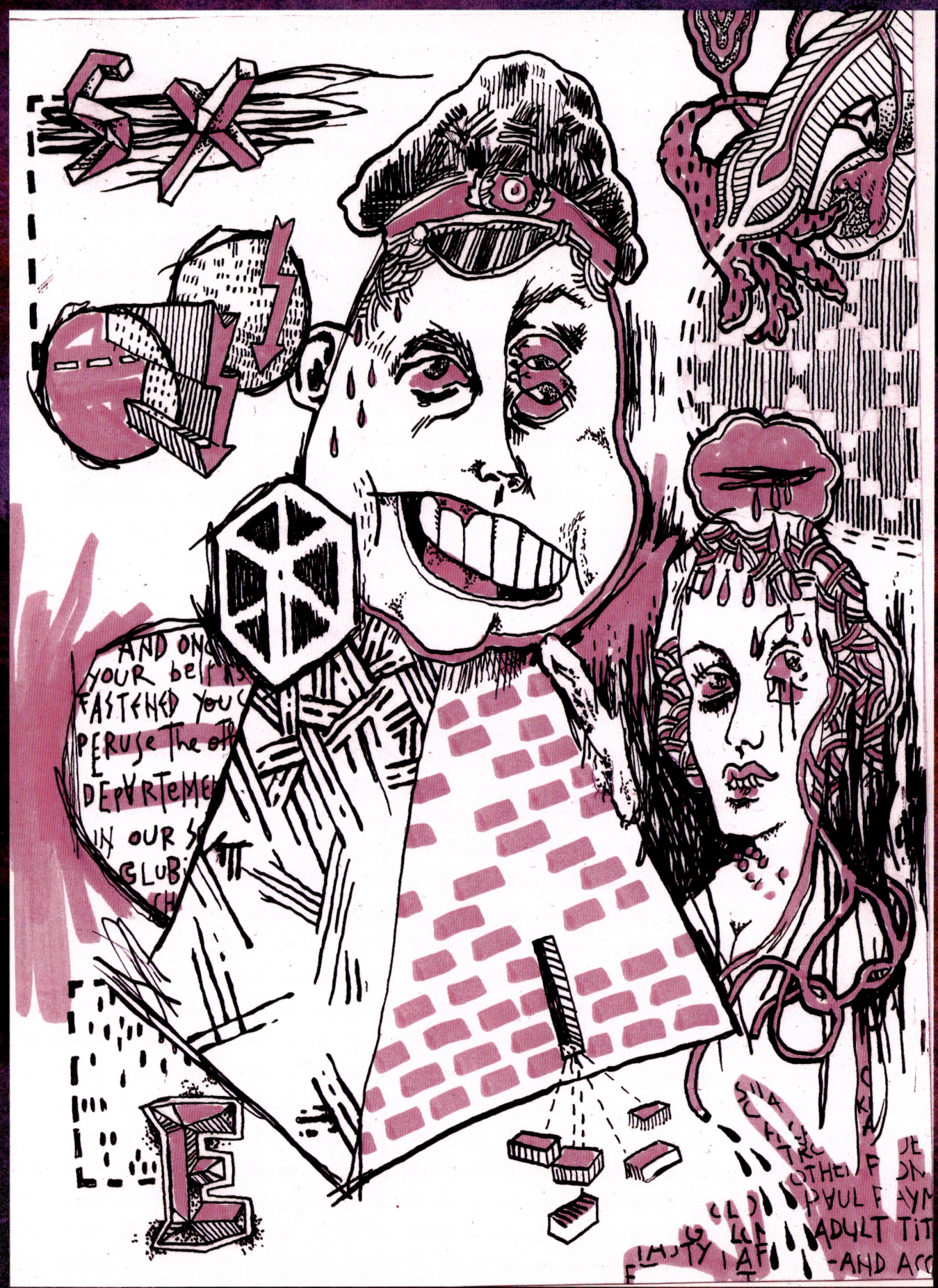

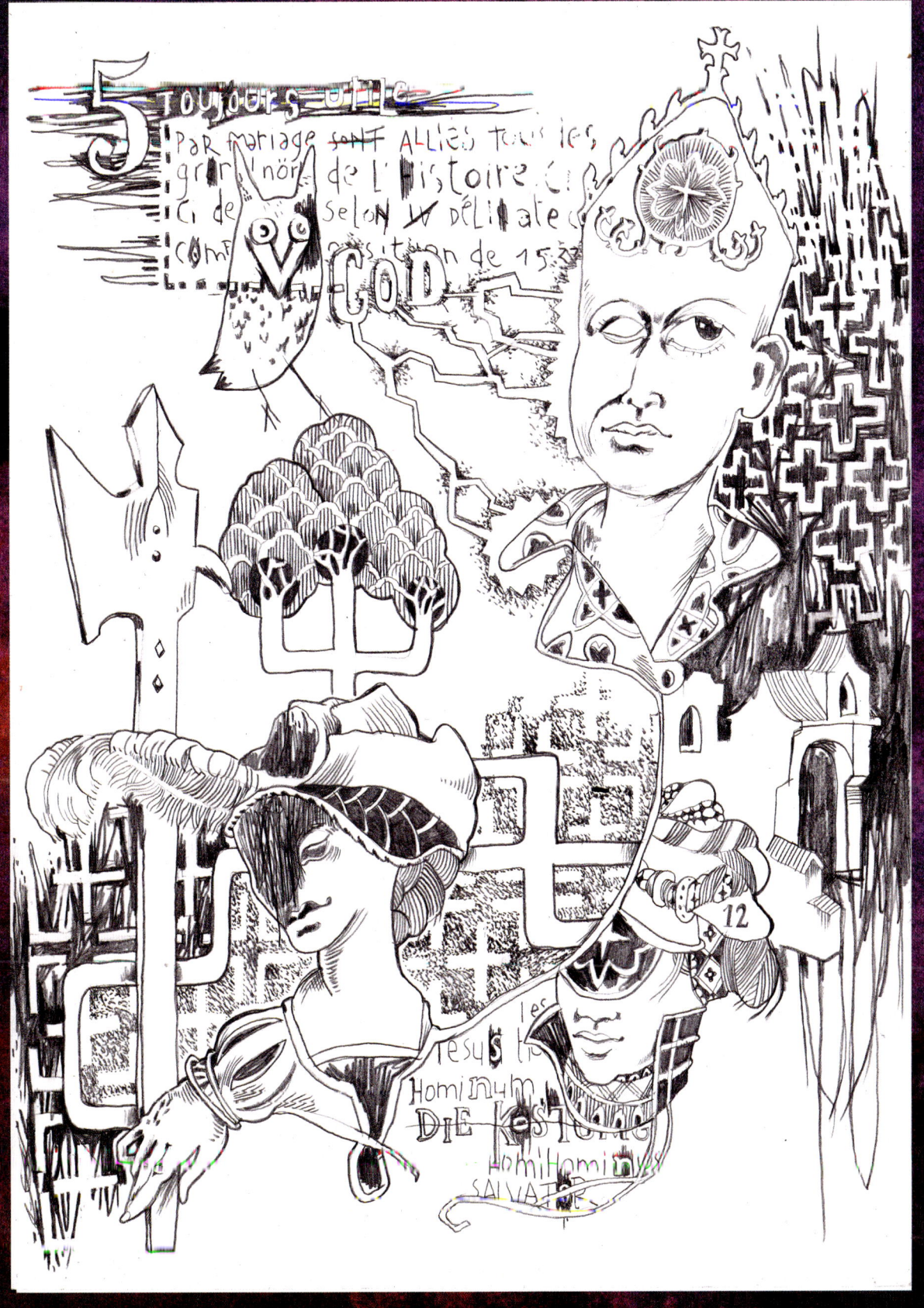

LEFT: *Pyramidical SX*. Ink and fluorescent marker on paper.
ABOVE: *Iesus Hominum Salvator*. Pencil on paper.
OVERLEAF, LEFT: *Electrik Nipple*. Pencil on paper.
OVERLEAF RIGHT: *Vide*. Ink and fluorescent marker on paper.

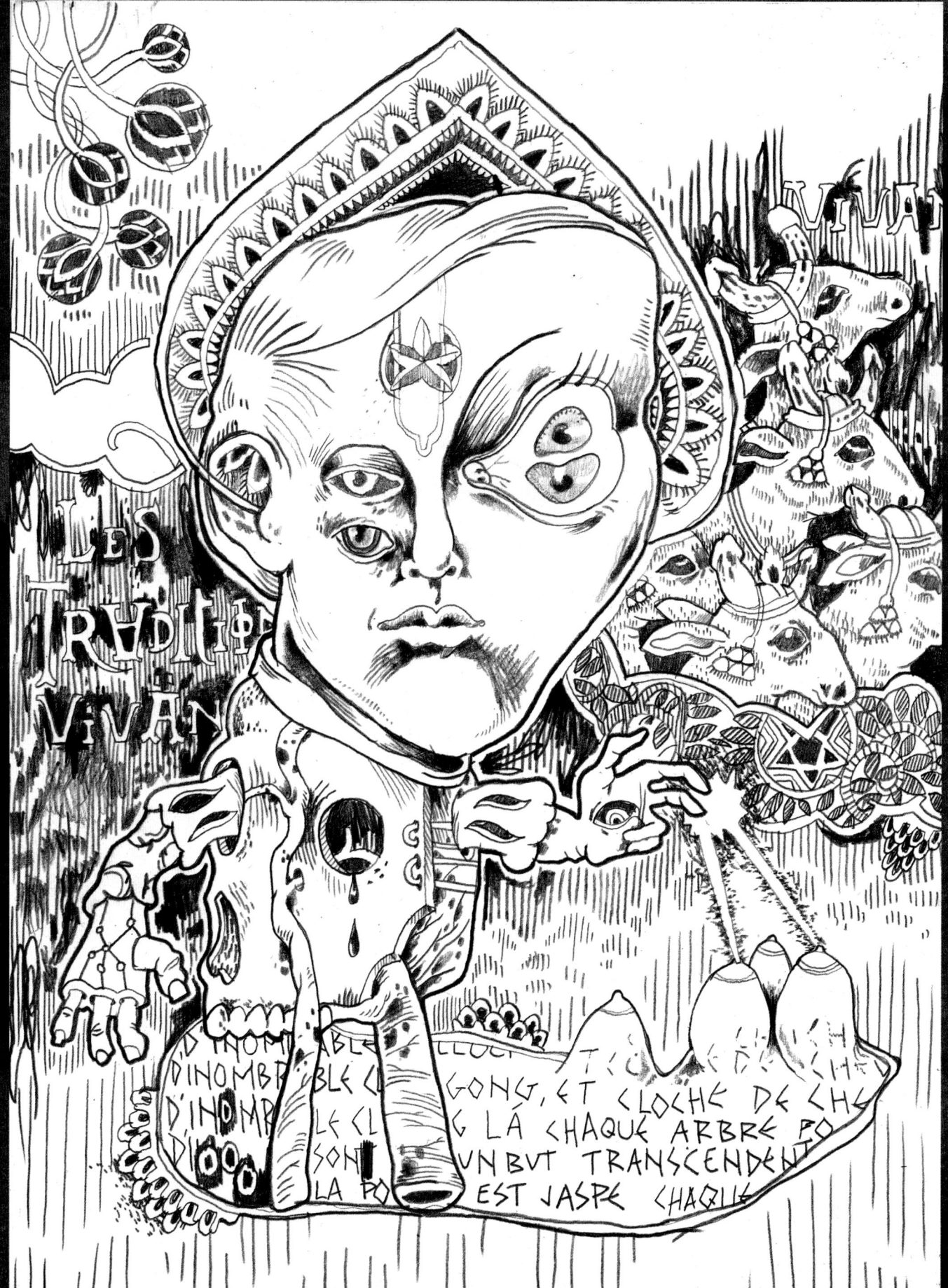

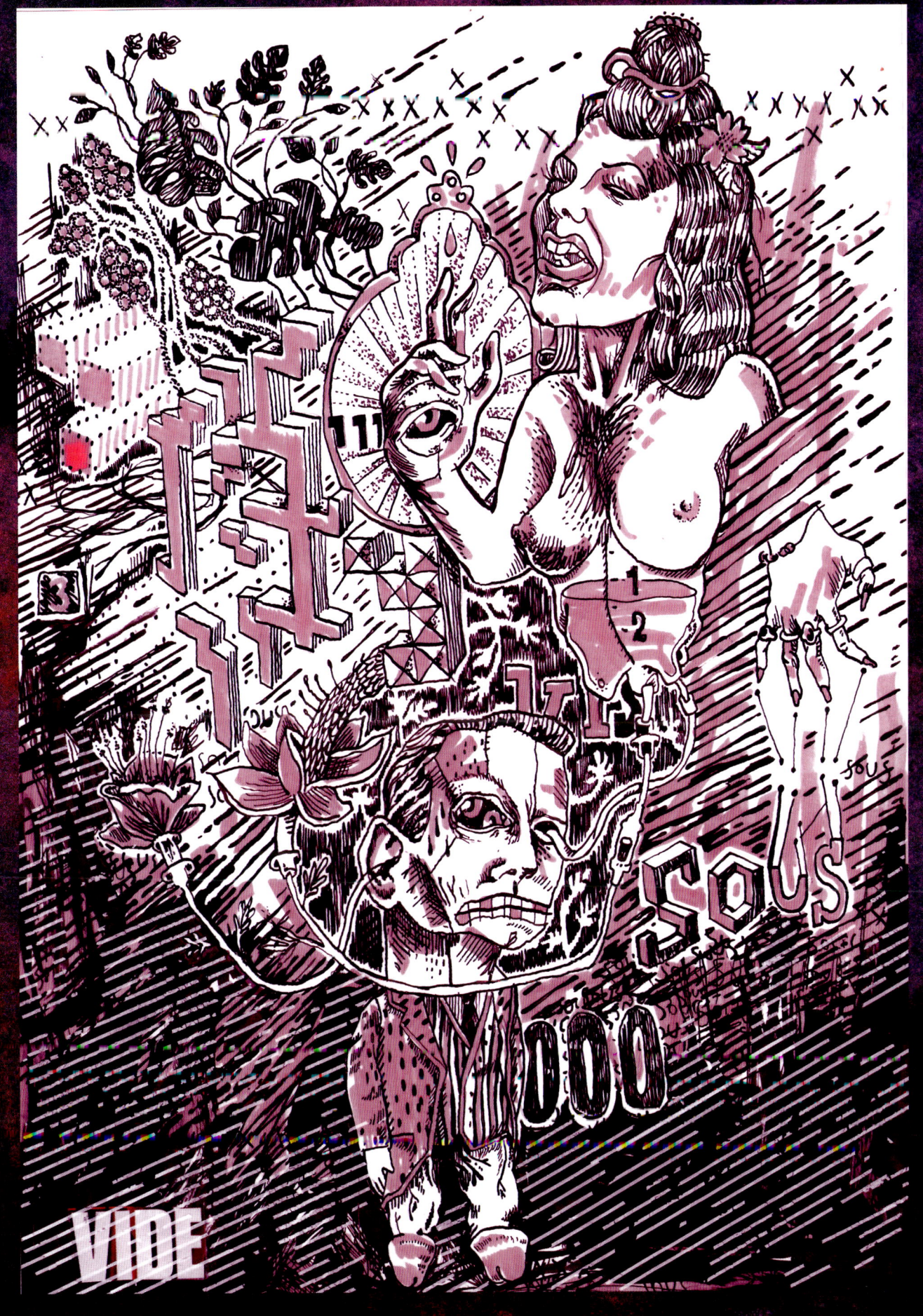

EL CARLO

BARCELONA, SPAIN.

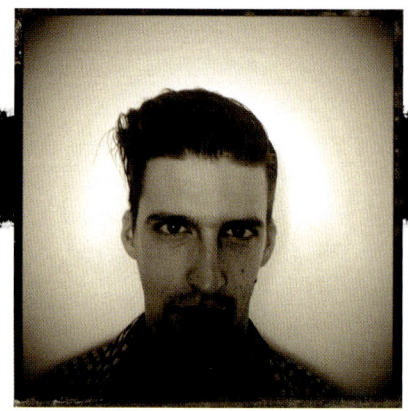

El Carlo was always into drawing from a young age and was always fascinated by tattoos. Taking the plunge into starting however meant "holding onto my balls… it was a scary time…hard to believe but it's all worked out in the end." He hated the early years, slaving away and earning only just enough to pay the rent. Now, however, working at Aloha Tattoos, he couldn't be happier. Tattooing, Carlo says, completely changed his drawing technique: "It helped me to simplify my line and to make my images more impactful. Over the years I managed to combine my natural style with something learnt and I think from that my 'look' emerged."

He draws and paints simply for the love of creating: "My art and my tattoos are my life; I earn my living doing the latter, but I do both also because it's a passion." He draws mostly in pen and ink, but recently has added linocuts. "It's a really fun way to work and the results are strangely satisfying." His influences are many, including punk and heavy metal, but amongst the "many, many" artists he names Monga, Rudi Fritsch, Chan, Rotor, Erik von Bartholomaus, Dave Ramirez and Victor Teantatus. He has shown his work extensively, including at the Cobra Negra tattoo gallery in Barcelona and in magazines including *Juxtapoz*, *Hey* and *Finerats*. "The tattoo scene has changed a lot in recent years," he says, "thanks to TV programmes, the Internet and the growth of the scene in general. I don't yet know whether that's a good or bad thing…it will be a few more years before we can tell."

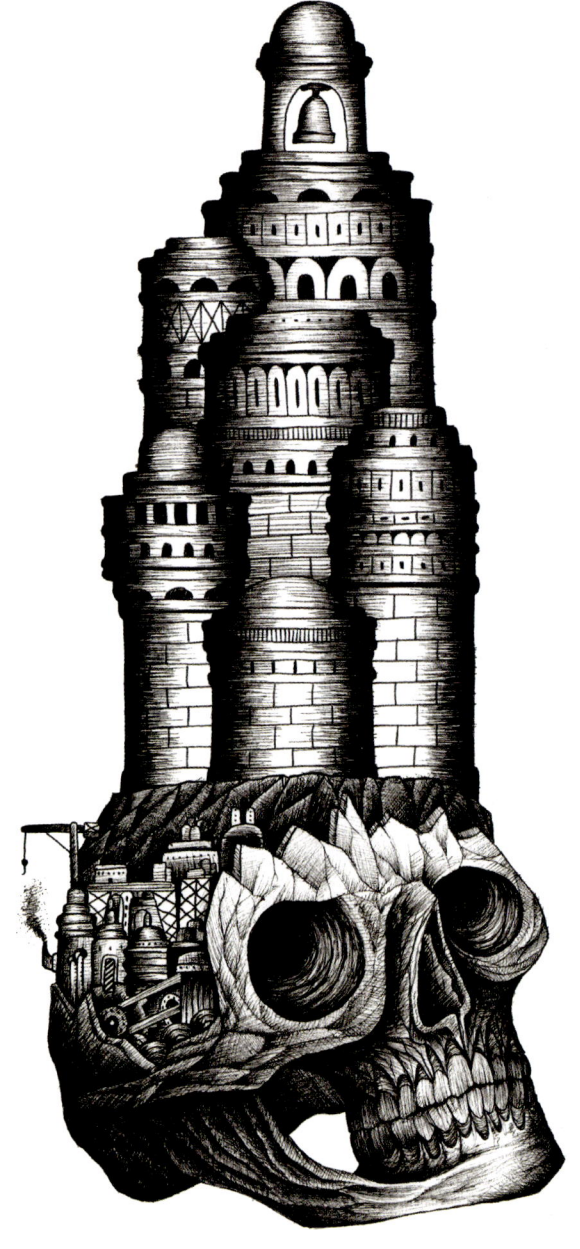

ABOVE: *SKULLTOWER*. PEN AND INK ON PAPER.
RIGHT: *PANZERBIRD*. PEN, INK AND LINOCUT.

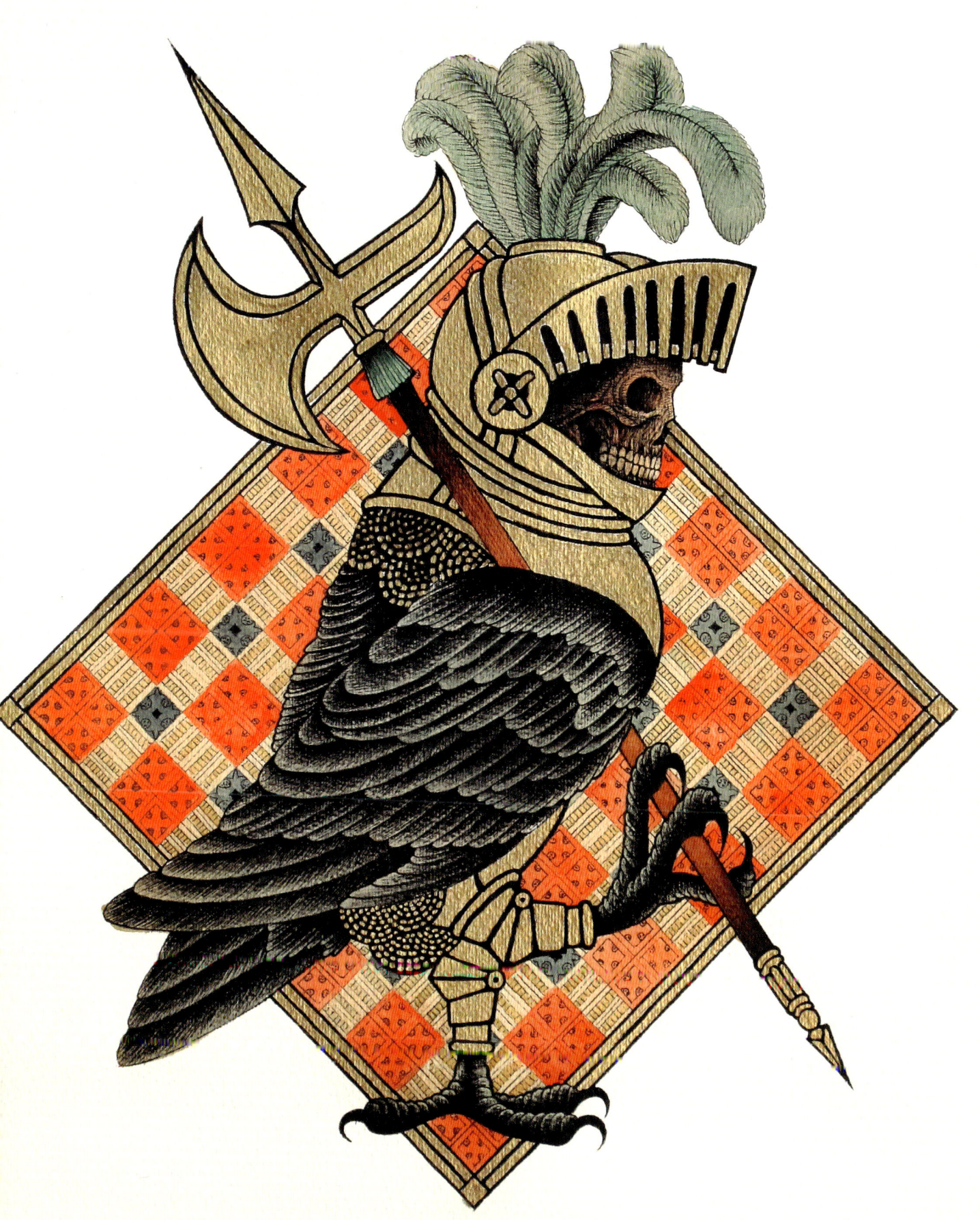

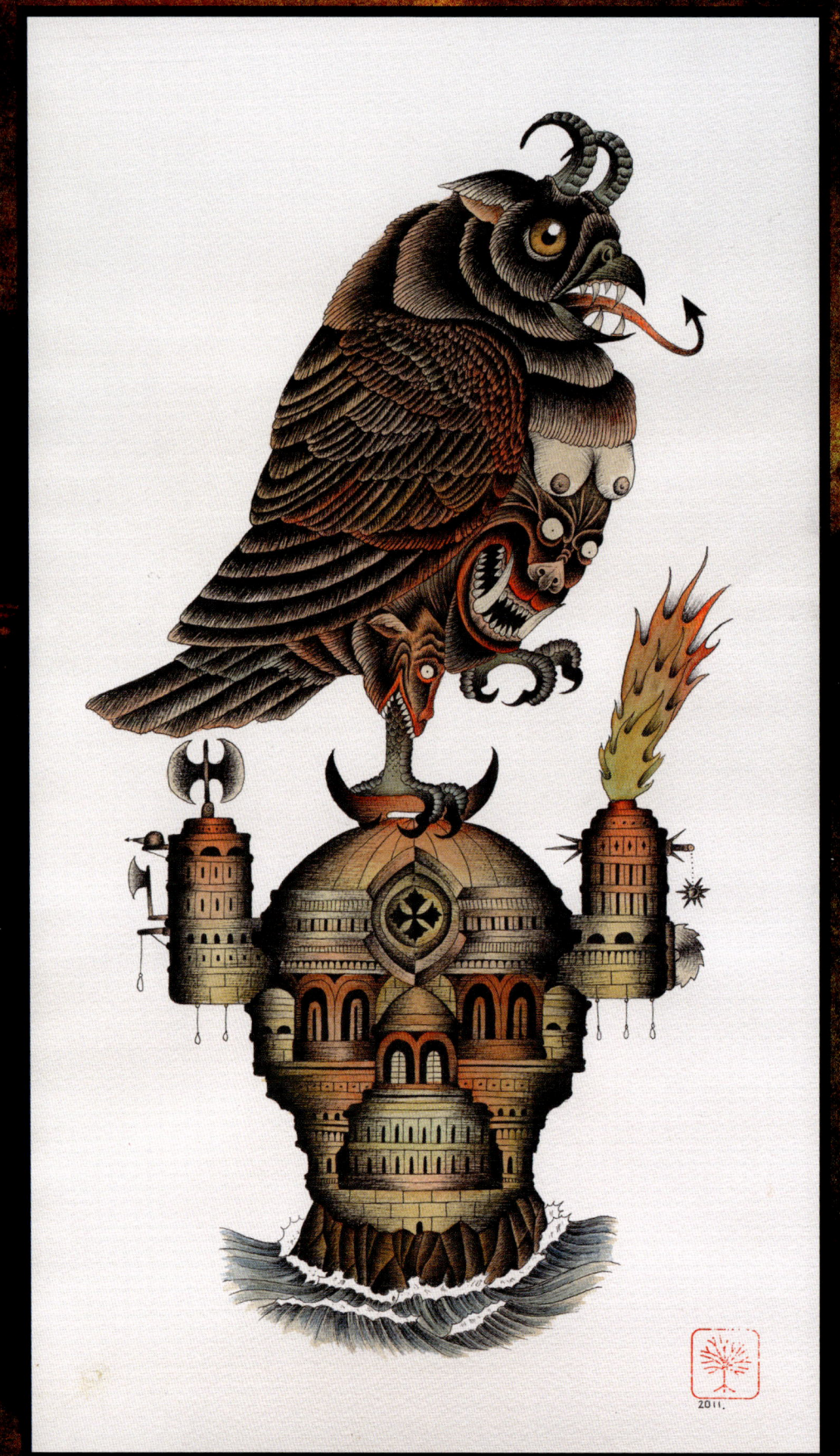

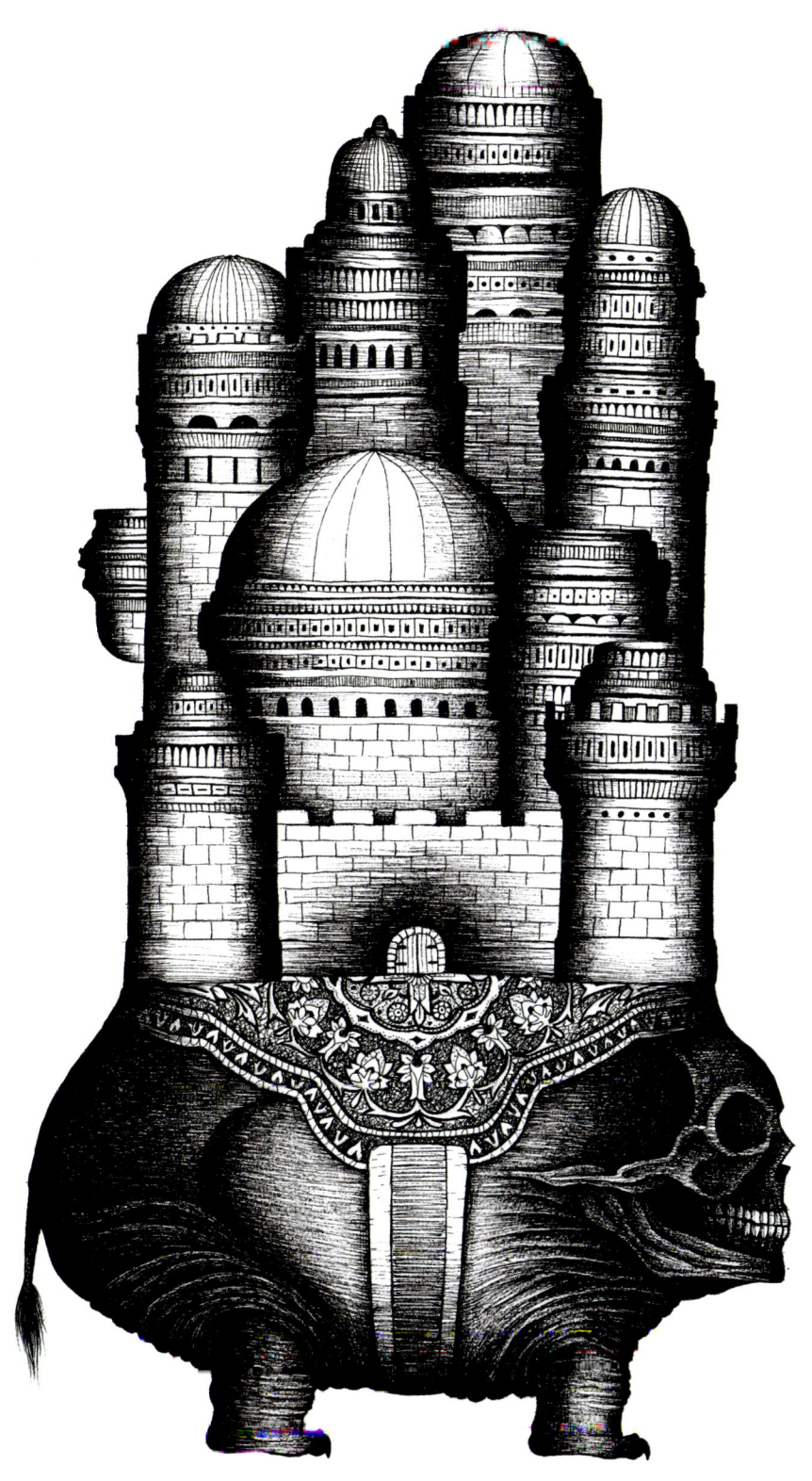

LEFT: *La Torre de la Muerte (The Tower of Death)*. Pen, ink and watercolour.
ABOVE: *Hippotower*. Pen and ink on paper.

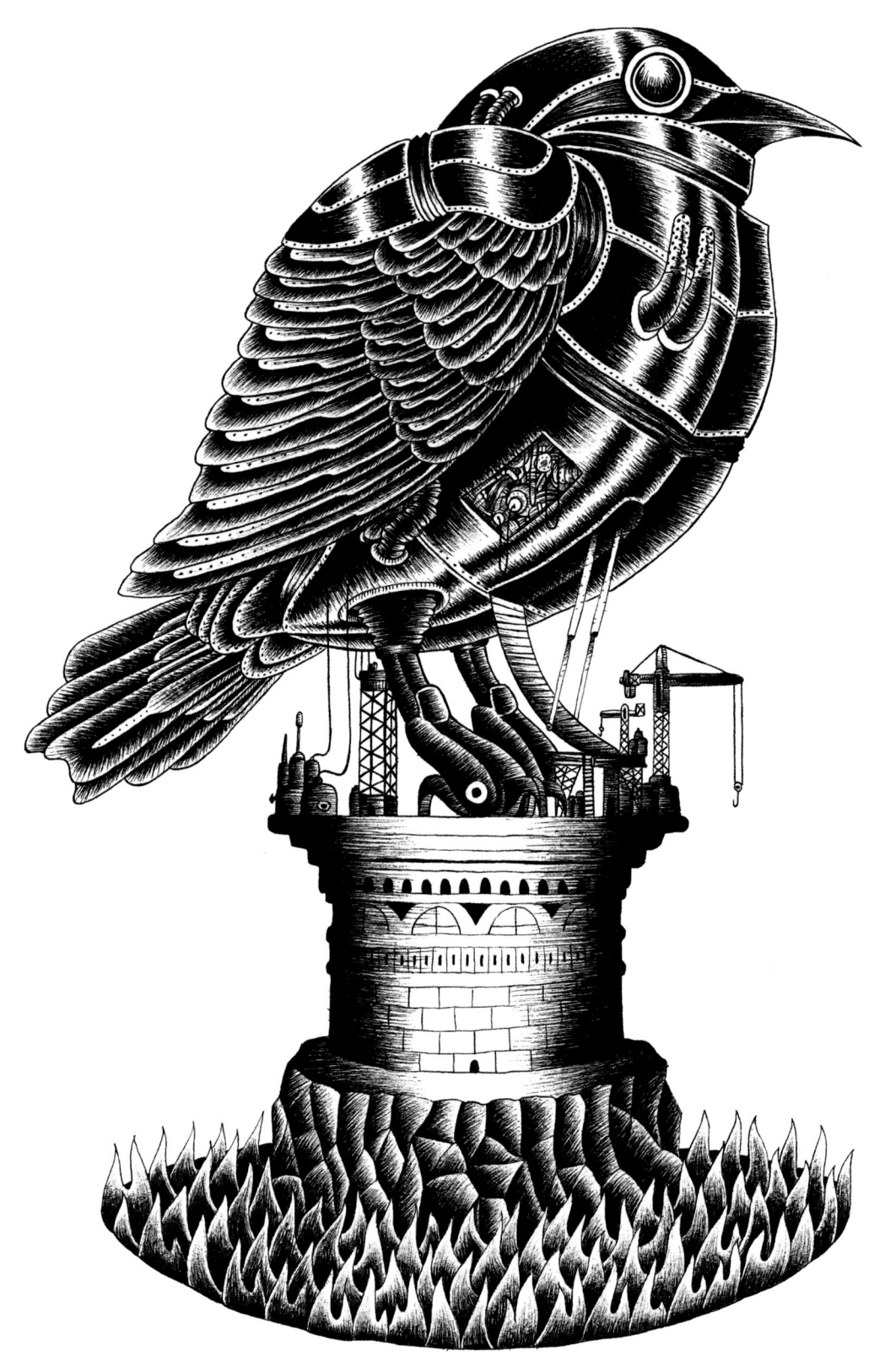

ABOVE: *Robot Bird*. Pen and ink on paper.
RIGHT: *Spider, Skull and Fly*. Pen, ink and linocut.

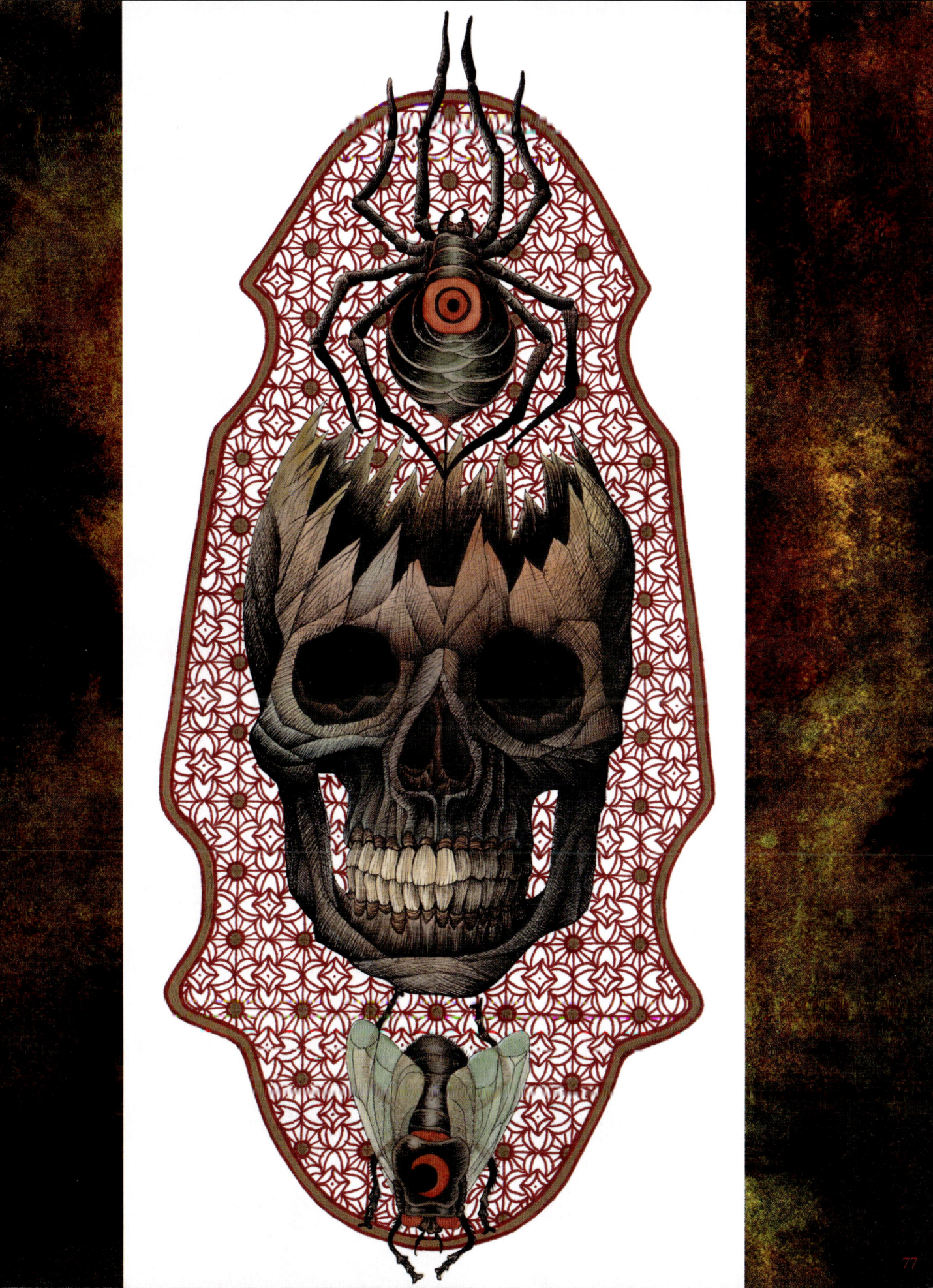

ENFRUNS

BARCELONA, SPAIN.

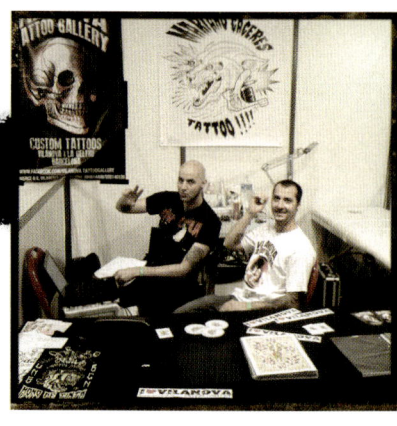

Remarkably, Sergi Enfruns is entirely self-taught. As a kid in Barcelona he had always drawn and painted, exploring different techniques by observing other artists. This is what led him to tattoo – it was a way of broadening his range, checking out some new techniques. He had just finished mastering airbrushing, and there was something about tattoo that grabbed him. "As with everything else I learnt I had to do it myself. I didn't have an apprenticeship or a mentor." He did however manage to get a spot at Vilanova Tattoo Gallery and that opened up loads of opportunities. "It really was like a big family and I'll always be hugely grateful to them." It also plugged Sergi into a network of other tattooists and he was soon doing guest spots around Europe. "I met some great people and had great experiences, like at Haunted Tattoo in London." Even with a busy schedule, Sergi finds time to draw and paint just for the pleasure of it. "I don't have as much times as I would like, but it's a great way to take a step away from tattoo and to try something new. I then find that some of those new techniques will find their way back to tattooing." Inspiration comes from many sources, in particular horror and science fiction movies. There are too many artists to mention "but if I had to name one, perhaps Frank Frazetta." One problem with being so versatile is that "my clients don't really know what to expect when it comes to my painting, but I can live with that." The changes in the tattoo scene in recent years have been a good thing according to Sergi. "Many artists have alighted on the scene out of frustration with the art business and establishment. They bring great new ways of doing things from the worlds of comics, graffiti and painting. There is some amazing talent there and this is going to ensure that tattoo will keep growing in impact and influence."

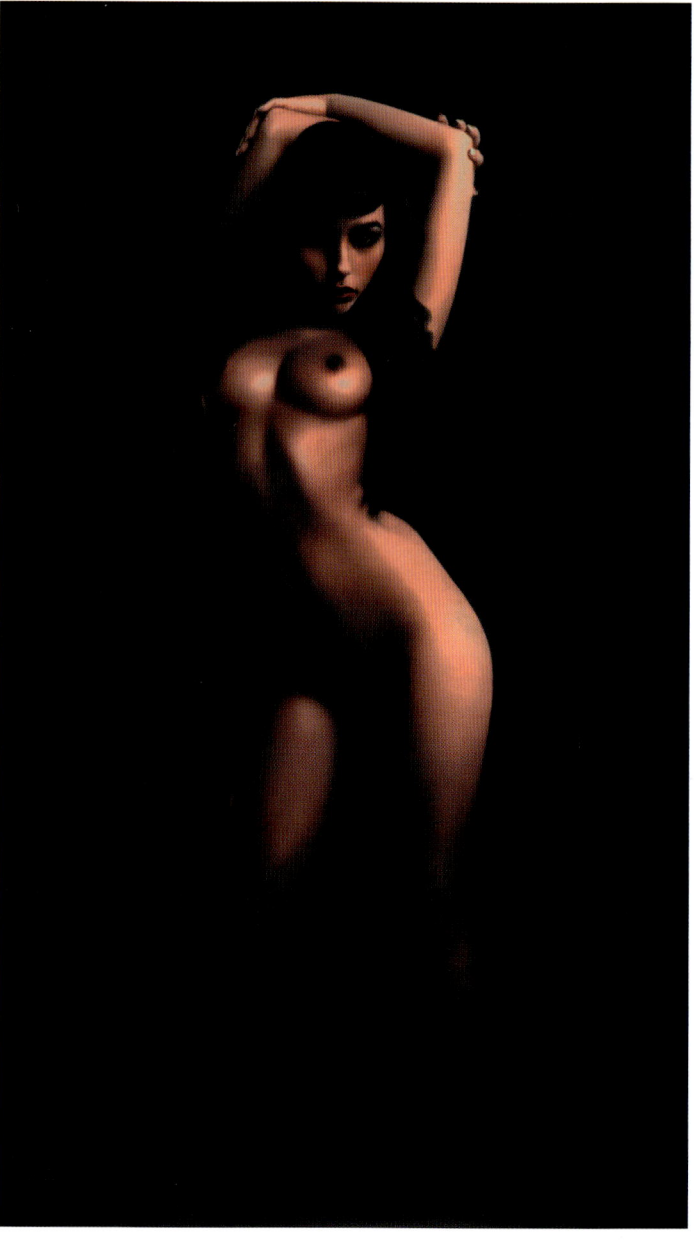

ABOVE: *Sexy Lady*. Acrylic on canvas.
RIGHT: *Nekro Skull*. Pencil on paper.
OVERLEAF: *Medusa*. Pencil and watercolour wash.

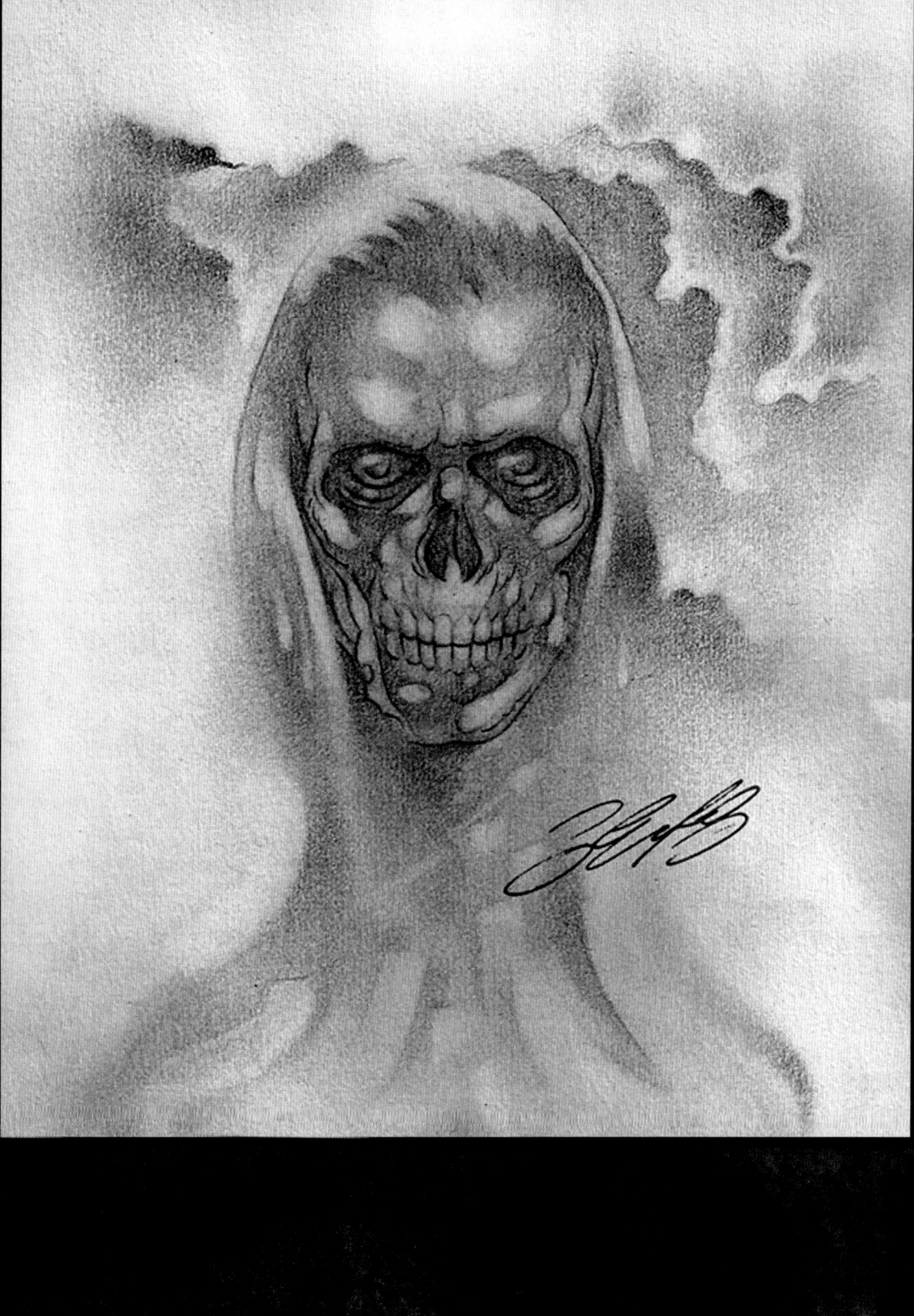

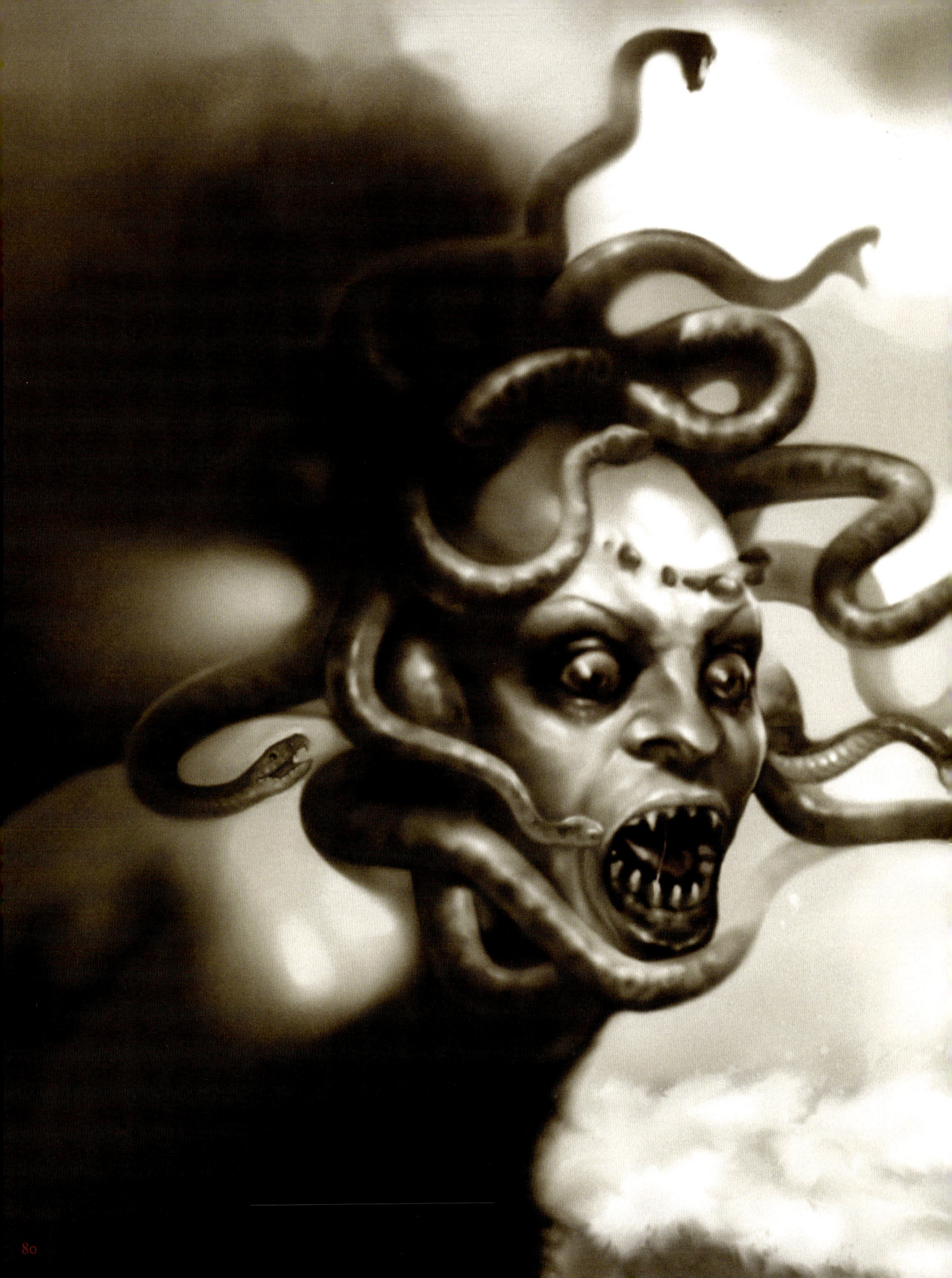

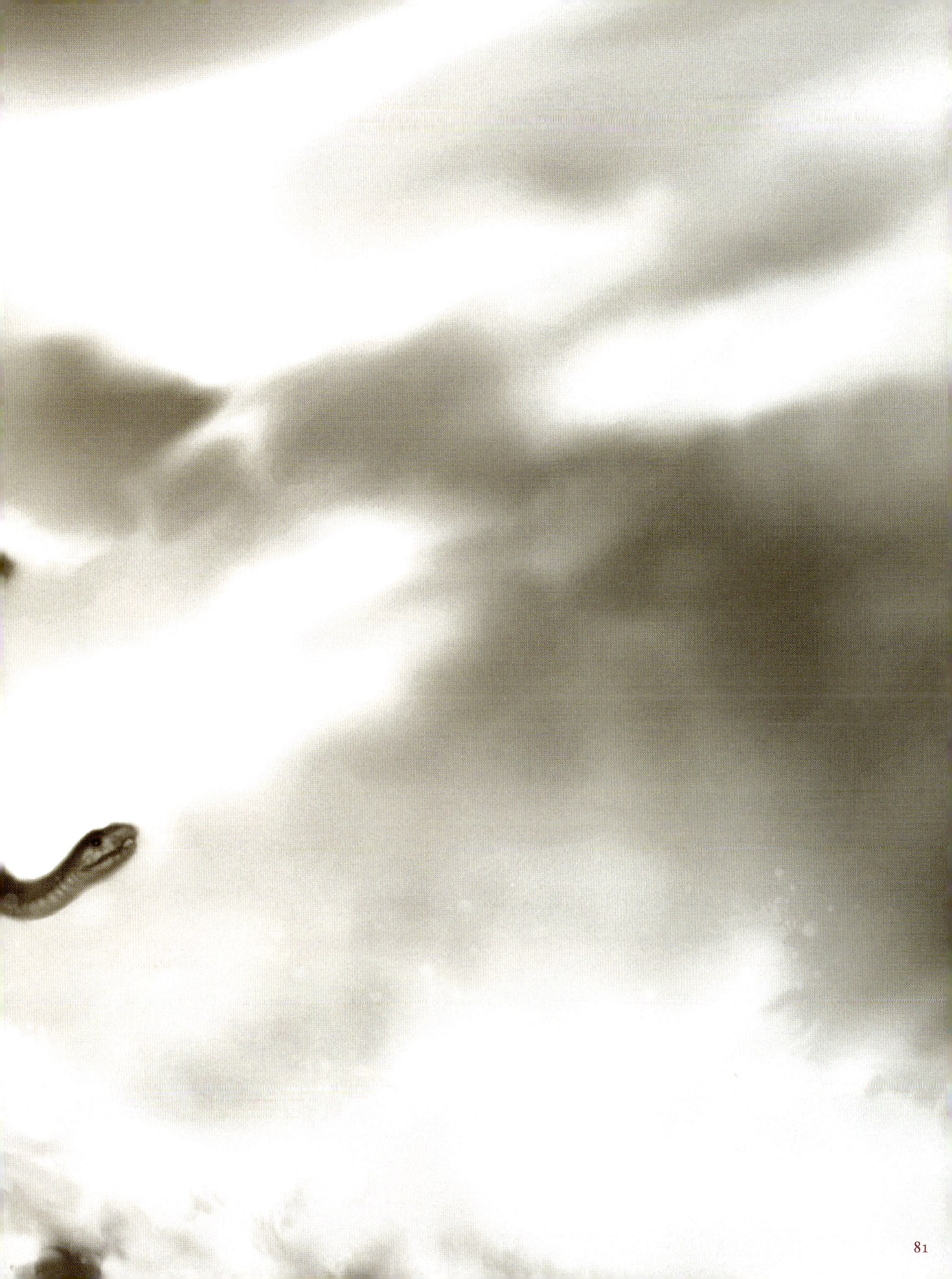

GAFFRON

GERMANY / ZÜRICH, SWITZERLAND.

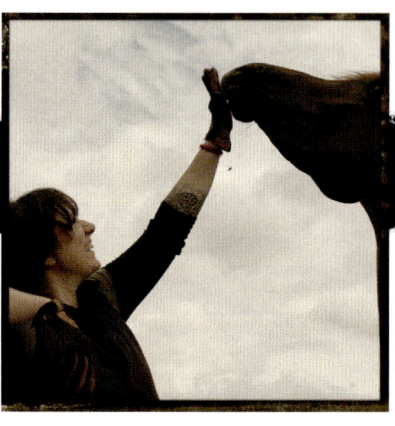

It was a fascination with the artistic possiblities that emerged in tattooing in the late '80s, "and being able to live the life I wanted, travelling, meeting people with a different view, living outside the tedious demands of the mainstream", that got Sabine into the scene. Born in Berlin, a natural self-taught artist, she remembers how tough it was at the start: "It was pre-Internet and information was hard to come by; being kicked out of tattoo shops for asking stupid questions was the norm. I was lucky because I knew Bernie Luther and he gave me an 'in', but it took a long time, and a lot of beatings." She started at one of the four tattoo shops in West Berlin, opened her own shop within two years, and two years later closed it down. "I realised that what I really wanted was to travel, so for ten years I worked my way around the world, working in many renowned tattoo shops in different cities." Today she is settled in Switzerland, where clients come to her private studio by word of mouth: "They know the kind of work I do, seek me out, and give me a lot of trust and freedom with the design." Tattooing has a very direct influence on her art: "I am incredibly anal about clear closed lines and sharp edges! It makes my art very graphic and probably makes it harder for me to stay loose and not over-polish things." The influence works in reverse however: "Hand-painting gives me more freedom in my tattooing, and opens up my creativity." Sabine is inspired "by the whole world: you just have to open your eyes", and in particular by the works of Mucha, the pre-Raphaelites, Turner, Klimt, and Chinese and Japanese art. Amongst her direct influences she cites Bernie Luther, the Leu Family, Paul Booth, Shige, Luke Atkinson, Fiona Long, Horiyoshi and Jacqueline Spoerle, "to name only a few." Her work has appeared in countless magazines, many books (including *Art of the Mark*, Miki Vialetto's *Folders* and *Bloodwork:Bodies*) and has been exhibited at most major tattoo conventions, as well as in Alex Grey's Microcosm Gallery. Of the scene she says: "Since I started it's exploded. Paradoxically the Internet has made things seem less connected; when you had to travel, rather than just check out a website, to see other artists' work, a lot of really strong friendships were built that remain to this day."

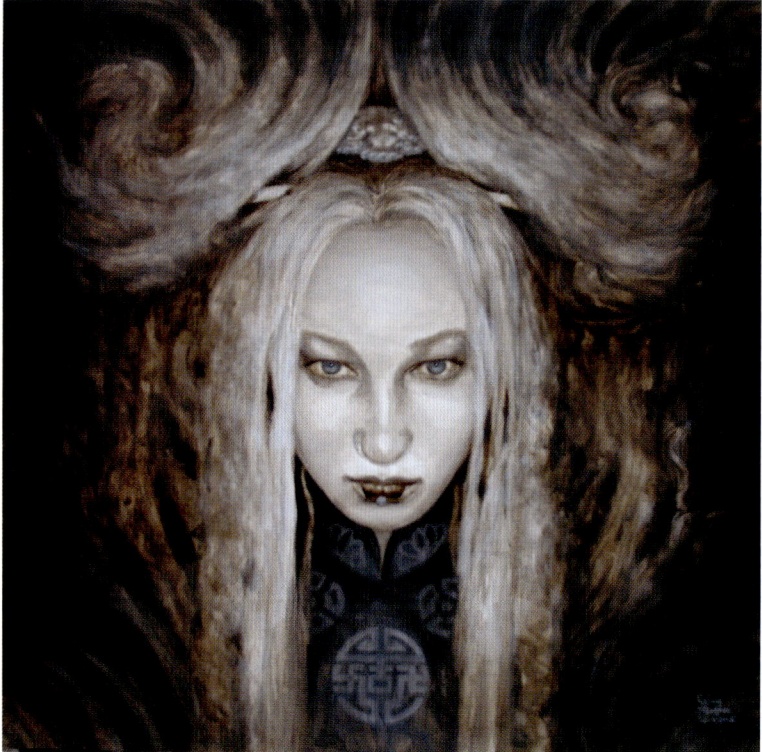

ABOVE: *Sarah*. Acrylic on canvas.
RIGHT: *Impossible Is An Opinion*. Acrylic on board.

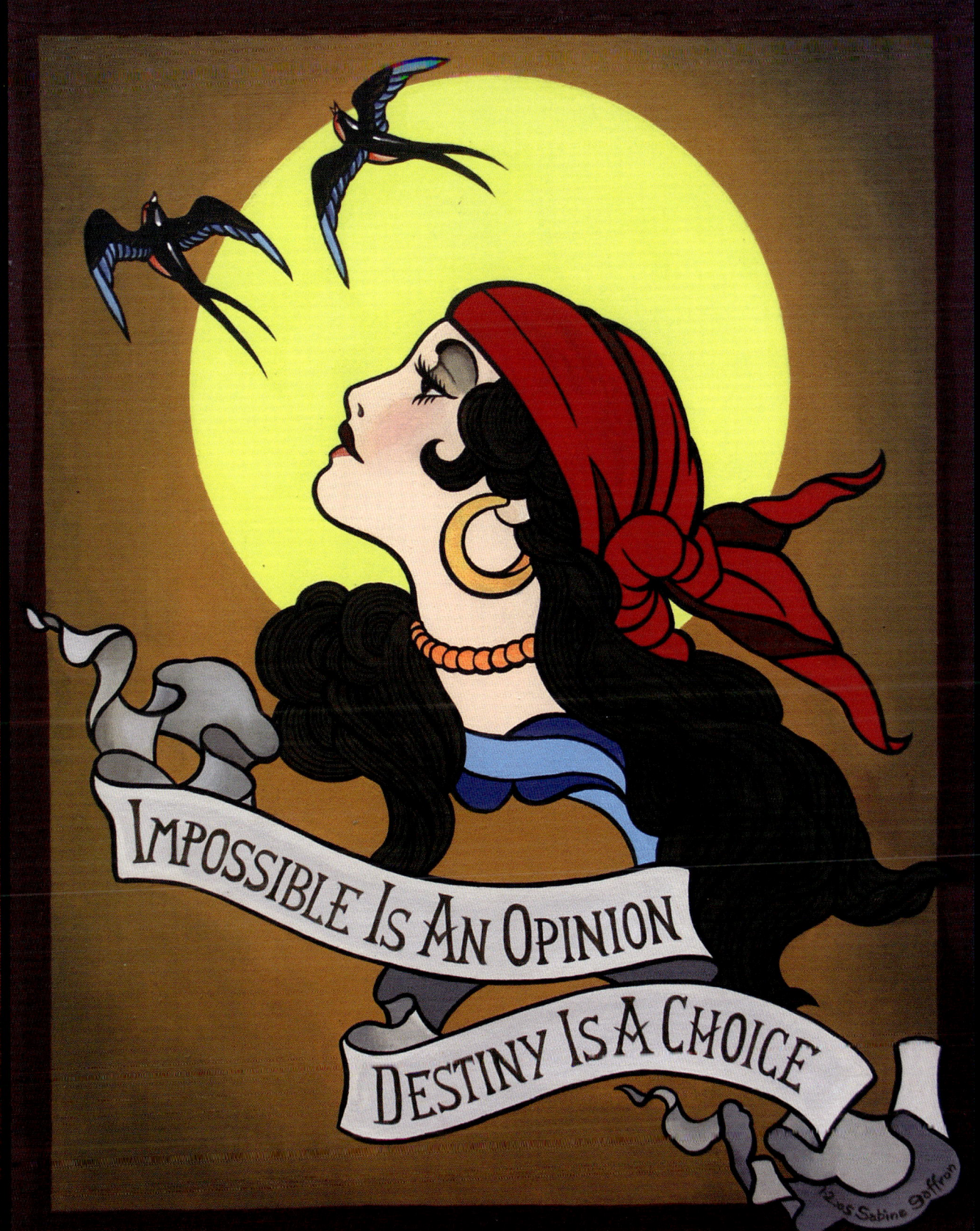

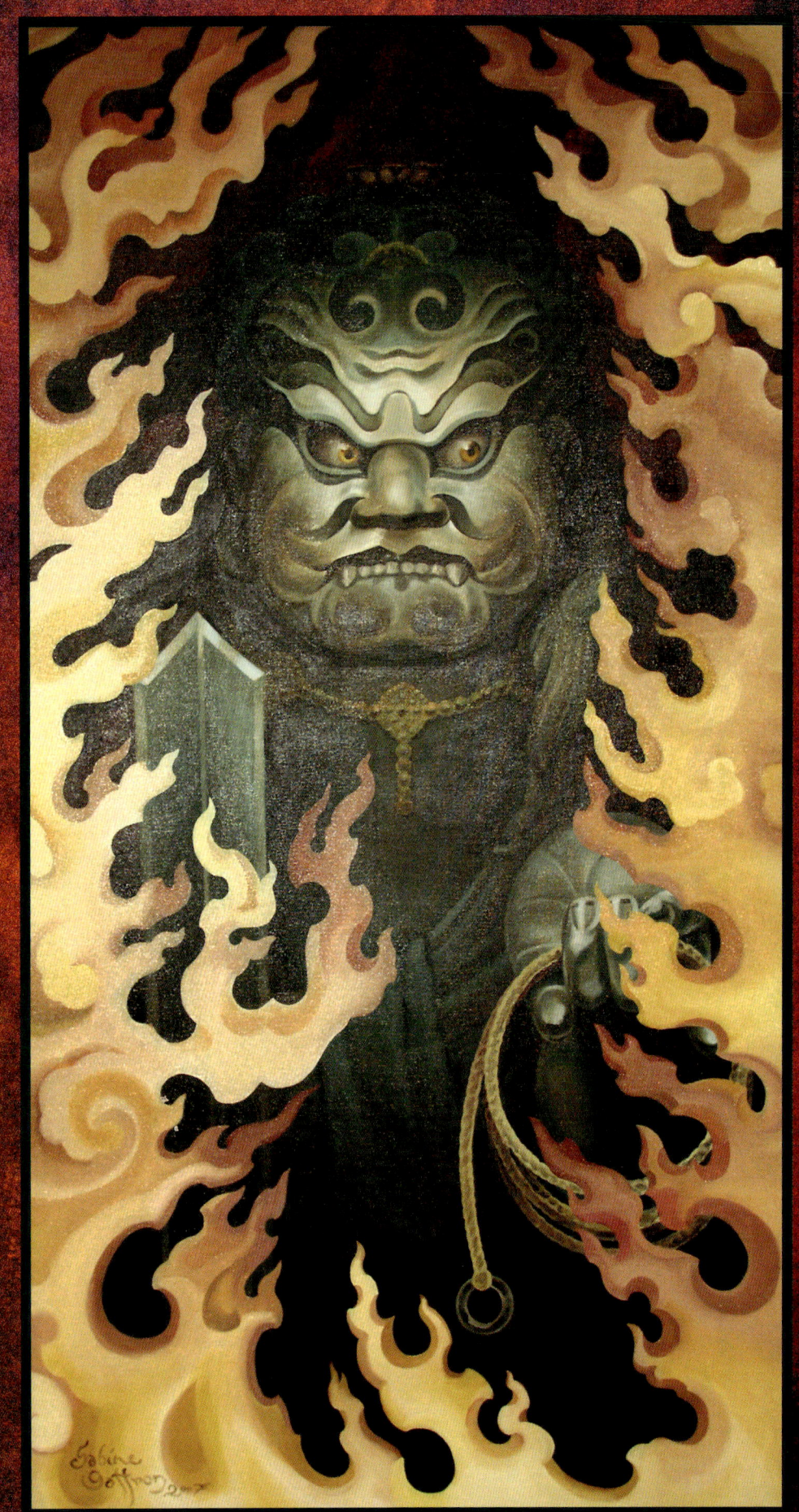

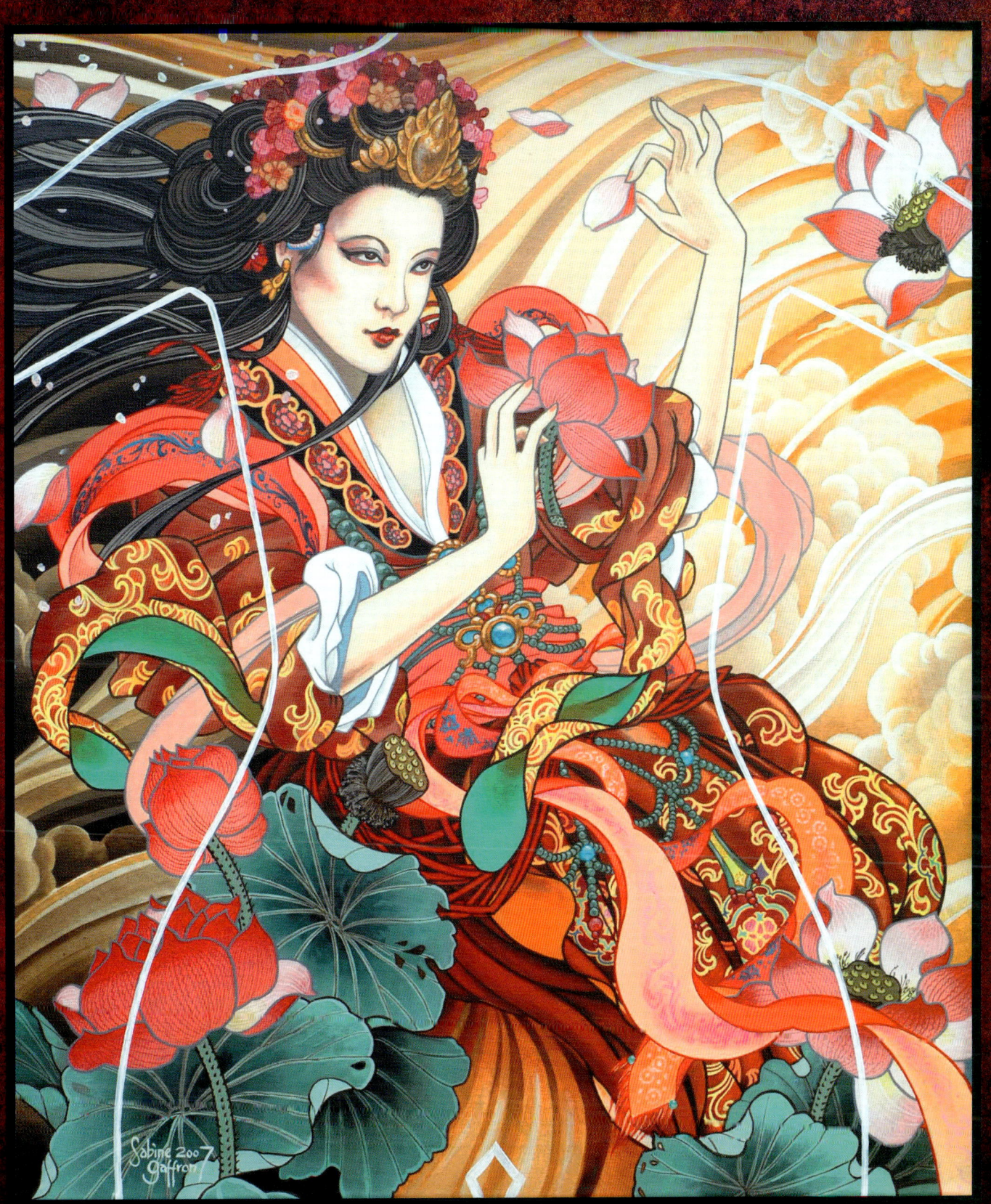

LEFT: *Fudo Myo*. Oil on board.
ABOVE: *Hope Flies*. Acrylic on canvas.

GANJI

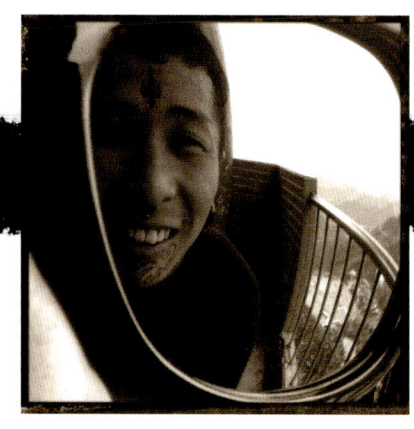

OSAKA, JAPAN.

"Tattoos are my life", says Ganji very simply. He didn't study fine art or design, but got into the scene "naturally, I just kind of flowed into it. I loved the art, wanted to do it and just made it happen." He began his apprenticeship at Crystal Skull Tattoo and then moved onto the renowned Three Tides Tattoo studio in Osaka, whose tattoo artists specialise in work inspired by the kustom scene. "My art is completely influenced by tattoo and viceversa" Ganji says, "I don't like to draw a distinction between the two. Those clients who get a tattoo from me are drawn to the art because they see the same style in both." His biggest influence? "That's easy - Grime," he says, referring the the US legend. When not tattooing Ganji collaborates with other media. He recently designed a set of toys and also created the tattoo backdrops for the recent video of Tsuchiya Anna's and Suga Shikao's track *S.ex*. His thoughts on the scene in Japan are straightforward "Tattoos are still coming into fashion. One thing's for sure, the number of people with tattoos in Japan will go on increasing for many years!"

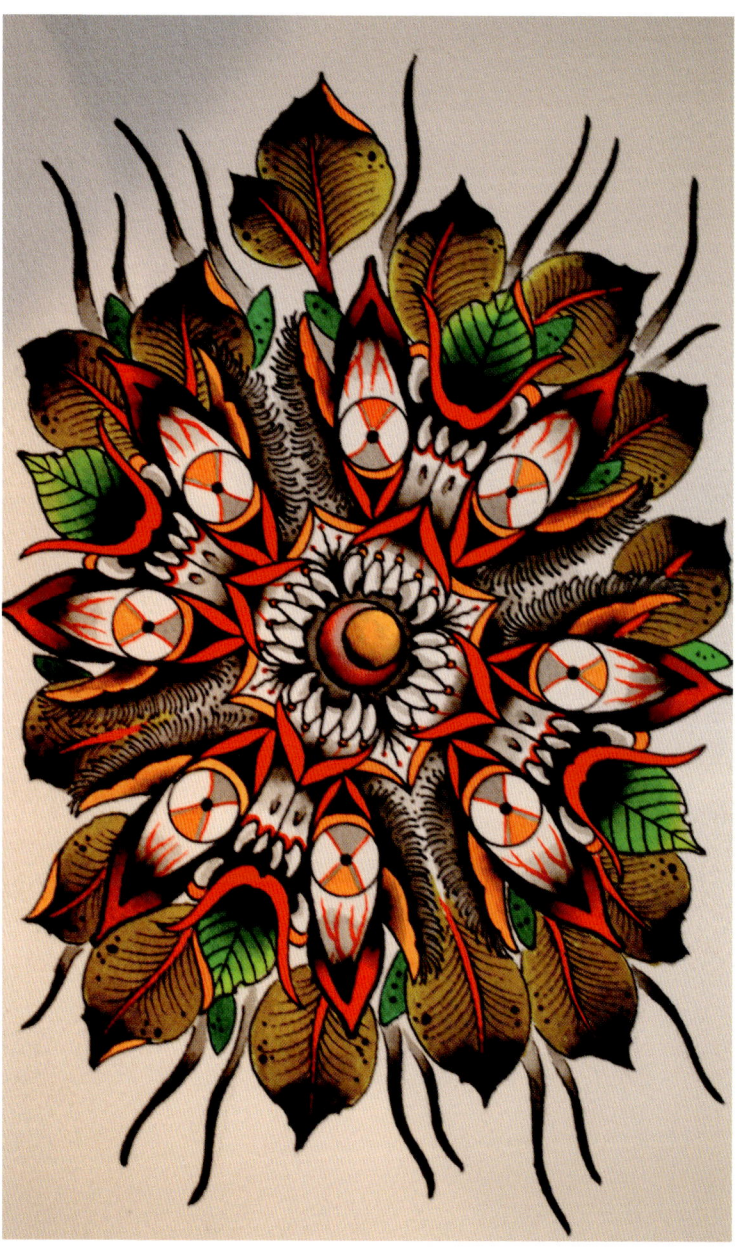

ABOVE: *Untitled*. PEN, INK AND WATERCOLOUR.
RIGHT: *Untitled*. PEN, INK AND WATERCOLOUR.

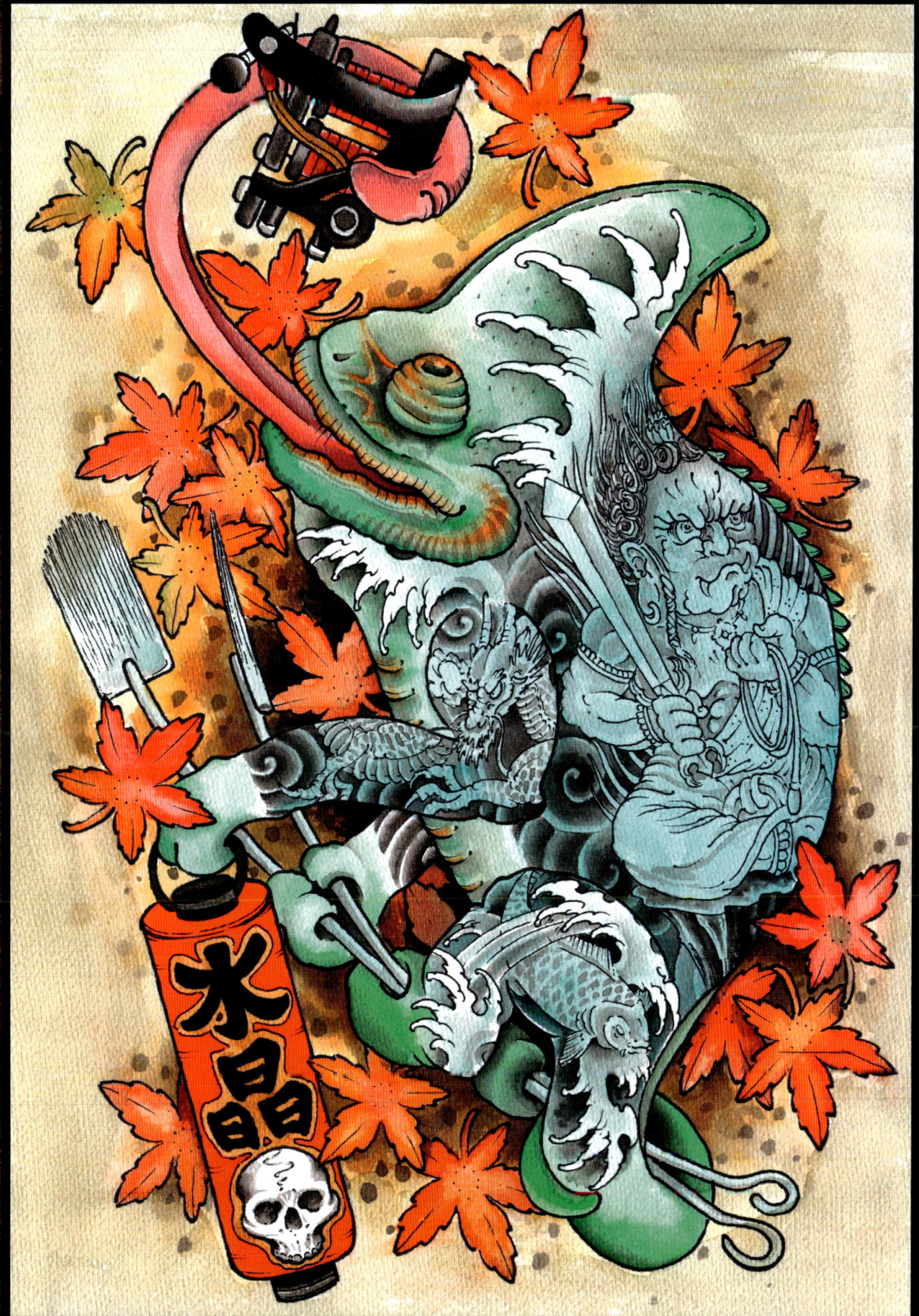

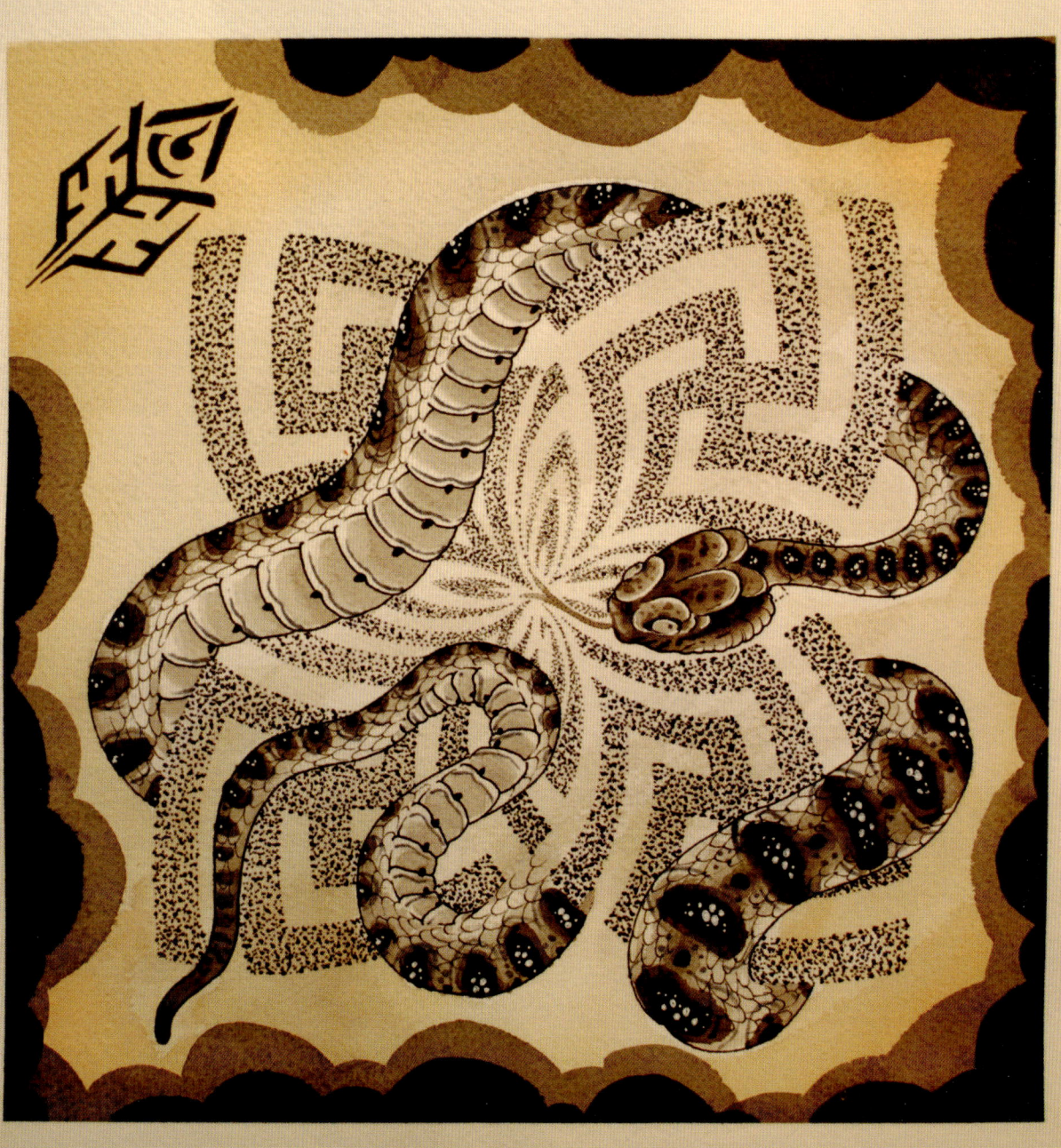

ABOVE: *Untitled*. PEN, INK AND WATERCOLOUR.
RIGHT: *Untitled*. PEN, INK AND WATERCOLOUR.

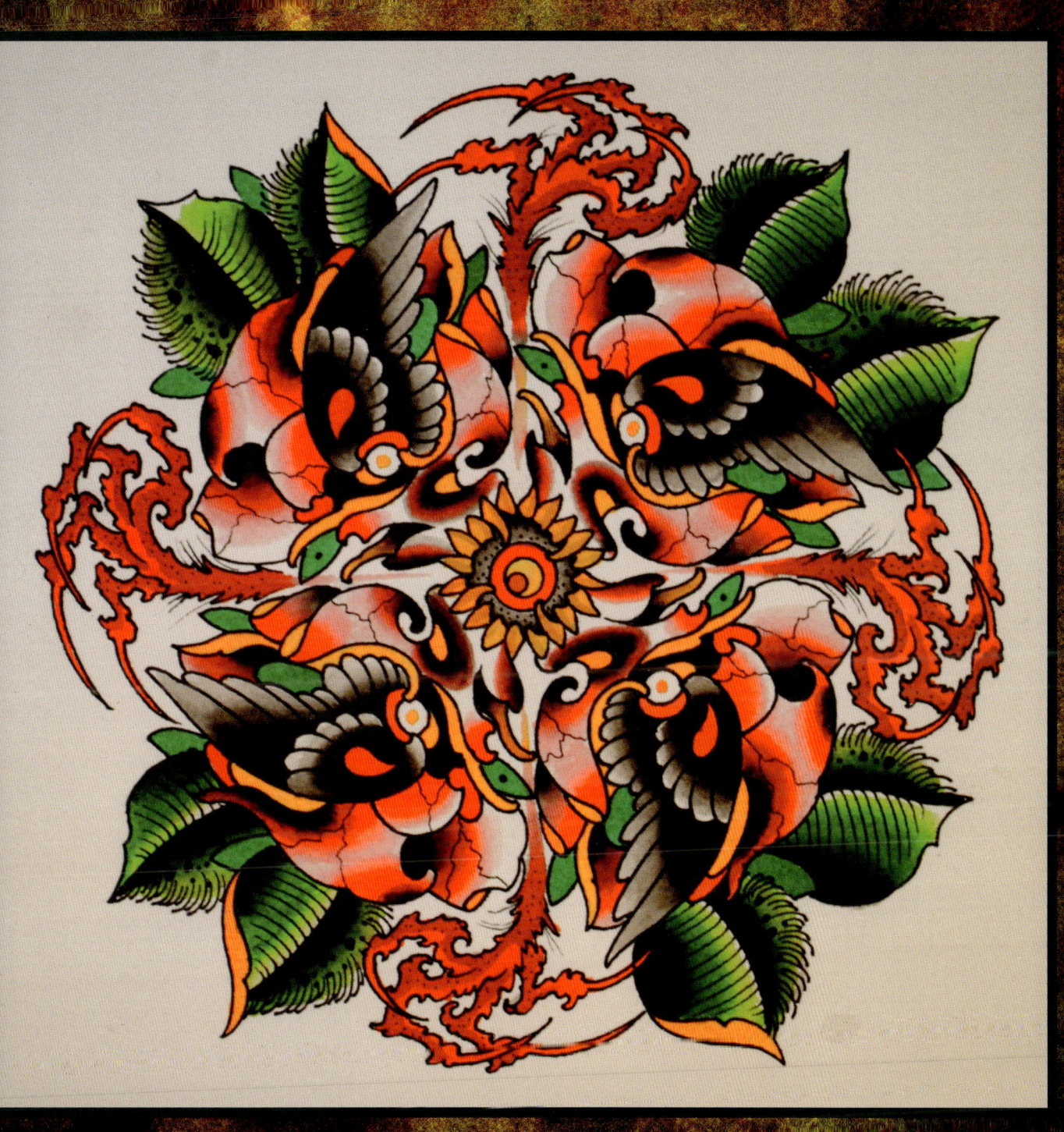

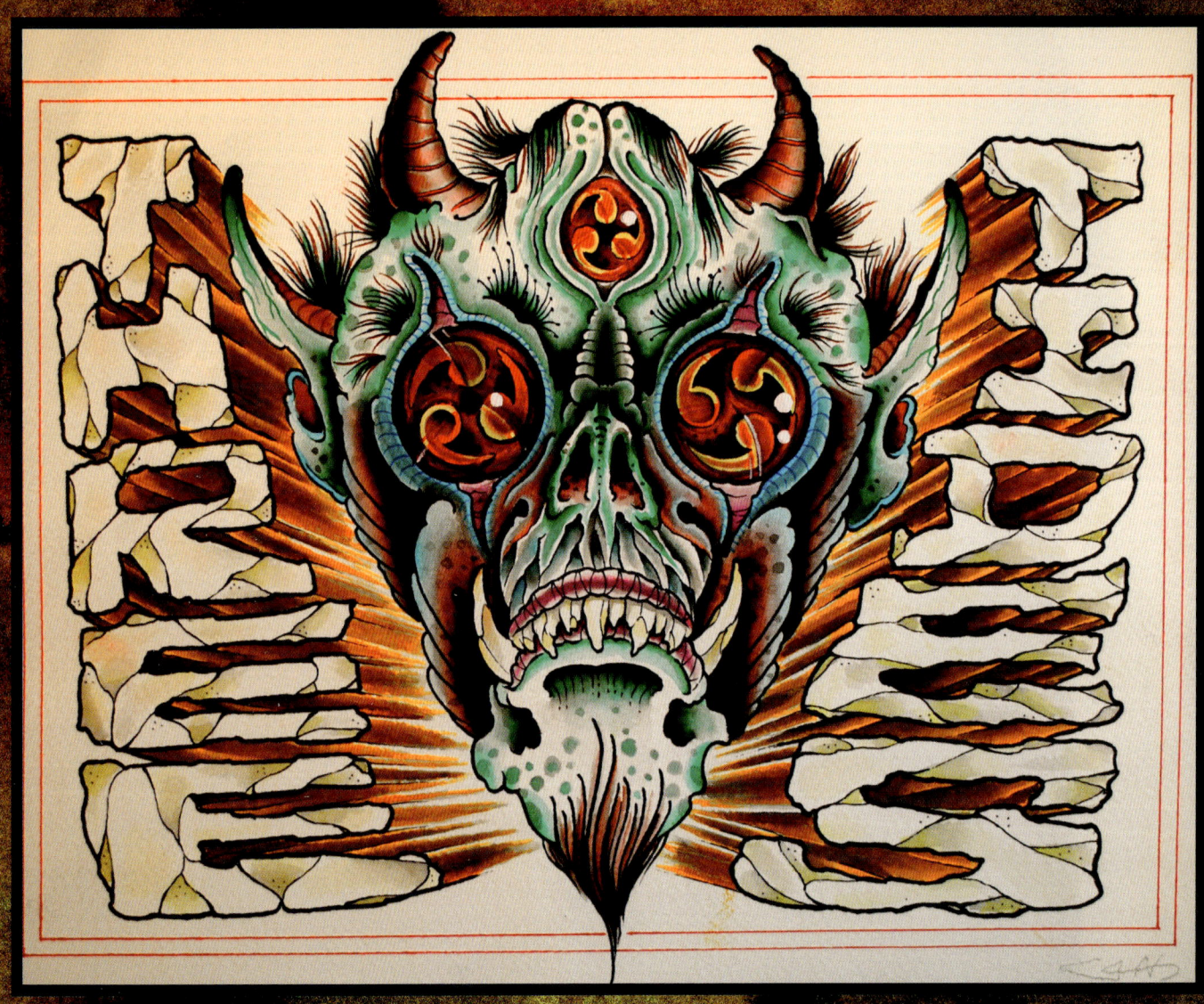

ABOVE: *Untitled*. pen, ink and watercolour.
RIGHT: *Untitled*. pen, ink and watercolour.

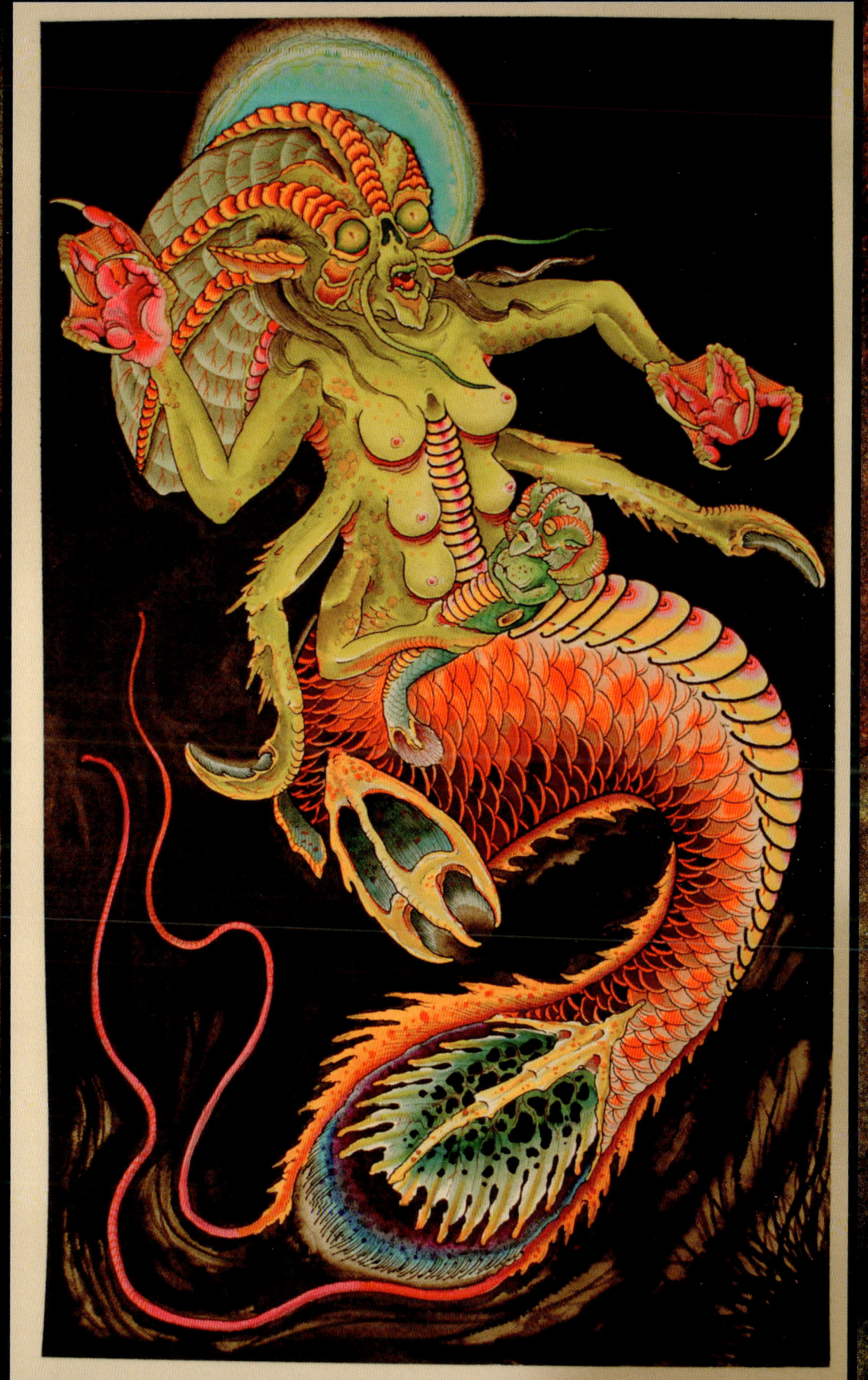

GIANT

SAN FRANCISCO, U.S.A

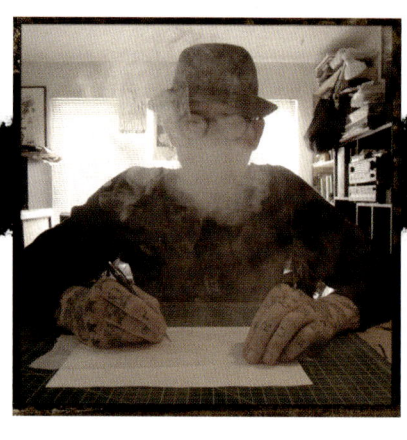

"You could say I'm a man of many paths," says Mike Giant philosophically. One can also say that he's already a legend amongst tattooists, graffiti artists, kustom artists and anyone into contemporary culture. He grew up in upstate New York, before moving to Albuquerque, New Mexico as a kid. That was a formative time. He was fascinated by the graffiti scene there – "those Albuquerque cinderblock walls which surrounded most properties were ideal canvases" – and by the Cholo culture from which most of it emanated. "Much of the graffiti was part of gang identity, a way of marking territory. I was thrilled by the symbolic language it contained. It was also something which had to be treated with respect. You know those symbols, like all things derived from old folklore, had and continue to have real meaning." Other influences at the time were the BMX scene, heavy metal, skateboarding, punk and hip-hop. Mike studied architecture for a while, but decided that wasn't for him. He left to go to San Francisco to design graphics for Think Skateboards. He spent ten years in the Bay Area: "It was a great time, but on one level I just seemed to be working to pay bills. I didn't have time to take advantage of the culture – so why be there? That was 2003. I looked around and decided to go to France with the intention of staying." In the event, France wasn't for him, and he returned to Albuquerque. "It was great to be back, close to family and it was super cheap, so I could travel loads." In Albuquerque he opened his legendary tattoo shop, Stay Gold and then was back in San Francisco, where his publishing firm, Skullz Press and renowned apparel brand, Rebel 8 (created with with Joshy D.), were born. In between he managed to travel – London, NYC, Tokyo, Amsterdam. He tattooed at some of the best shops in the US: East Side Tattoo, New Skool Tattoo, Everlasting and Tattoo 13. He considered going back to art school, but there was too much going on with his art, including collaborations with Shepard Fairey. Of his art and inspirations he says, "I'm influenced by everything around me…it's all interconnected…you can chose what you surround yourself with to some degree. In the end, I find solace when making art, in the personal focus that artistic concentration gives you. When there are few distractions, I get a lot done." Today Mike has retired from tattooing and is focusing on his fine art, exhibited in major galleries around the world. He loves mixing images that are heavy with meaning, history and symbolism, with the abstract and expressionistic. One thing remains consistent: everything is still black and white: "I like the simplicity of inking black with Sharpies on white paper; and one other thing – I'm colour-blind."

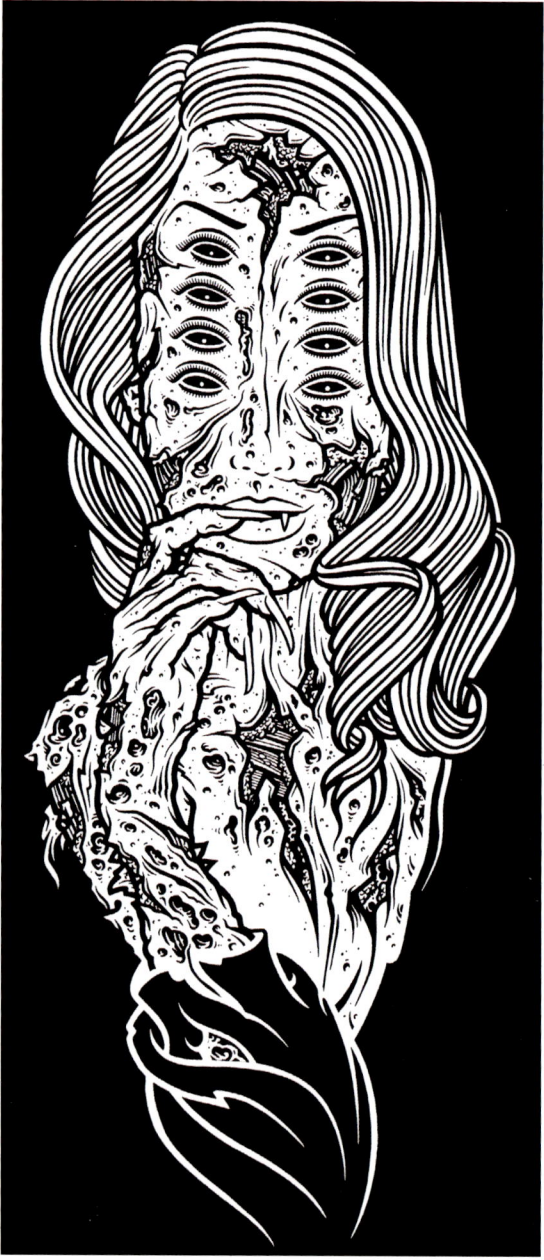

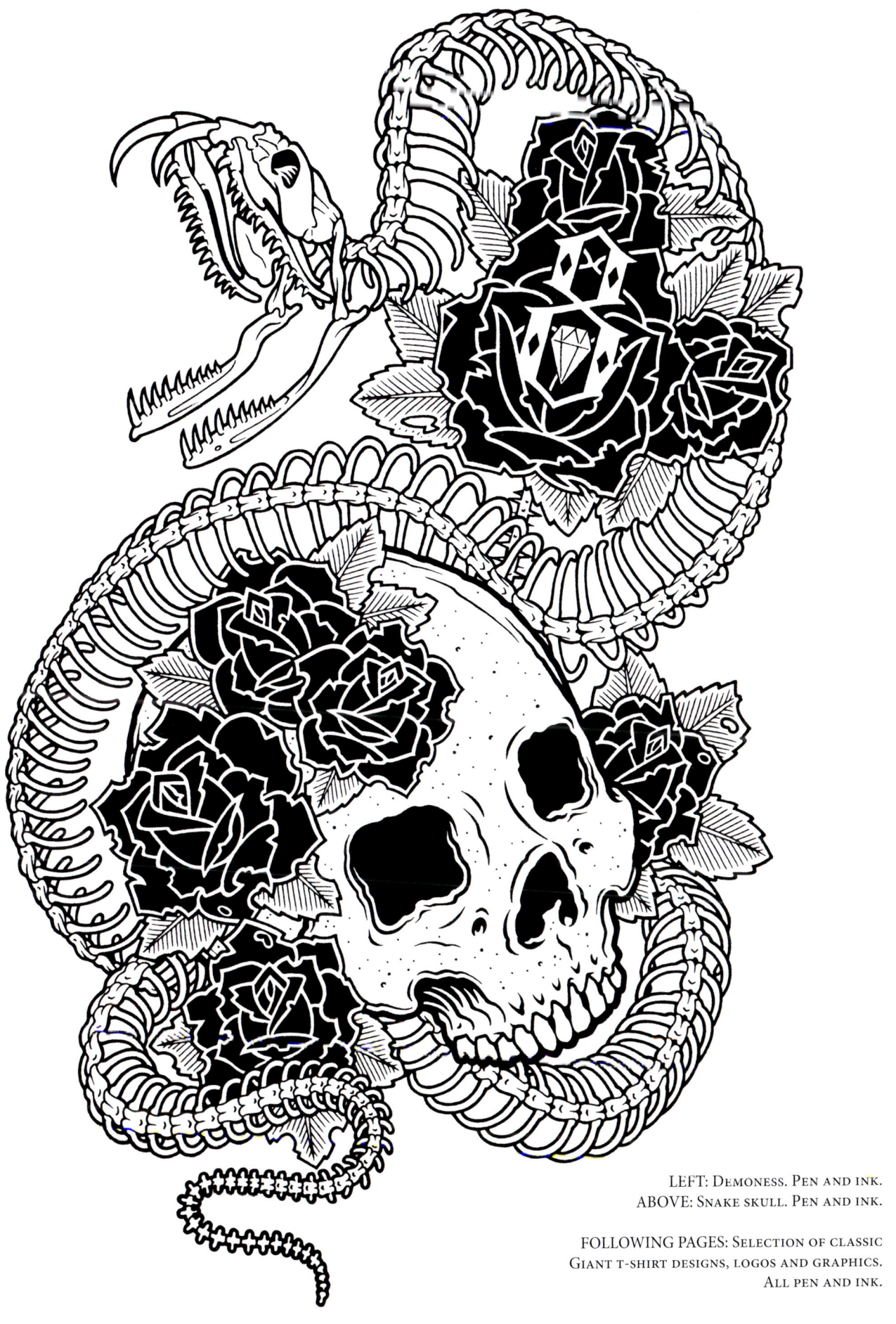

LEFT: Demoness. Pen and ink.
ABOVE: Snake skull. Pen and ink.

FOLLOWING PAGES: Selection of classic
Giant t-shirt designs, logos and graphics.
All pen and ink.

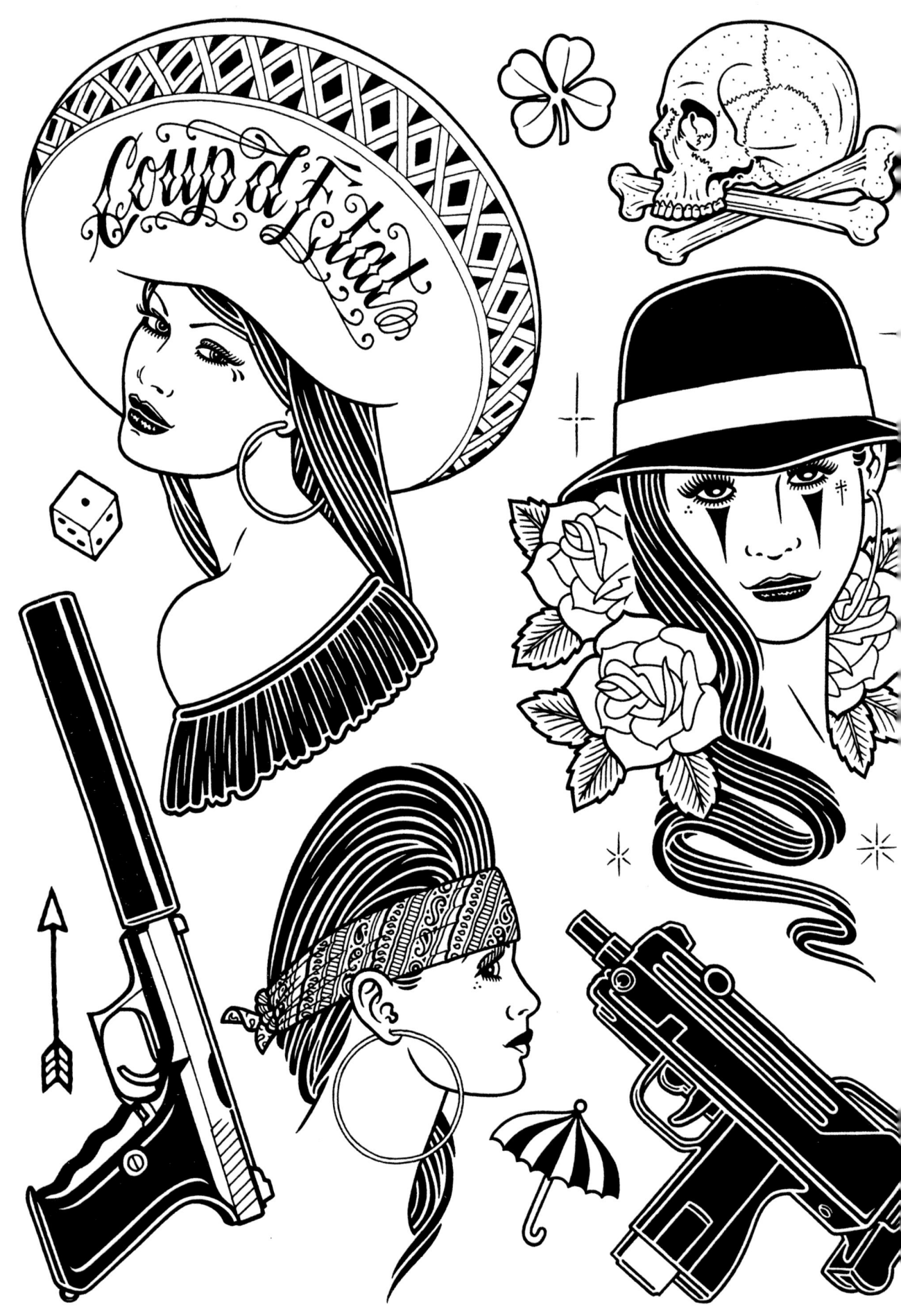

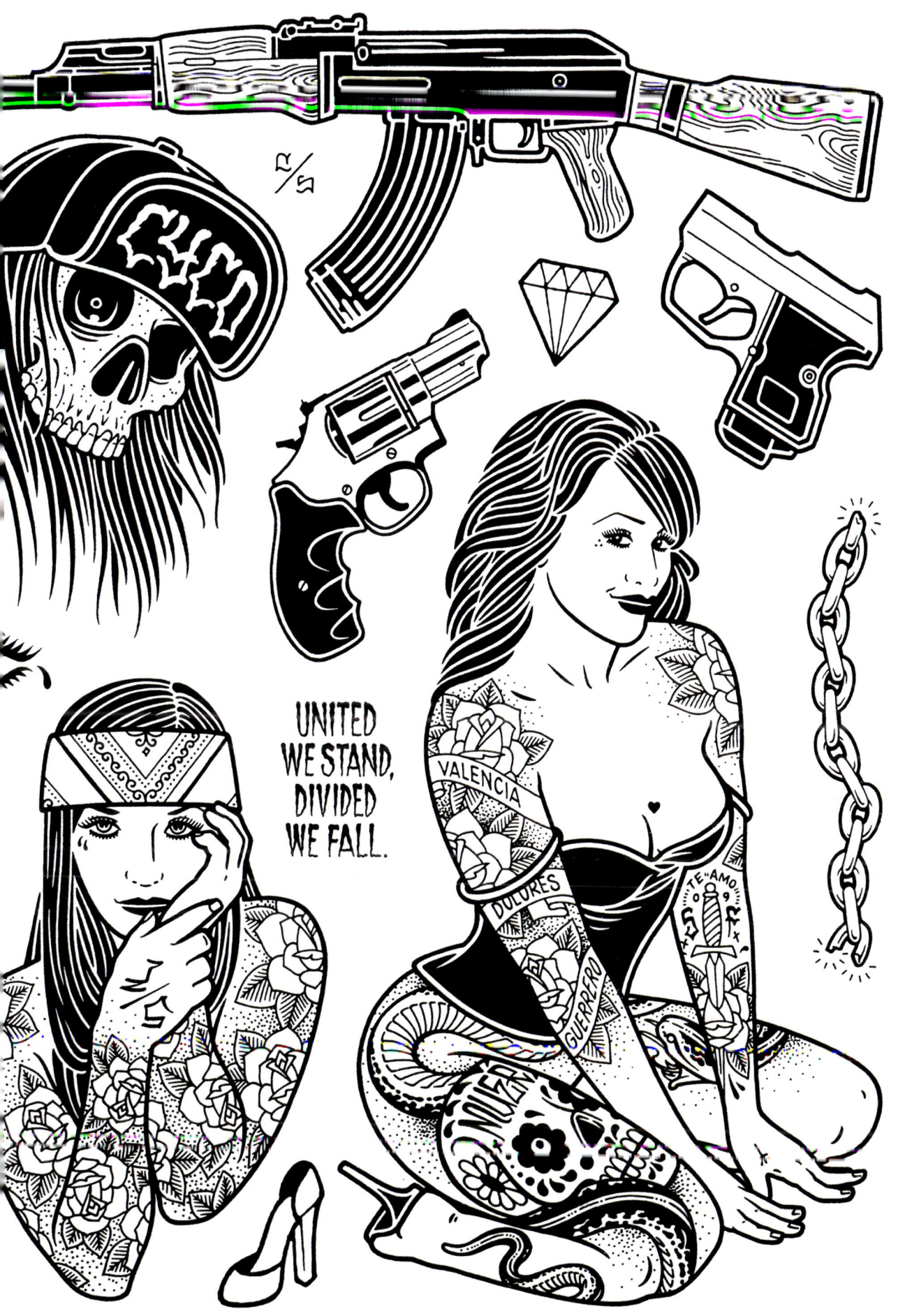

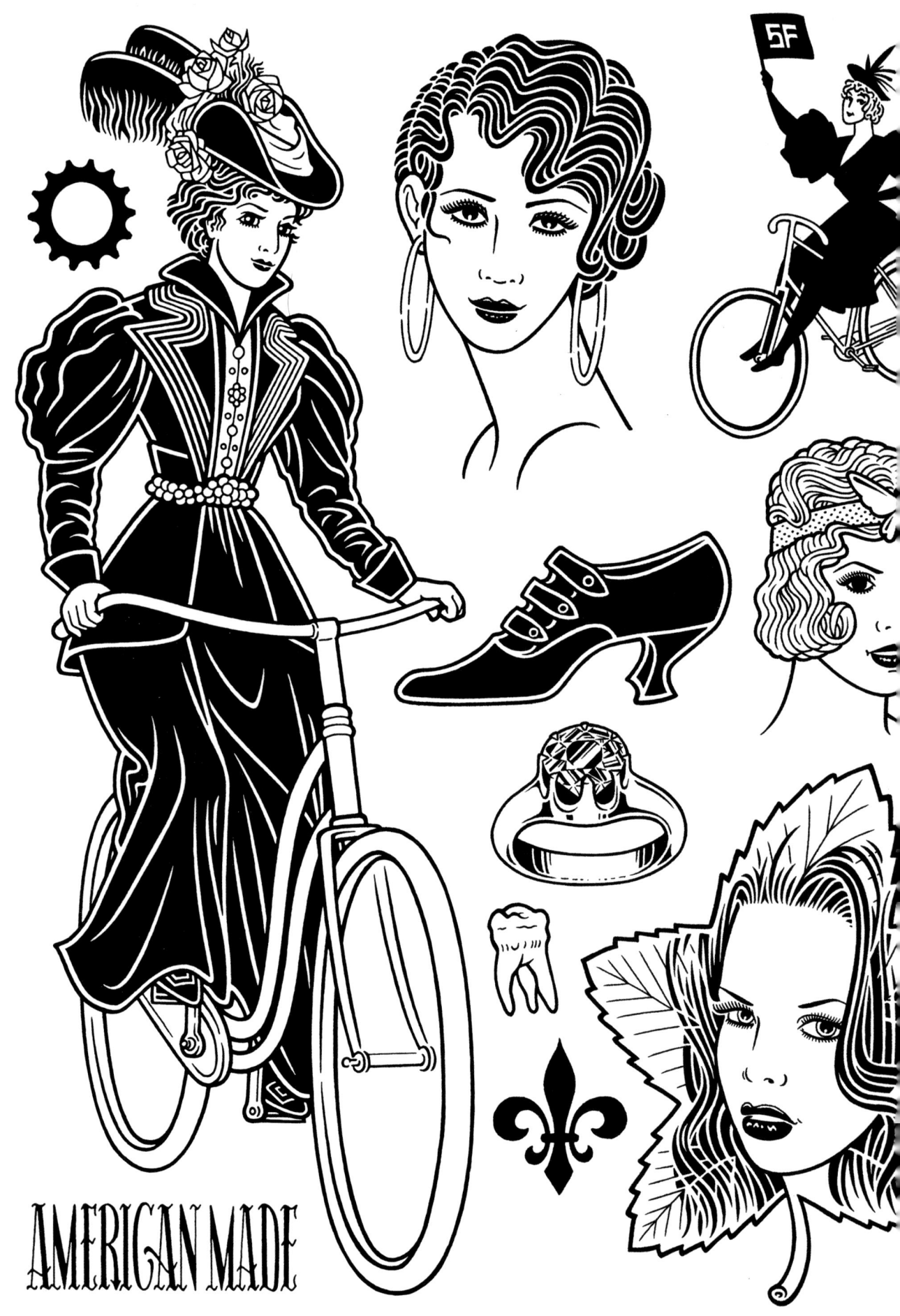

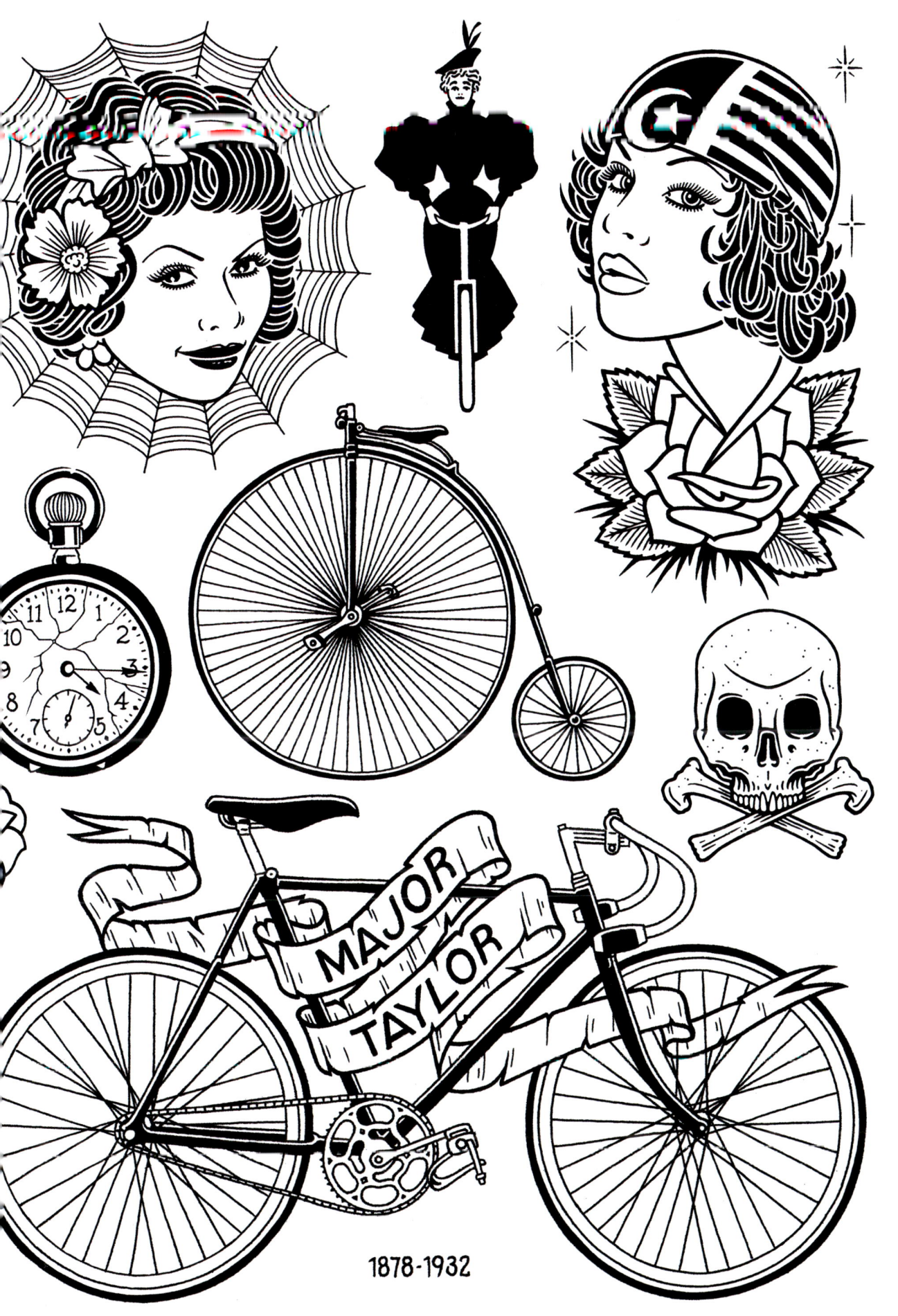

GRAVES

TRANSYLVANIA / LONDON, UK.

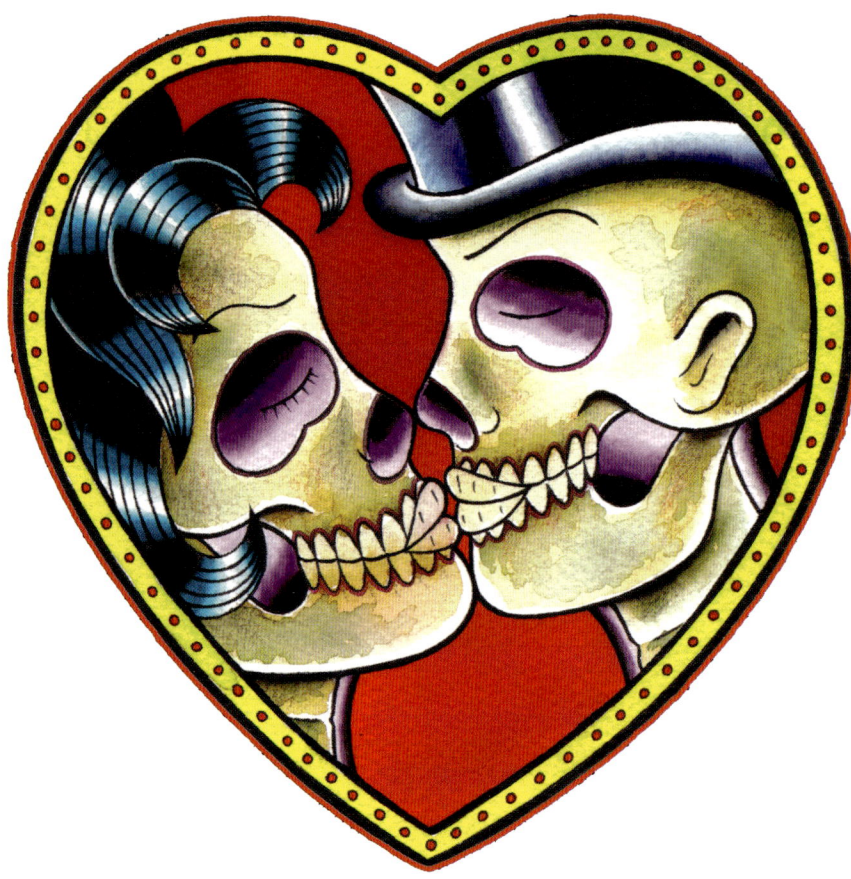

"As a kid I was always drawing monsters; I was then trying to think of how I could keep doing this as a career...I did a couple of years of technical drawing, decided that wasn't for me, and moved onto comic book school in Barcelona; when I discovered what was lurking in the world of tattoo I decided I had to give it a shout." Allan was lucky to have Patricio Sadowsky, a tattoo artist, moving into his flat when he was starting out. "I'm very grateful to him; he taught me a whole lot at the start." Allan was soon working in a shop, then, after travelling around the world tattooing in many cities, he founded the renowned Haunted Tattoos in London. Allan's art, as well as his tattoos, are influenced heavily by '80s culture, "especially the use of colour and composition, which you see in movie posters from the period." His art pieces and tattoo pieces feed into each other "I recycle techniques from the art into my tattoo work and viceversa." Much of his tattoo work is of horror comic-style tattoos from the pre-code '50s, "rather like old school tattoos with loads of black contrast and strong colours." Current inspiration includes Gary Pullin, Graham Ingles, Bernie Wrightson "and loads of comics!" An impressario by nature (as well as Haunted and his art, Allan is involved in numerous publishing projects), Allan is always trying new things. "I like to see my career as a ghost train, not knowing what's ahead of me." Clients for his art are essentially those for his tattoos. "Mine are the best clients a tattoo artist could imagine....not least because they let me draw horrible and spooky things on them!" Of the scene he says: "It's now moving so fast, it's hard to keep track of what's happening...like Instagram, where you can get instant feedback even before finishing a piece."

ABOVE: *Kiss Of Death*. Pen, ink and watercolour.
RIGHT: *Tiki*. Pen, ink and watercolour.
OVERLEAF: *Bat*. Pen, ink and digital.

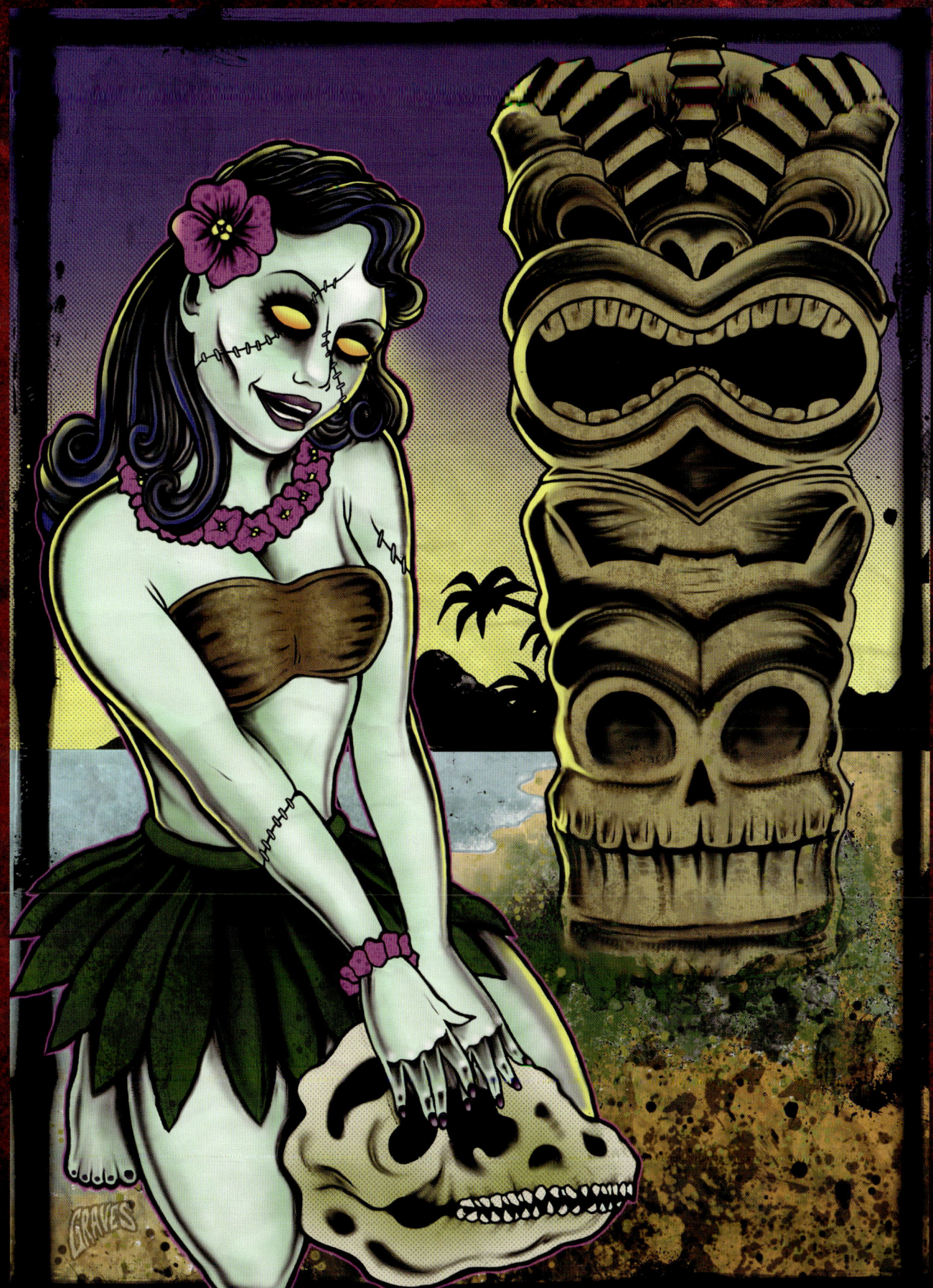

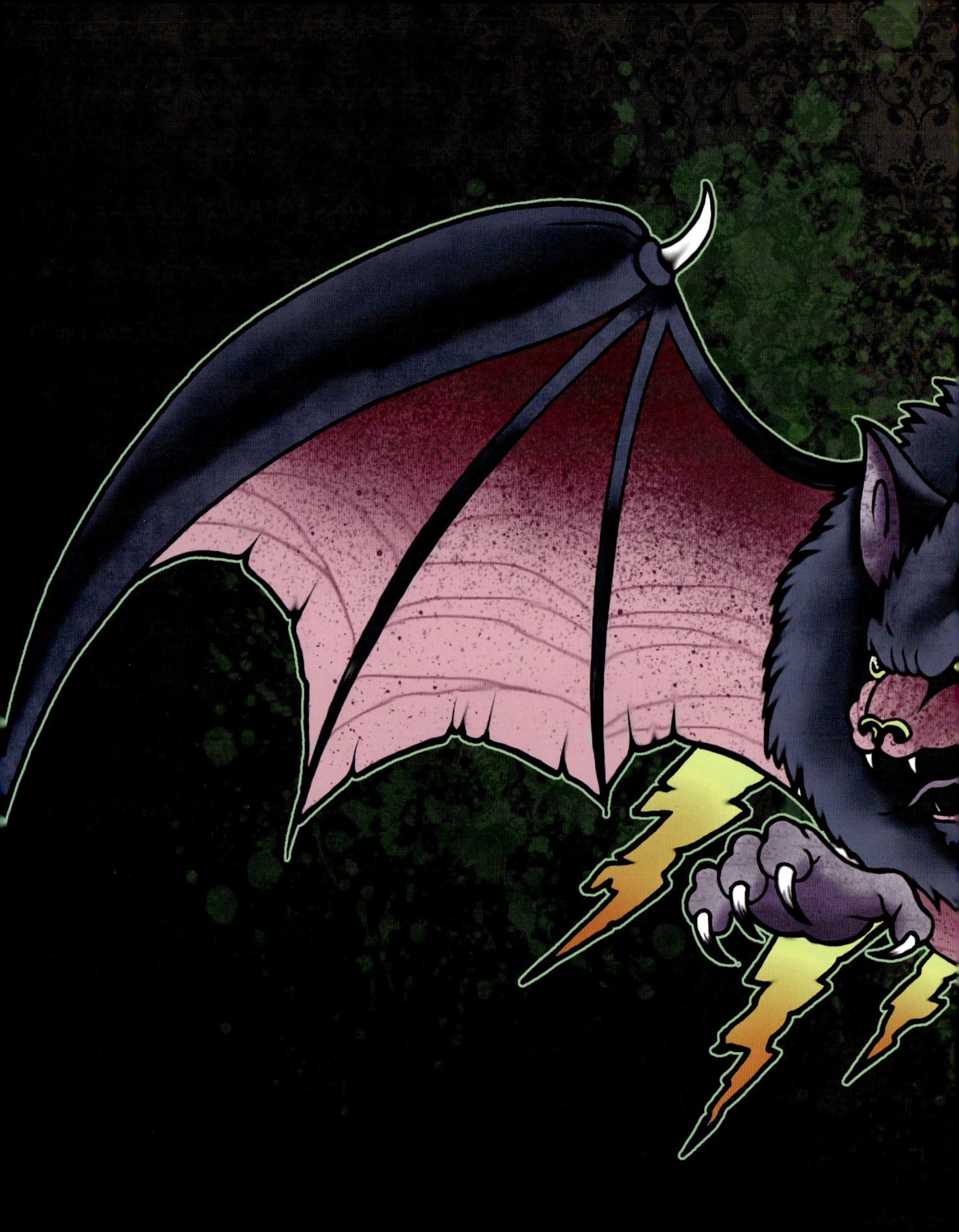

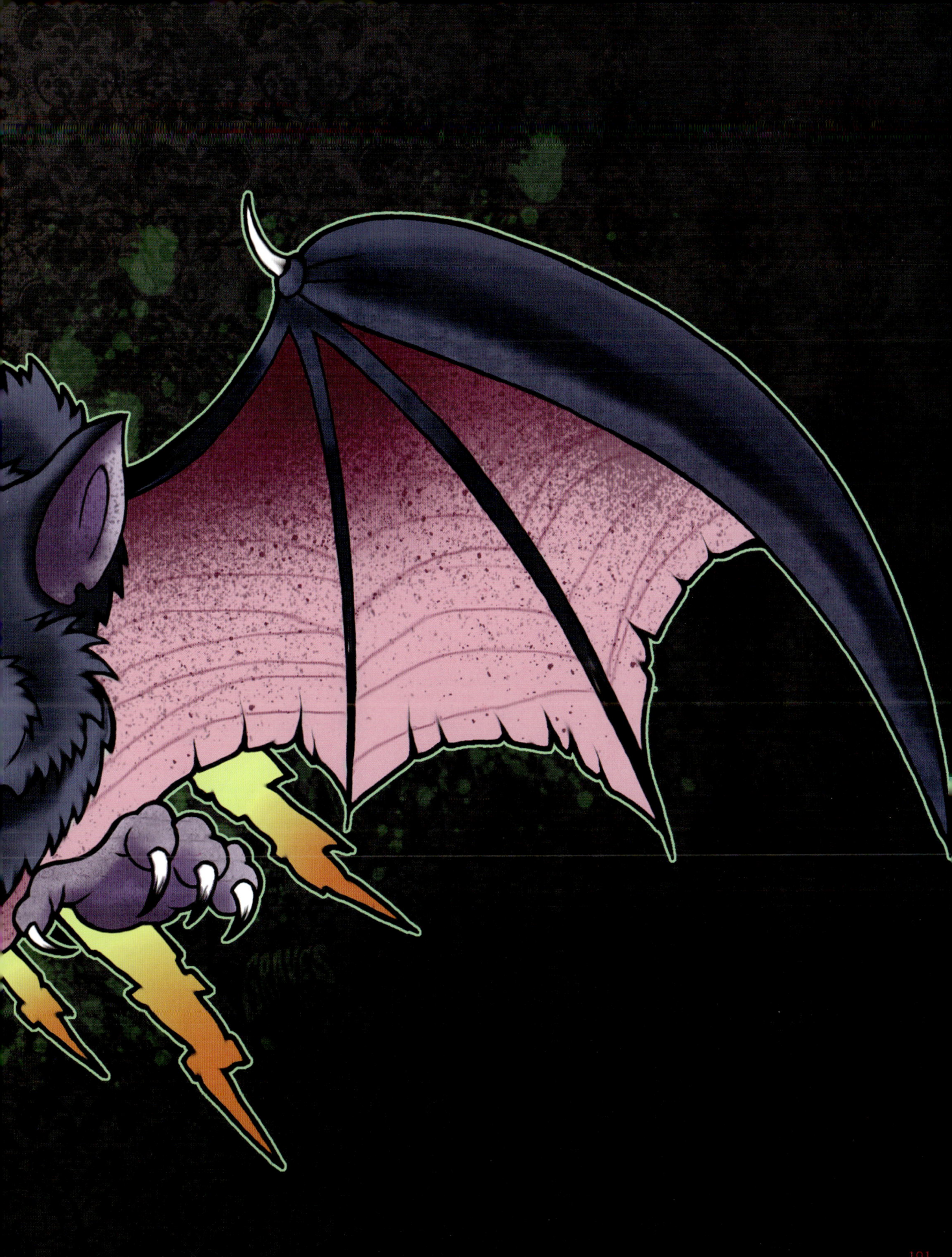

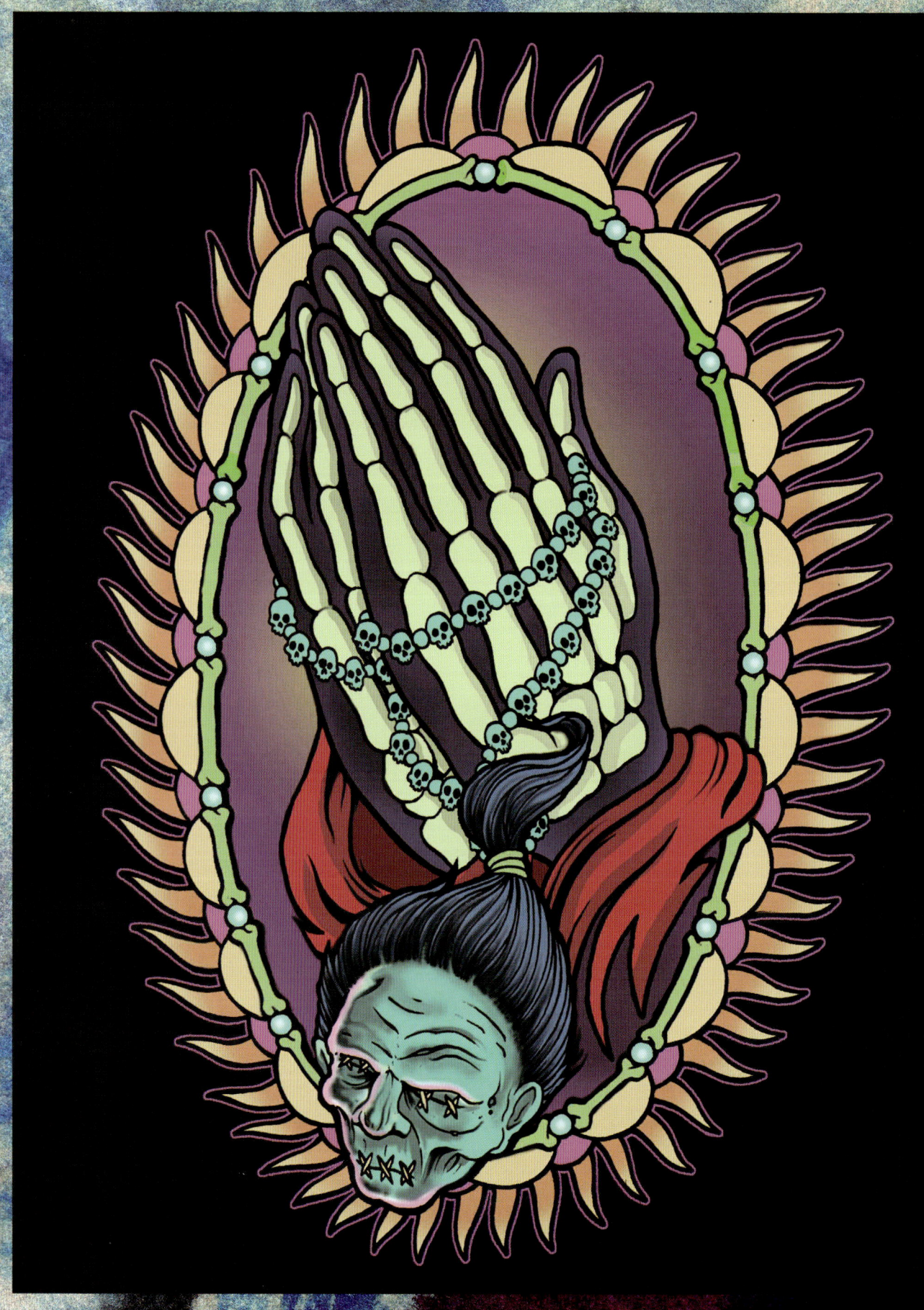

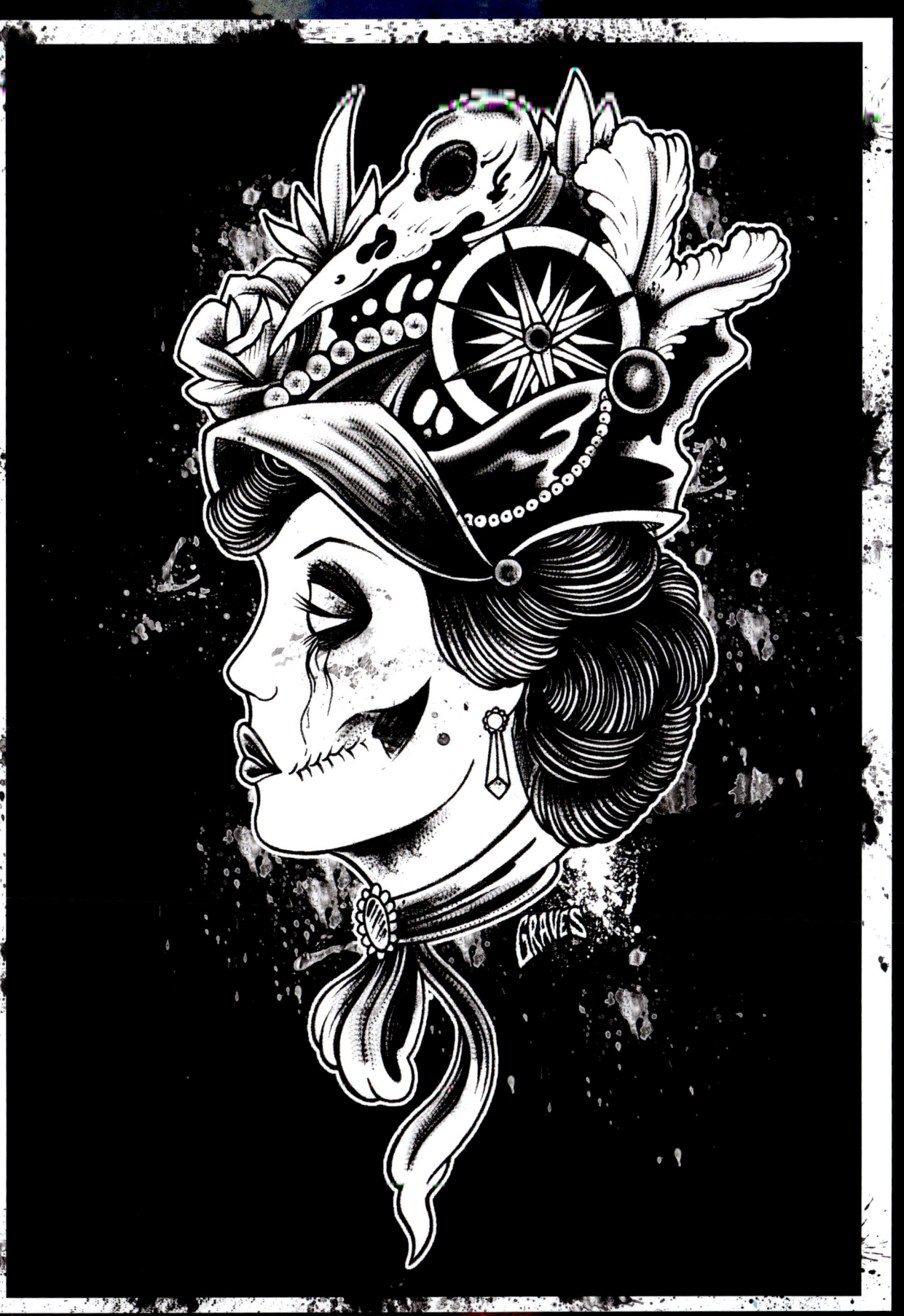

LEFT: *Praying for evil*. Pen, ink and digital.
ABOVE: *Victorian Undead*. Pen and ink.

JOÃO

BRAZIL / LONDON, UK.

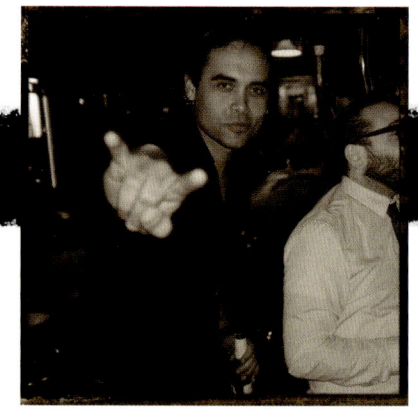

It was his friends, who recognised João's special talent for drawing, who encouraged him to take up tattoo and "comics and heavy metal music." Originally from Brazil, João is now London-based. "I still consider Mauricio Teodoro, from São Paulo, one of my major influences, and he remains that to this day; I still get ideas from Cuz." The early days in northern Brazil were tough; "then when I started to travel and work with different artists, I began to develop a deeper understanding of the art. But like any artist one never stops learning." Today he is inspired both by tattooists and influences from outside the scene, including comics, heavy metal, the baroque, the Renaissance and classicism: "yeah pretty much the whole of Western art! It's importat to bring outside ideas in, so as to give one's art more 'identity'." João works traditionally, using coil machines, with only the occasional foray into yo-yo rotaries. The artworks he creates primarily for pleasure and "to preserve the now." His art clients are his tattoo clients also "I owe them everything! I couldn't live my life without them!" The scene, João says, has always been in motion. He celebrates the incredible quality of work these days, adding "the rules remain the same. Only the hard workers will reach the top, the lazy ones will keep scratching the bottom. No sacrifice, no victory!"

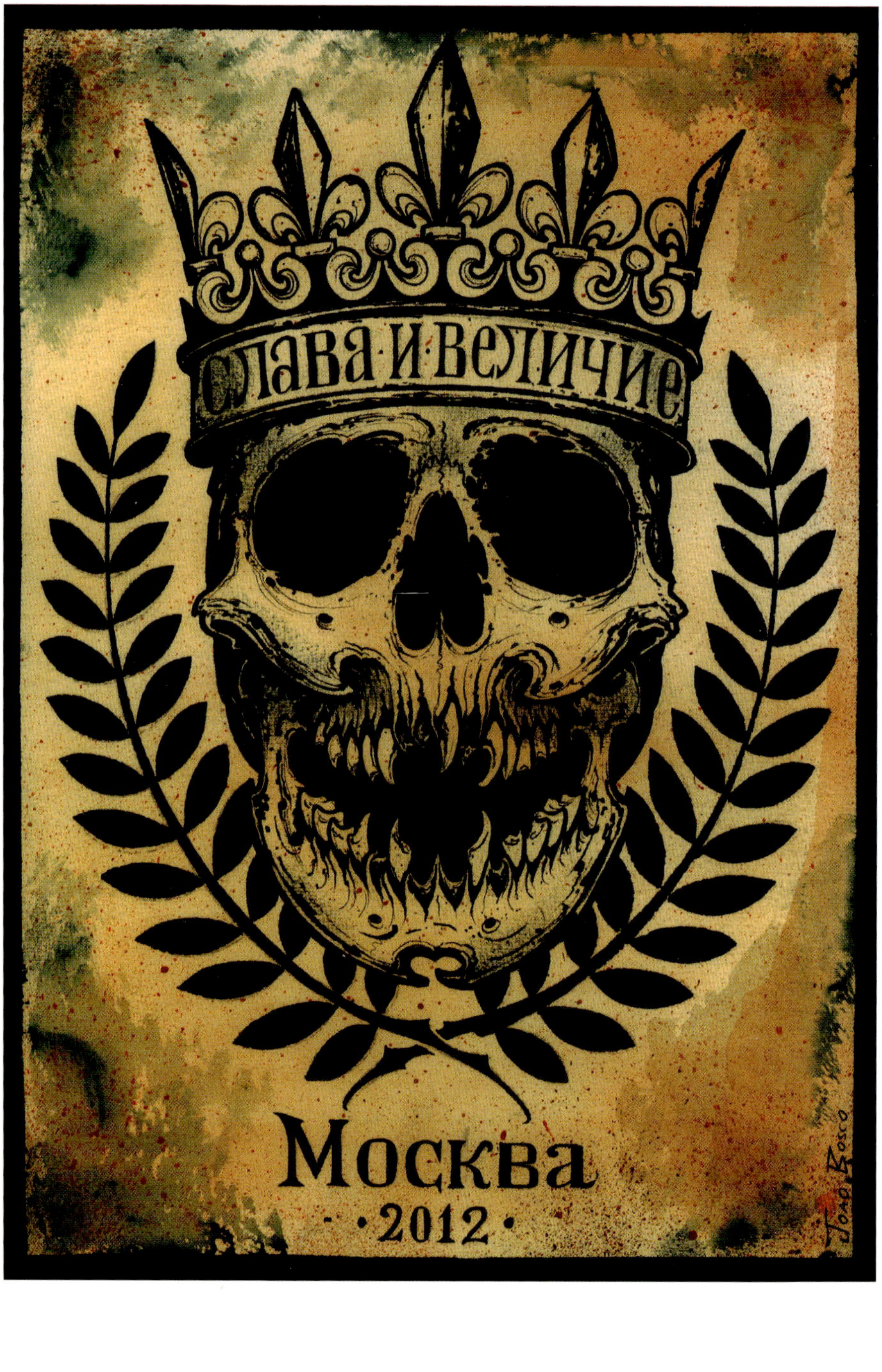

RIGHT: *Skull King*. Pen and ink, watercolour wash.
FAR RIGHT: *Snake Skull*. Pen and ink, watercolour wash.

OVERLEAF:
LEFT: *Eagle*. Pen and ink, watercolour wash.
RIGHT: *Dragon*. Pen and ink, watercolour wash.

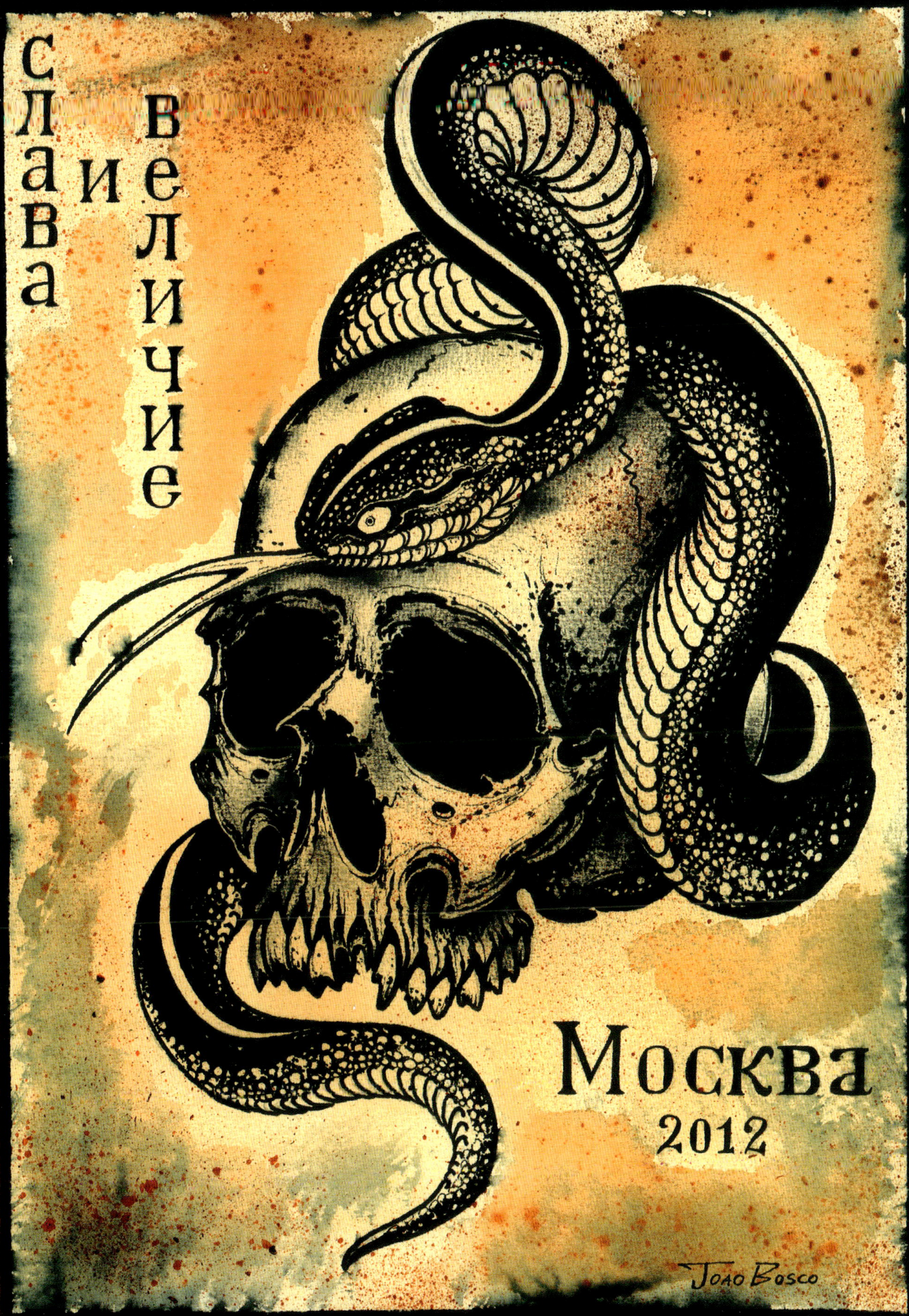

слава и величие

Москва
2012

João Bosco

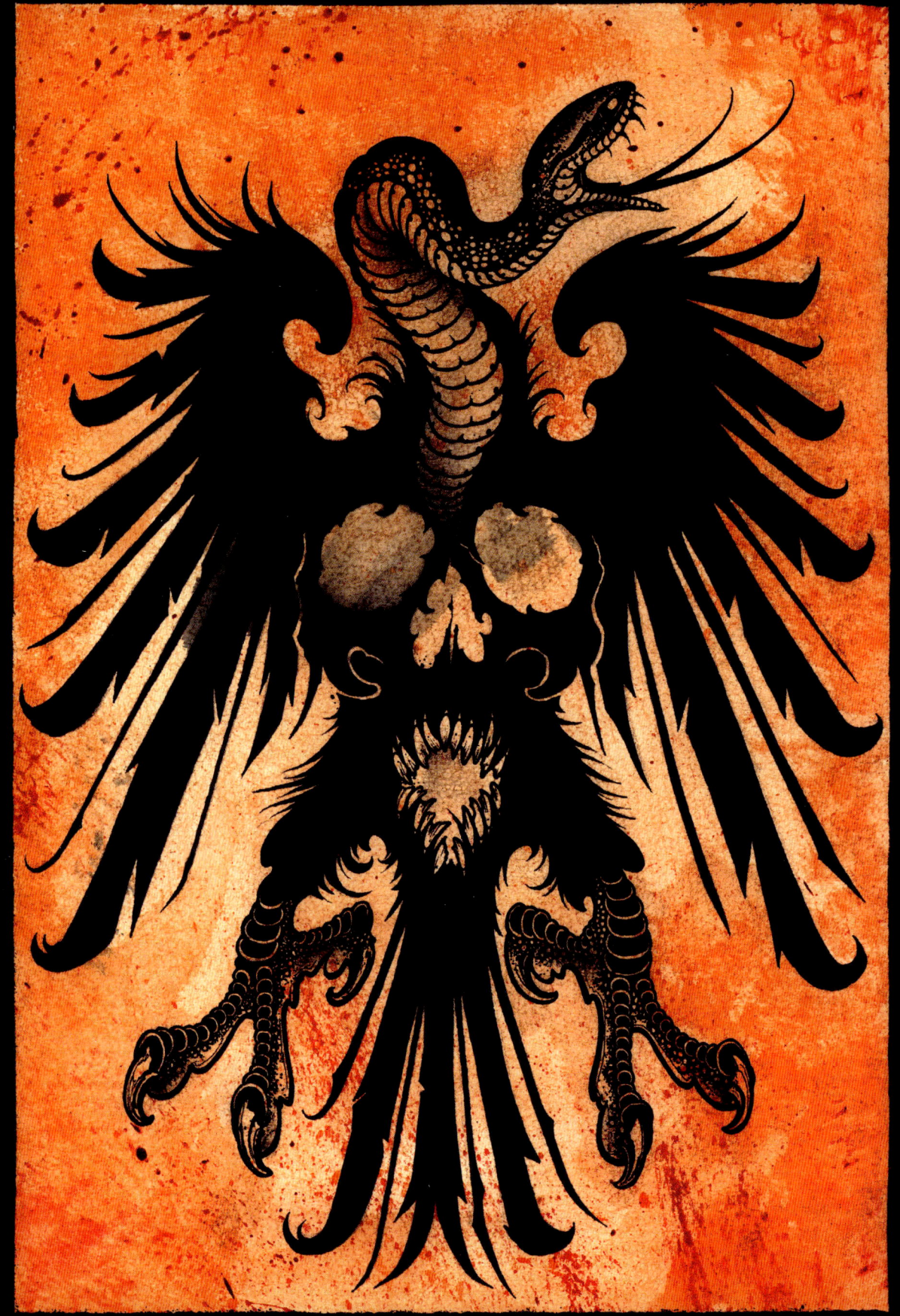

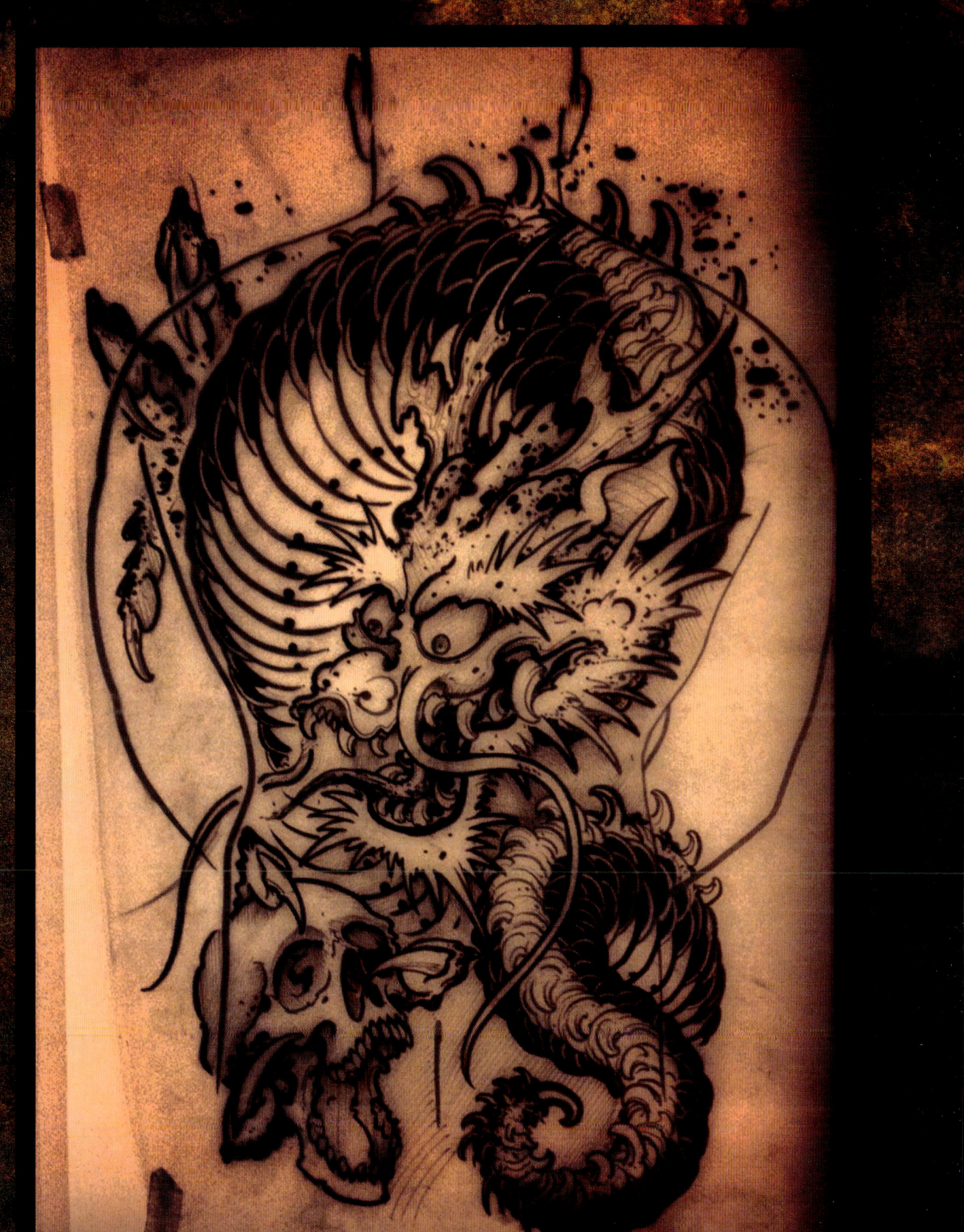

JONDIX

BARCELONA, SPAIN.

The spark that got Jondix into tattoo was getting inked at the famous Tin Tin shop in Paris: "There was a magic in that place that left a deep impression on me. Environments like those where art, fun and professionalism coincide are now so rare." When he started, eveything was difficult. Those were the days before the Internet and Jondix stayed up many nights "figuring our how I would do the next tattoo...in those days I would do anything to learn something new." He first worked at LTW Barcelona, where he spent a few years of learning and fun. "Three years ago I quit to go private. I have my client base that follows me everywhere. Also, now that I'm older I find I have little time for shop politics. I also like to do conventions (they also make it difficult to be shop-based) and need all the time I have to produce the tattoos I have in my mind." Jondix spent eight years at architecture school in Barcelona, where Emil Troeger was his art teacher. This has informed many of his complex and mysterious designs. He doesn't draw a distinction between his art, his tattoo and indeed his life. "My life is my 'art' as I do what I feel...I don't pretend, or try to fit in, or follow a trend, or whatever....all my designs, art or tattoo, come from my way of life and from my insights." The influences and inspirations are many and include: "Hendrix, Mati Klarwein (whom I met in person before he died – he had a huge impact on me), and, at the moment, Fllip and Xed."

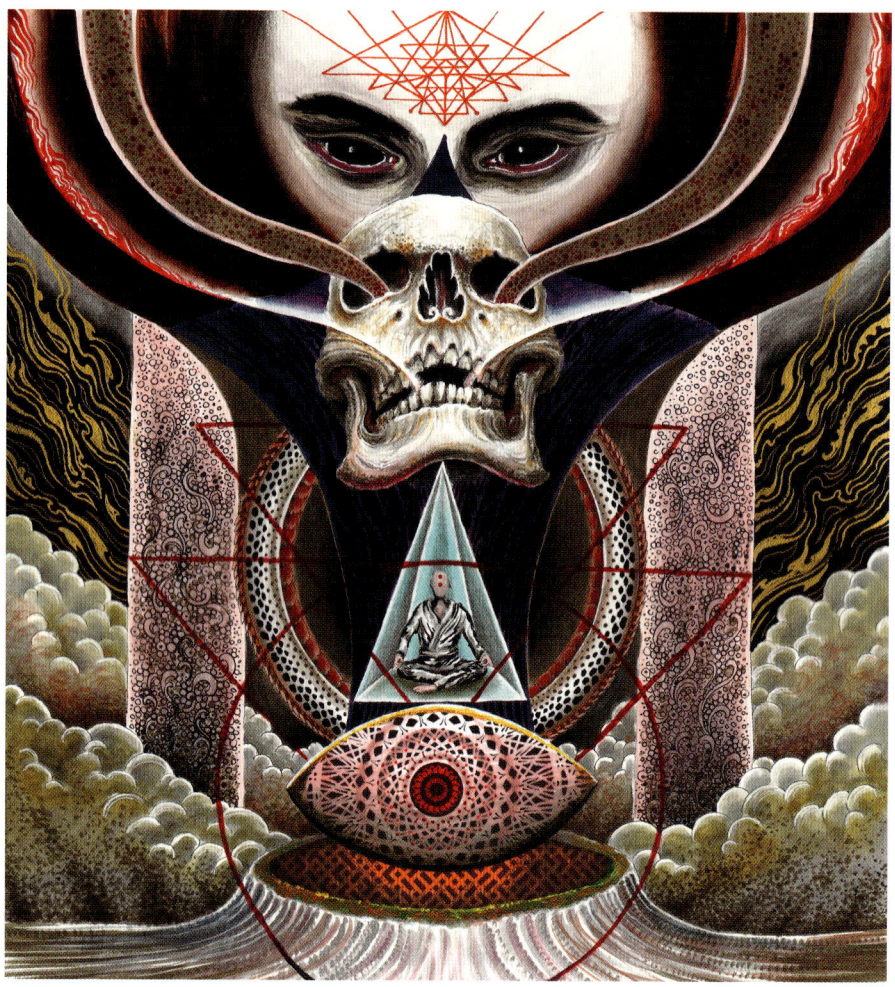

ABOVE: *Purified in Blood*. Pen, ink, watercolour and pastels.
RIGHT: *Aeons' Gate*. Pen, ink, watercolour and pastels.

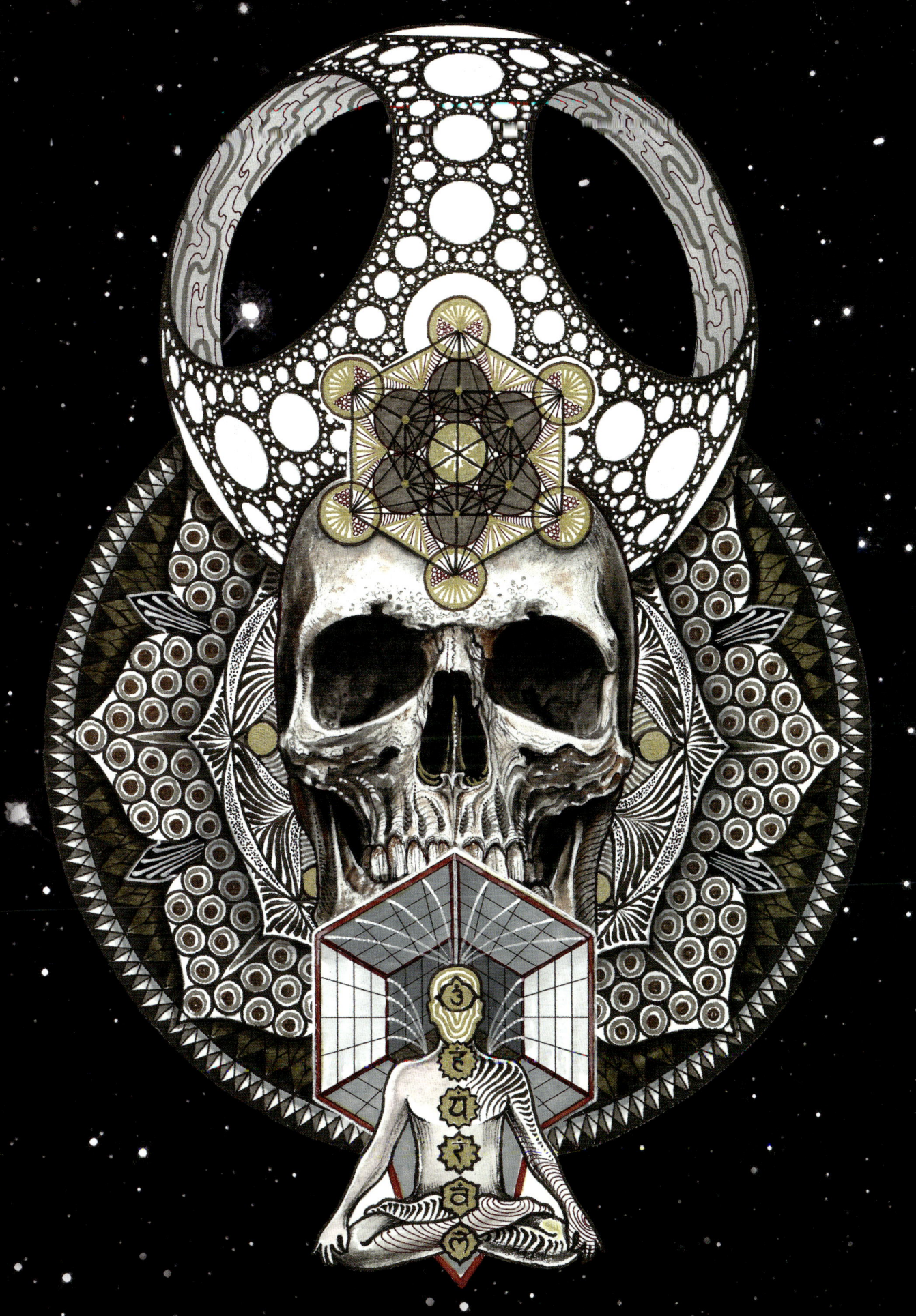

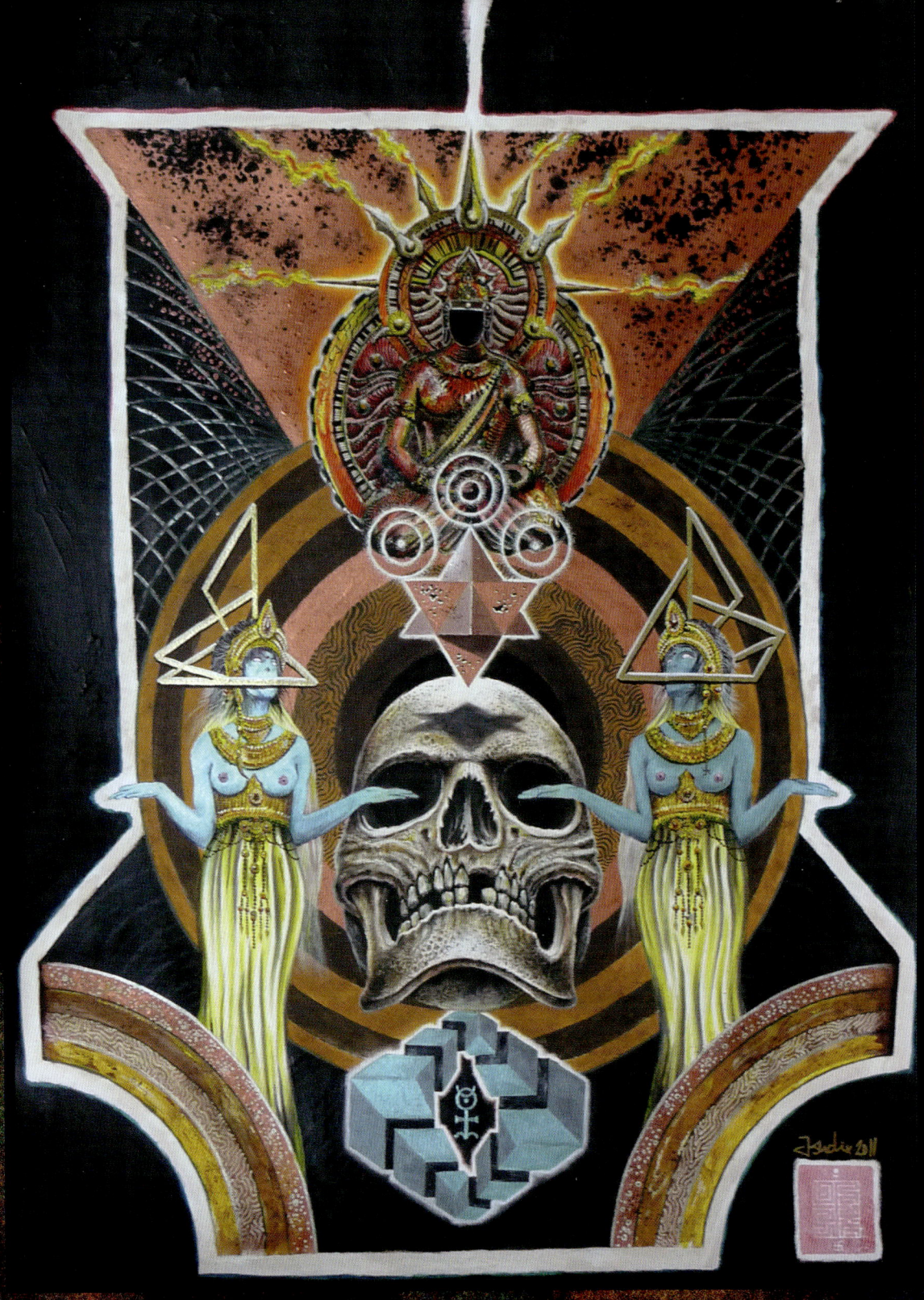

ABOVE: *Liberation*. Pen, ink, watercolours and pastels.
RIGHT: *Holy Mountain*. Pen, ink, watercolours and pastels.

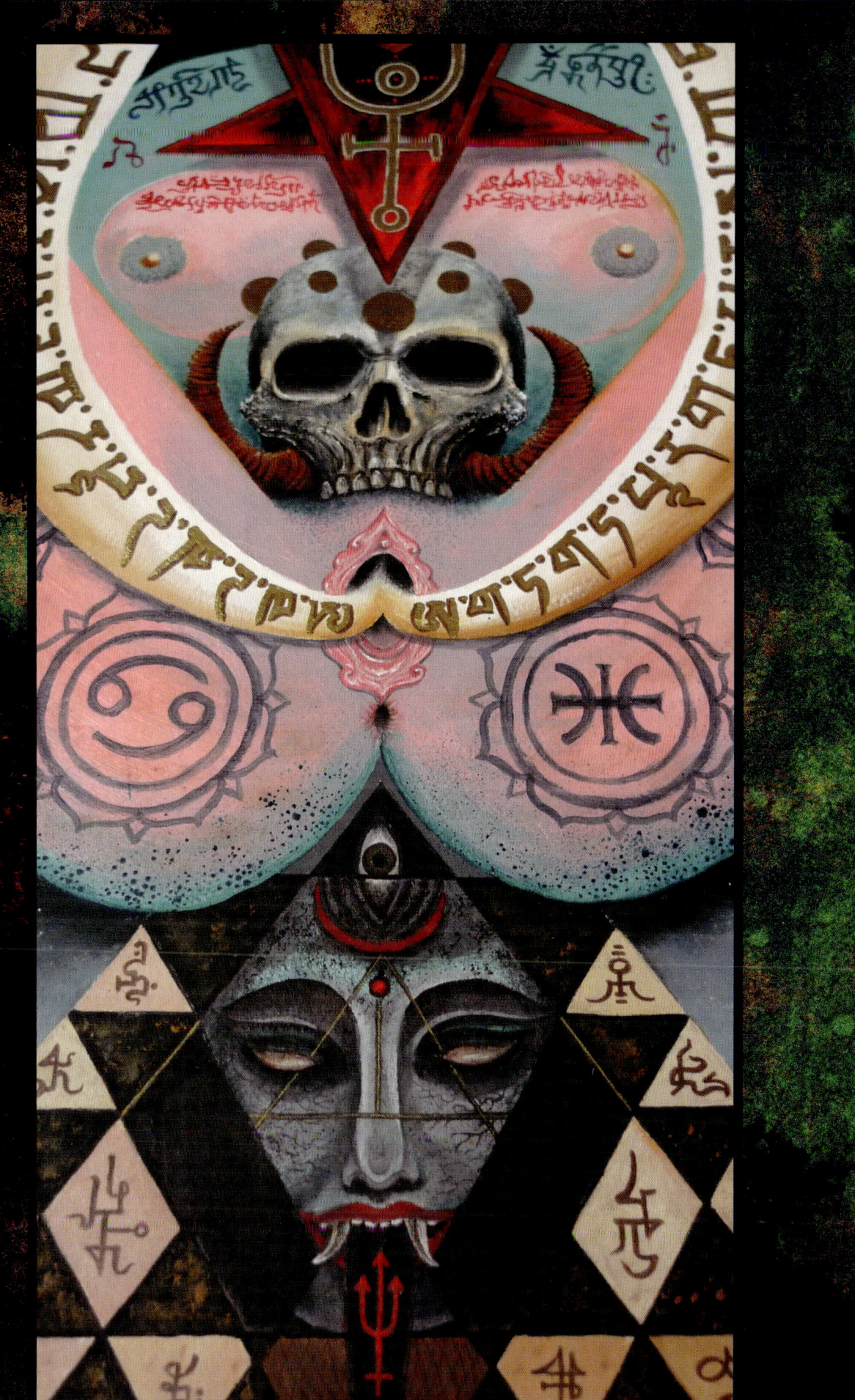

JØRGENSEN

COPENHAGEN, DENMARK.

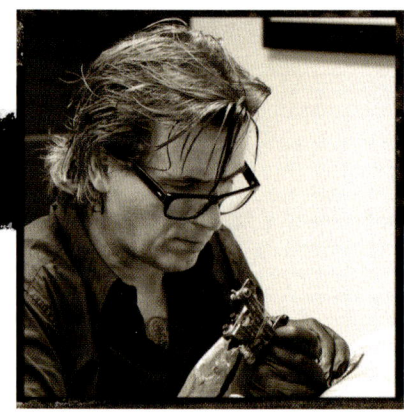

Henning Jørgensen grew up in the red light district in Copenhagen, Denmark, where all the tattoo shops were, and remembers being obsessed with the art from about the age of 12; "When I turned 18 the first thing I did was get an apprenticeship. That was in 1979." Back then the scene was really rough and maybe the standards were not as high as today. It was more important to put in really strong colours than to do fantastic artwork. I tried to come across as convincingly professional and, well, somehow it worked." His first shop was Tattoo John in Istedgade and then he had a stroke of luck, being invited to join the late Tattoo Ole in Nyhavn in 1982. A year later he took the plunge and opened his own shop, Royal Tattoo, in Helsingør. Mostly self-taught, Henning draws particular inspiration from Japanese artists like Kuniyoshi, Kyosai and Yoshitoshi, as well as "all those people I am so fortunate to meet in daily life." Of the scene he says "It has exploded in recent years – nobody would have predicted this even five years ago. There are too sides to this: on the one hand many people are getting into the trade for the wrong reasons, the scene suffers and there is a loss of mystery; on the other there are some fantastic new artists and seeing their work gives great inspiration... there is a feeling that we can keep pushing boundaries, that anything is possible. I feel pretty previleged to be a part of the movement right now."

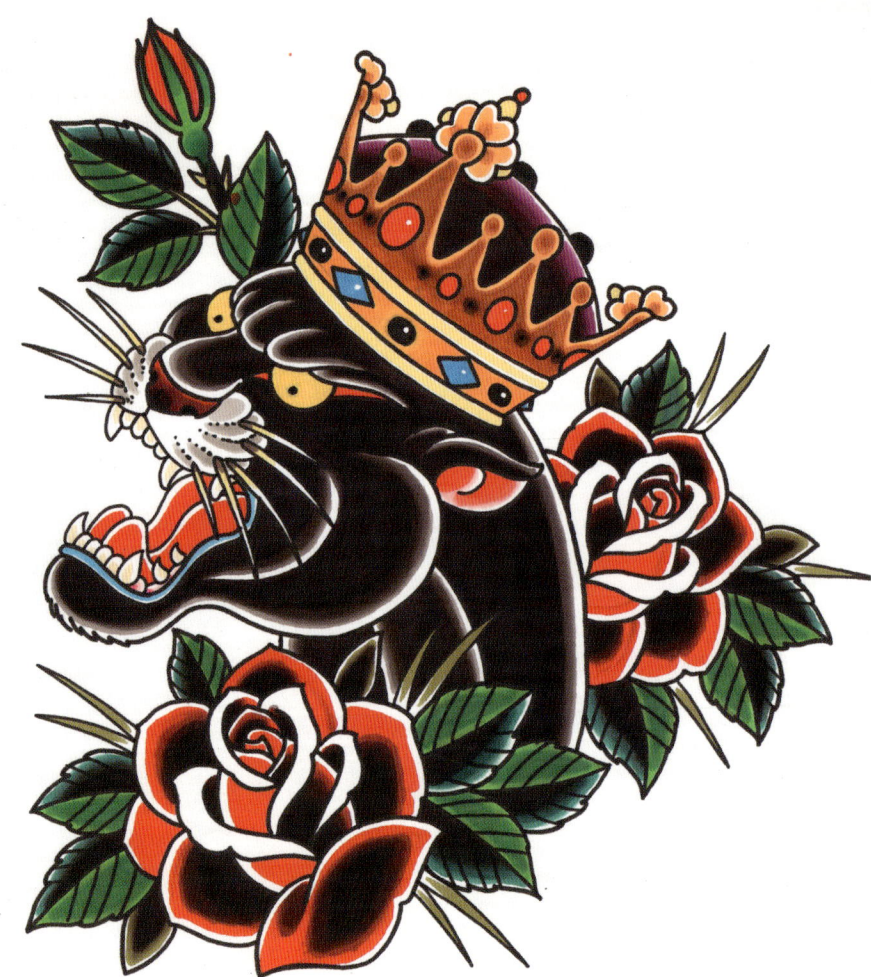

ABOVE: *Crowned Panther*. Ink and marker pens.
RIGHT: *Lotus Tiger*. Ink and marker pens.

OVERLEAF:
LEFT: *Dragon Year*. Ink and marker pens.
RIGHT: *Snaked Skull*. Ink and marker pens.

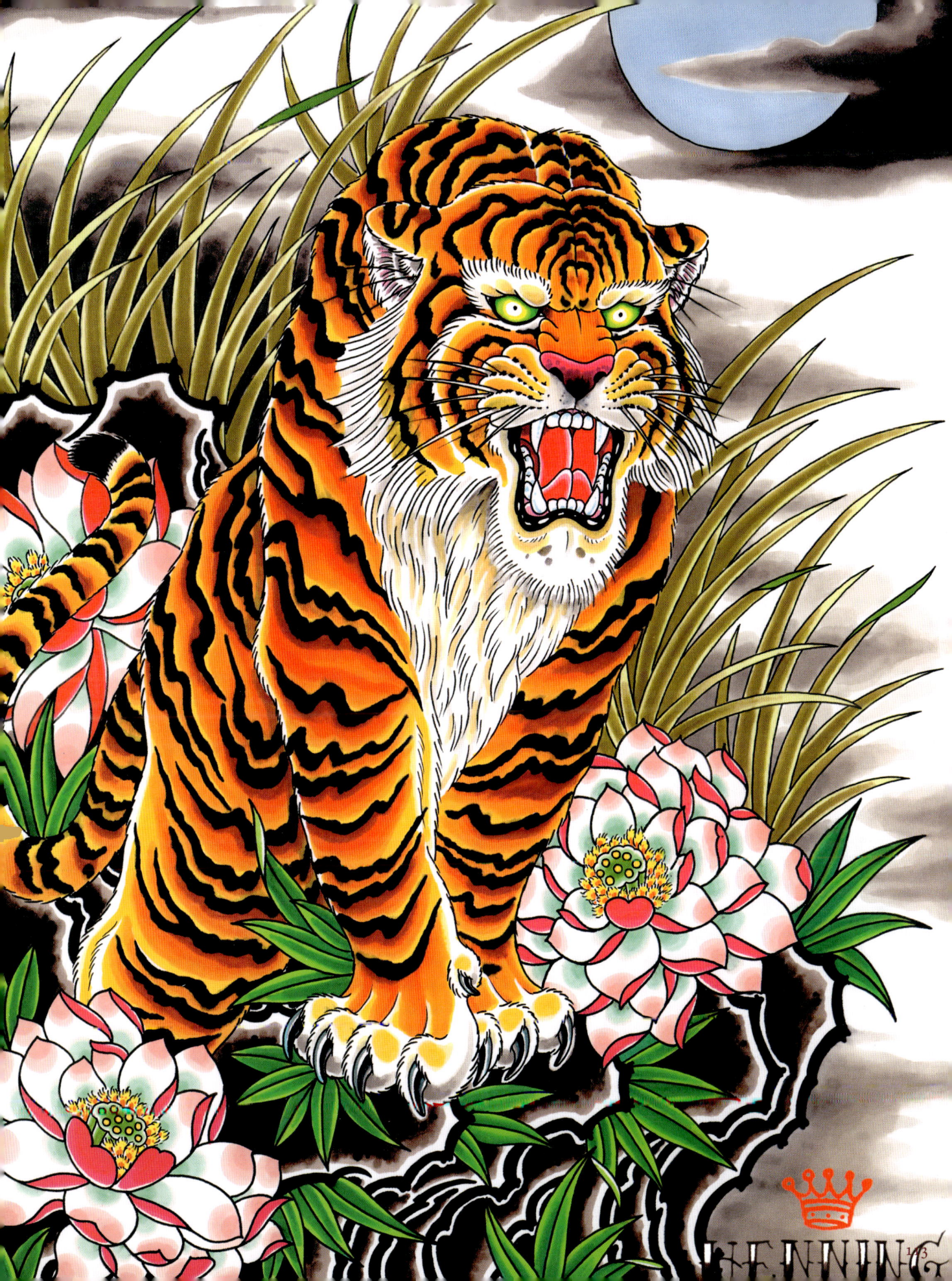

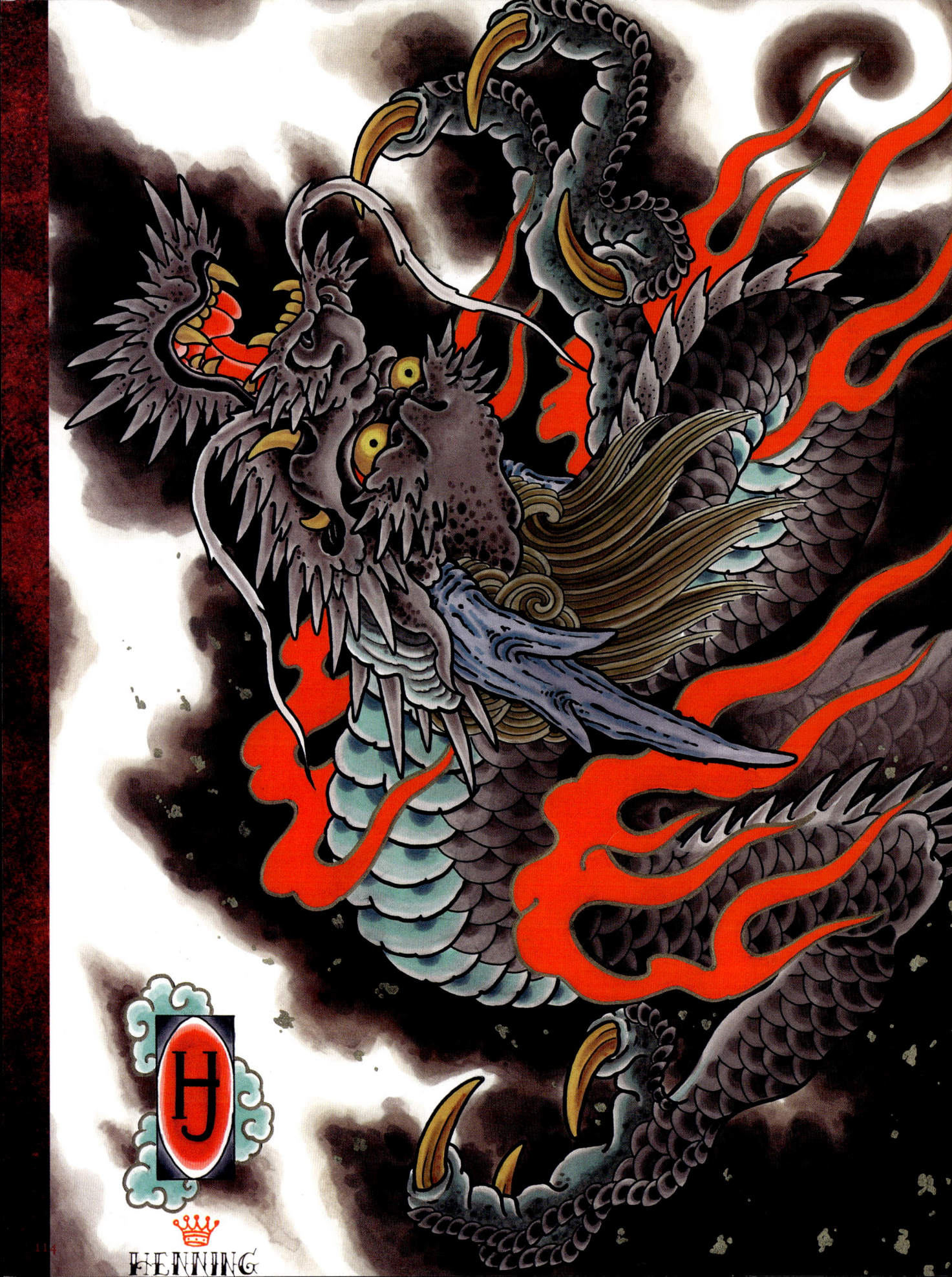

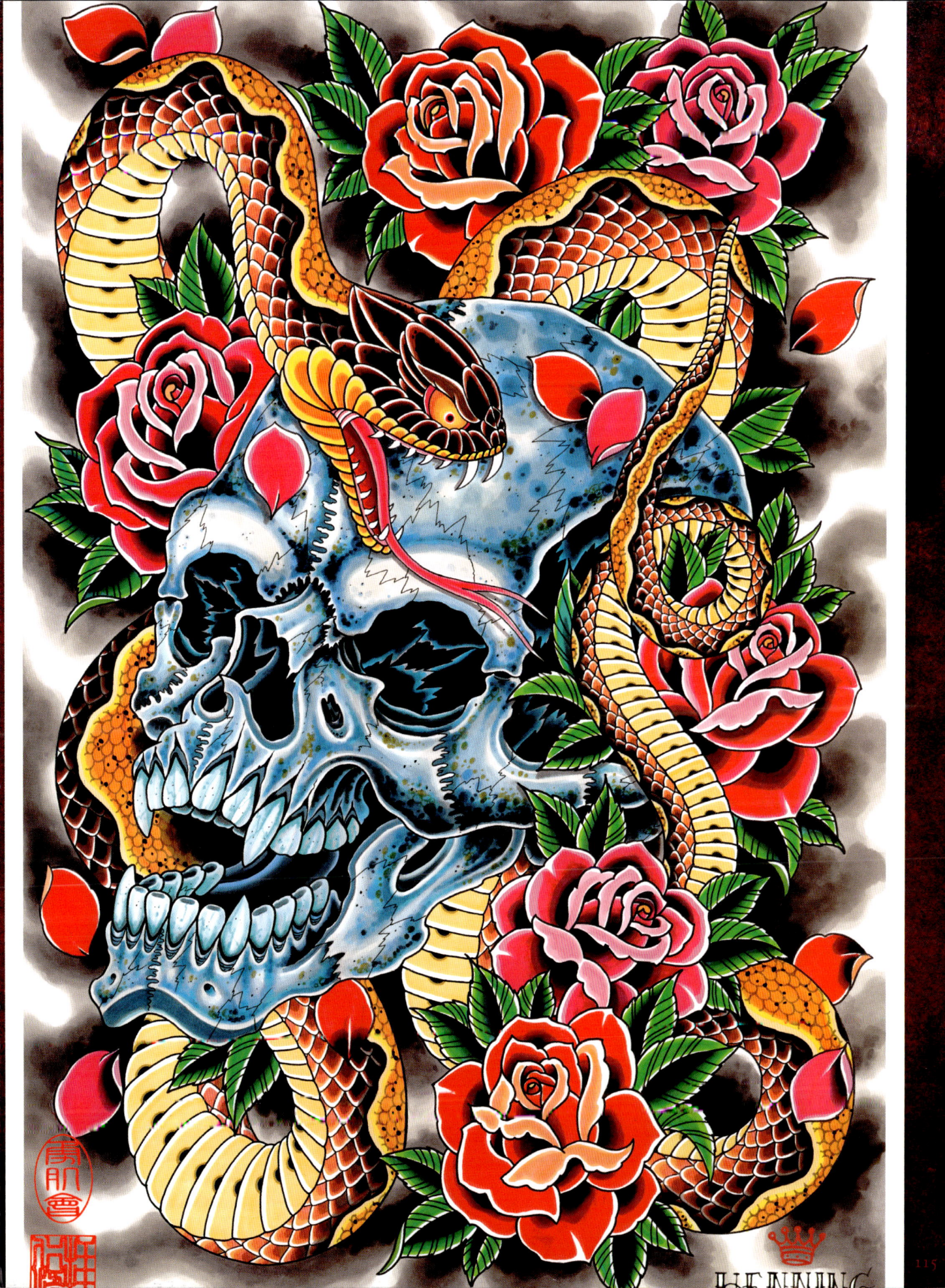

KEZAM

BARCELONA, SPAIN.

"From an early age I loved Japanese engravings, comics, stamps, animation...but it was the Japanese stuff that I tended to draw again and again", says Barcelona-based Kezam. Entirely self-taught he began to do graffiti from the age of 14 or so: "It was a way of escaping the less creative aspects of my neighbourhood." He first came into contact with the world of tattoo during his military service and with three friends he established a tattoo studio in the small town in southern Spain where they were posted. "That experience taught me all the clichés in tattoo and allowed me to work them out of my system." He apprenticed with a friend's brother who ran a piercing studio, cleaning tubes and needles, but occasionally he could try his hand at a Kanji design; "then slowly I began to really understand the world of tattoo." He then studied some of the masters hard – Ed Hardy, Horiyoshi III, Eddie Deutsche, Filip Leu, Bernie Luther, Marcus Pacheco (to name a few) – and then joined Augustin Cavalieri's outfit, where he worked with Javi Castaño. In 2007 Kezam made a seminal trip to Japan, where he met with masters such as Gifu Horihide, Shodai Horimasa and Horikoi, and first really began to understand classic Japanese tattoo. As a result of that trip he established a highly individual style. A few years later he was invited to join Javi Castaño at Barcelona Electric; "I jumped at the chance – and every day I learn something new and inspirational, not just for my tattooing, but for my other artworks."

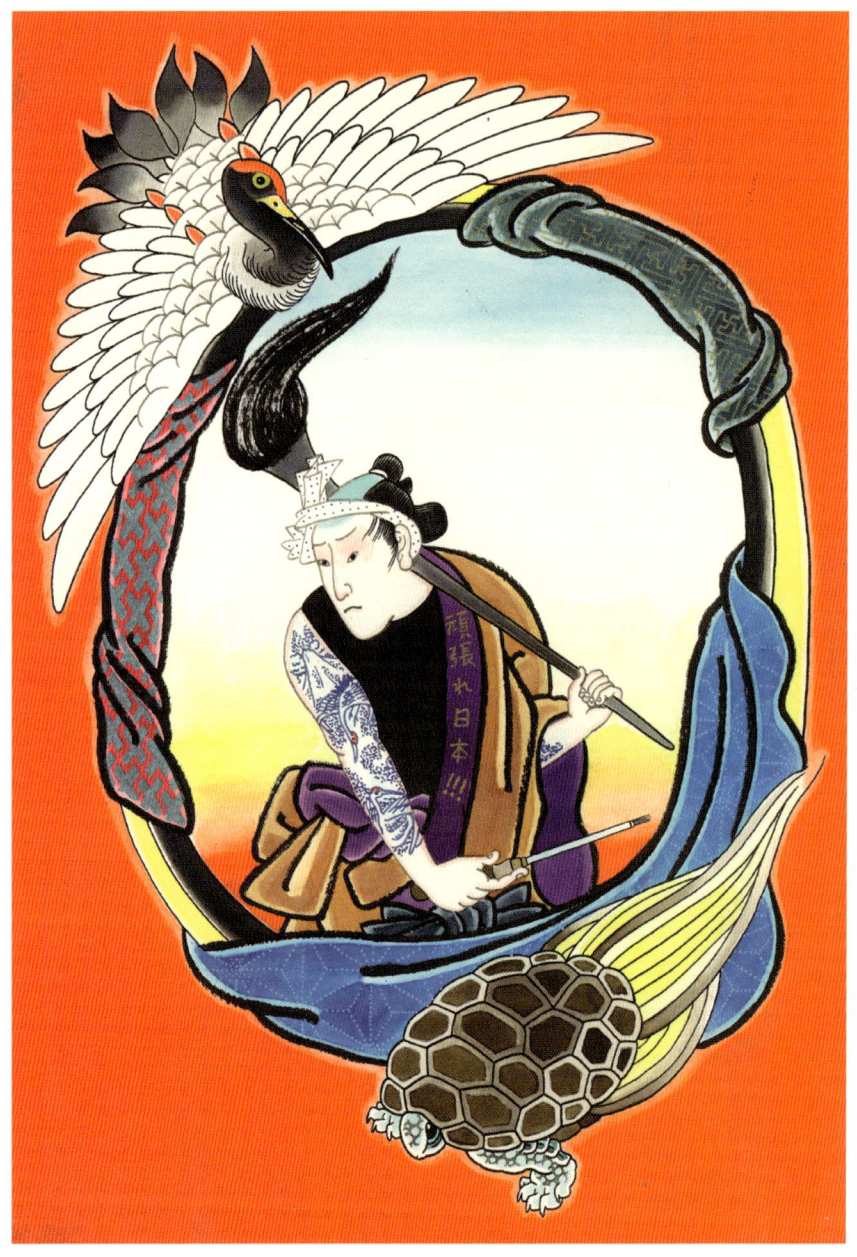

ABOVE: *Gambare Japan*. PEN, ACRYLIC AND WATERCOLOUR.
RIGHT: *Fugen Bosatsu*. PEN, ACRYLIC AND WATERCOLOUR.

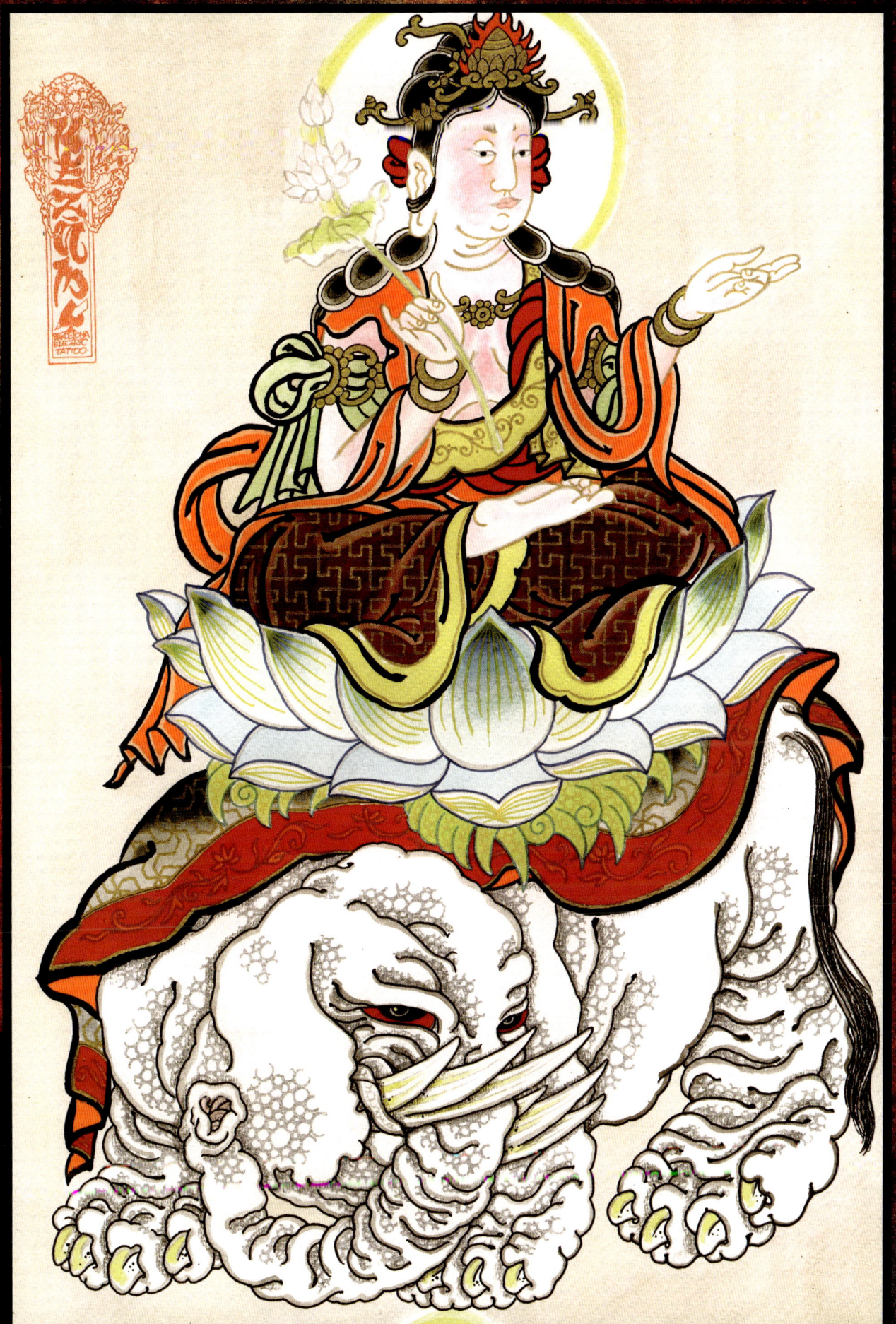

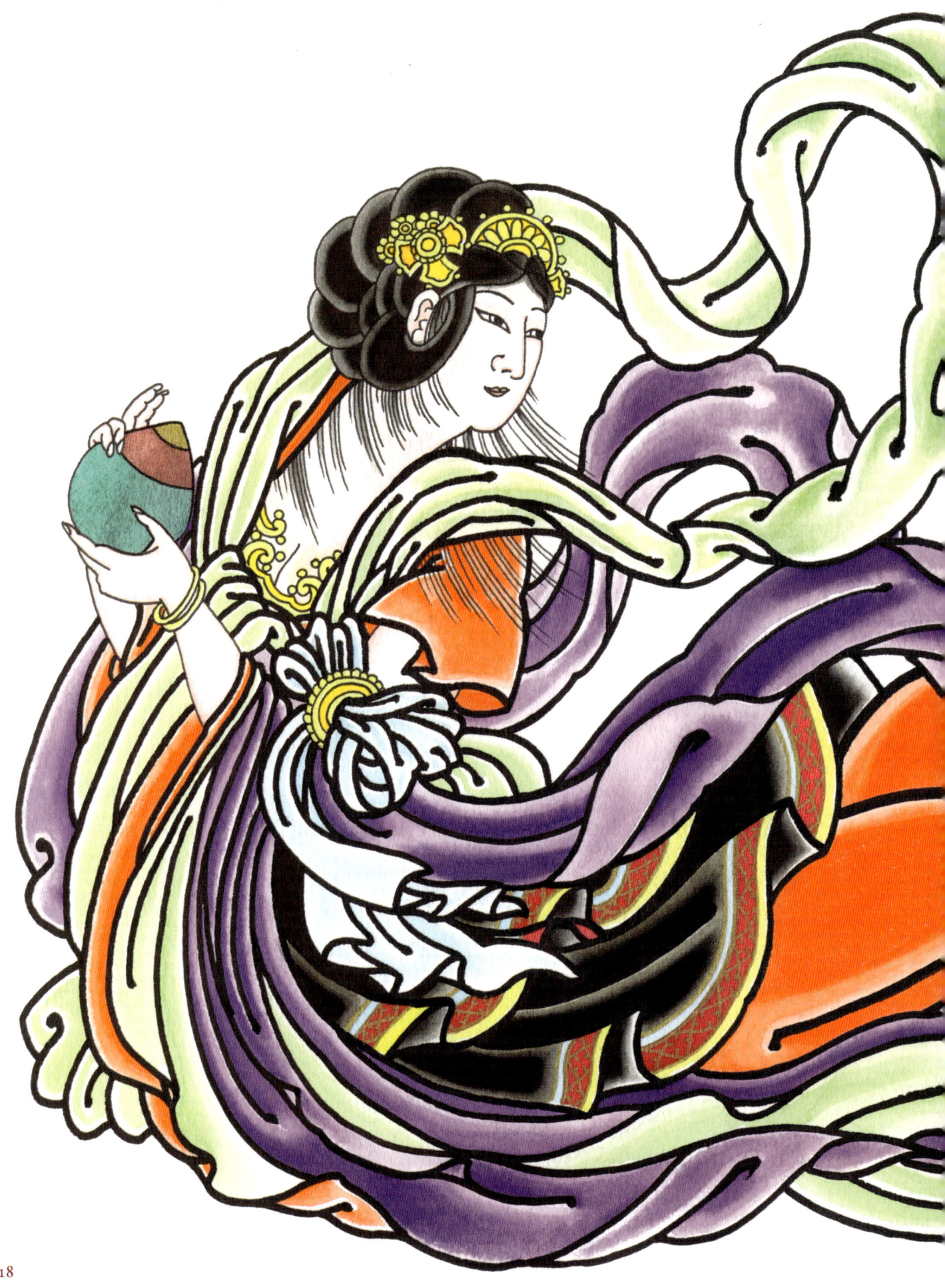

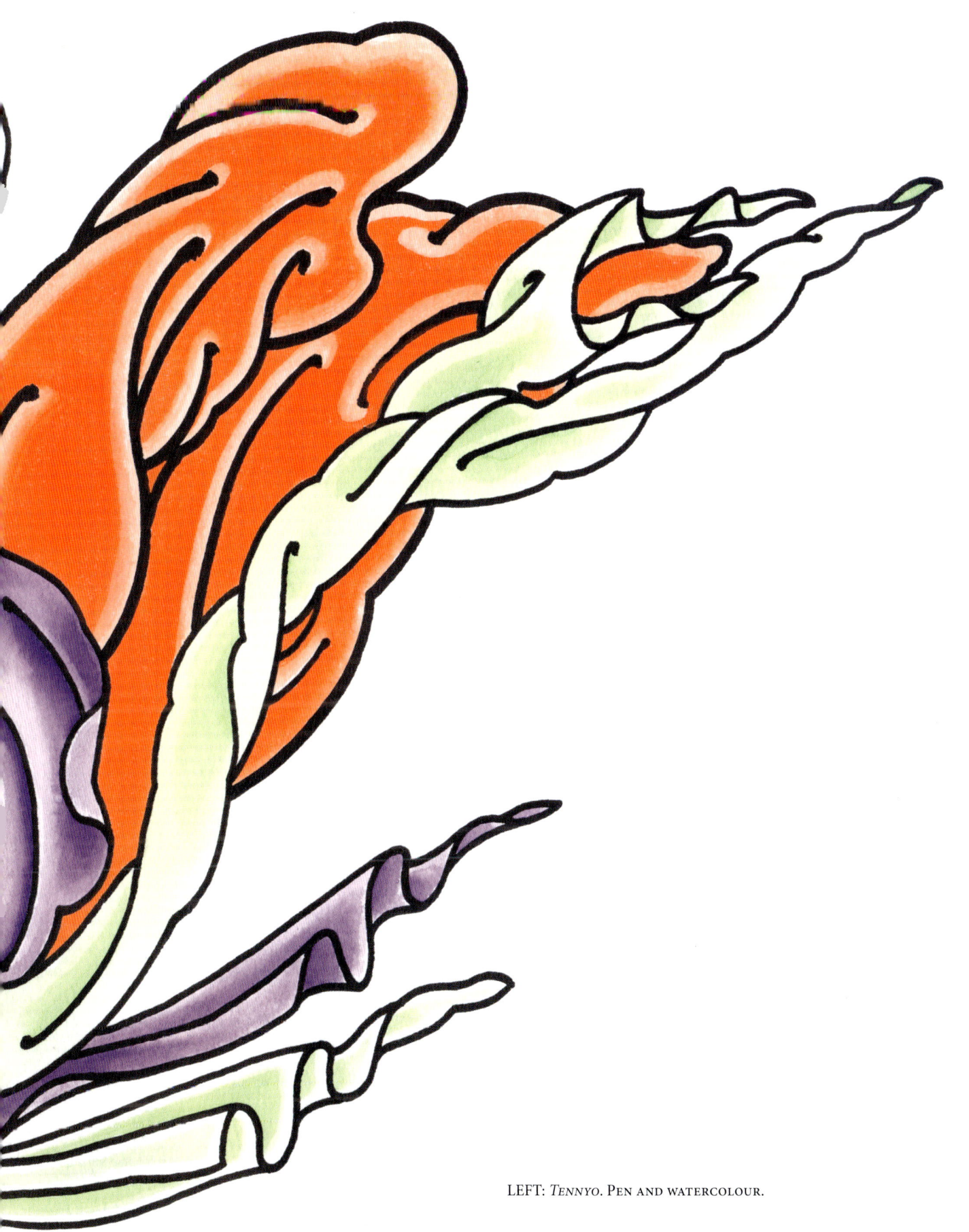

LEFT: *Tennyo*. Pen and watercolour.

KYLE

USA / BRIGHTON, UK.

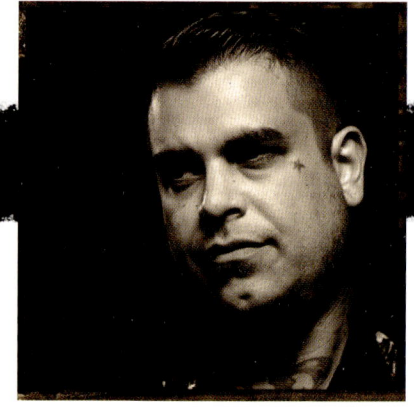

The dye of Phil's future was cast when, aged five and living in the USA, a neighbour arrived from England covered in tattoos. "I knew then that, the moment I could, I would do the same. In the meantime I used to cover myself with 'lick 'n' stick' tattoos sold in bubble gum packs." Holidays spent with two uncles, both architects, in France got Phil into drawing at the age of ten: "They provided supplies and showed me techniques; I would disappear for hours with paper and pencils." Aged 13, Phil discovered punk rock. "Many of the bands, like G.B.H., The Cro Mags and Agnostic Front, were covered in tattoos. At 15 I got my first one. It was the early '80s and there were few regulations. The world was beginning to change. I realised I had to do this full-time." Living in Maryland, just outside Baltimore, Phil spent four years hassling tattoo parlours, before getting his first apprenticeship at Main Street Tattoo. He moved on to Tony Olivas's Sacred Heart Tattoo in Atlanta before two long road trips up and down both East and West Coast US. "Then, after a stint at Permanent Productions in Cincinnati Ohio, I decided it was time to try Europe, and tattooed in France (Nice and Brittany), before alighting on Brighton, on England's south coast. The town just grabbed me, I felt instantly at home – seafront, fantastic light and buzzing with creativity. I said to myself 'One day I will open a shop here.' " In 2007 he did, and also got involved with tv show London Ink for the Discovery Channel. The shop, Magnum Opus, also includes a gallery space, where Phil puts on many art shows and gigs. Of his own art he says "With both the paintings and the tattoos I try and reflect the old school traditions of tattoo. It's a way of giving back to tattooing what it has given to me."

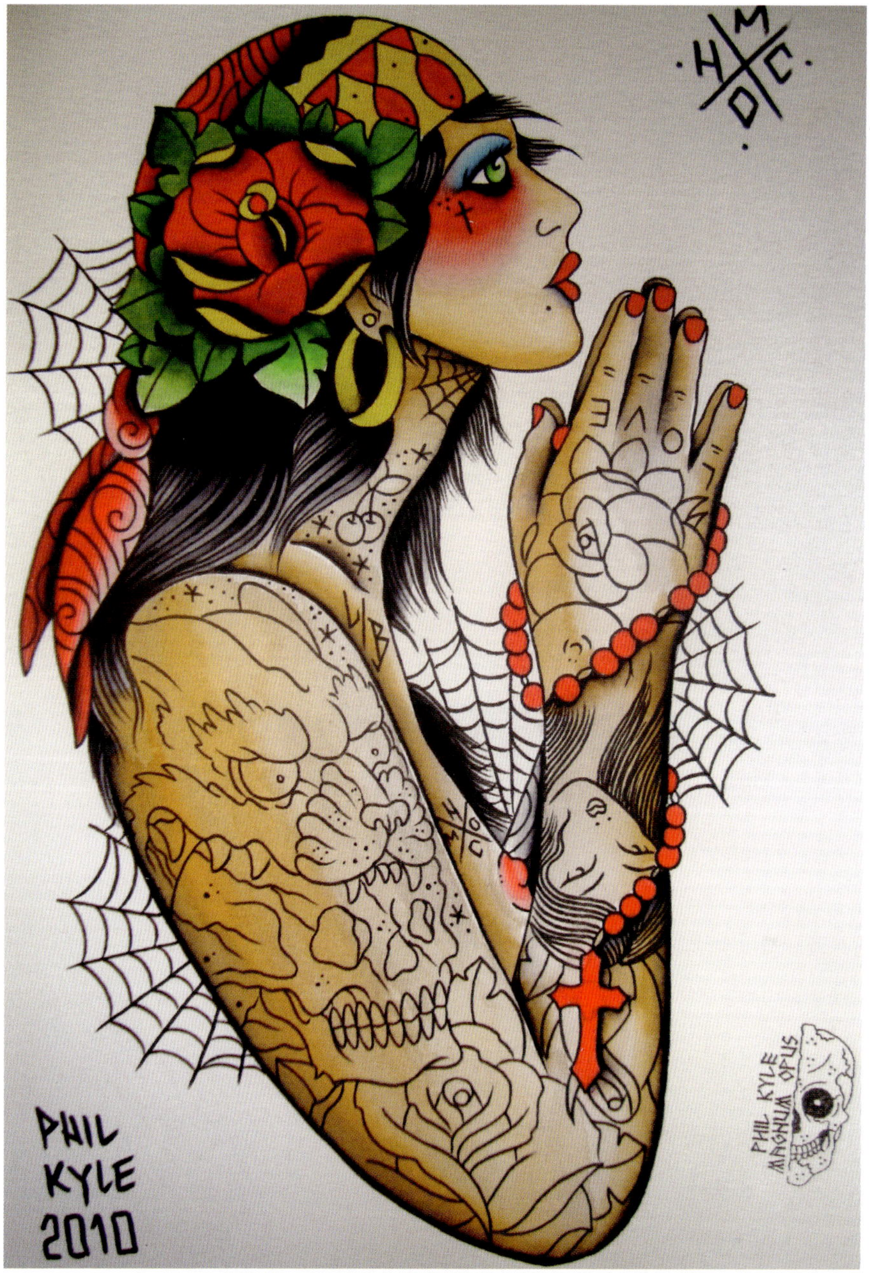

ABOVE: *Gypsy Prayer*. Pen, ink and watercolour.
RIGHT: *Wedding*. Pen, ink and watercolour.

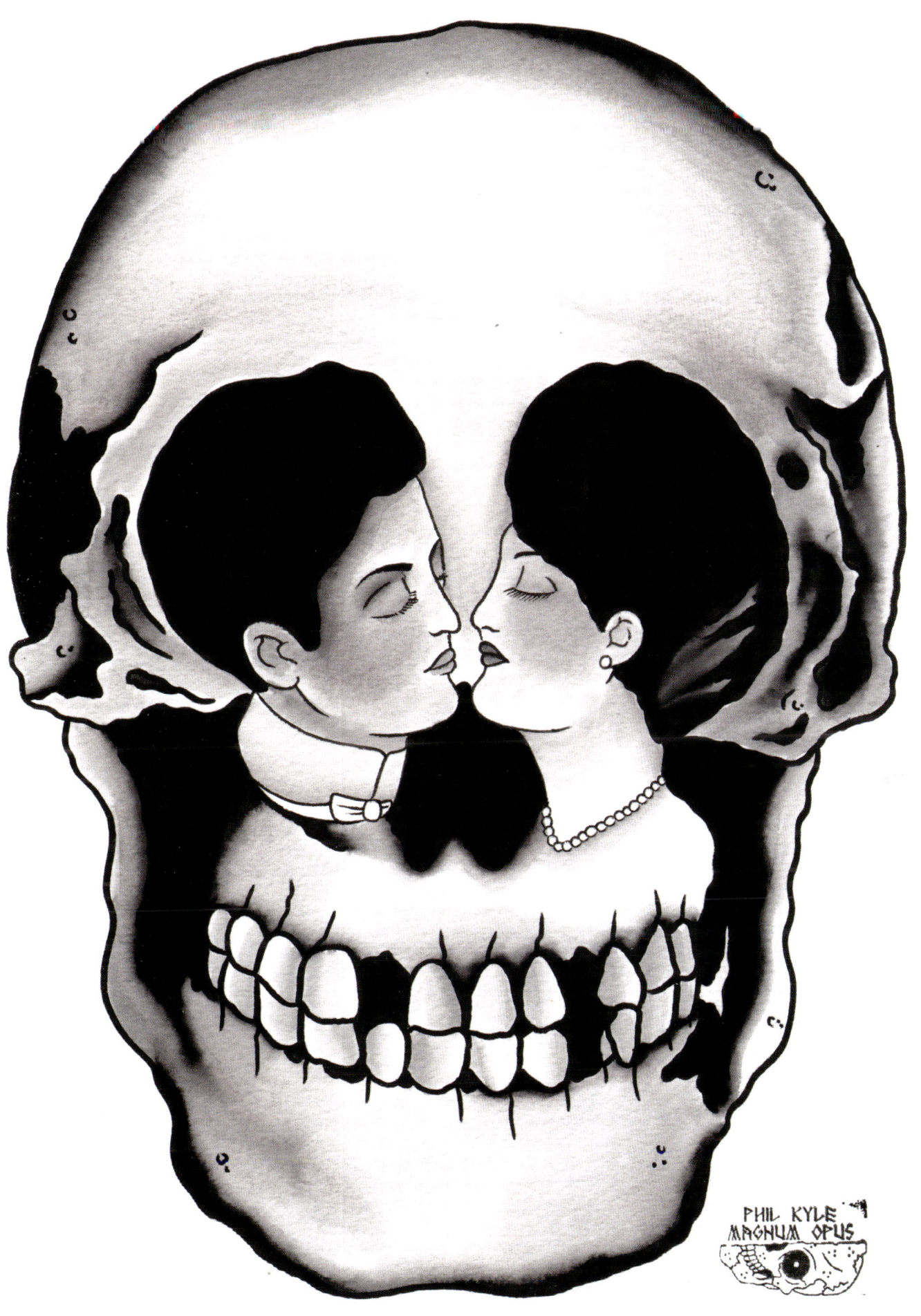

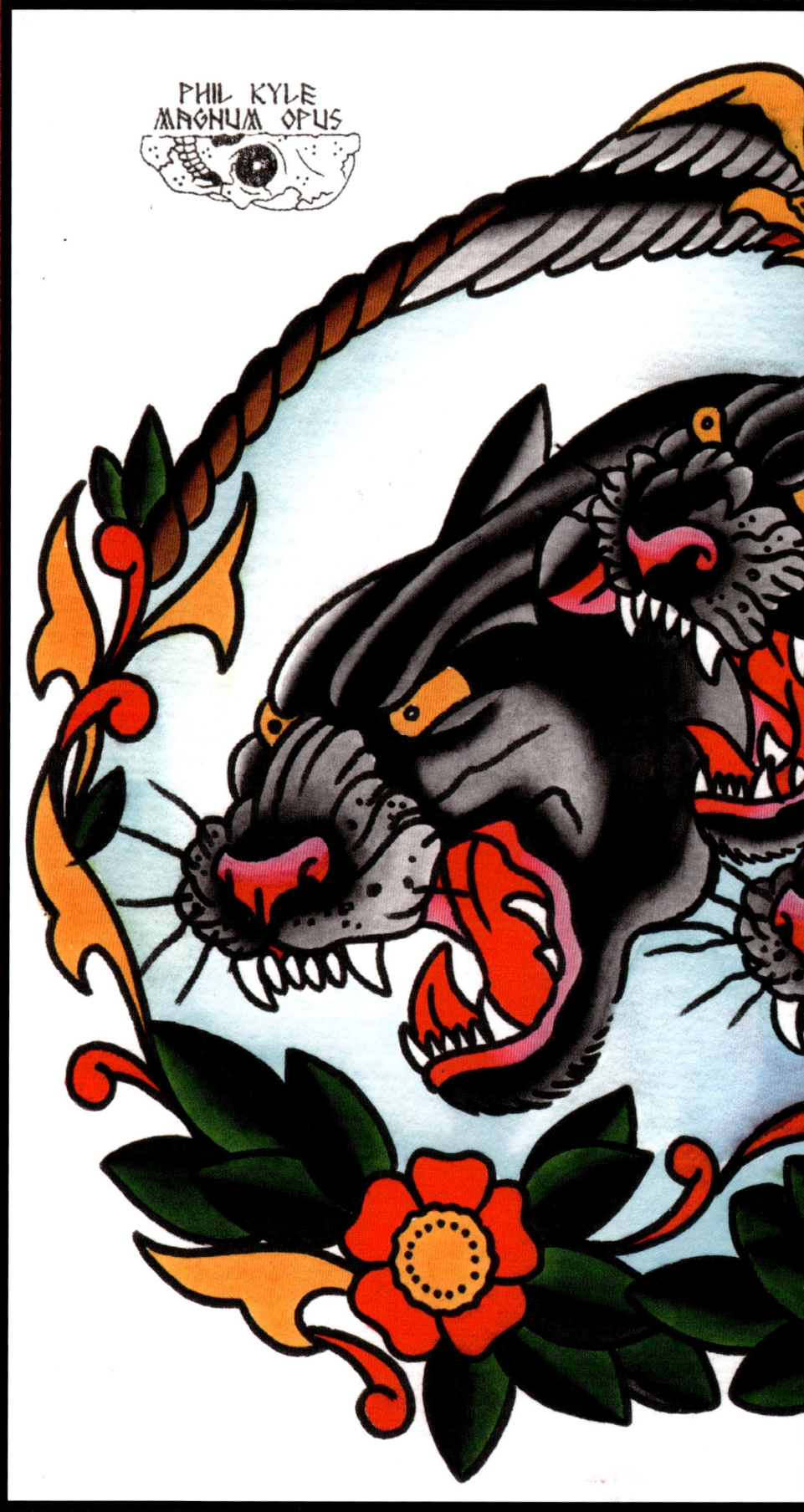

RIGHT: *Panthers*. Pen, ink and marker pens.

OVERLEAF:
LEFT: *Elephant Man*. Pen and ink.
RIGHT: *Eastern Sun*. Pen and ink.

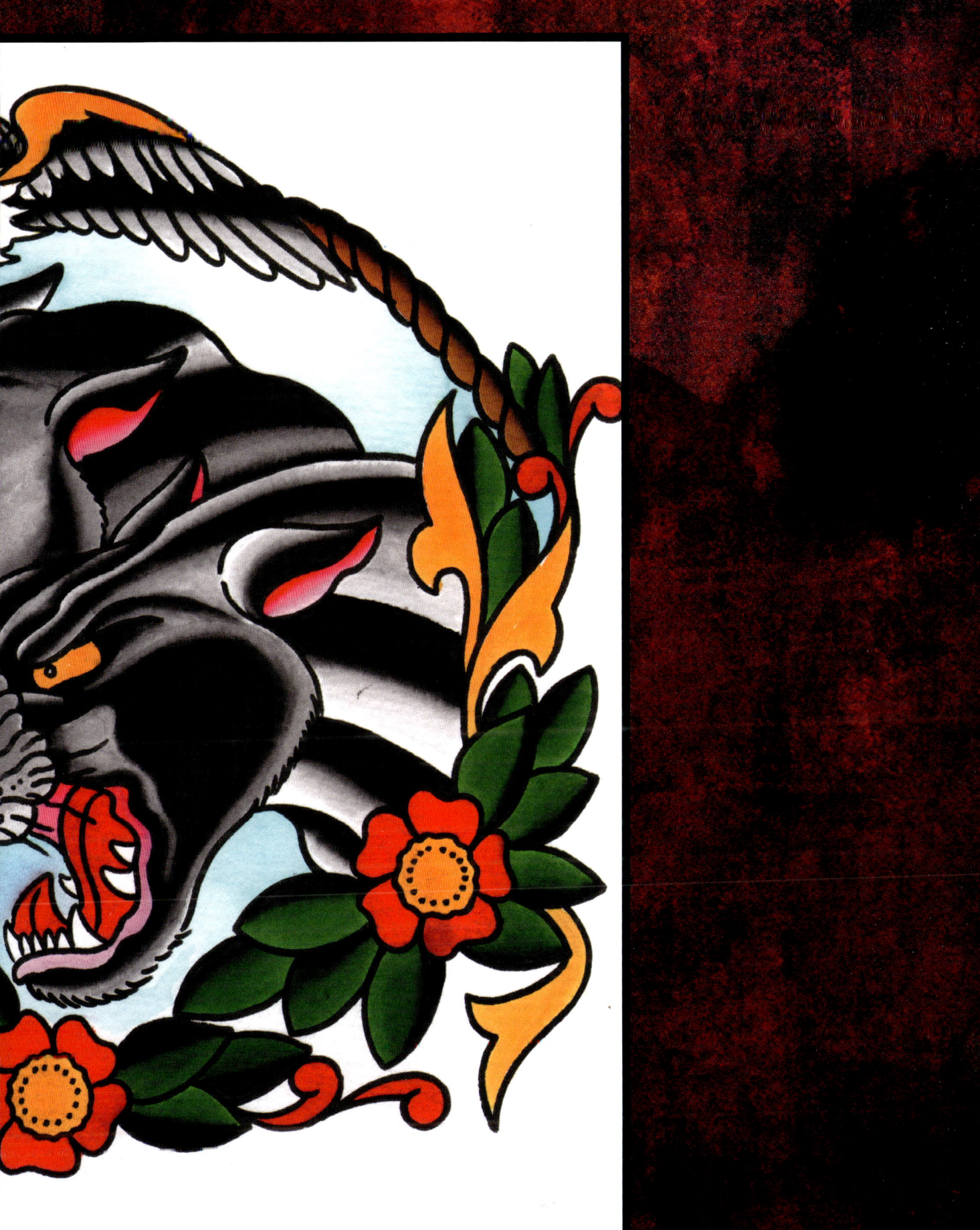

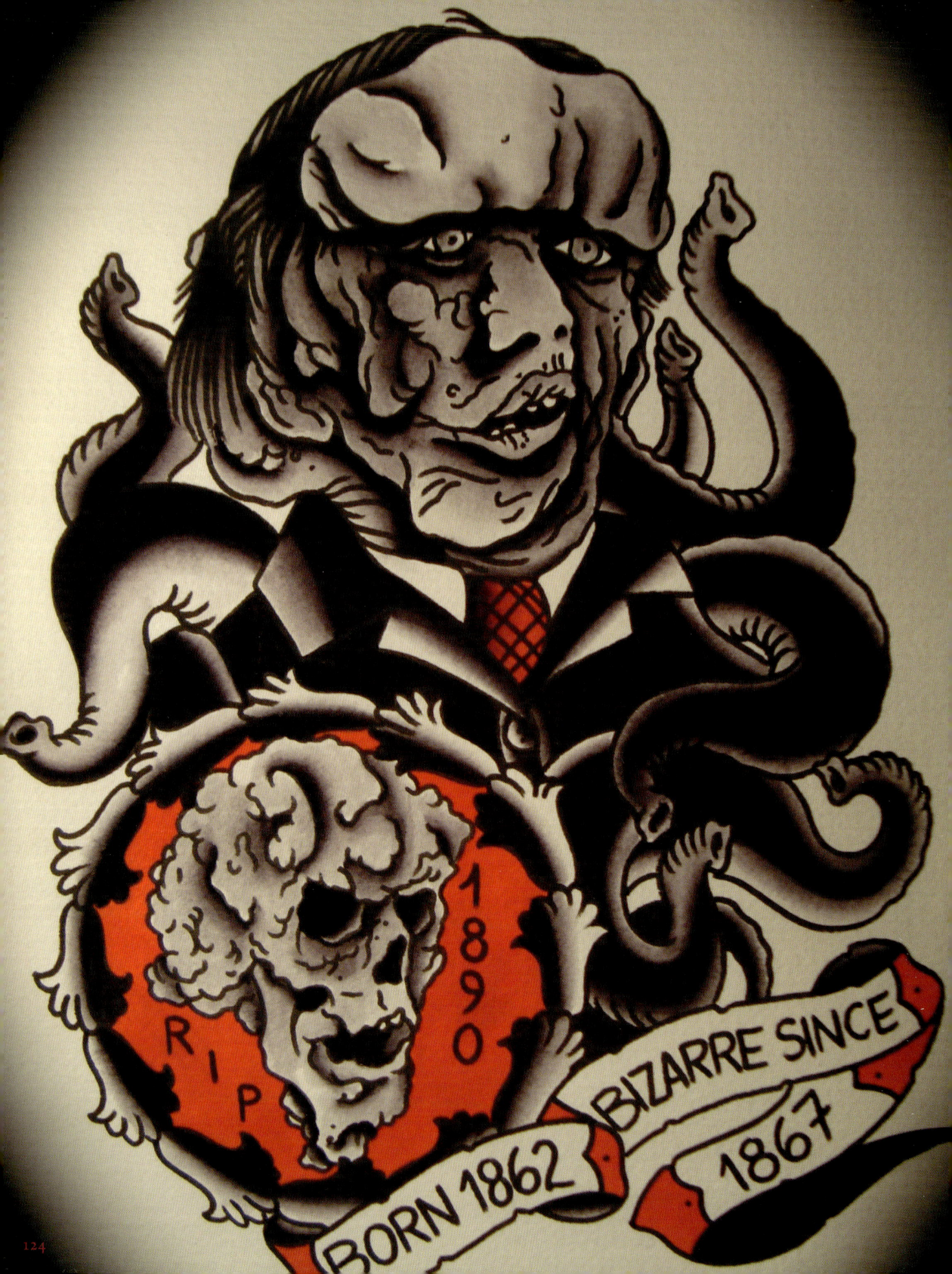

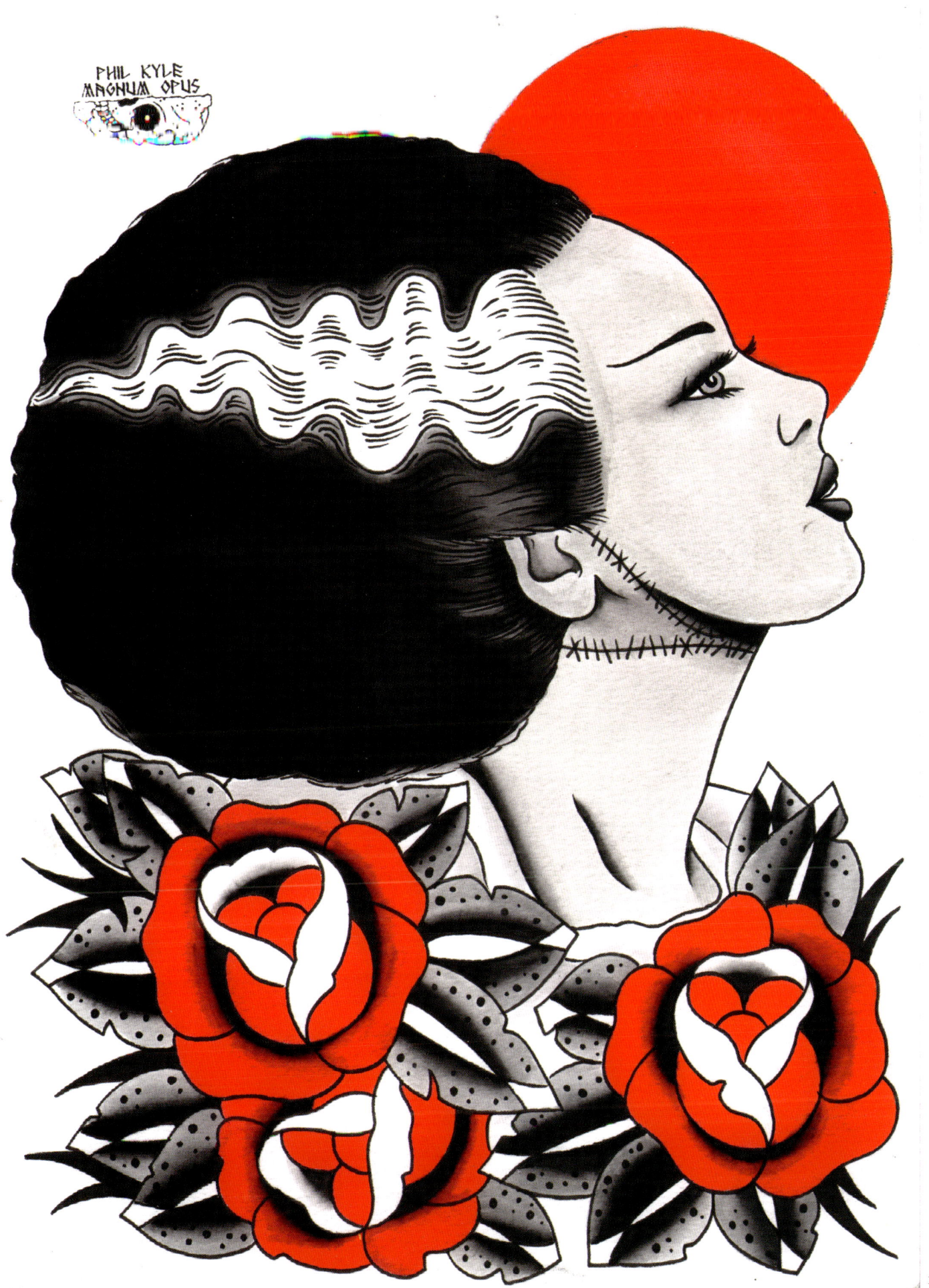

MONGA

BARCELONA, SPAIN.

"When I was young it was the smoking guitar of Ace Freshley (from Kiss) that suddenly lit up my path in life....and even now it's that same spark that keeps me smouldering along empty roads," says Monga rather mysteriously. "Getting going was really tough...times that seemed never ending......like being stuck in a cave without an exit. But then on the verge of loosing hope, the monsters in my cave showed me the way to the promised land."

Monga may sometimes talk in riddles, but at other times he is amazingly focused. "I have never worked in the sense of working to live. From a very young age I decided to devote myself to tattoo so as to be beholden to no one except my personal demons." Monga learnt to draw by tattooing, not the other way round. His art is still directly connected to tattoo, although he also experimented with the collages and photomontages of Punk. His daily influences are his fellow tattooists at Aloha Tattoos, which Monga set up, together with the Cobra Negra Tattoo Gallery, in 1992. More broadly his father and brother have been hugely significant. "I owe them both enormously...my brother has more artistic talent than me, so it's lucky he decided to become a writer!" The list of inspirations is too long, "but includes Hermann Hesse, Charles Bukowski, Martin Scorsese, Robert Crumb, Milo Aukerman, Keo Buenavista, Ed Hardy and Erik Von Bartholomaus." Monga regrets not having more time for art, "I love just to paint, but only seem to find time when I'm asked for an exhibition, so my paintings get sold and are dispersed all over the world. I've only got the few I gave my wife and the really bad ones." Extensively published, Monga has also exhibited across Europe and the US. Of the scene today he says "there are quite a lot of donkeys masquerading as zebras....I'm not sure where things are going...I'm just holding onto Ace Freshley's spark."

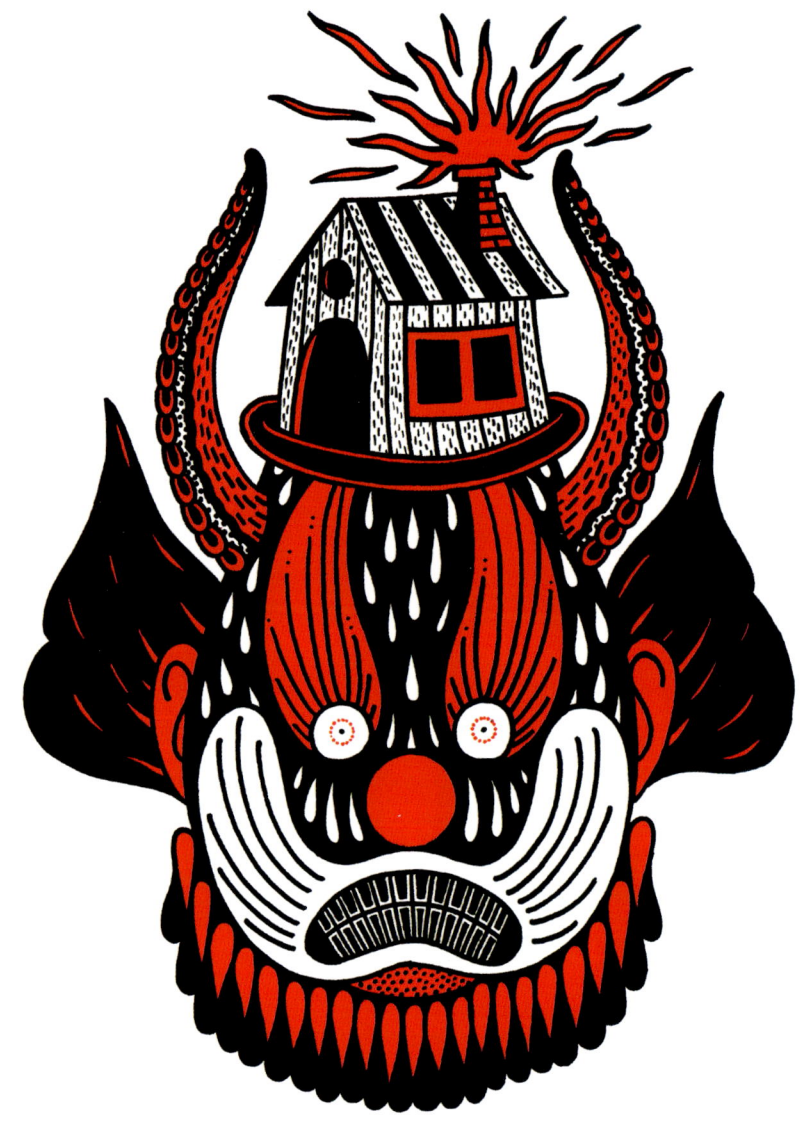

ABOVE: *Four Faces (Face 2)*. Silkscreen on Somerset Velvet White.
RIGHT: *Four Faces (Face 3)*. Silkscreen on Somerset Velvet White.

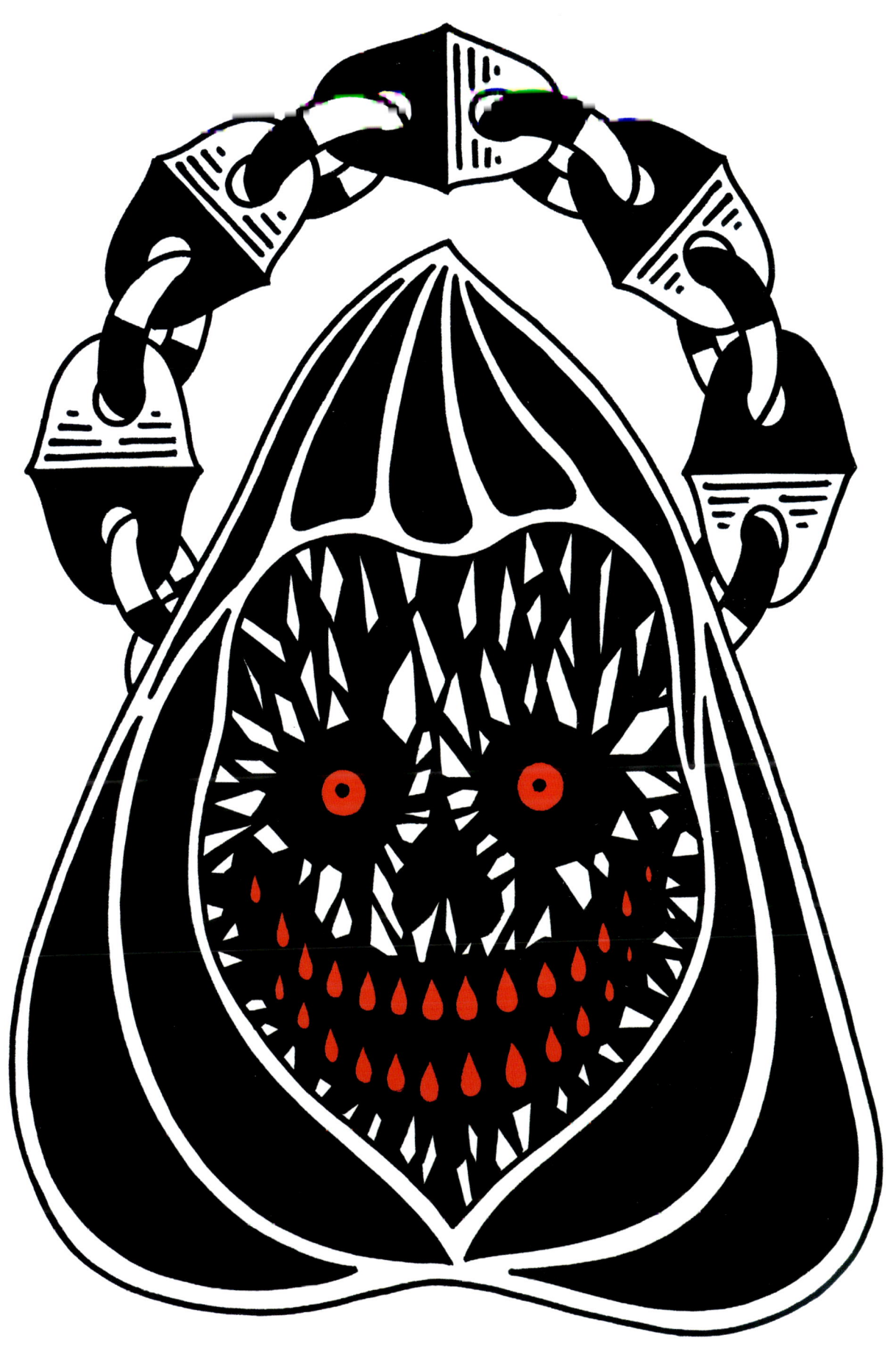

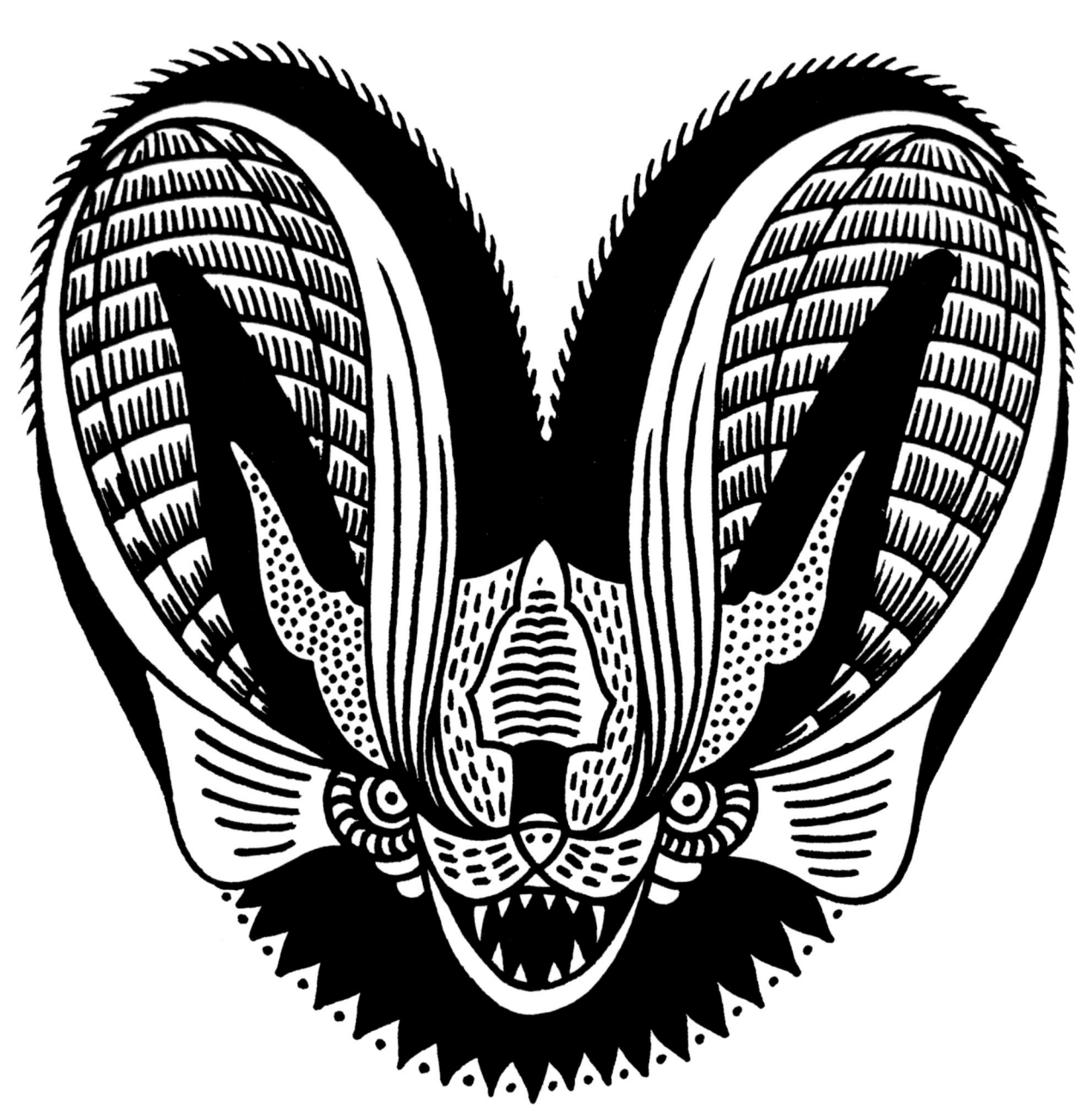

ABOVE: *Bat Head I*. Silkscreen on Somerset Velvet White.
ABOVE RIGHT: *Bat Head II*. Silkscreen on Somerset Velvet White.
BELOW RIGHT: *Bat Head III*. Silkscreen on Somerset Velvet White.

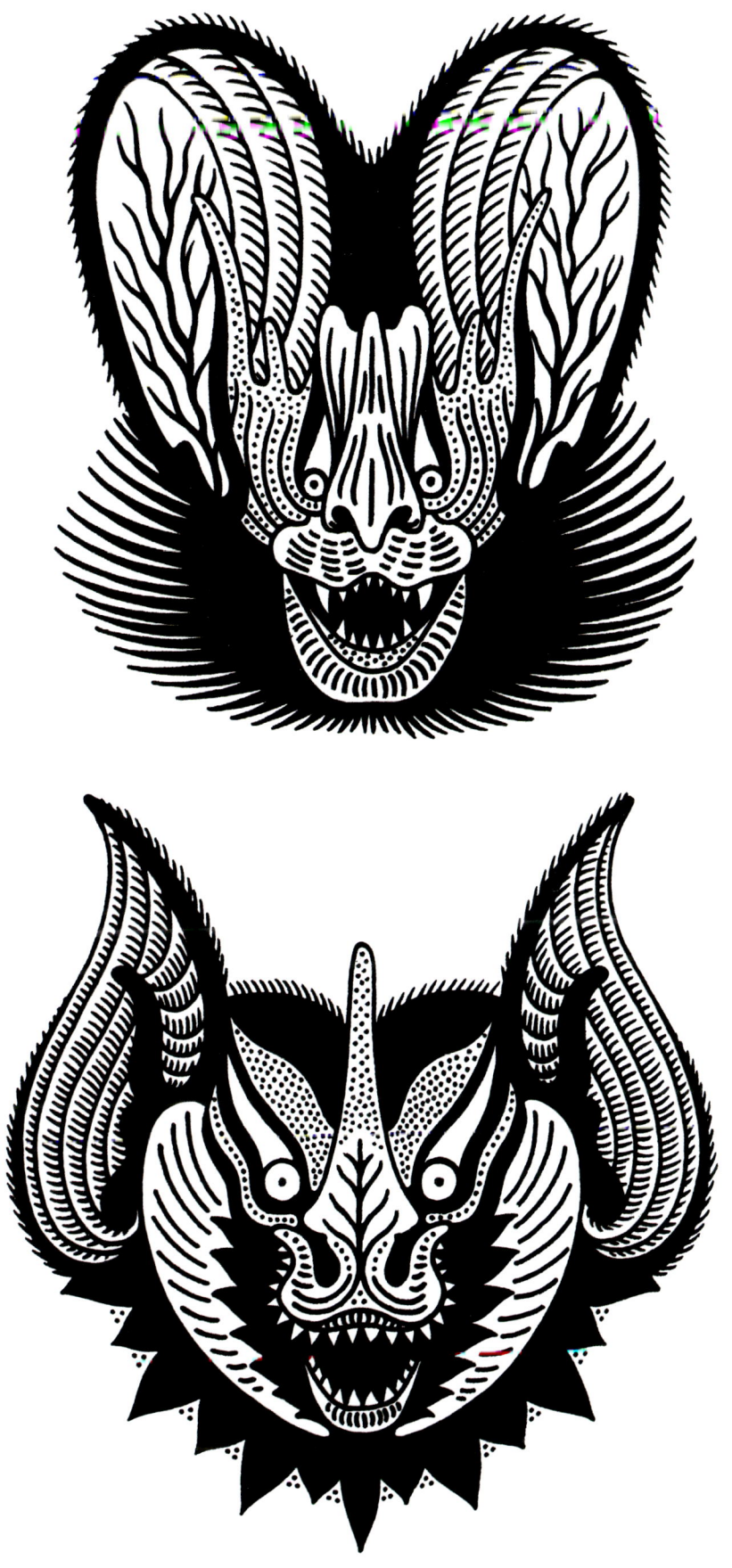

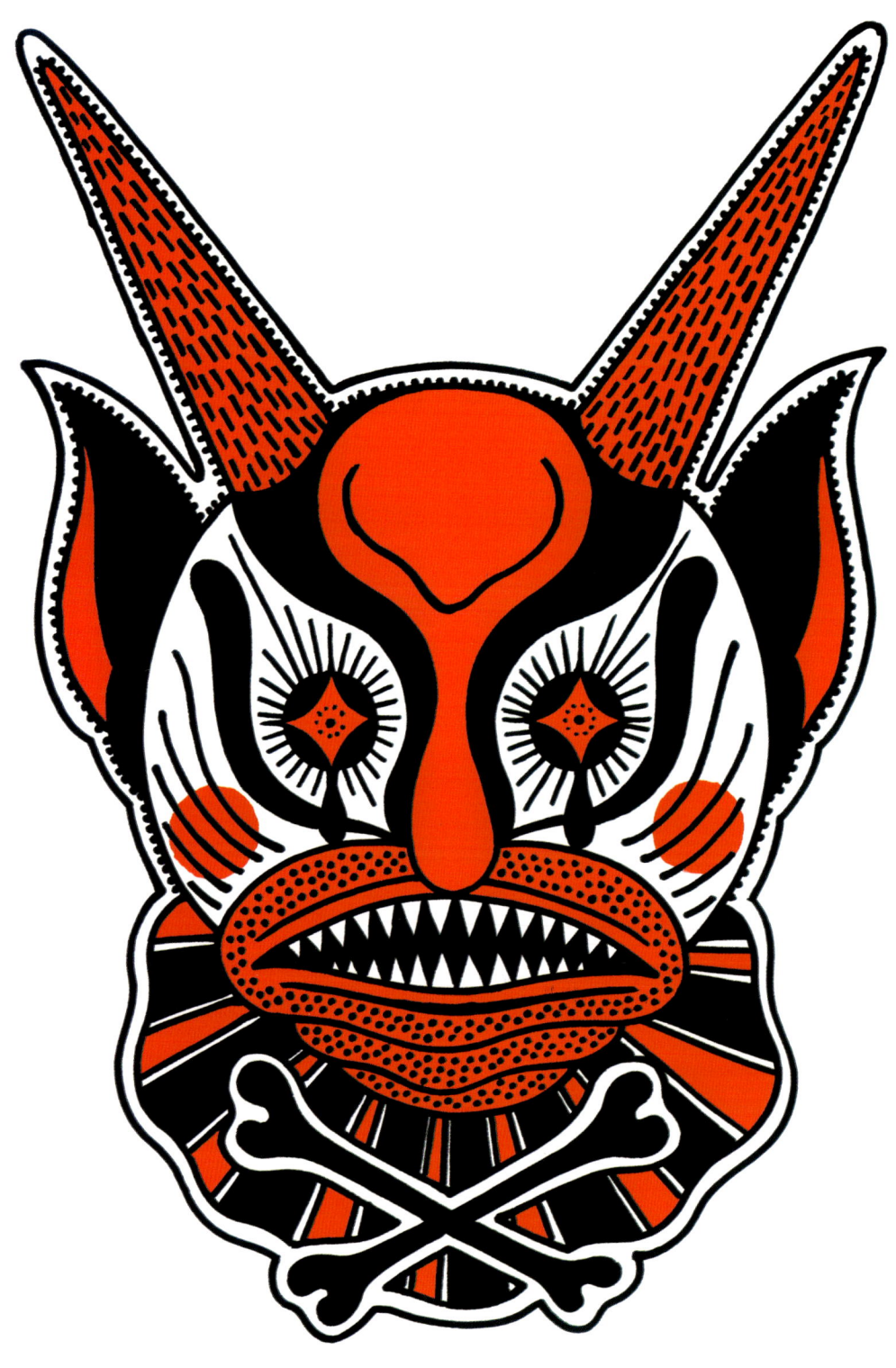

ABOVE: *Running with the Devil*. Silkscreen on Somerset Velvet White.
RIGHT: *Seduction of the Innocent*. Silkscreen on Somerset Velvet White.

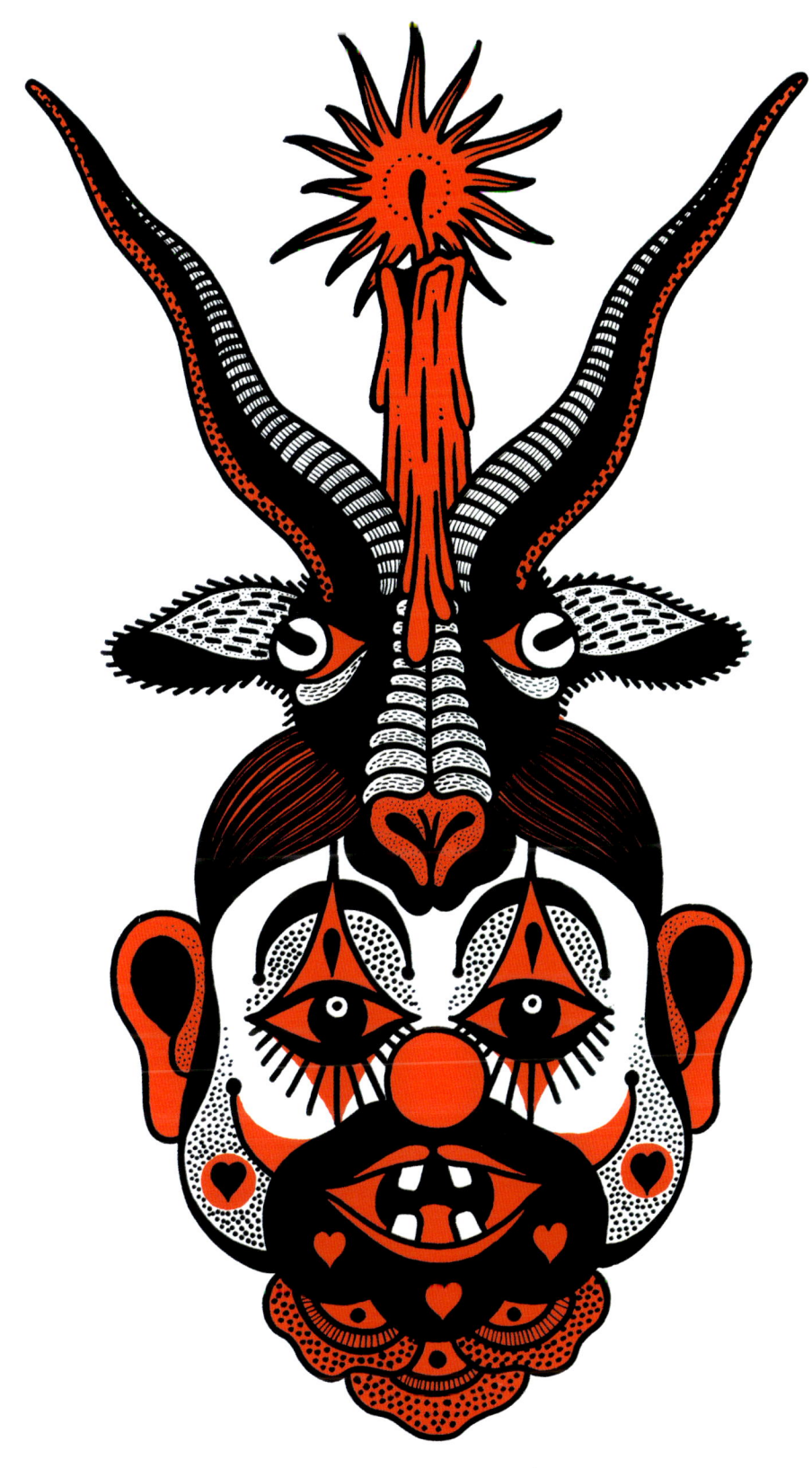

MONTEZ

NM / SAN FRANCISCO, USA.

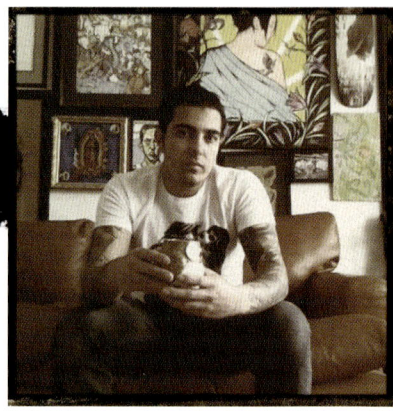

"Being from the US South West and surrounded by Cholo culture, I was always around tattoos growing up. In those days it was cholos, bikers and army vets who had tattoos. I was none of those, so the last thing I expected was that I would end up making tattoos my life; it's almost as though tattoos found me," says Derick of his early years. He tripped into the scene whilst living in Albuquerque, doing medical care work and also painting graffiti; Mike Giant was a friend and Derick got a tattoo by him and then started helping him out around his shop, Stay Gold, before finally becoming apprenticed. "Starting out was all trial and error; no matter if you have someone advising you what lines to pull this or that way, what machines to buy, which ink to use....in the end it's all down to skin time."

Having initially been a graffiti artist, Derick says he found the transition to a smaller medium difficult. The move to San Francisco also forced his art to translate to smaller canvases. "Both my tattoos and paintings have a very illustrated look to them. When you tattoo every day, it's hard not to have programmed into your brain certain elements of shading, layout and design. Tattooing is obviously much more restricted than painting, but I also find it goes the other way: the tattoo influences clearly spill over into my painting work." Derrick cites many artists whose work has inspired, including Mike Giant, Henry Lewis, Juan Puente, Jason Kundell, Patrick Conlon and Robert Ryan. His favourite dead artists include Seurat, John John Jesse and Gustave Dore. Derrick also loves early 1800s architecture and industrial design from the 1920s-1940s: "There is an an attention to detail you just don't see any more." He has shown in galleries all over the world, including in San Francisco, Beijing, Seoul and Istanbul, to name a few.

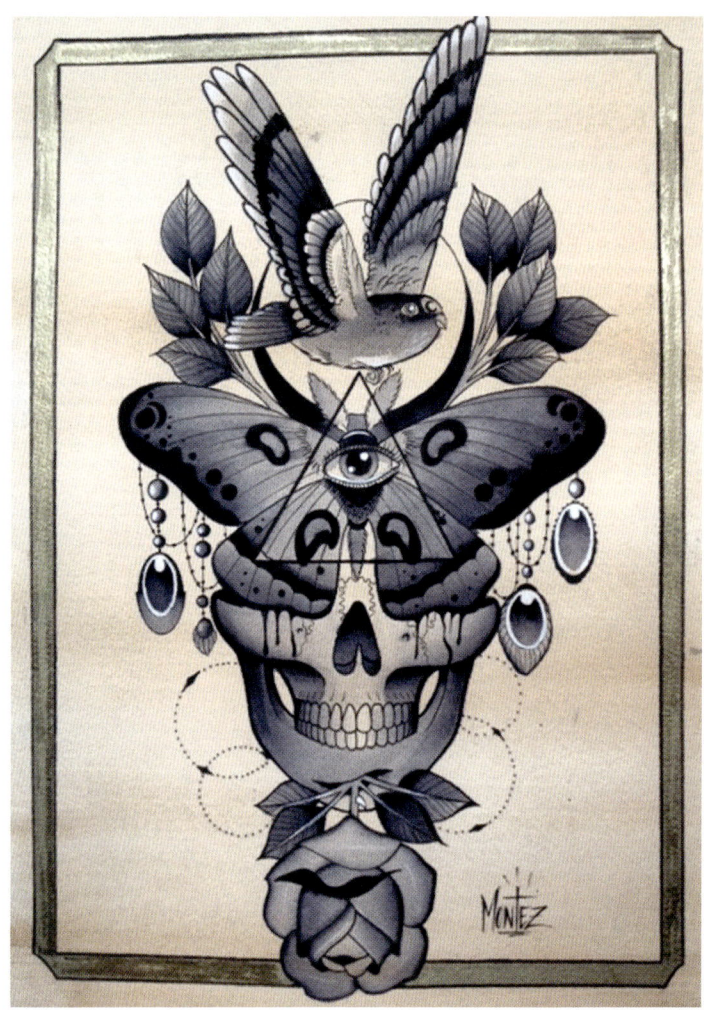

ABOVE: *The All-Seeing Eye*. Pen, ink and watercolour.
RIGHT: *Sioux*. pen, ink and watercolour.

OVERLEAF:
LEFT: *Cockerell, Skull and Anchor*. Pen and ink.
RIGHT: *Dreams*. Pen and ink.

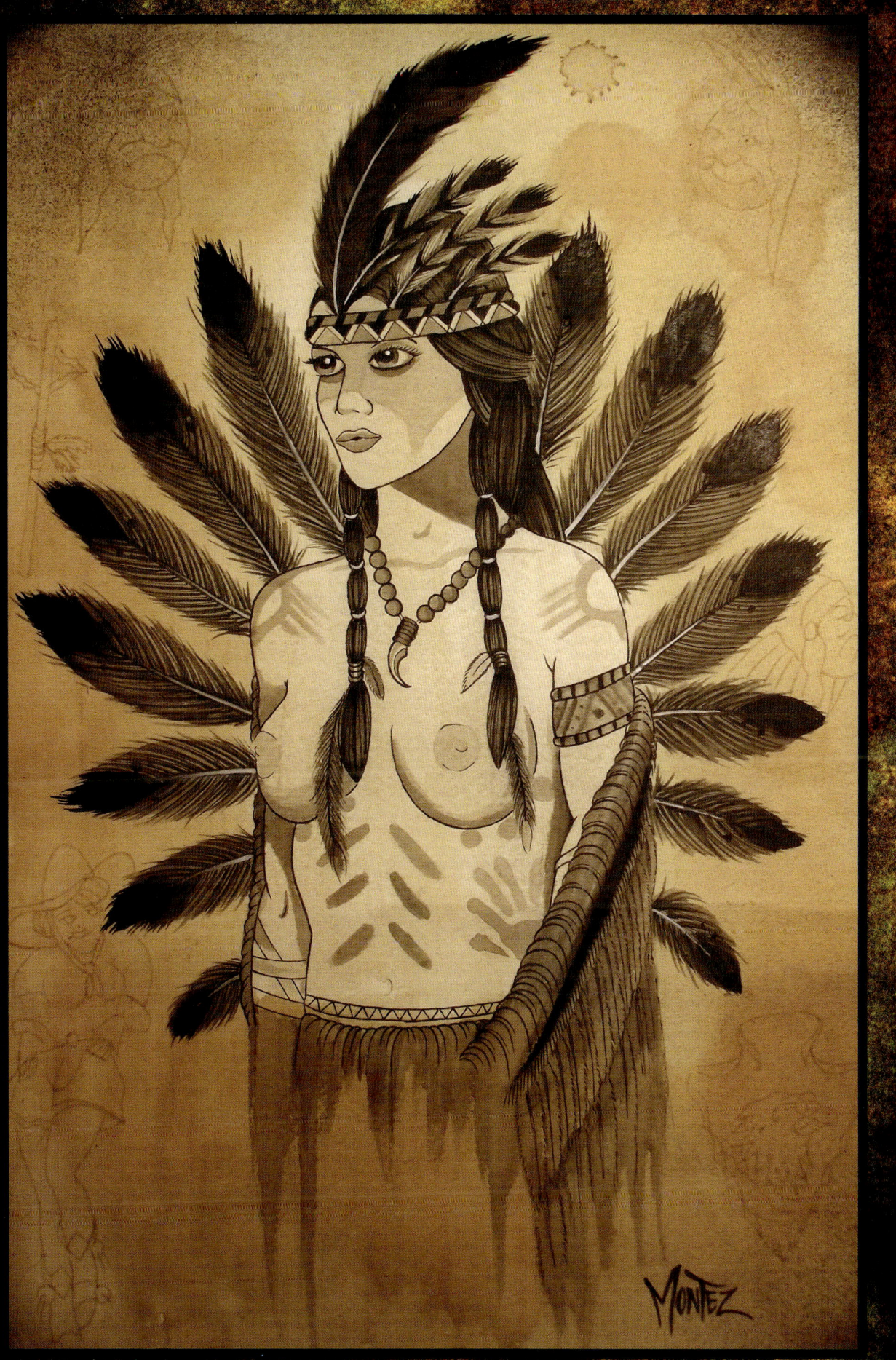

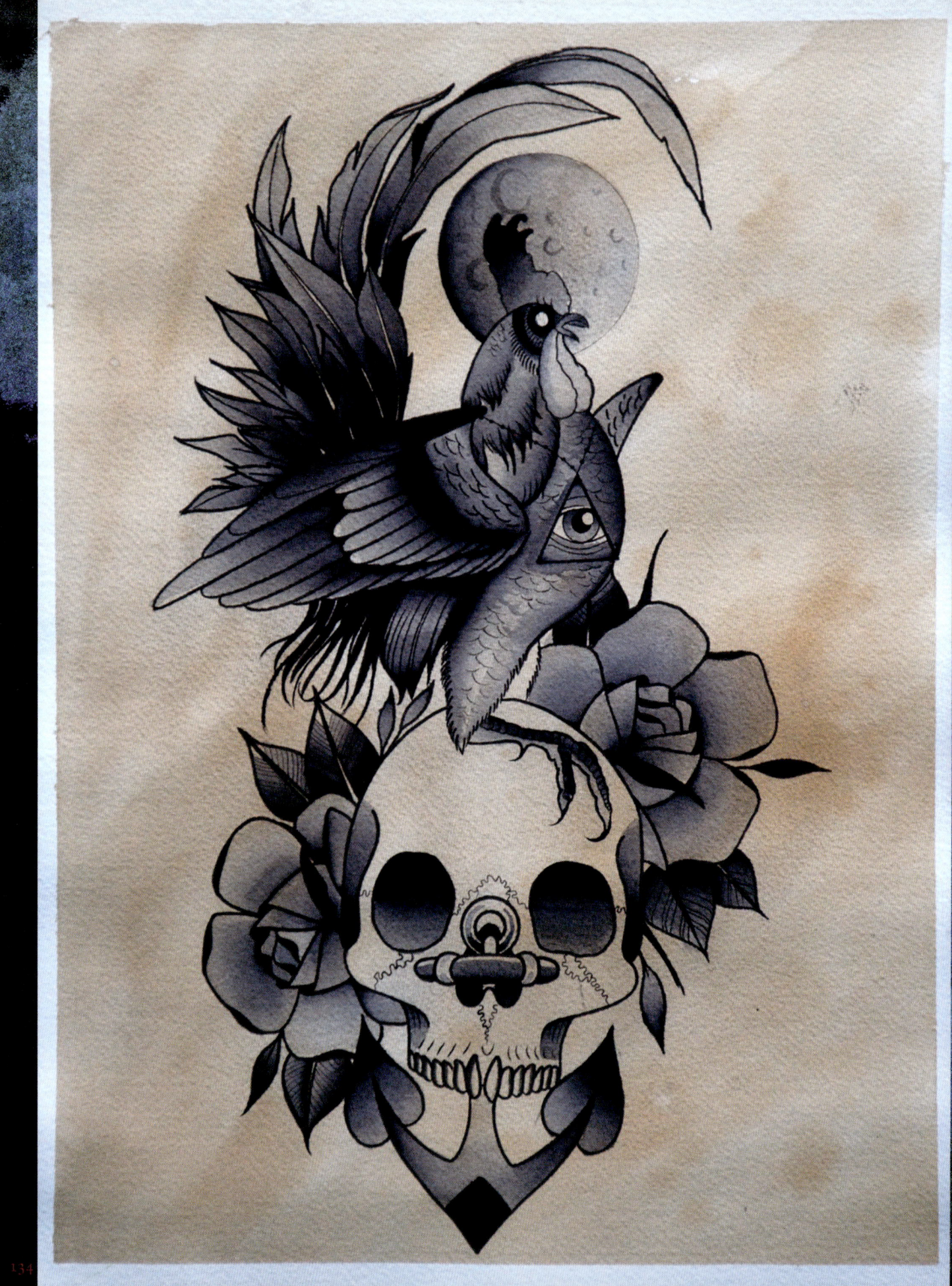

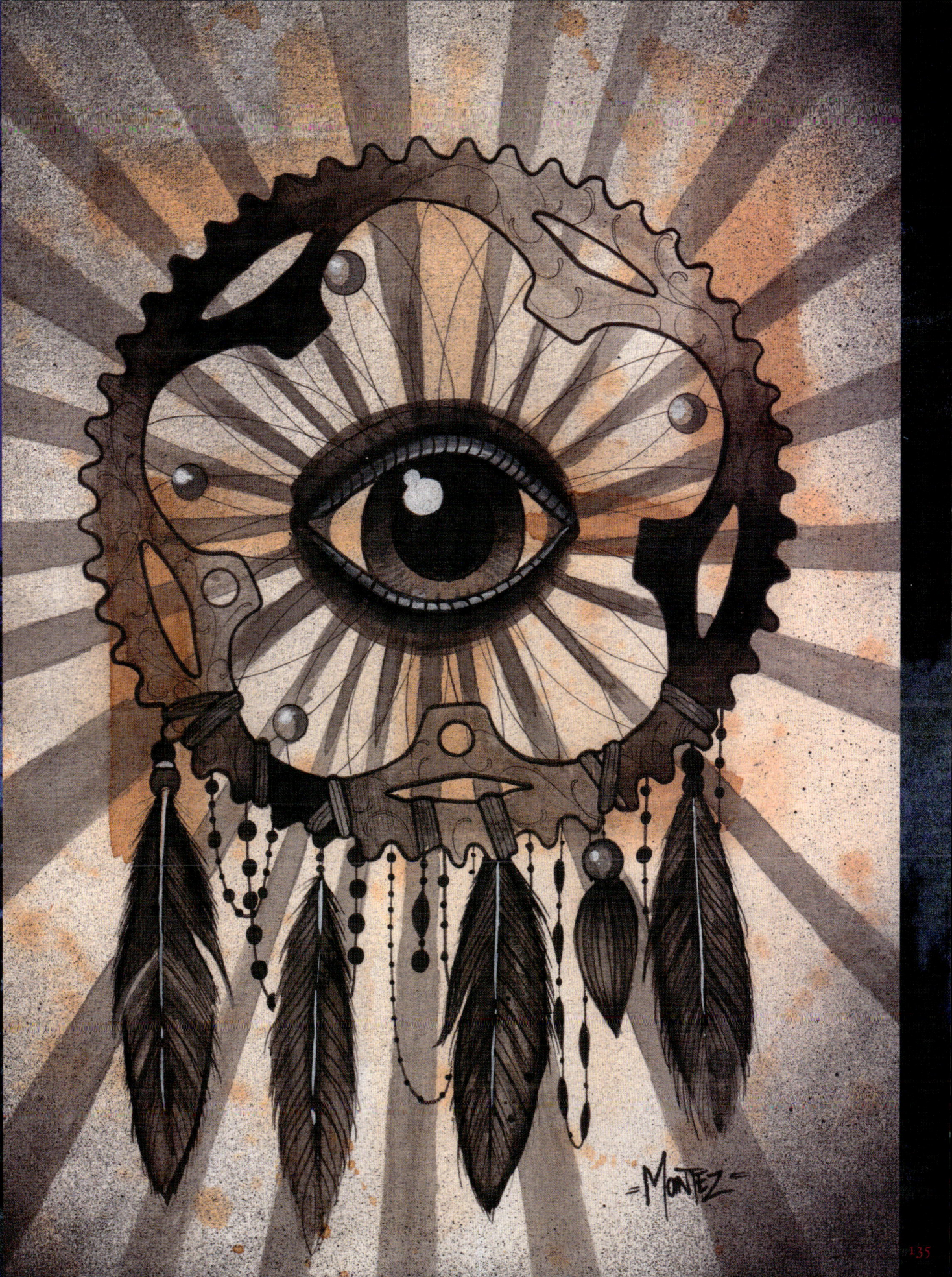

OLIVE

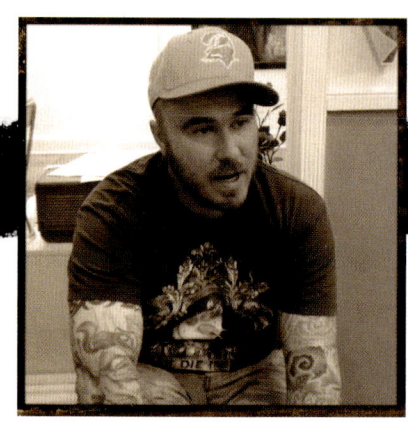

SARASOTA FL, USA.

"There wasn't a spark or moment of truth that got me into creating tattoos; it was just that I was already heavily tattoed and thought I could offer something more than I was able to get at the time – there just wasn't anyone around who was doing what I was after." That was ten years ago and Scott was trying to get a cartoony-graffiti style tattoo: "That's when I realised I had something new to offer. It was a no brainer: tattoos are awesome, why wouldn't I want to be a part of this industry?" The hardest part was finding an apprenticeship: "It was years of 'no', 'no,no', 'no, maybe', 'maybe' and then finally I got my foot in the door. But I was broke and had to make pizza part time; I couldn't wait to get out of that, but it was a waiting game."

Scott apprenticed with Travis Franklin in Sarasota, Florida at Oddity Tattoo and has stayed. Having mastered the art, he now has time to also paint. "With my paintings its oil or acrylics. Tattoo definitely feeds the art, particularly when it comes to contrasts. I also find that it has made my linework a lot cleaner, so the techniques have translated. However I also like to keep a distinction, so my paintings don't immediately look like they've come out of tattoo and my tattoos don't look like paintings!" Scott cites Travis Franklin as his major influence: "I have attended art classes at a few different colleges in Florida, but never for more than a year; the apprenticeship with Travis was the real study." Amongst other tattooists it's Jesse Smith, Scotty Munster, Tanane Whitfield, Kelly Doty, Curtis Burgess, Jason Stephan and Jimmy Lajnen. For his paintings he has been inspired by Scott Musgrove, Joe Sorren, Nathan Ota, Scribe and Daniel Fleres, and then "of course there are those other massive influences: Dr Seuss, Pixar and Dreamworks films, Disney, Ninja Turtles and the cartoons I watch with my son."

Scott says he doesn't think too much about how the scene is evolving: "I just go to work, tattoo, come home, draw, and go back the next day and repeat. I don't travel much, so it's hard to know what's really going on out there." In addition to Oddity Tattoo, Scott is represented by the Glitch Gallery in Richmond, Virginia.

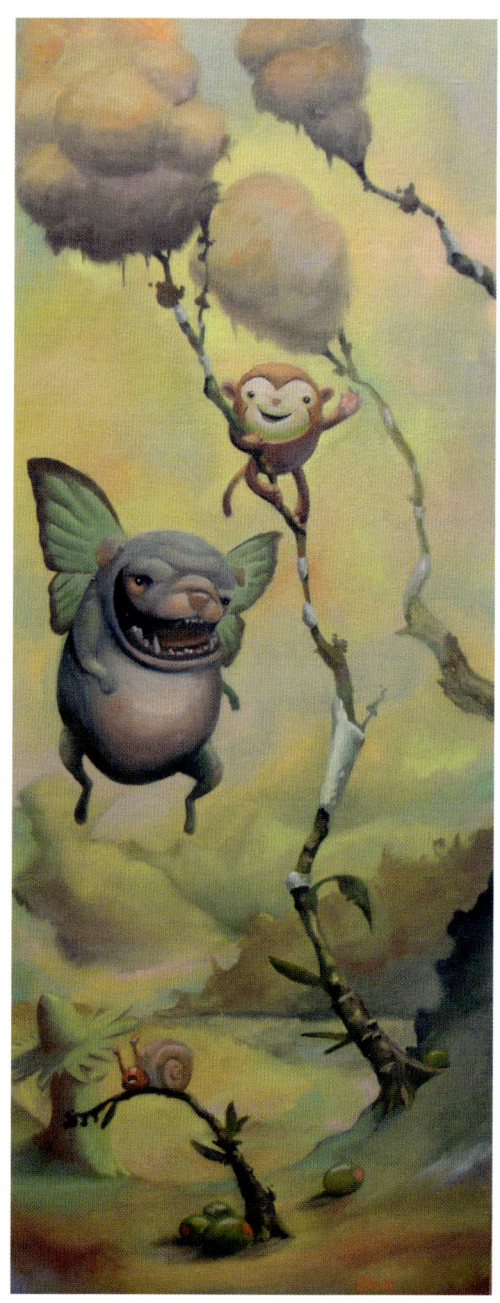

ABOVE: *Olive Island at Sunset*. Acrylic on canva
RIGHT: *Brinks*. Acrylic on canvas.

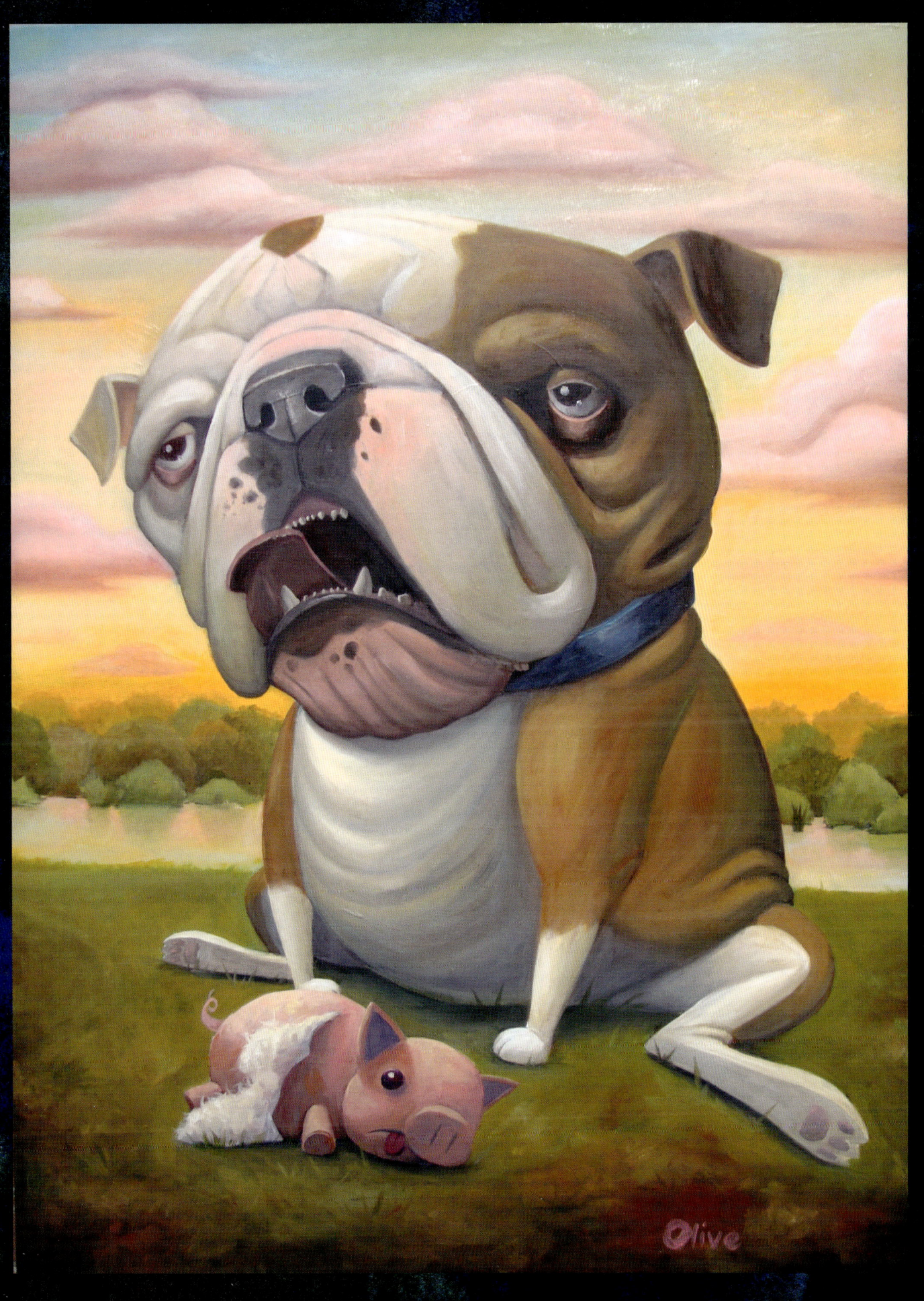

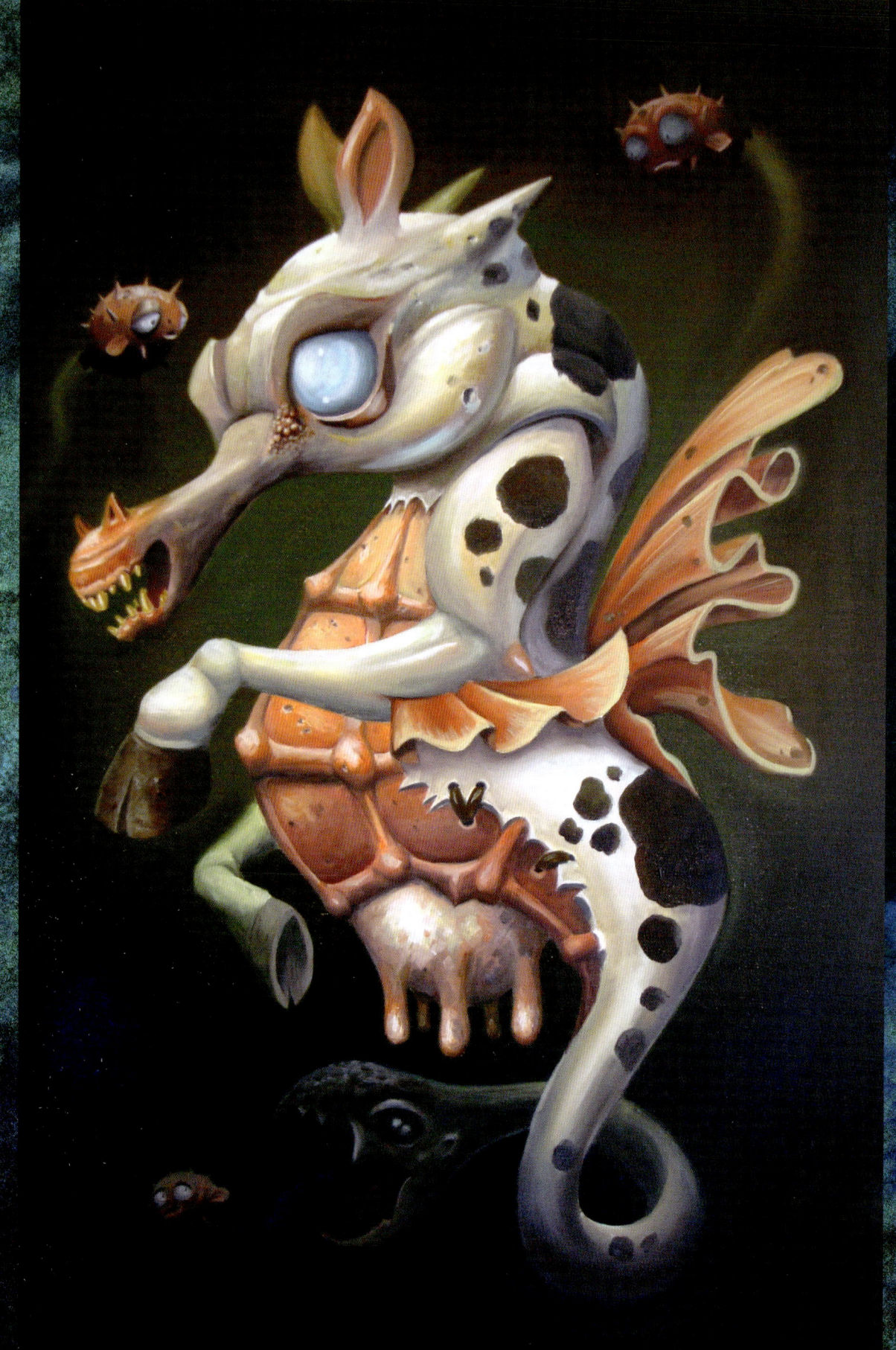

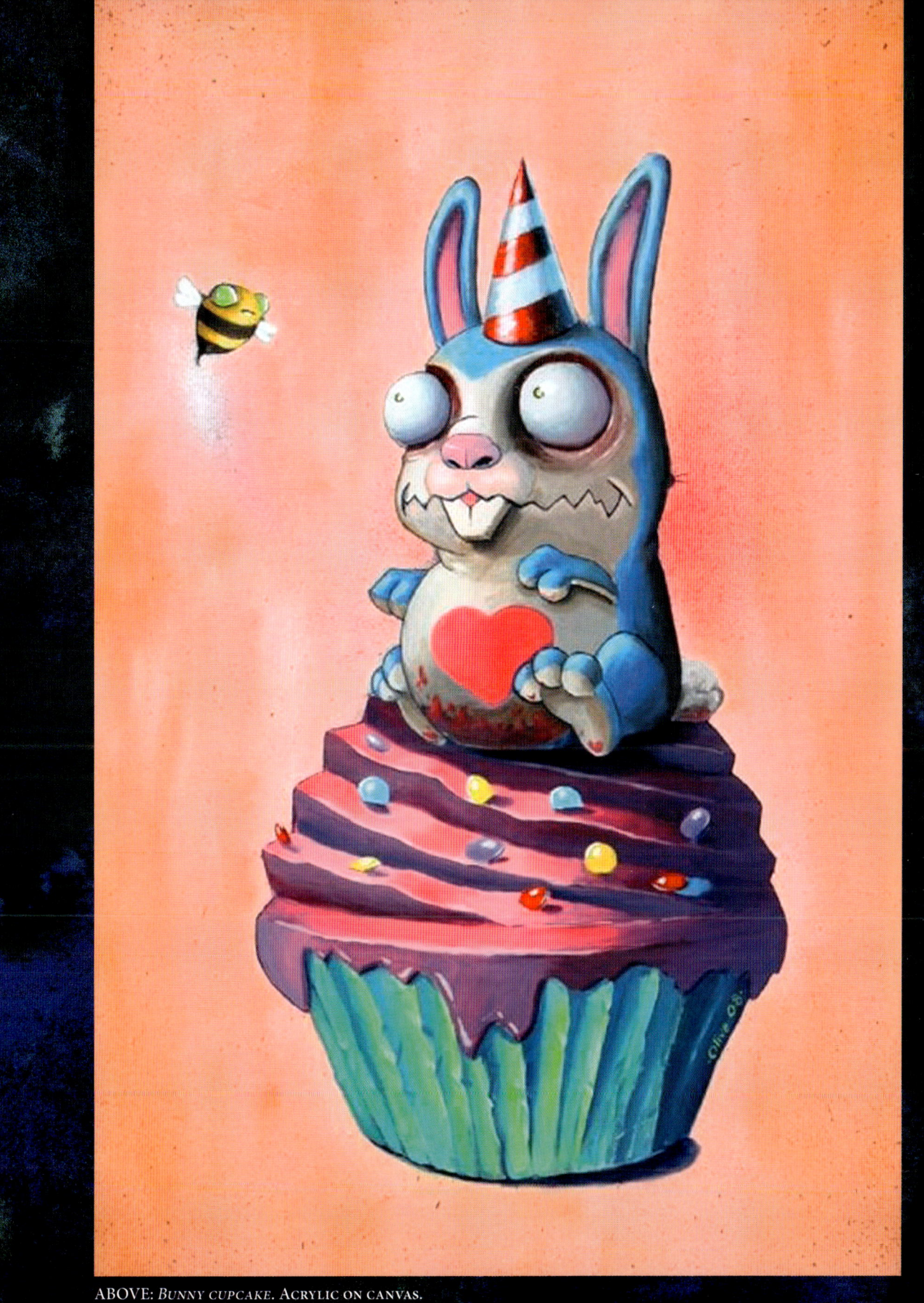

ABOVE: *Bunny cupcake*. Acrylic on canvas.
LEFT: *Zombie Sea Cow*. Acrylic on canvas.

REINKE

GERMANY / LONDON, UK.

It was coming across Sandy Pullman's book *The Japanese Tattoo* that created the spark. Alex was 14 and that was that. He began by teaching himself whilst studing art and design at university. Reinke then practiced in Plettenberg, Germany, before deciding to go to Japan to get a body suit tattoo from the master, Horiyoshi III. They became friends and Alex became his apprentice. Today he works in London, but the influence of Japan touches on everything he does. "Because I am steeped in the Japanese tradition and have made that my specialism, my art and tattoo are completely intertwined. All the designs, and the stories behind them, are similar. For my tattoos I use rotaries and Tebori as well as Japanese hand tools. For my art, it is Japanese inks, papers and brushes. I have also just started creating silk scroll paintings." The biggest influence of all on Reinke's art is his mentor, Horiyoshi III followed by artists like Kuniyoshi, Yoshitoshi and Kyosai "and loads of others in the woodblock print tradition." Reinke's work has been widely shown, in tattoo conventions and magazines. His growing client base is drawn by the fact that he is the only student of Horiyoshi III working in Europe. They are also, says Reinke, increasingly middle-aged and middle-class. Of the scene he says "There's way too much to say about that....It's changed dramatically in recent years.... Where is it going? Who knows? Maybe it's heading straight to Hell!"

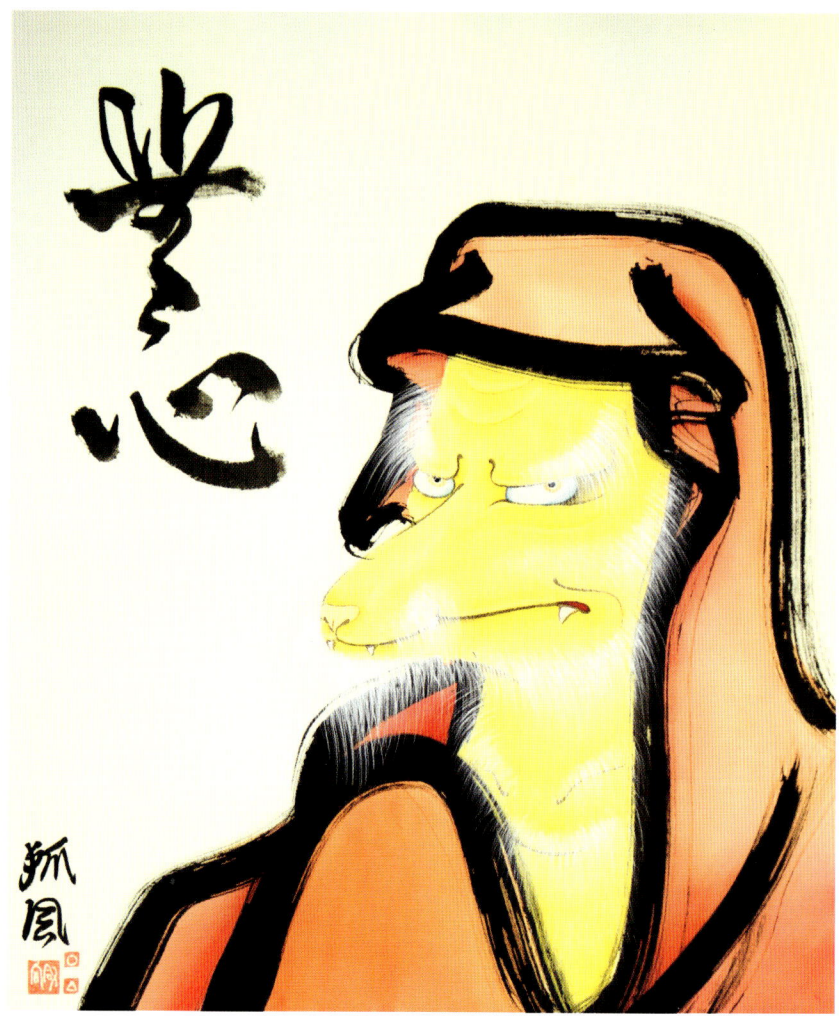

ABOVE: *Wiley Fox*. Brush and ink.
RIGHT: *The Crimson Curse*. Brush and ink.

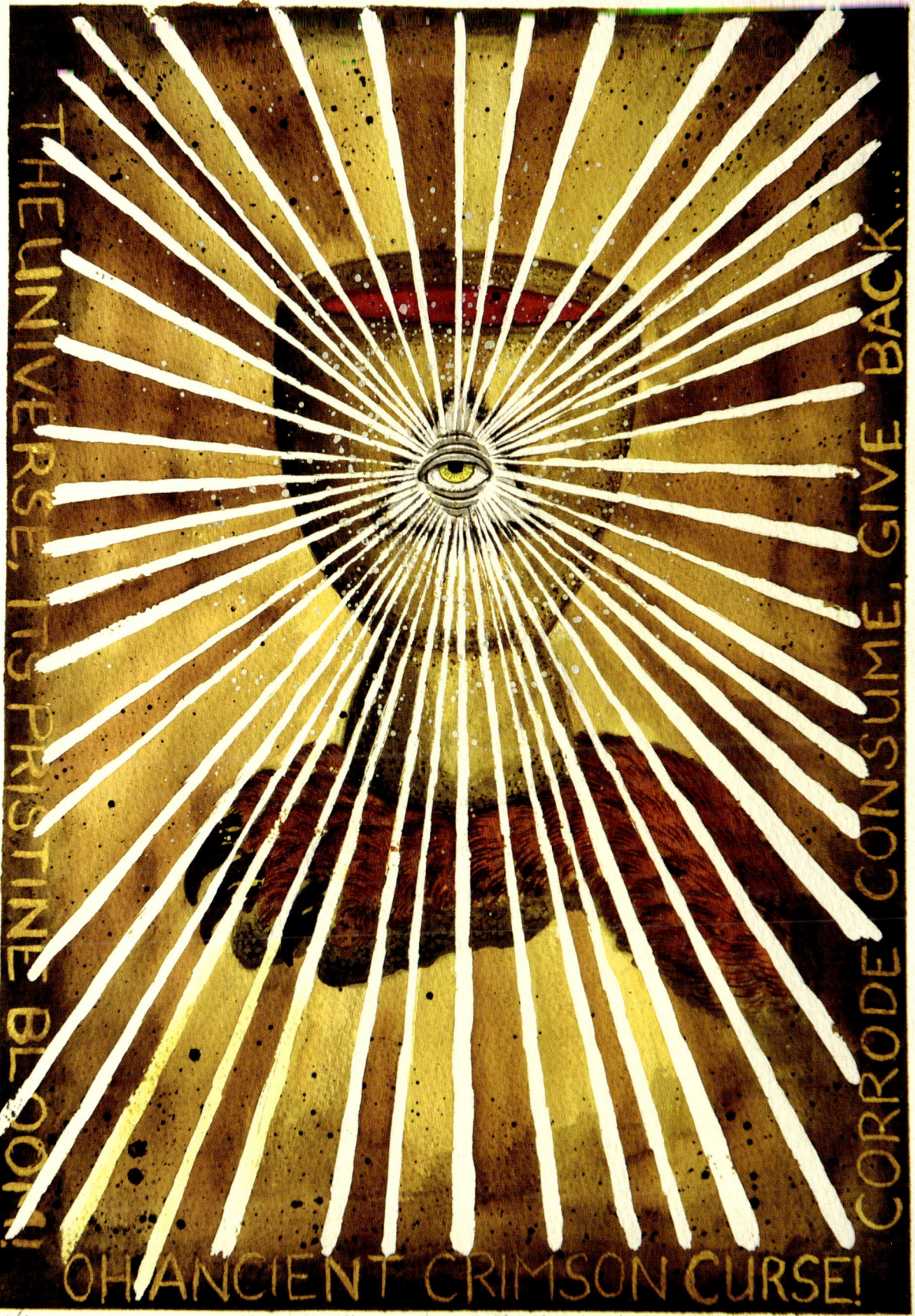

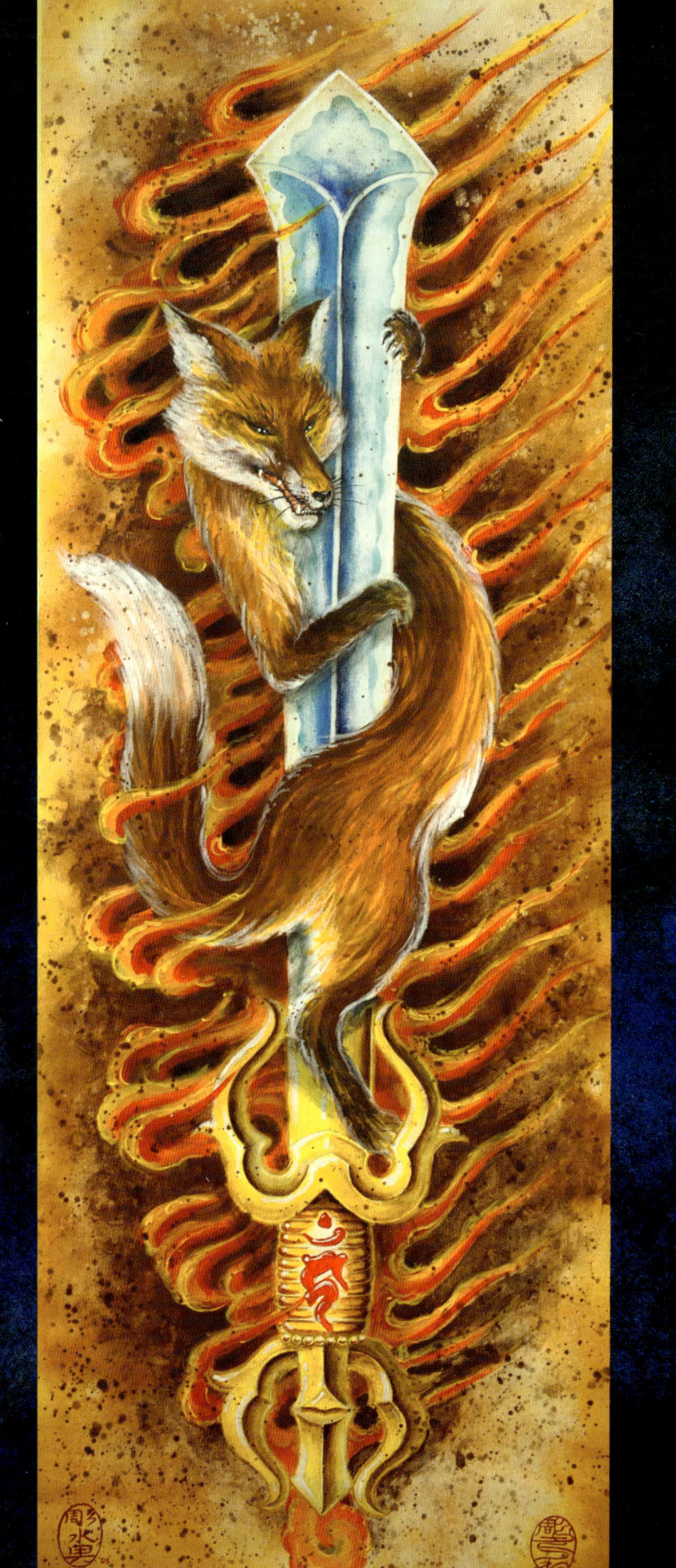

RIGHT: *Fox and Dagger.*
Brush and ink.
FAR RIGHT: *Skull.*
Brush and ink.

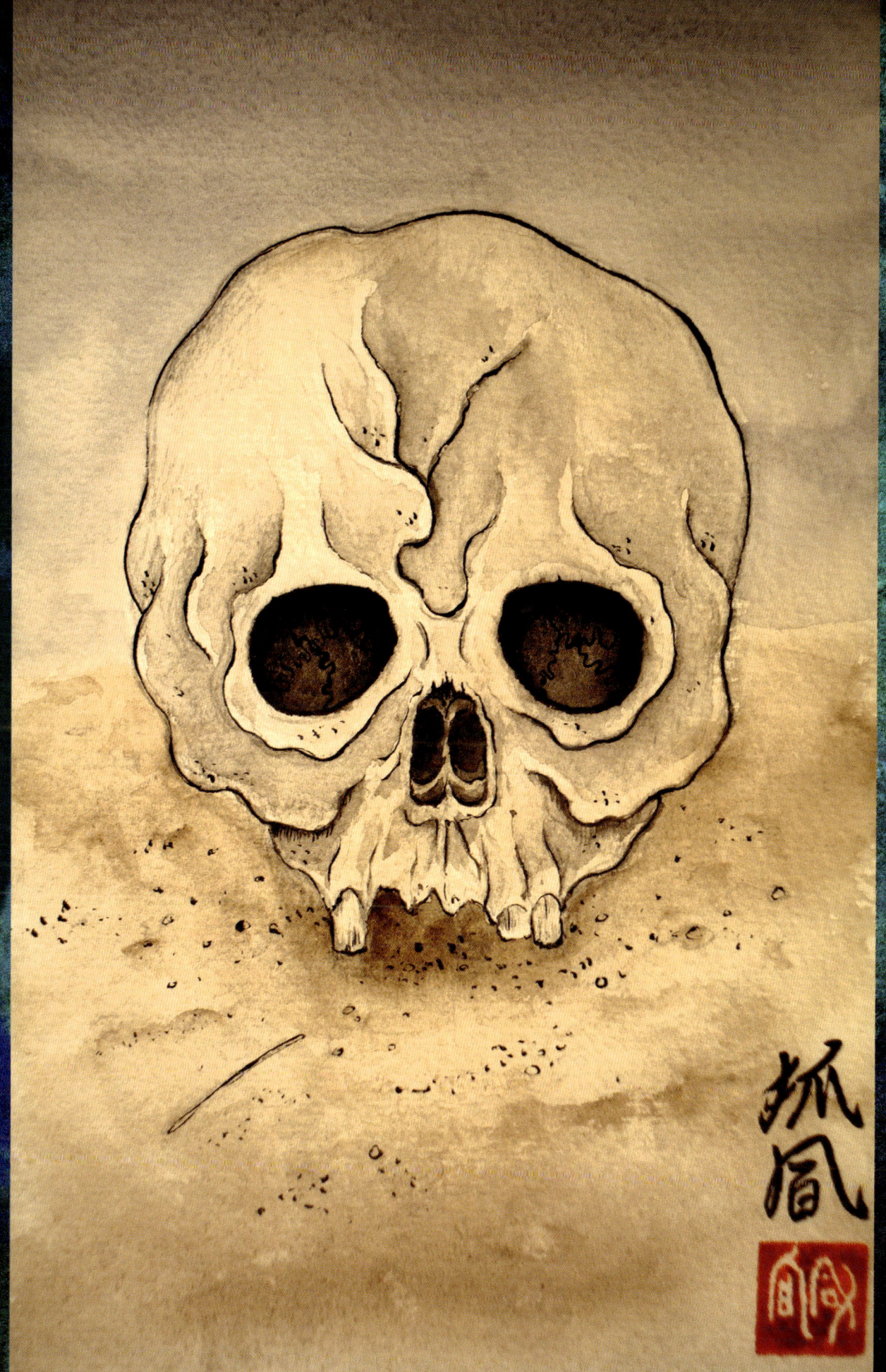

RICO

BRAZIL / IWATE, JAPAN.

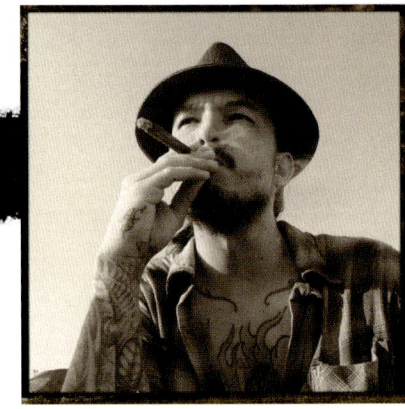

"It was all those tattoos I saw as a kid on the beach in Rio that did it" says Rico, "and then when I got into skateboarding I got in touch with people also into tattoos." He started when he was 17: "I was lucky and quickly got to know all sorts of people in Rio's underground culture; just to get access to equipment back then was a mission." For the first three years he tattooed out of his mum's house in Vila Isabel, before landing a job at Tyes Tattoo in Ipanema. That's where he refined his technique. For six and a half years Rico lived and worked in New York, before moving to Japan where he now runs a tattoo studio with his wife, Shion. "I now do machine work and some Tebori" says Rico, "and most of my clients here are working-class people and fellow tattooists...and a lot of members of the Angry Back Club!" His influences are many: "there are so many good people out there now and I learn something from each one I come across. If I had to name a couple of artists it would be Yokosuka Horihide as the biggest influence on my tattoos and Kuniyoshi for my paintings." Rico is a regular at many tattoo conventions in South America, USA, Europe and Japan. His work has been extensively published in magazines, including *Tattoo Life*, *Tattoo Tribal* and Japan's *Tattoo Burst*. The explosion of the scene in recent years he thinks is a good thing. "It's led to higher quality work than before. The younger generation is quick to catch up and they know how to evolve the art in the right way. I think tattoos are going to get better and better, provided everyone keeps their feet on the ground."

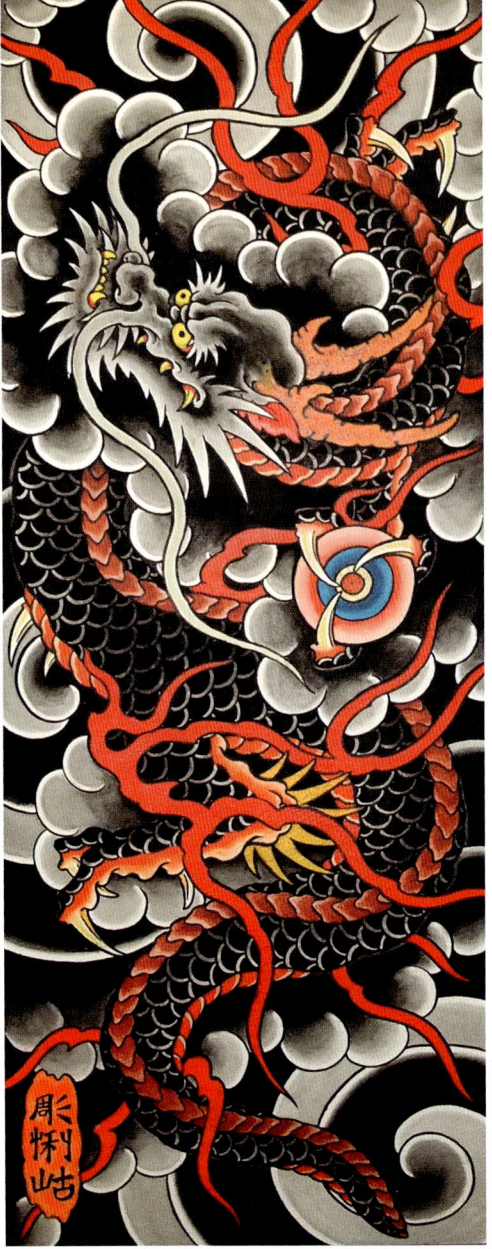

RIGHT: *Dragon*. Pen, ink and watercolour.
FAR RIGHT: *Hanai Mask*. Pen, ink and watercolour.

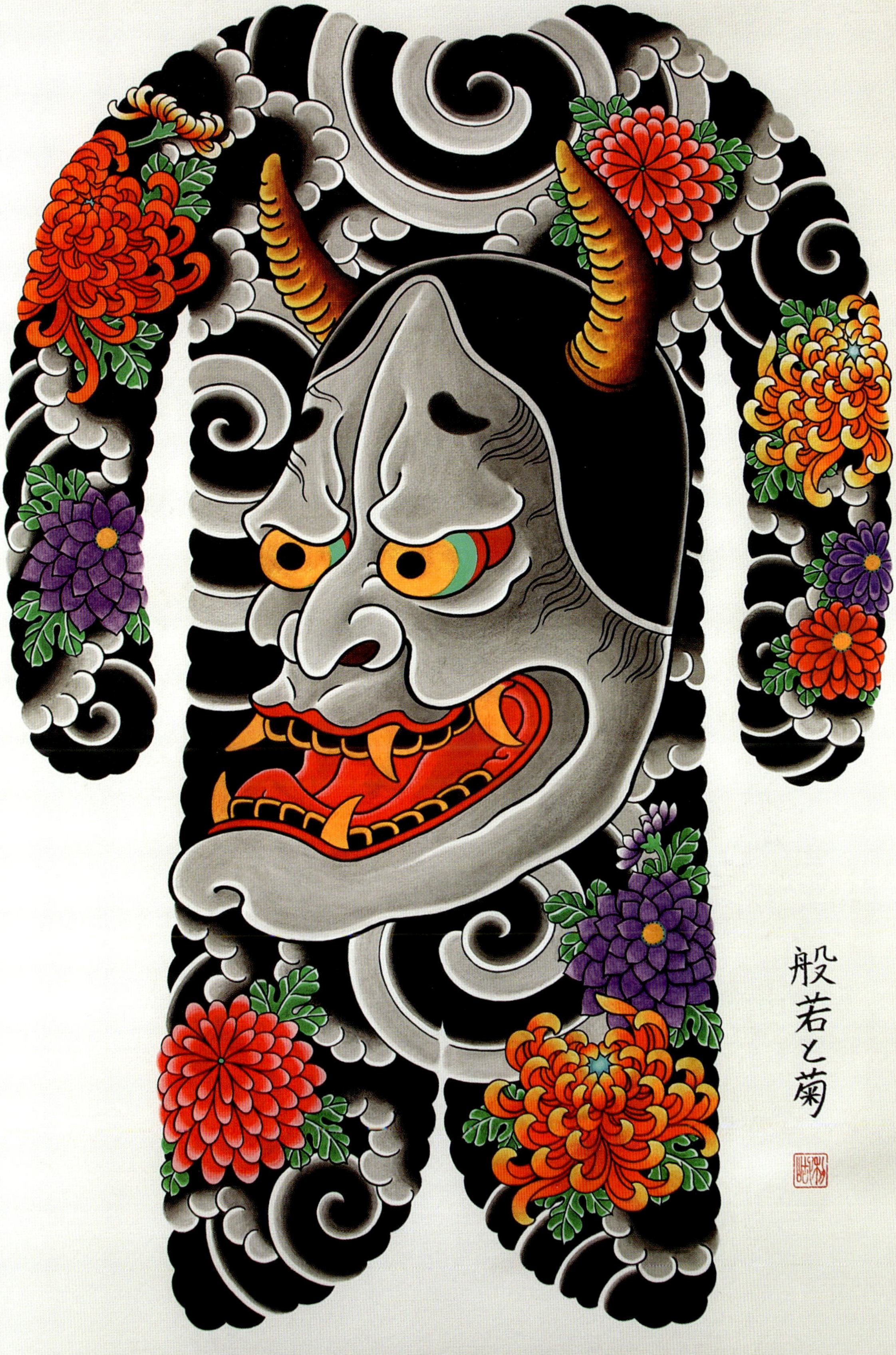

般若と菊

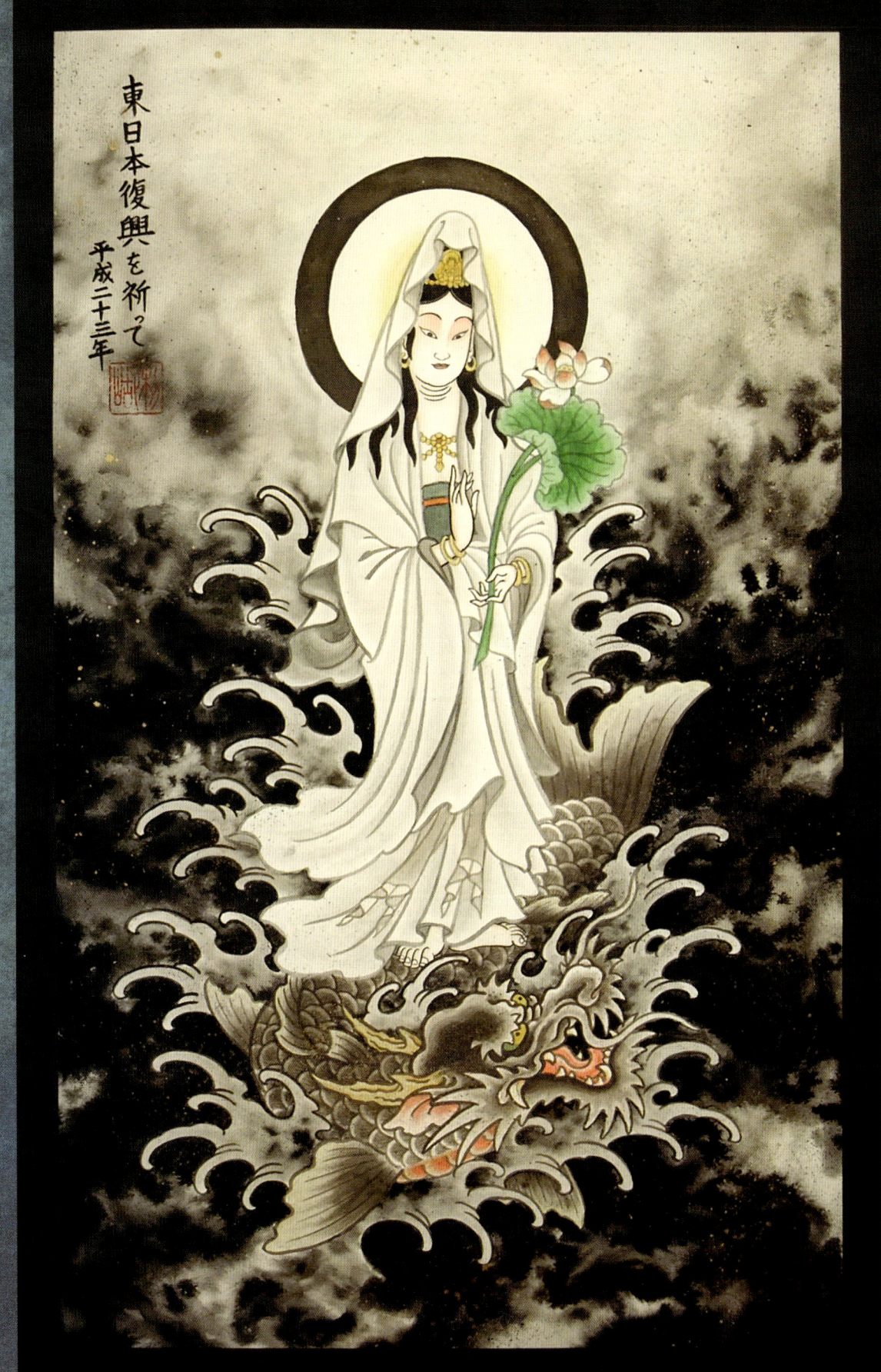

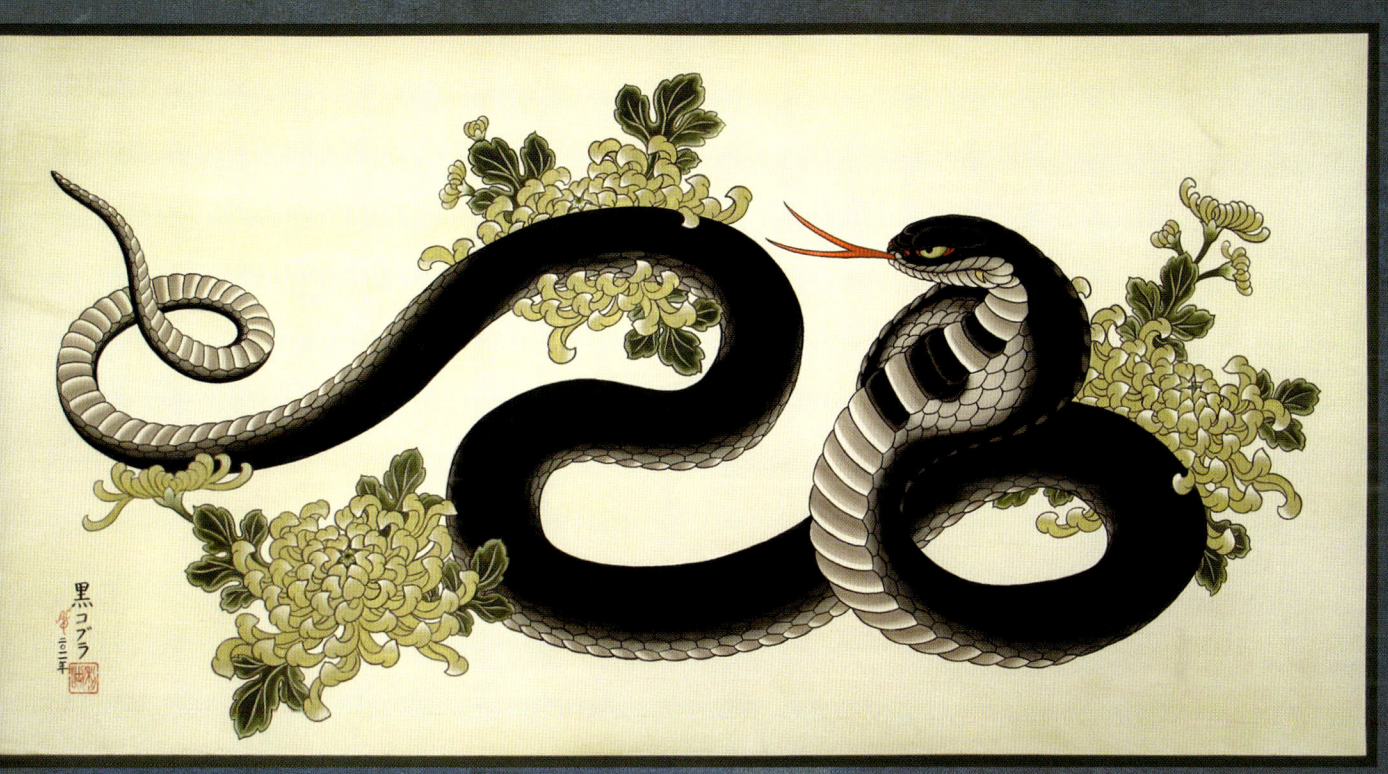

LEFT: *Lotus Goddess*. Pen, ink and watercolour.
ABOVE: *Cobra*. Pen, ink and watercolour.

ROBINSON

BRIGHTON, UK.

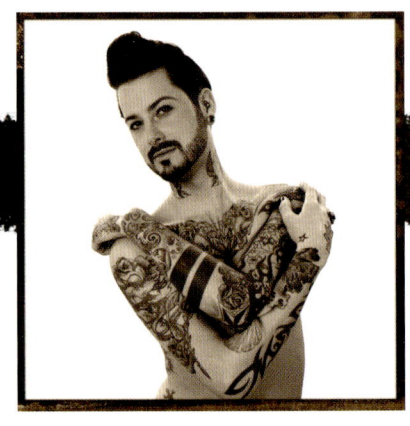

Growing up in a small fishing village on the Dorset coast in southern England, James decided from a very young age that he wanted to be a tattoo artist. "I don't know where the idea came from; my school was bemused." The scene was so hard to get into that James first pursued illustration as a way to earn a living. He moved to Brighton, expecting that a studio there would take him on, but "it was really hard to get people to look at my work." James decided that the only way to start, and also to follow his father's advice ("be sure to have a trade") was to teach himself. "I bought a basic kit off the Internet, researched cross-contamination and sterilization and started practicing on every inch of skin I could reach…that got me my first job in a tattoo studio." That was 2008; three years later, with an inheritance from his grandmother, James opened Gilded Cage tattoo – a boutique, gallery space and tattoo studio – in the heart of Brighton's gay neighbourhood. Early influences on James's style were Jo Harrison and Jeff Gogue – "They tattooed in the same way I illustrate, with an almost painterly quality" – although now he looks for inspiration from art, objects and people from outside the scene. His art and tattoo are intertwined – "if I'm not tattooing I'm drawing; when I do work for a gallery show, most will be linked to a tattoo aesthetic." His techniques, says James, are constantly evolving. Early on everything was coloured pencil, particularly for birds (for which he is renowned), then he went through fazes exploring oils, sculpture, jewellery design and watercolour; "each one has somehow influenced the way I tattoo." Of the scene he says "The culture of studios feeling they own tattooists is gone; people research their artist and find where they are. Standards have got to such a level, it's hard to imagine they could improve further!" James has been featured widely (notably a naked shoot in *Skin* a few years back) and his client base travel far to be inked by him; "I was humbled recently by one guy who came over from Australia!"

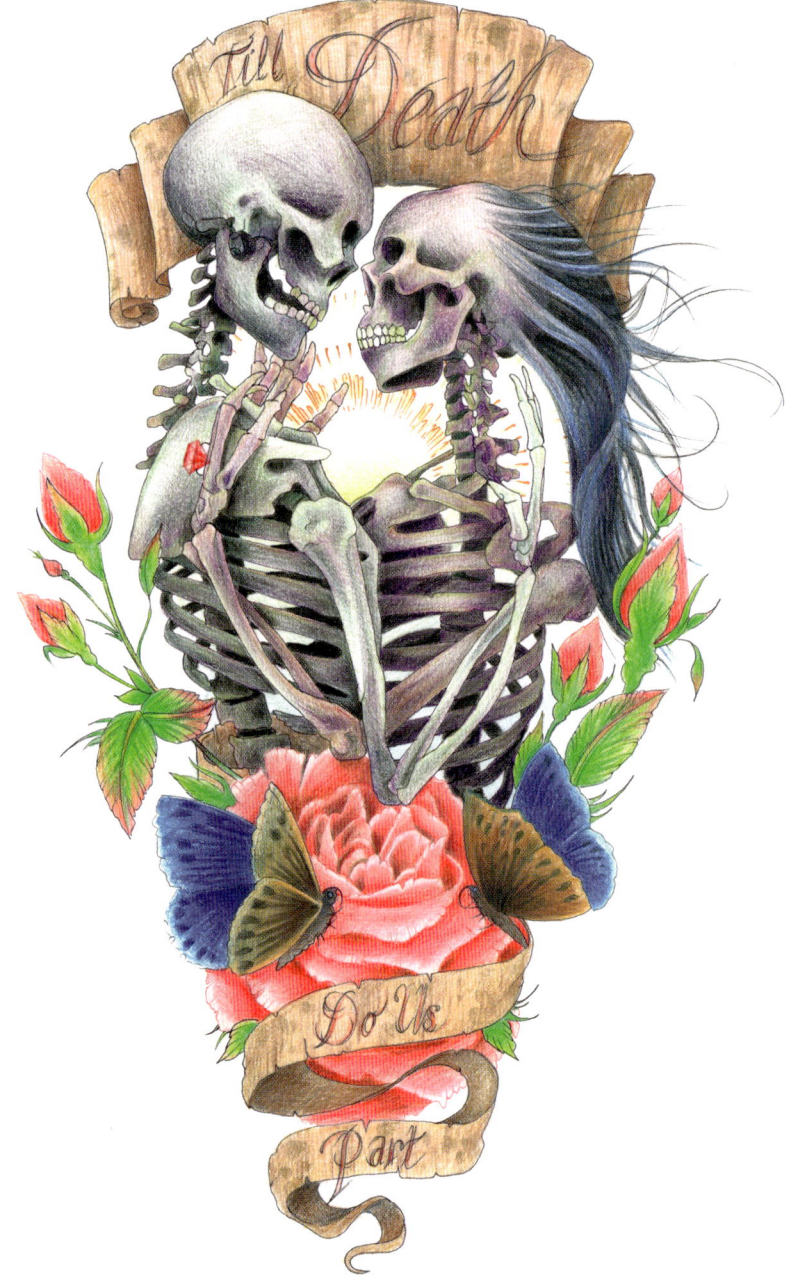

ABOVE: *Till Death Do Us Part*. Coloured pencils.
RIGHT: *Skeleton Virgin Mary*. Coloured pencils.

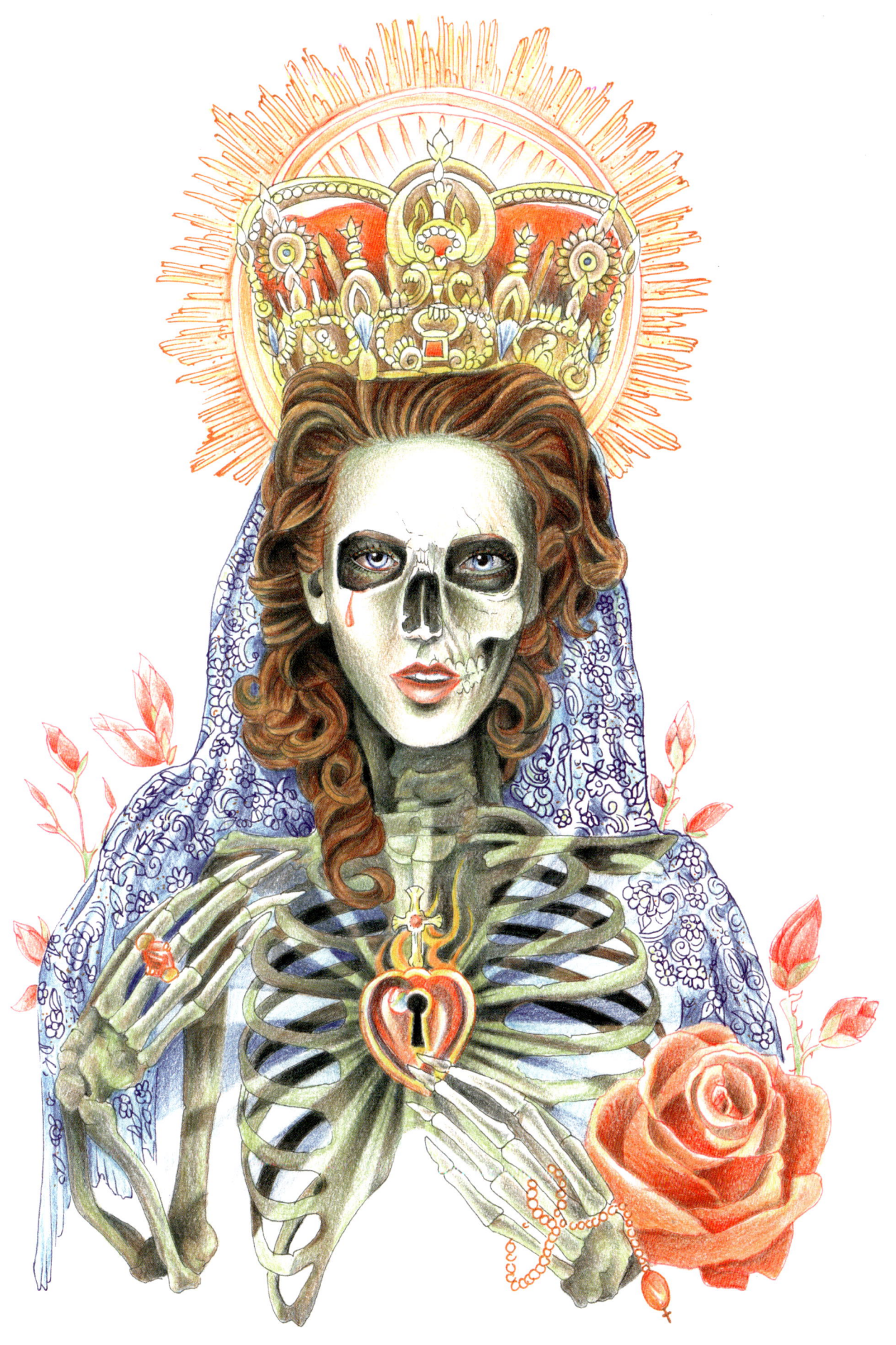

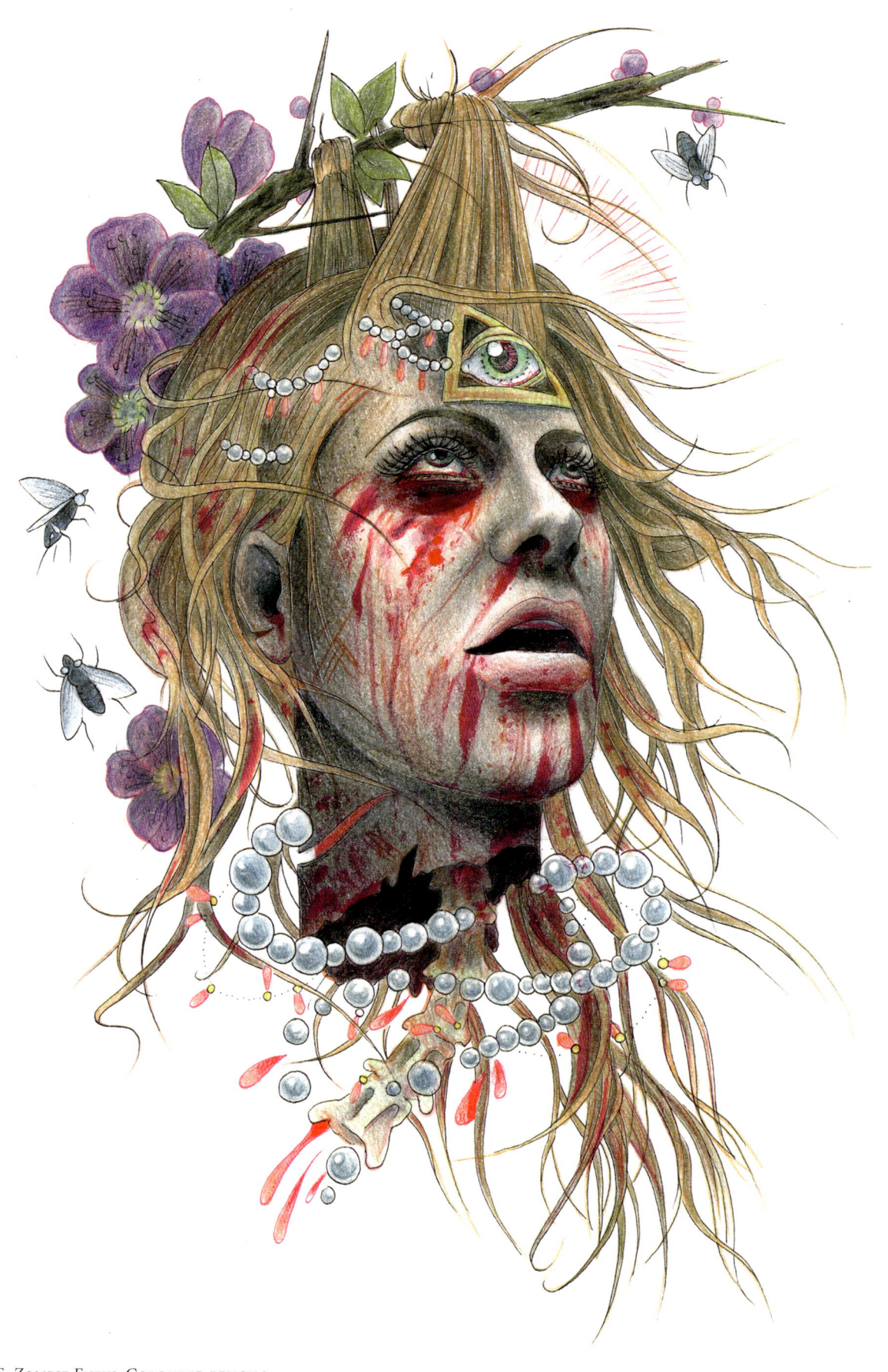

ABOVE: *Zombie Enfys*. Coloured pencils.
RIGHT: *Autumn Owl*. Coloured pencils.

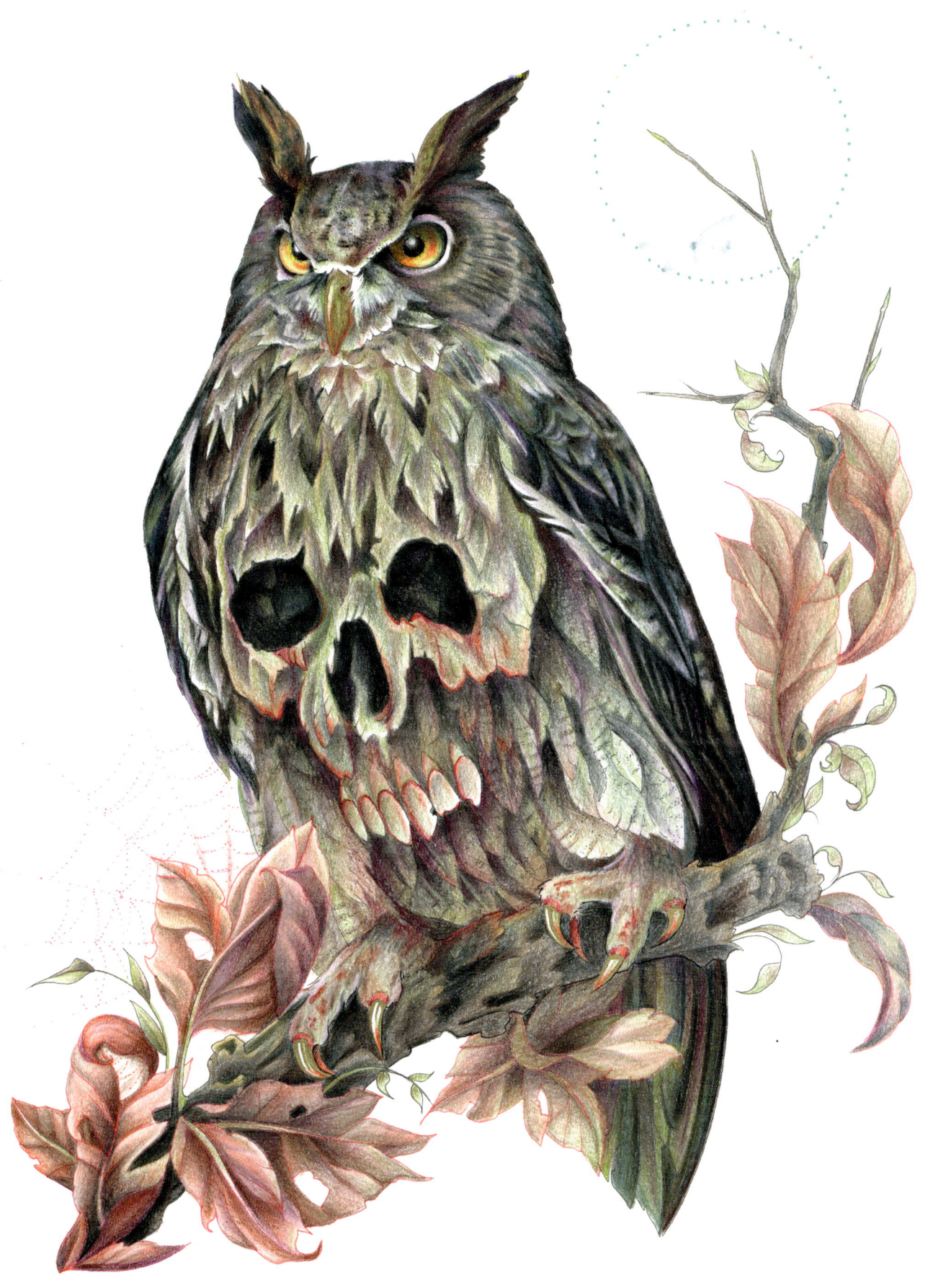

ROTOR

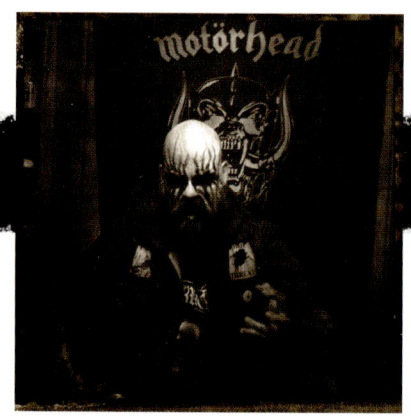

BARCELONA, SPAIN.

"When I discovered tattoo it was like the gates of hell opened and I found I rather liked it" says Rotor. He trained in graphic arts and murals in Barcelona and had been working as a professional illustrator, but hanging out with tattooing friends. He was fascinated by the distinct rules governing the art as opposed to the greater freedom which illustration allowed him, "but at the same time, knowing how to draw is hugely useful to the tattoo artist." He apprenticed at Aloha Tattoos before joining the shop: "An amazing bunch of guys; I feel really proud to be part of that group... they are real innovators."

It's inevitable that his art is now mostly influenced by tattoo as the latter takes up almost all his time and energy. "It's rare that I can find a gap to just drawn or paint, but when I do, I do it for pleasure rather than to commission; that said I find that my regular clients also tend to buy this work." His greatest influences are other artists – "too many to mention" – and also movies and comics. Social networking has, he thinks, had the greatest influence in the tattoo world recently: "It has allowed me to disseminate my work worldwide, and that in turn has meant it has been featured in printed magazines far and wide as well as in online shows....in that sense I am the child of these recent changes!"

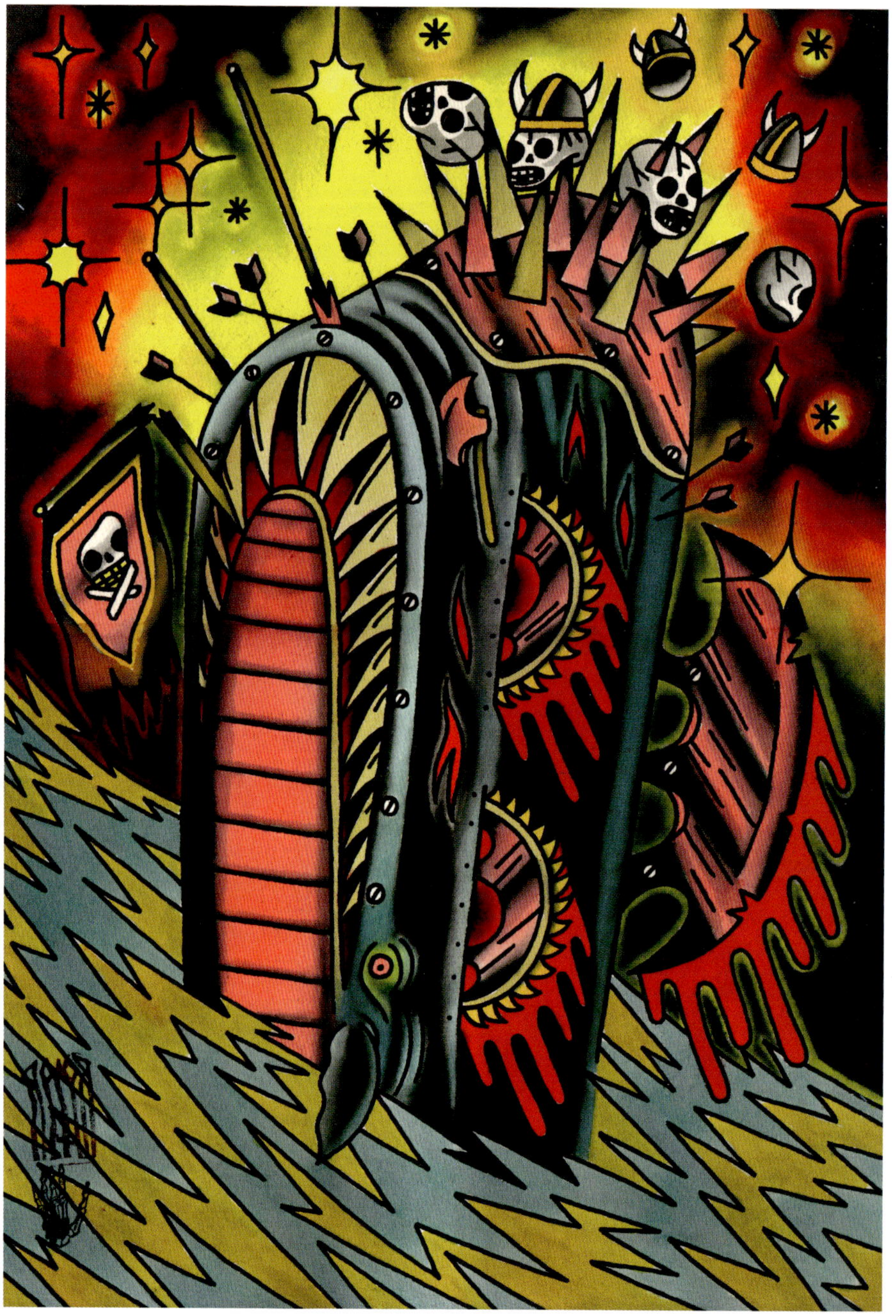

ABOVE: *Ballena Viking*. Pen and ink; digital.
RIGHT: *Warrior*. Pen and ink; digital.

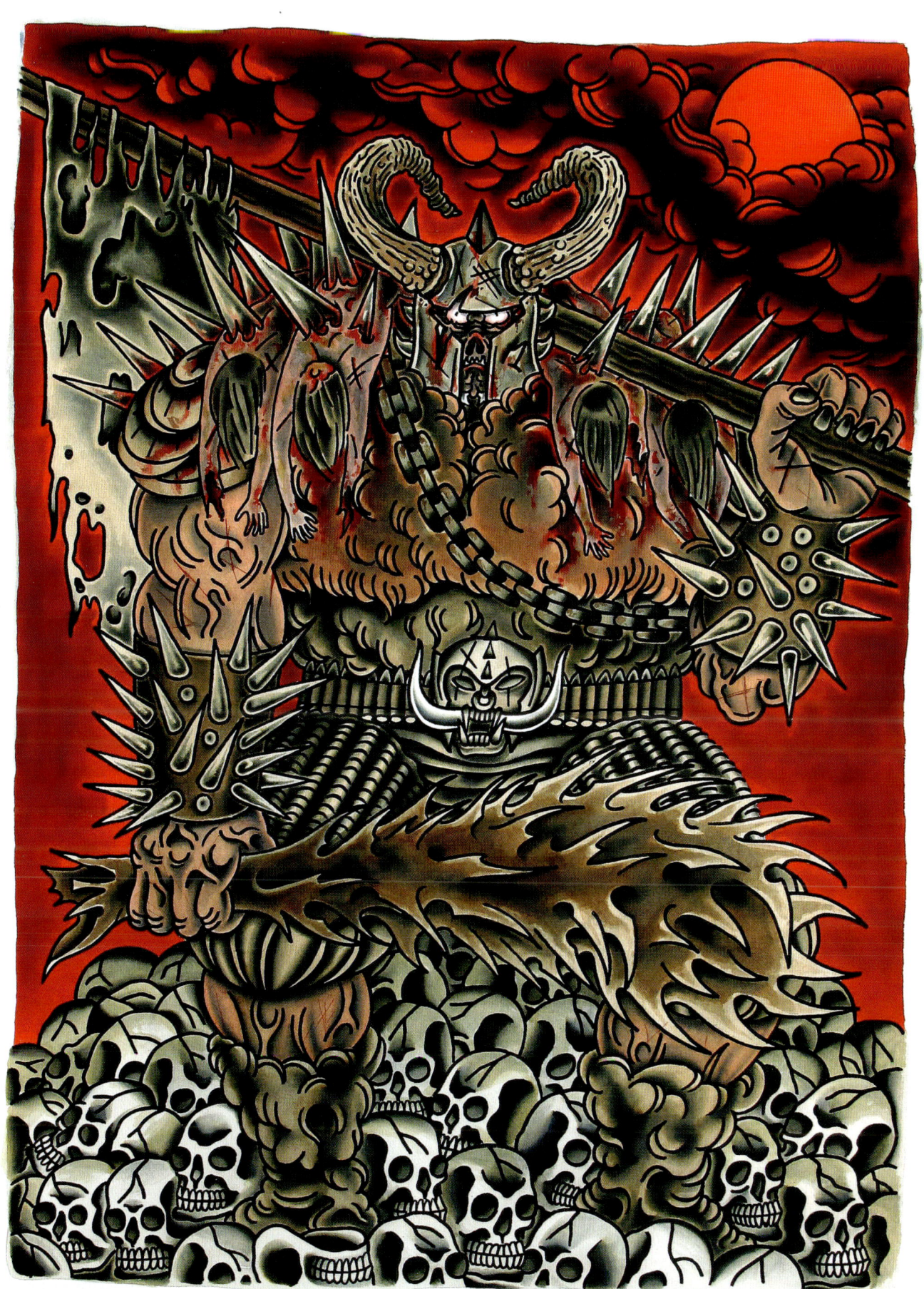

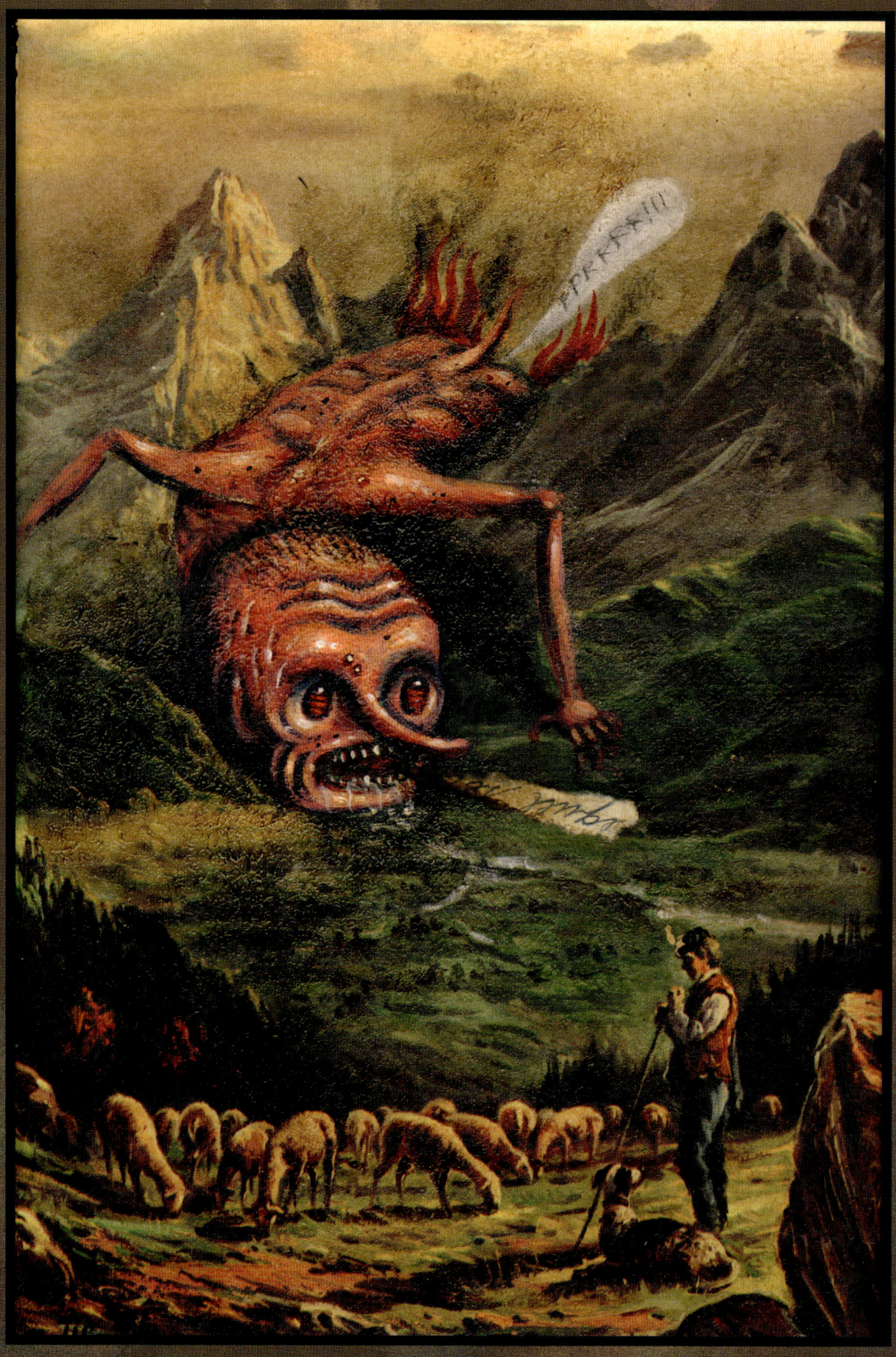

ABOVE: *The Quiet Shepherd*. Oil on canvas.
RIGHT: *The Cottage Fire*. Oil on canvas.

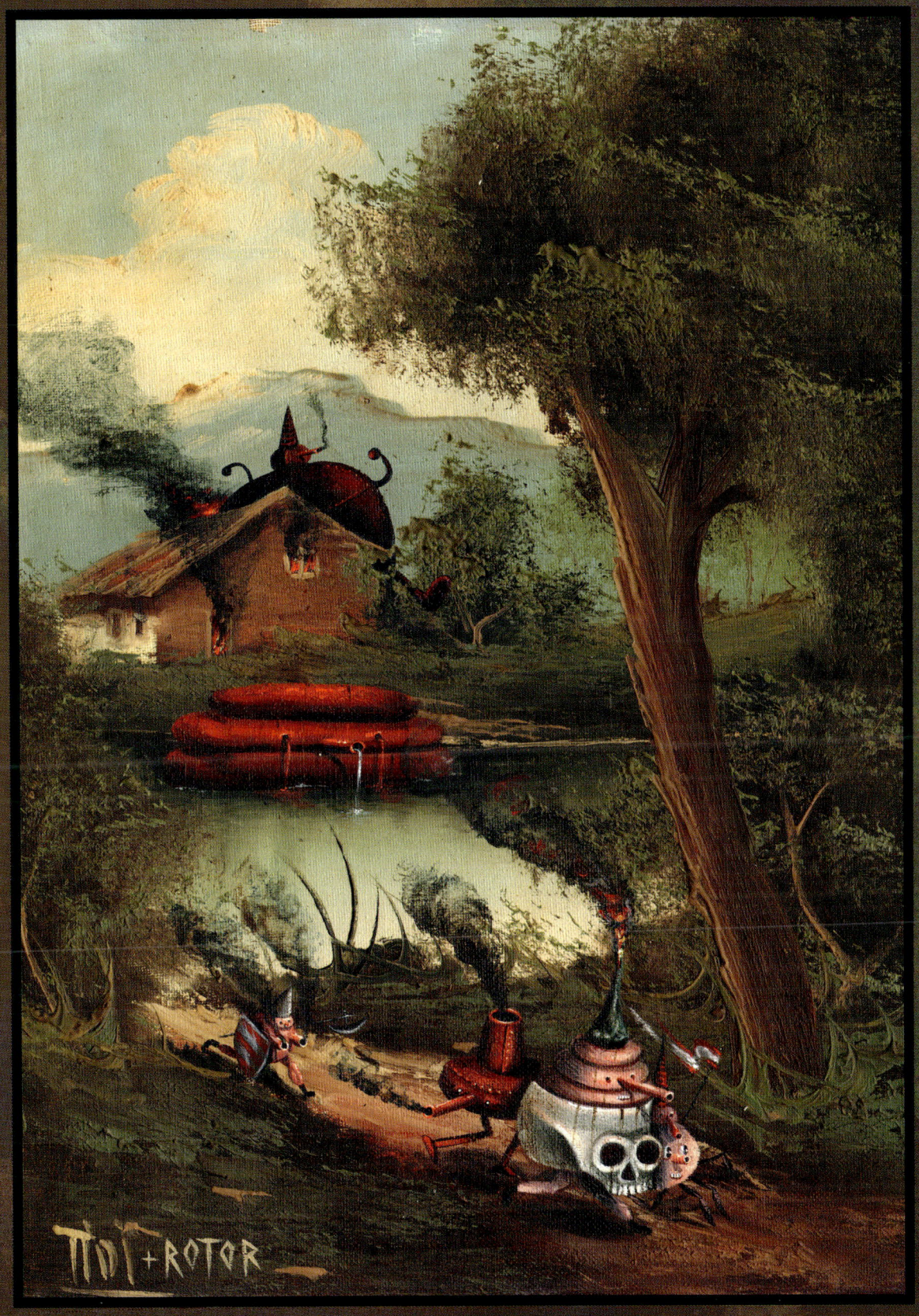

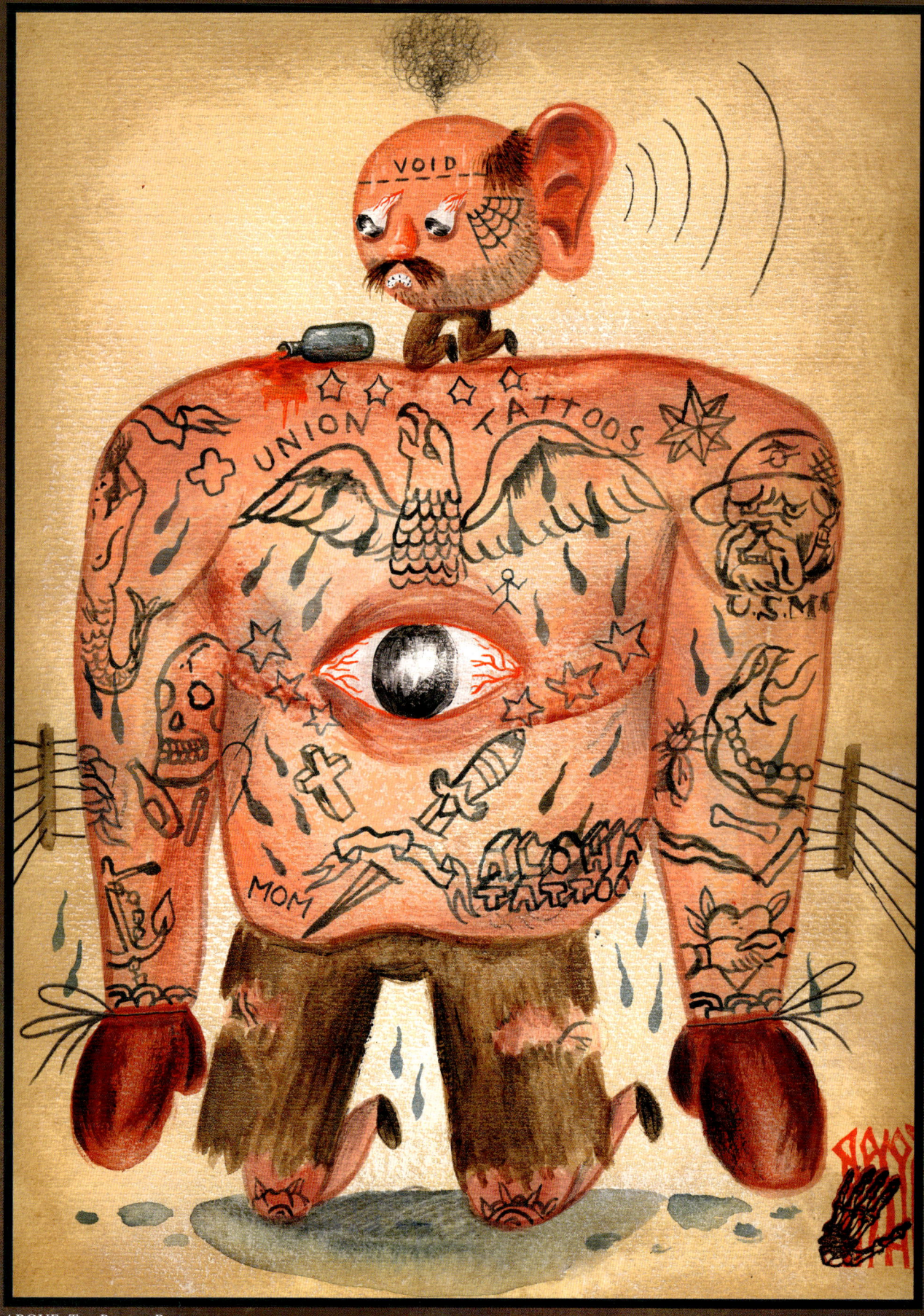

ABOVE: *The Boxer*. Pen and watercolour.
RIGHT: *The Communist*. Pen and watercolour.

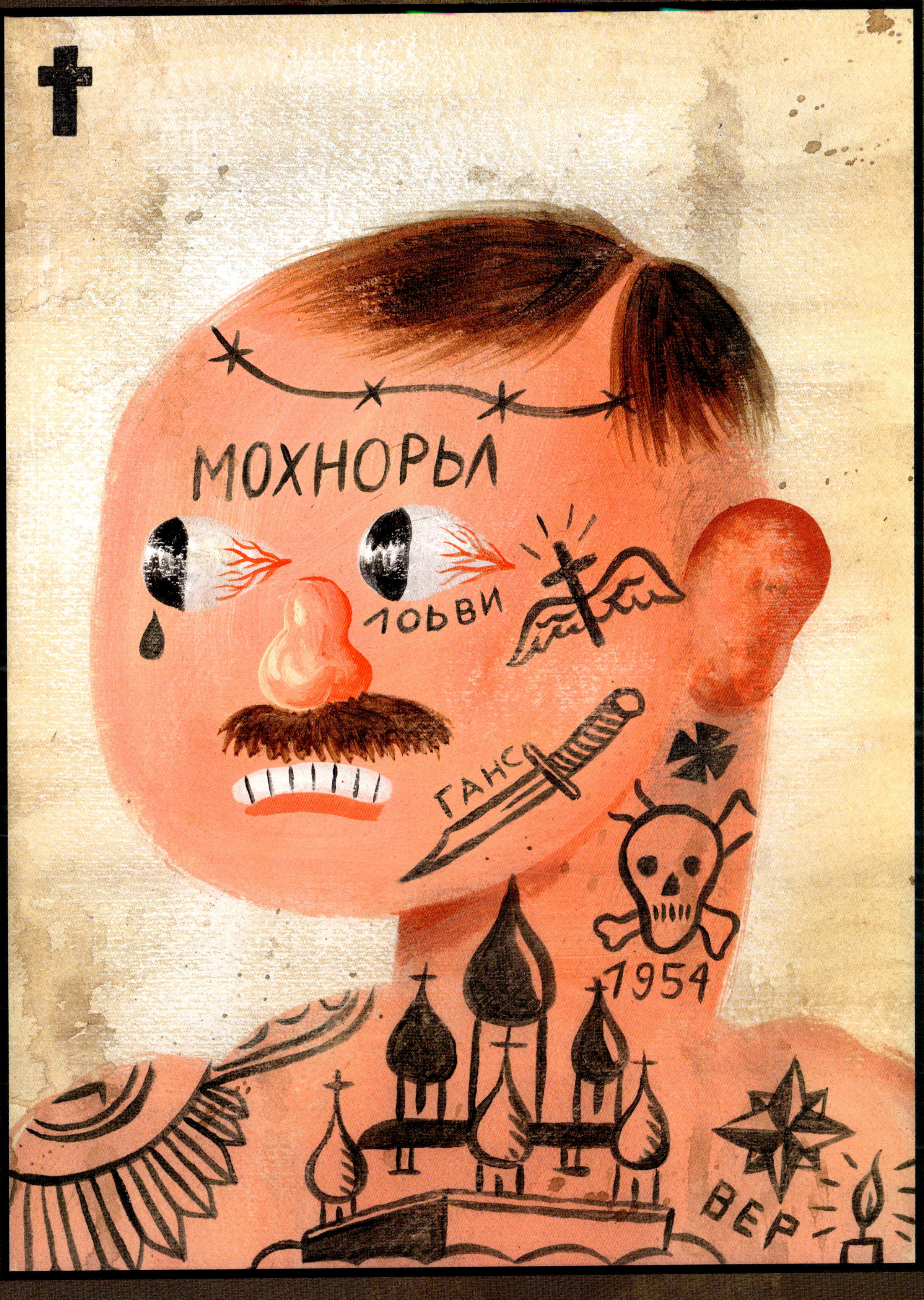

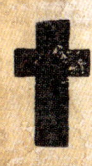

SENTO

VALENCIA, SPAIN.

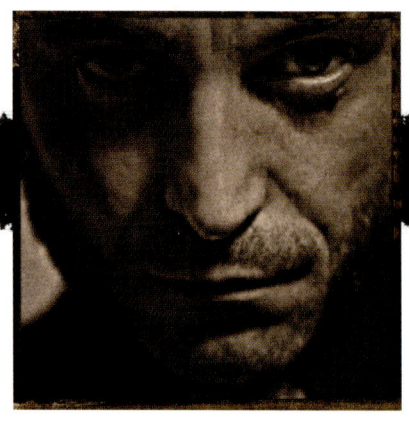

"A lot of tattooists of about my age will tell you that it used to be much harder, and they're not wrong!" says Sento, "....no Internet, only one or two magazines, only one or two tattoo shops in town who wouldn't tell you how to treat needles, or where to buy equipment. In the end if you wanted to start, the only way was to experiment on your own skin or your friends'." That was in 1998, when Sento sort of stumbled out of illustration and into tattoo. He managed to get a placement in a big commercial shop and then travelled the world tattooing at various studios, before opening his own, Three Pirate Studio in Valencia.

Sento is proud to be self-taught. He considers himself to be a tattooist who occasionally paints, not a tattoo artist. "Listen, I have so little time to do art, to explore art, to think about it deeply....it's when I find the time and then I do it for myself or for an artshow, and in the case of those it's at most one or two every two years." His art is completely rooted in tattoo. When we ask whether there are any specific artists who have influenced him, he prefers not to name names, "better just to see the work." The techniques he uses are very traditional, typically watercolours on archival paper mounted on wood, with brass tacks or rivets framing the work, or 3-D pieces involving found objects with resin models in interesting juxtapositions . Mexican art and woodcuts and *dia de los muertos* iconography are a major inspiration. "I am drawn more and more," he says "to religious art and the darker stuff."

Sento has exhibited widely in Spain and also at shows in the US and Canada. The scene has recently "gone crazy, there's too much stuff going on! Don't get me wrong, I'm not saying it's a bad thing, rather a double-edged sword, a case of too much too soon perhaps. Will it continue its exponential growth ? I don't know! The only thing I can tell you is that the future is uncertain!"

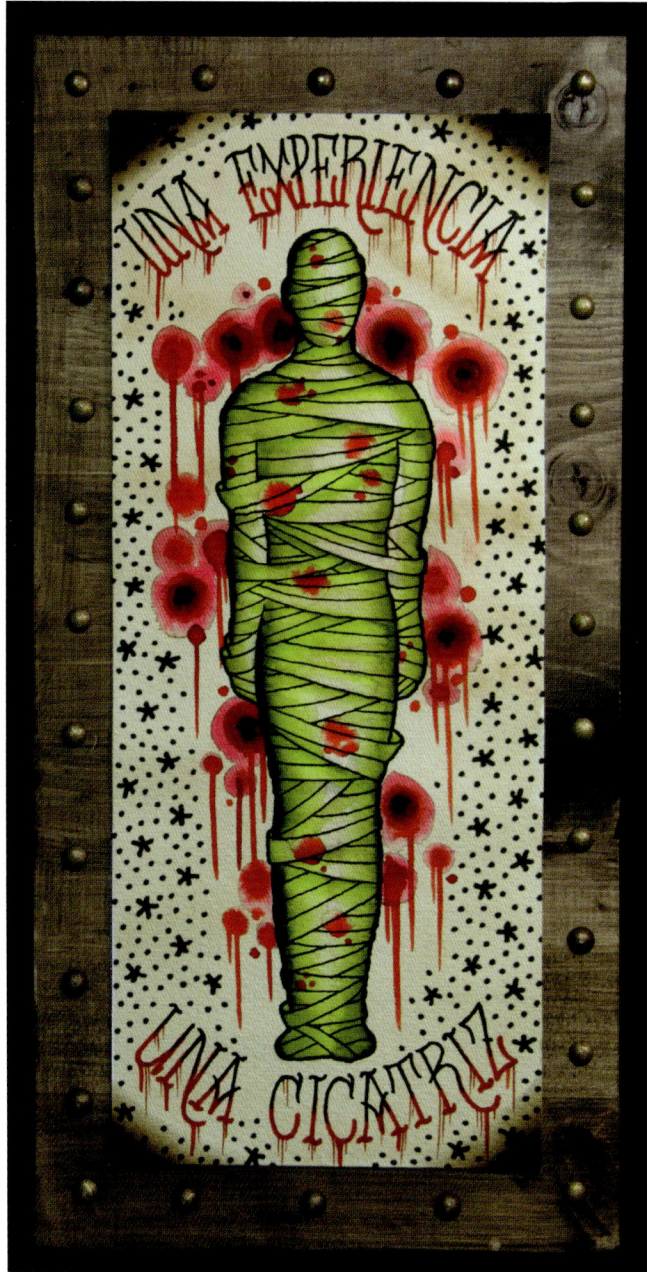

RIGHT: *Una Experiencia, Una Cicatriz (Experience, With a Scar)*. Watercolour on archival paper.
FAR RIGHT: *New World Order Christ*. Ink on wood and acrylic.

OVERLEAF:
LEFT: *High Heel On Top*. Pen and ink.
RIGHT: *Waiting Heart*. Resin, iron cage and bracket.

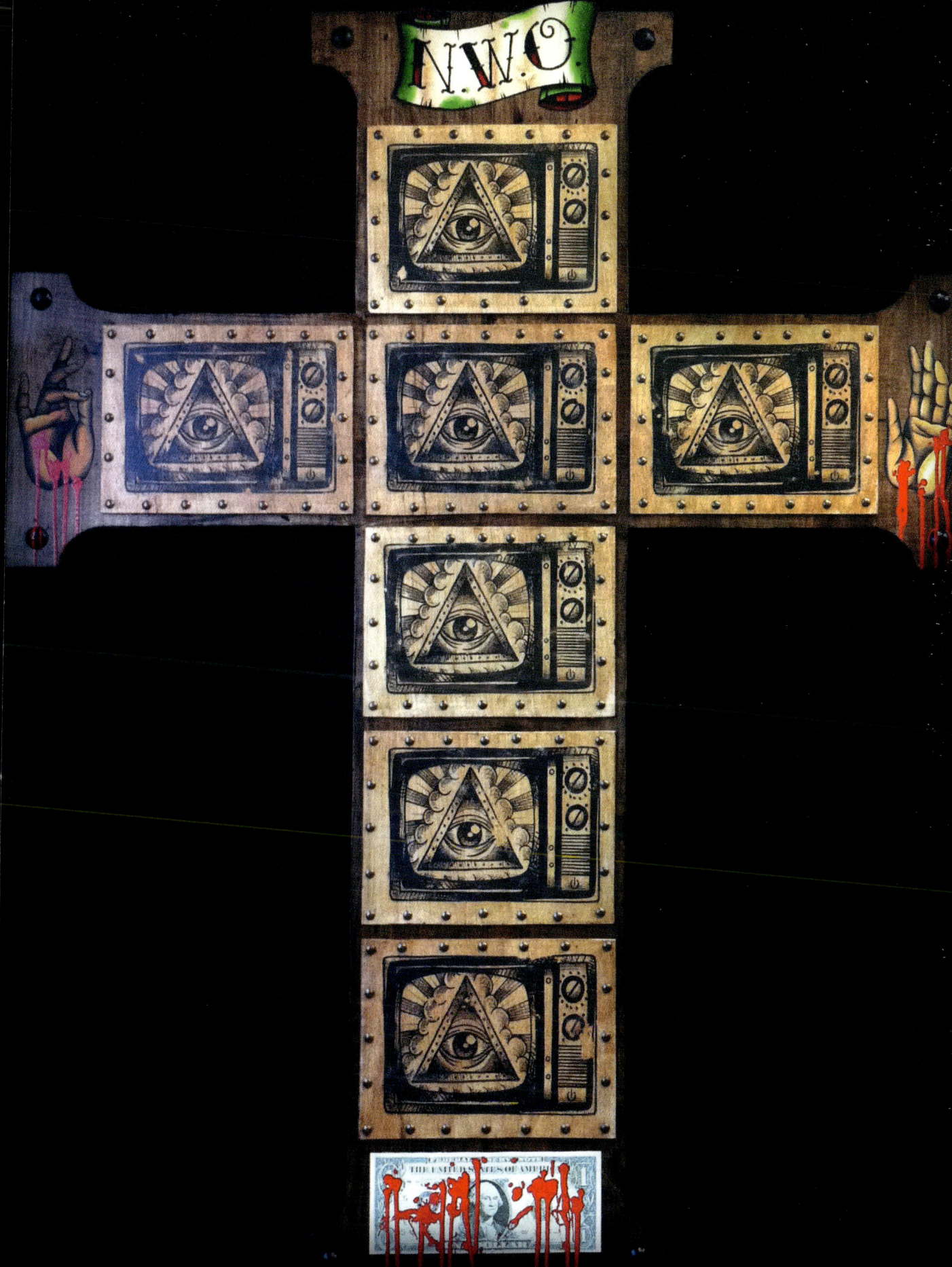

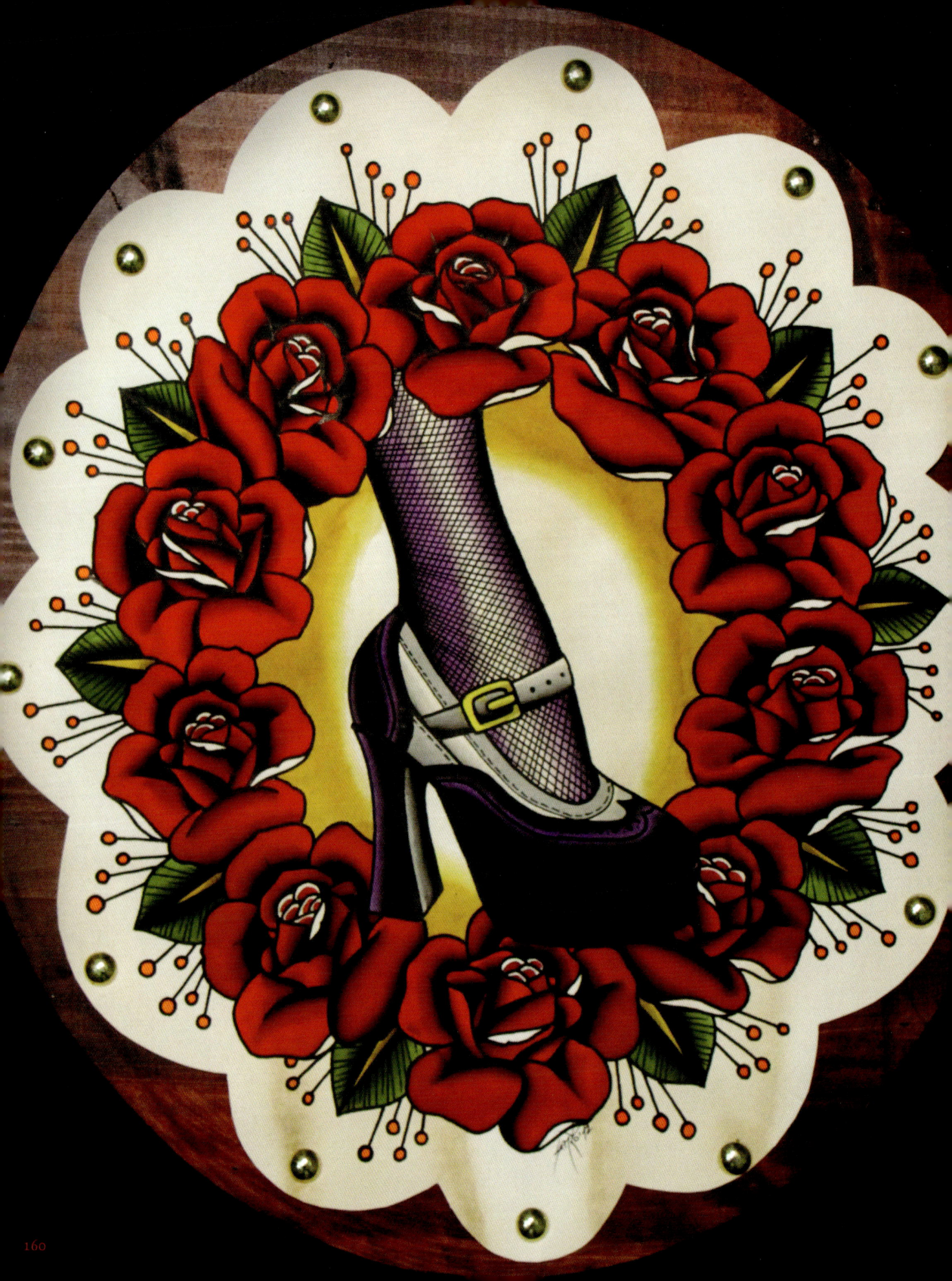

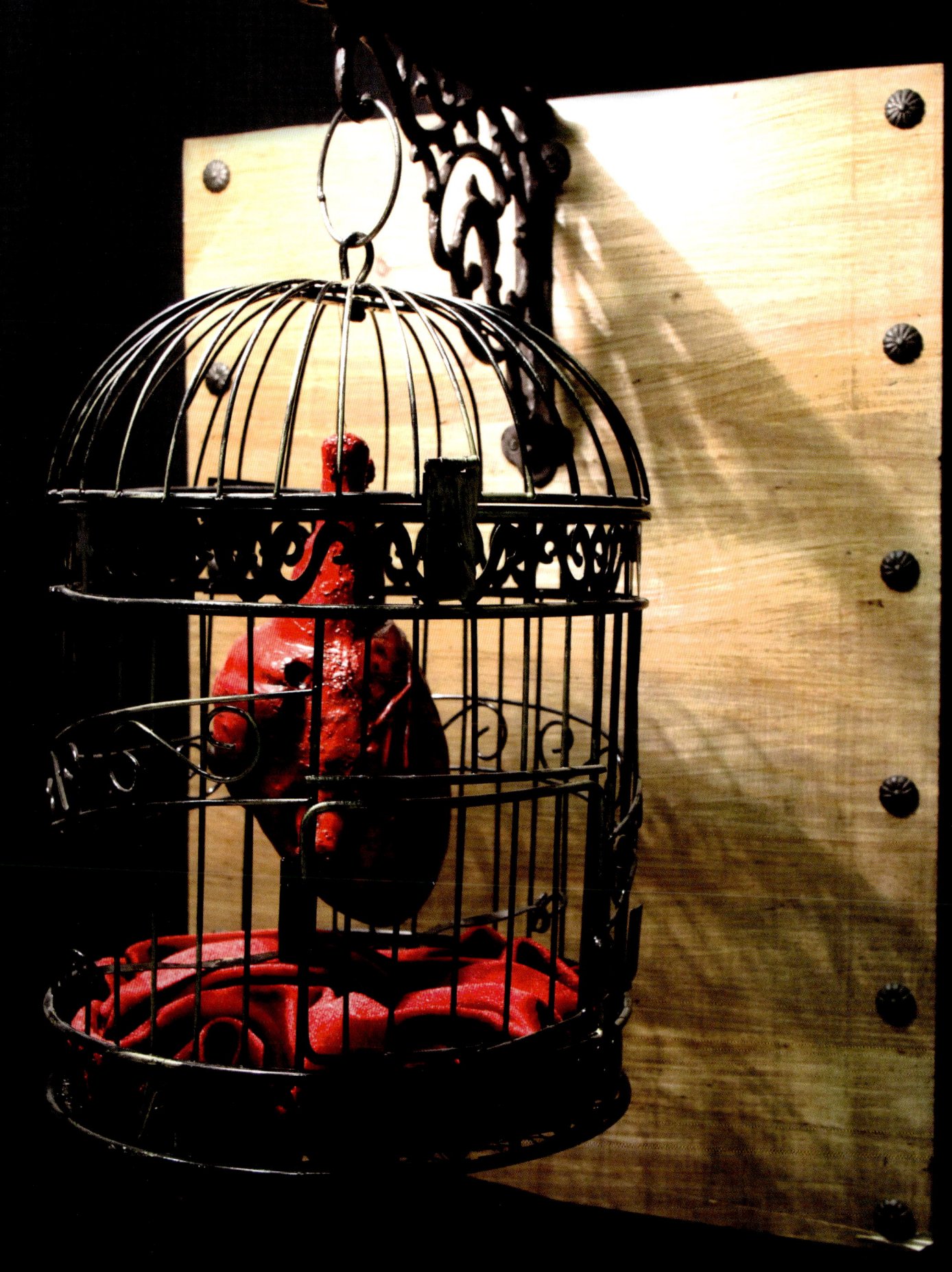

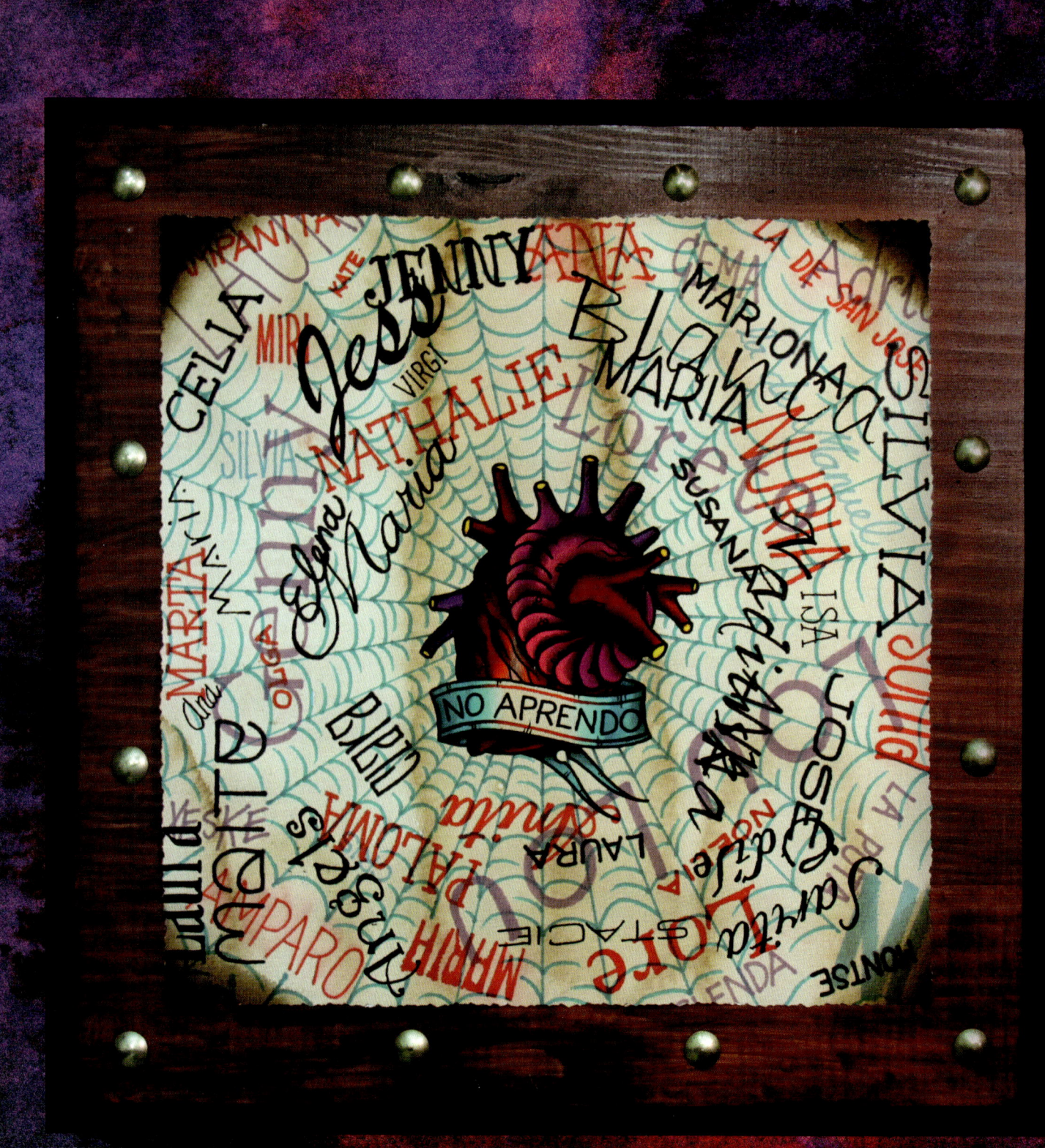

ABOVE: *No Aprendo (I Never Learn)*. Watercolour on archival paper, ink and brass studs on wood.
RIGHT: *Sugarskull Bouquet*. Dia de los muertos sugarskull, silk flowers and wood.

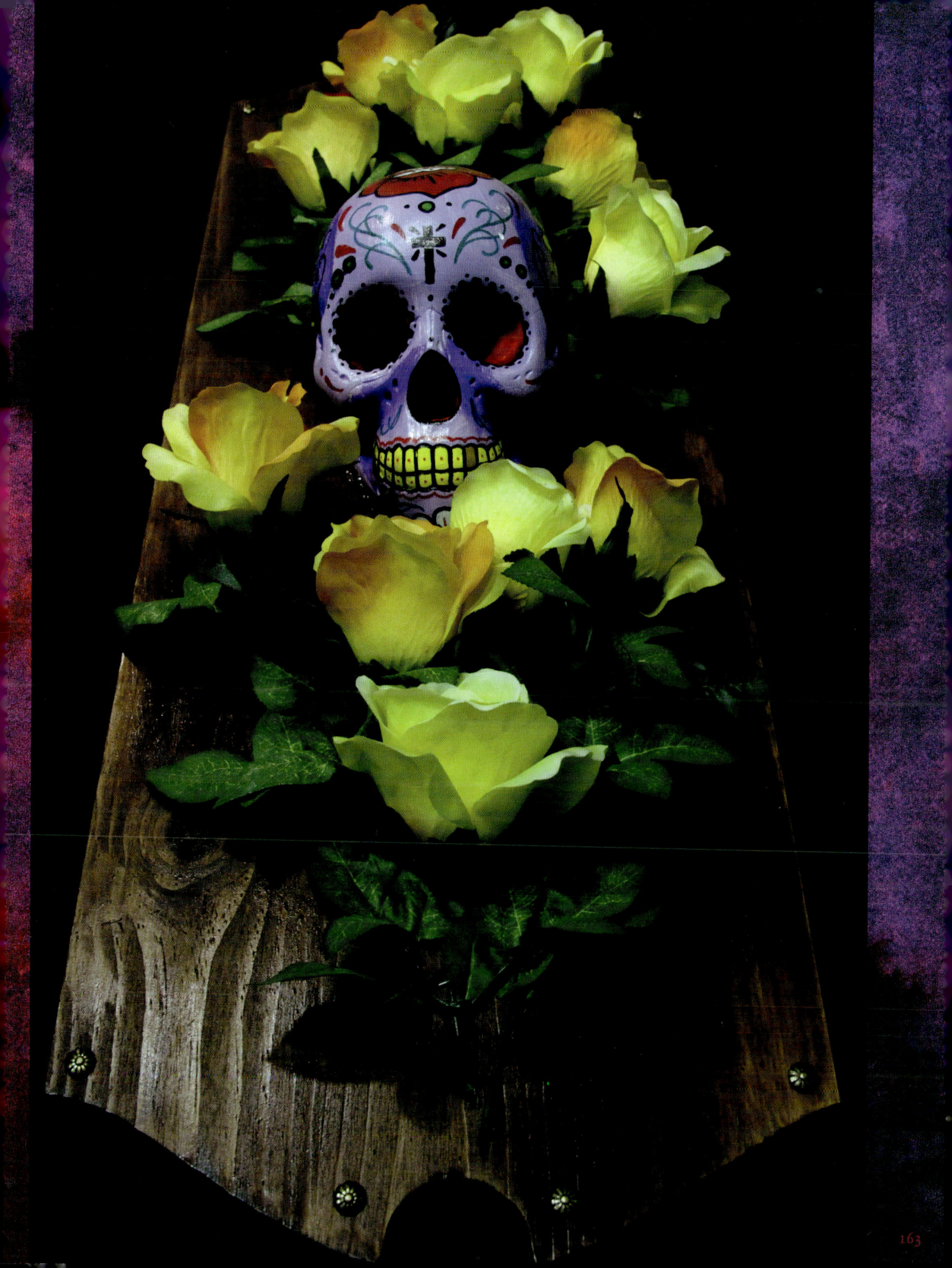

SERRA

BRAZIL / LONDON, UK.

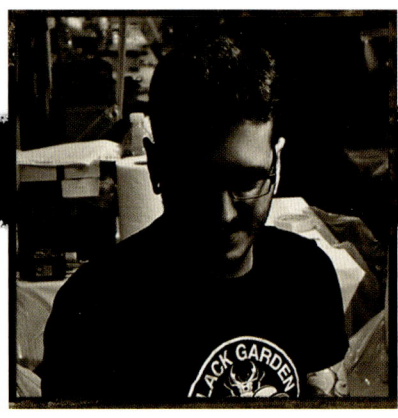

Tutti Serra first dreamt of becoming a tattooist as a kid in São Paulo, Brazil, but didn't put his plan into action until he moved to London aged 20. "I was exceptionally lucky; never did I think I would fall on my feet, but after only a few goes of findng a place to start I came across Cesar Mesquita and Rodrigo Souto in their studio and we became firm friends. After only a few meetings Cesar offered me the opportunity to become his tattoo apprentice. It was one of the best days of my life." Tutti worked fantastically hard at the shop during the day, picking up techniques and tricks, and then in the evenings he would practice on his friends. A few months later he began tattooing full-time and quickly acquired a reputation for his very clean and resolved designs in the American tradition. His mentors observed what a natural Tutti is and Rodrigo, Cesar and Tutti opened a shop together, Black Garden Tattoo. "Almost all of my time is spent tattooing, so I get very little time for art. What I create is not far removed from flash; it's a way of exploring new concepts and resolved designs; I like going for a complete look, to which you couldn't add or take anything away." Of the scene Tutti says: "It's been pumping ever since I became involved, so its hard for me to get a perspective on whether its changed for better or worse. I just know how lucky I've been and really I'm enjoyng the ride, trying to get better and better, but not thinking any more than one week ahead!"

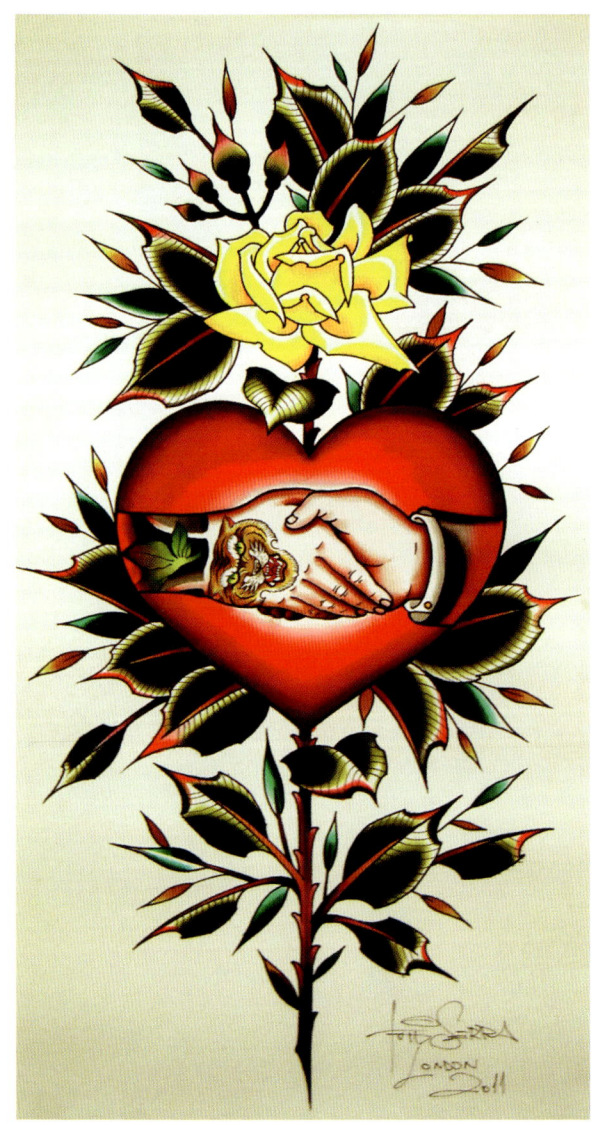

ABOVE: *Rose Heart*. Pen, ink and watercolour.
RIGHT: *Eagle Sioux*. Pen and ink.

OVERLEAF:
LEFT: *Peacock*. Ink on tracing paper.
RIGHT: *Jungle Parrots*. Ink on tracing paper.

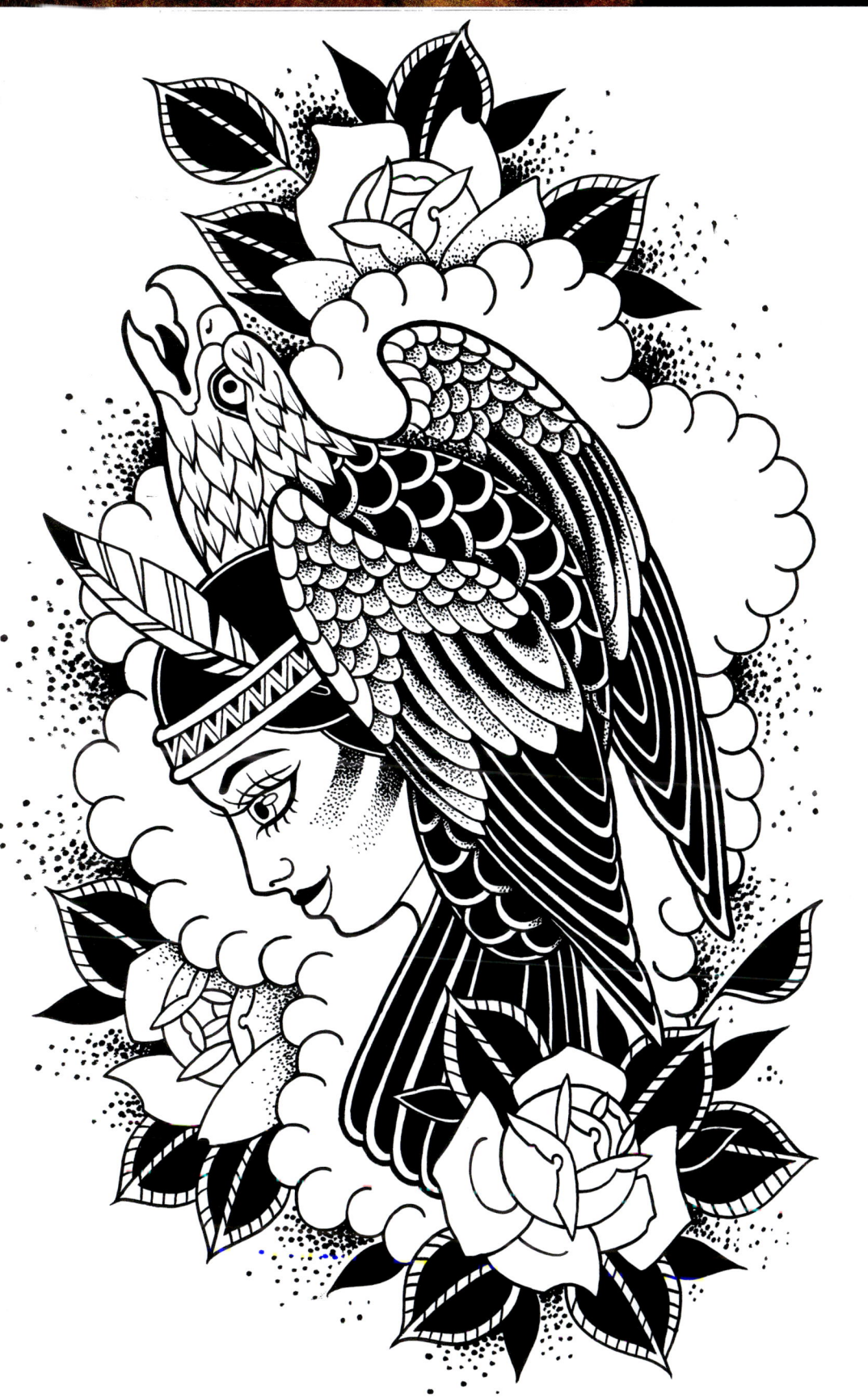

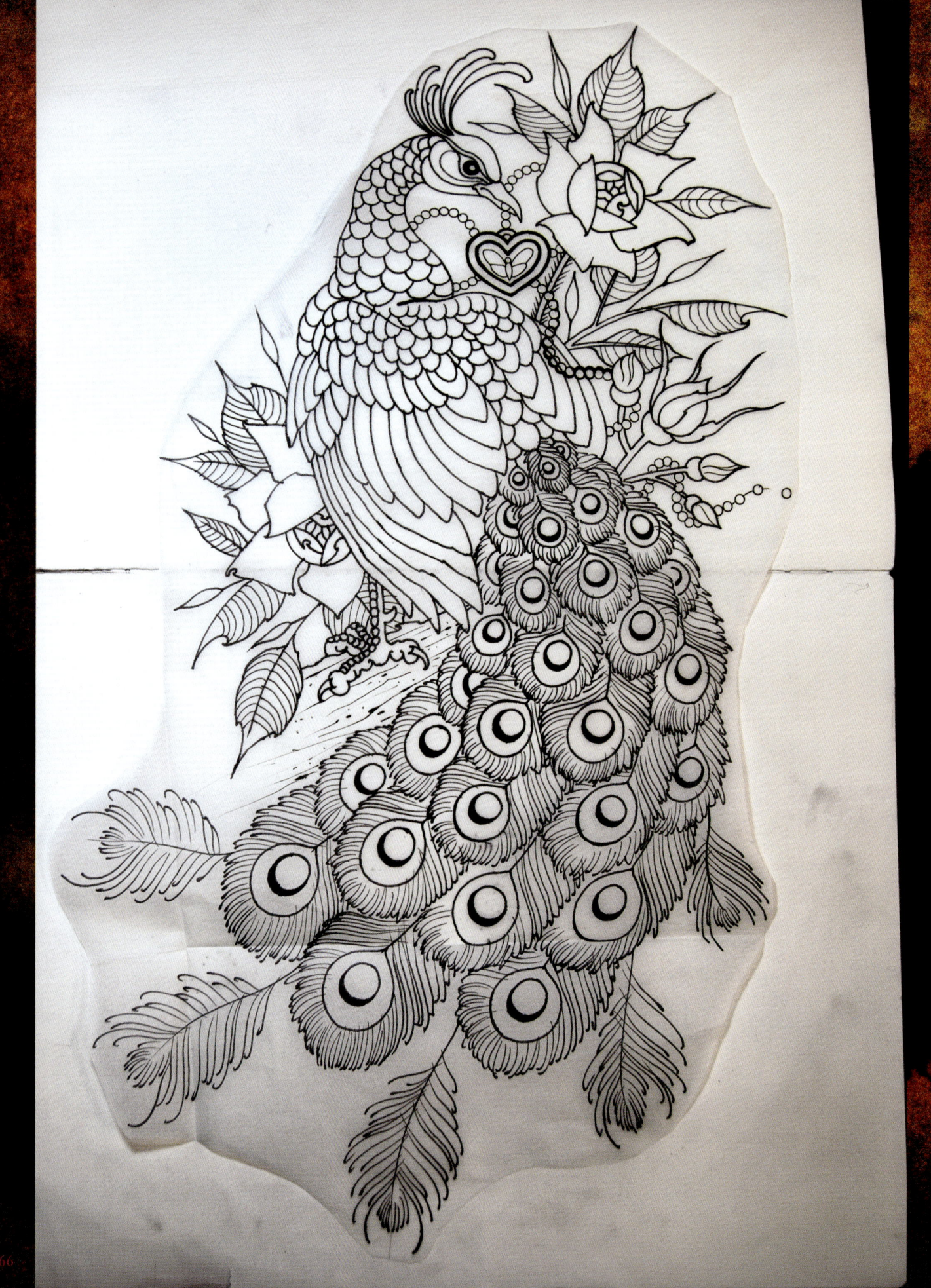

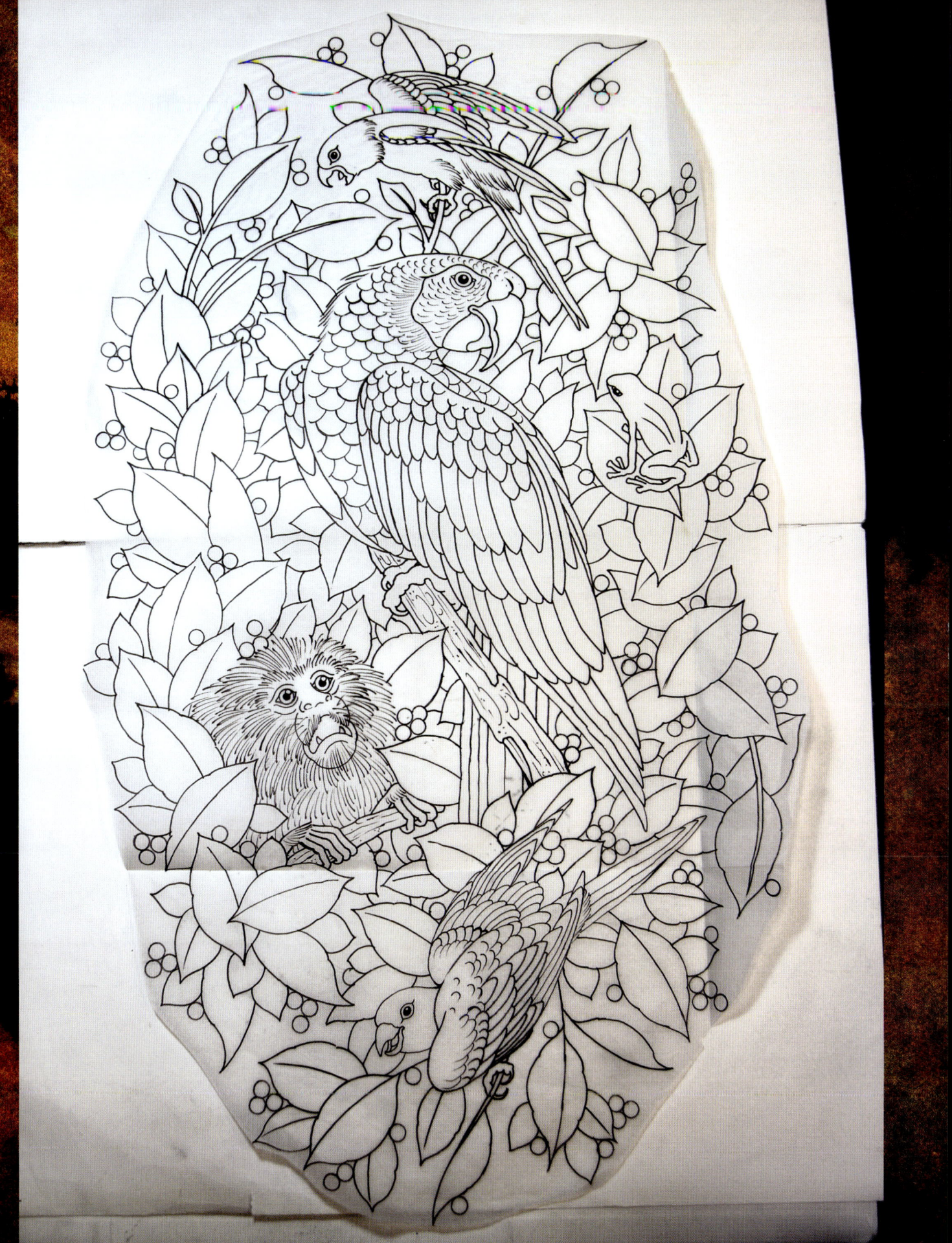

SINNES

LUXEMBOURG.

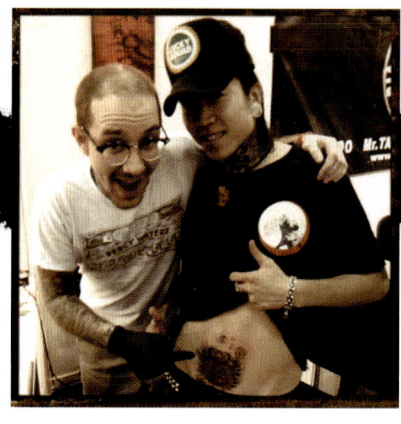

"What I love about this business is that thing of putting my mark on someone else, you know, like a legal tag", says Dan Sinnes. Growing up in the Luxembourg countryside he, rather unusually, apprenticed as an optician. That didn't last long and Dan returned to his early enthusiasm for drawing, became interested in tattooing scripts and Japanese mythology and then got into Shunga tattoo. Off the back of his drawing skills, he managed to get an apprenticeship in a tattoo shop in southern Luxembourg. "Yeah, it was harder in those days than now, finding good supplies and also design ideas as inspiration to develop your own style." Today Dan works from his own shop, Electric Avenue in Luxembourg. "Tattoo is my life, day in and day out. When I find gaps to do some art, it's all for pleasure; it's tough though, to find the time." Dan carries the techniques of tattoo into his artworks, using lining and shading to create the image and finishing in watercolour. For his prints he aims to achieve images with a certain droll humour: a skull made rather less threatening with a woolly hat, a Buddha-type figure with a head like a penis helmet, a serious Germanic heraldic eagle holding a pair of sunglasses in its talons. Influences are "heaps of good tattoo artists" and inspiration comes from "books, tv and travelling – seeing the work of others." Extensively published in tattoo magazines in Europe, the US, Australia and Japan, Dan is pretty calm about changes to the scene. "Yeah, tattoos are a lot more popular and that's good in some ways and bad in others. I'll just keep on tattooing whichever way it turns!"

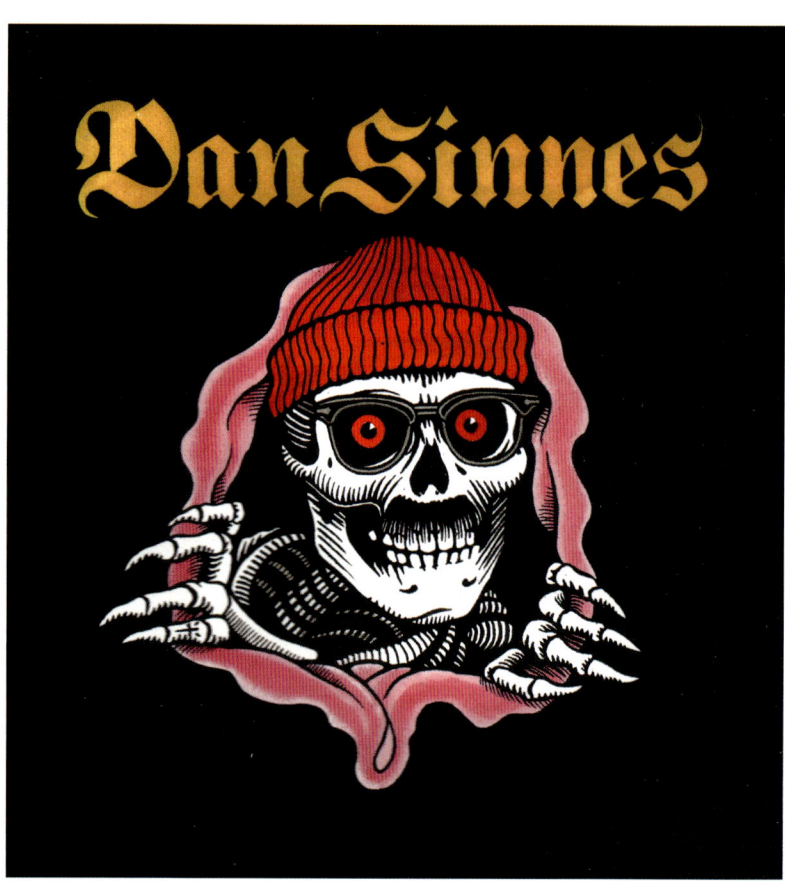

ABOVE: *Boned Sinreaper.*. Pen, ink and watercolour.
RIGHT: *Japanese Kirin (Dragon-horse)*. Pen, ink and watercolour.

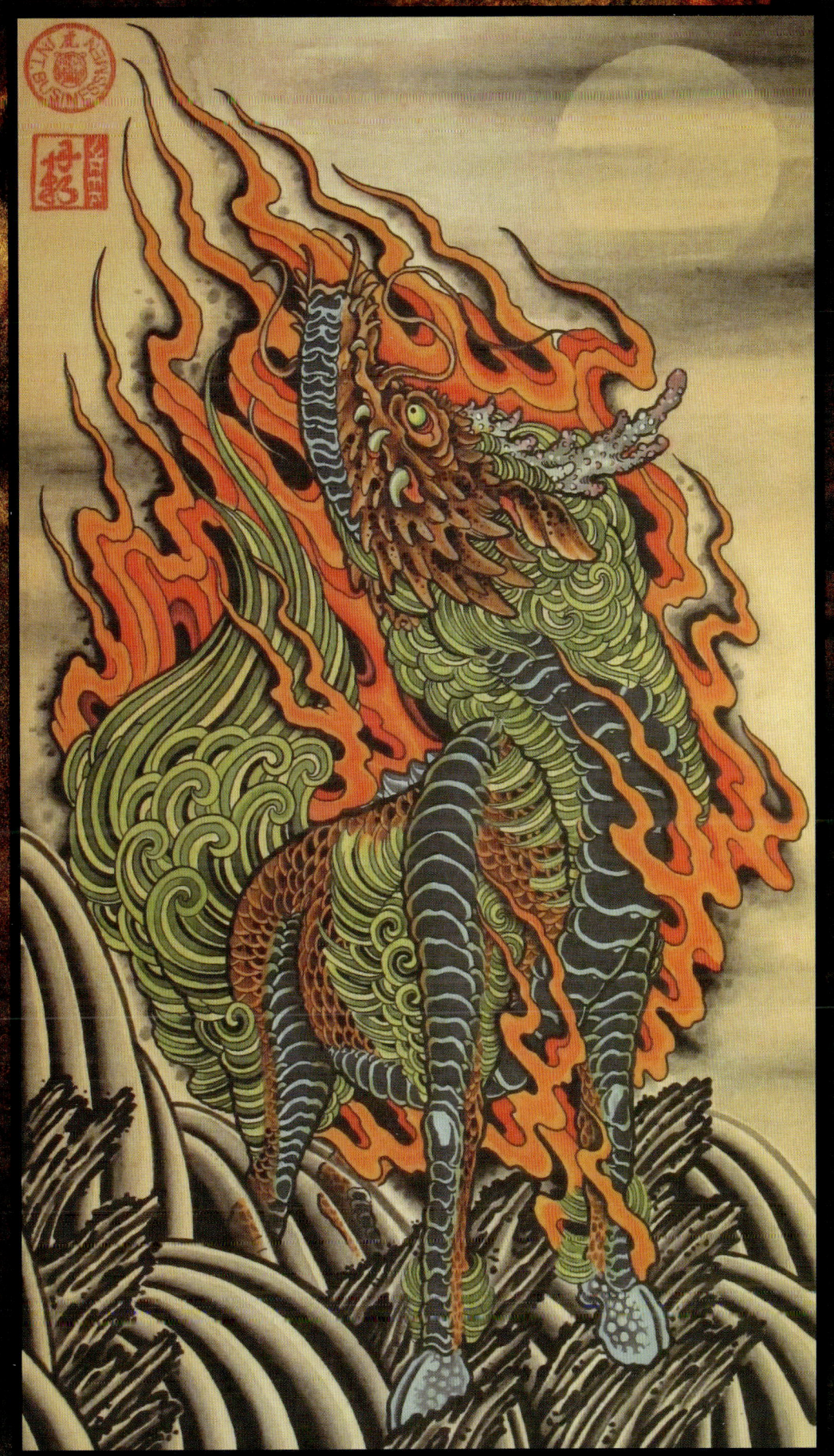

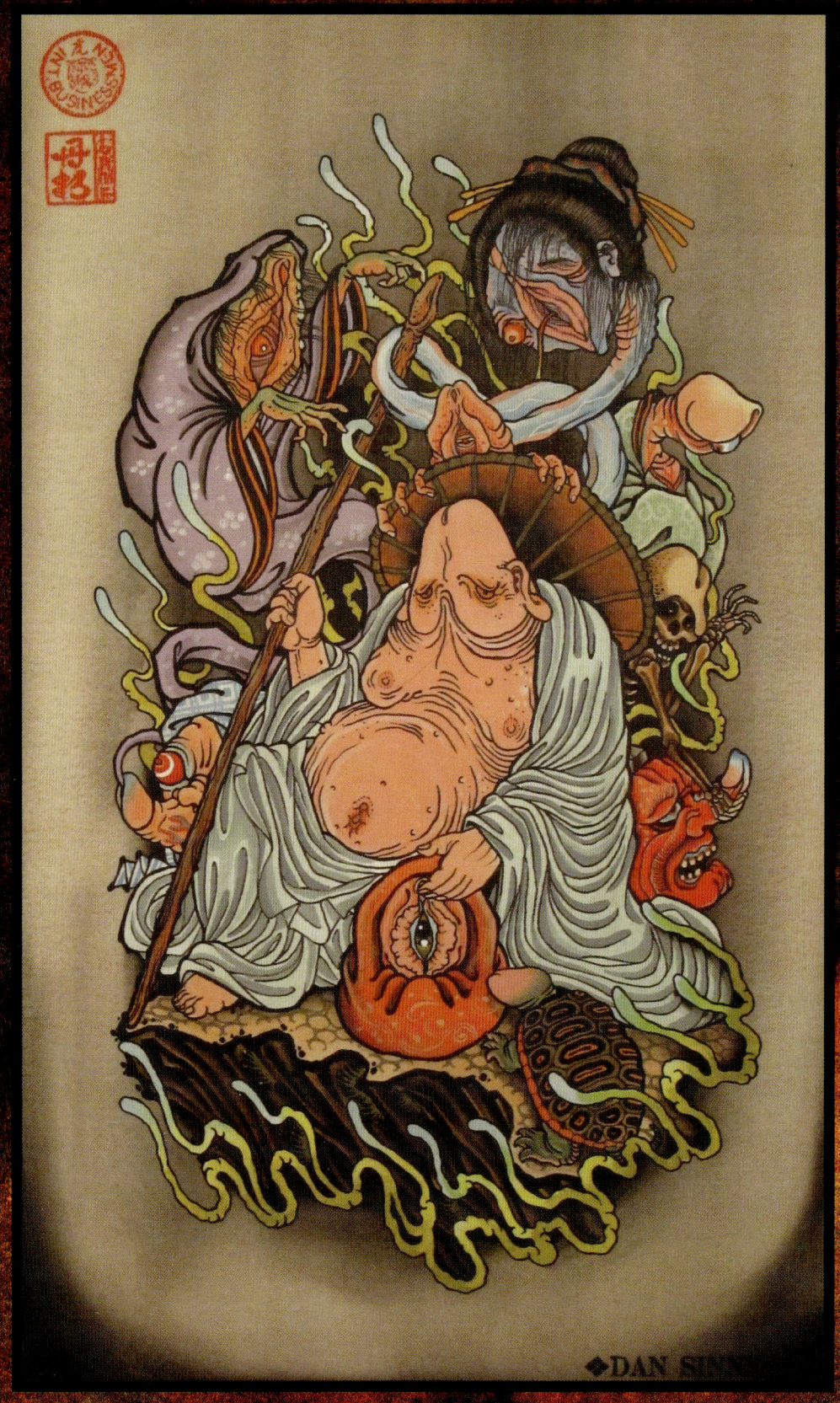

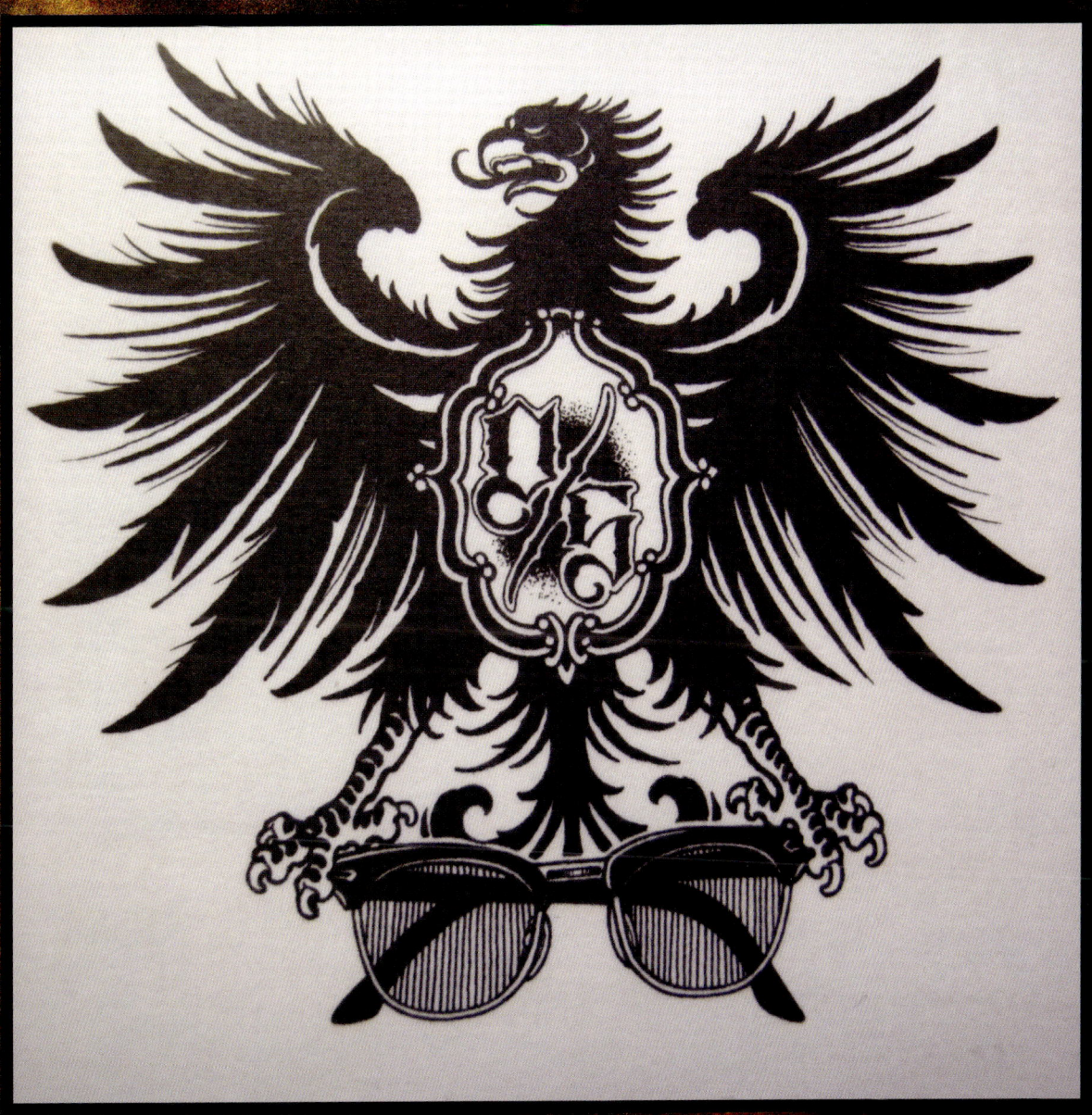

LEFT: *Shungasquad No 1 (Vagina-Penis Painting)*. Pen, ink and watercolour.
ABOVE: *Optical Sin Crest*. Pen and ink.

SMITH

SAN FRANCISCO, USA.

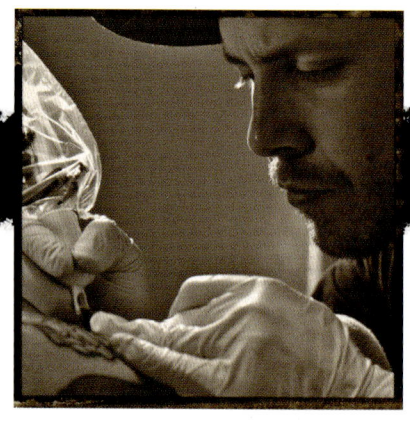

"The way I got into tattooing was definitely the wrong way. I had never intended on becoming a full-time artist. I always enjoyed creating art, had stumbled on this fella tatooing out of his house and I just learnt from him, being flattered that people would let me decorate their bodies with stuff that could last a lifetime. I should have got an apprenticeship, and learnt not just the art but proper sterilization and hygiene. A botched tattoo is nothing compared to some of the diseases I could have given friends and others because of my ignorance." Luckily no one came to any harm and Jesse did get enough experience to devote himself to tattoo full-time after studying illustration at Virgina Commonwealth University. Today he is based at Loose Screw Tattoo in Richmond, where his clients come to get "something a little different from the norm." His style has been hugely influenced by graffiti and lowbrow as well as the traditions of tattoo. Amongst individual artists he cites Greg 'Craola' Simkins, Scribe, Jime' Litwalk, Gunnar, Jason Stephan, Toast and Electric Pick. His techniue involves a lot of layering. "I used to think that a tattoo should be done in one pass, but through painting I learnt that laying down a base of colour gives you a good idea as to what you need to do to the whole piece to create cohesion; having the opportunity to work back into a piece can make a ton of difference." The experience of tattooing has in turn made its way into his art. "When you design for the body, you have to add 'flow' to your work and you have to open up the design so that it's a lot more legible," explains Jesse, "and that has changed the way I paint." The pleasure of creating art is that Jesse doesn't do it to commission, unlike his tattoos, and he can paint "unedited, straight from my brain; I try to keep the art in that space." Jesse's work has been featured in over 50 magazines, books and blogs and he has been exhibited widely, mostly in West Coast galleries. The scene, he says, has changed a ton in the last five years. "There are sooooooo many great artists now; it feels like I stumble upon a new amazing talent every single week."

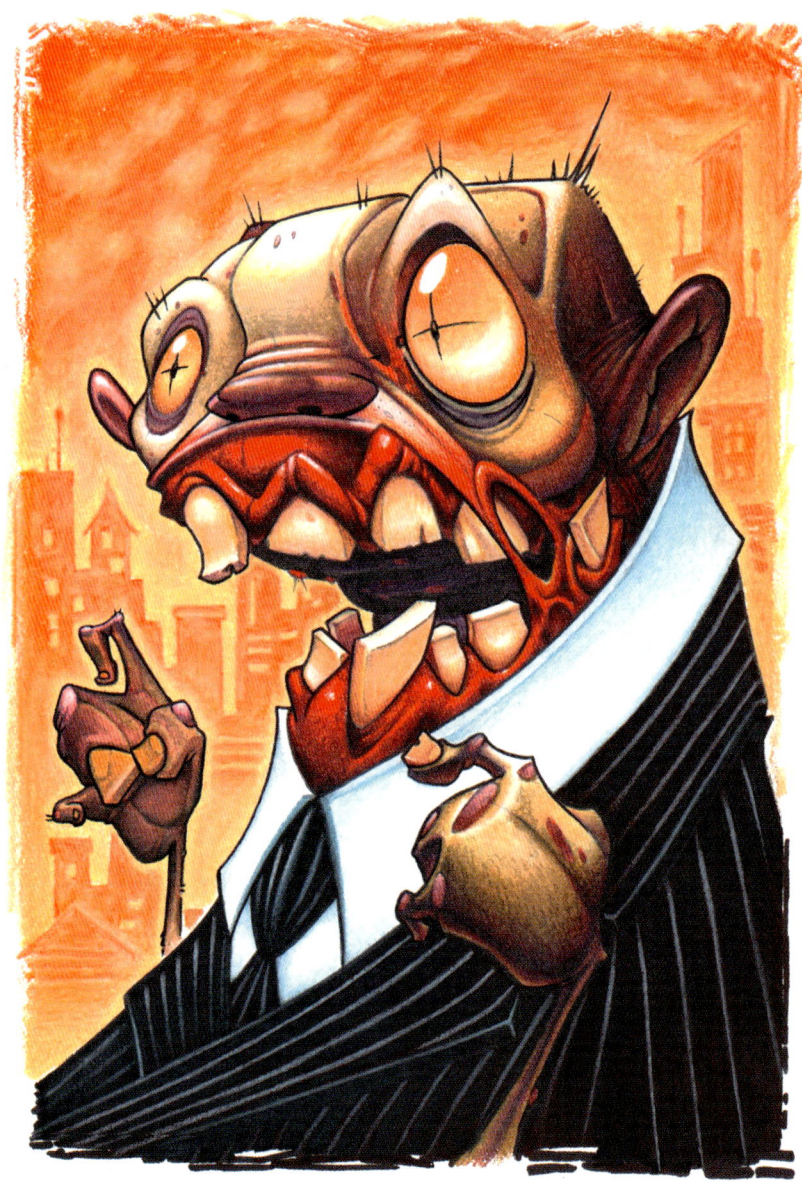

ABOVE: *Quank*. Pen, ink and watercolour.
RIGHT: *Demon Killer*. Acrylic on board.

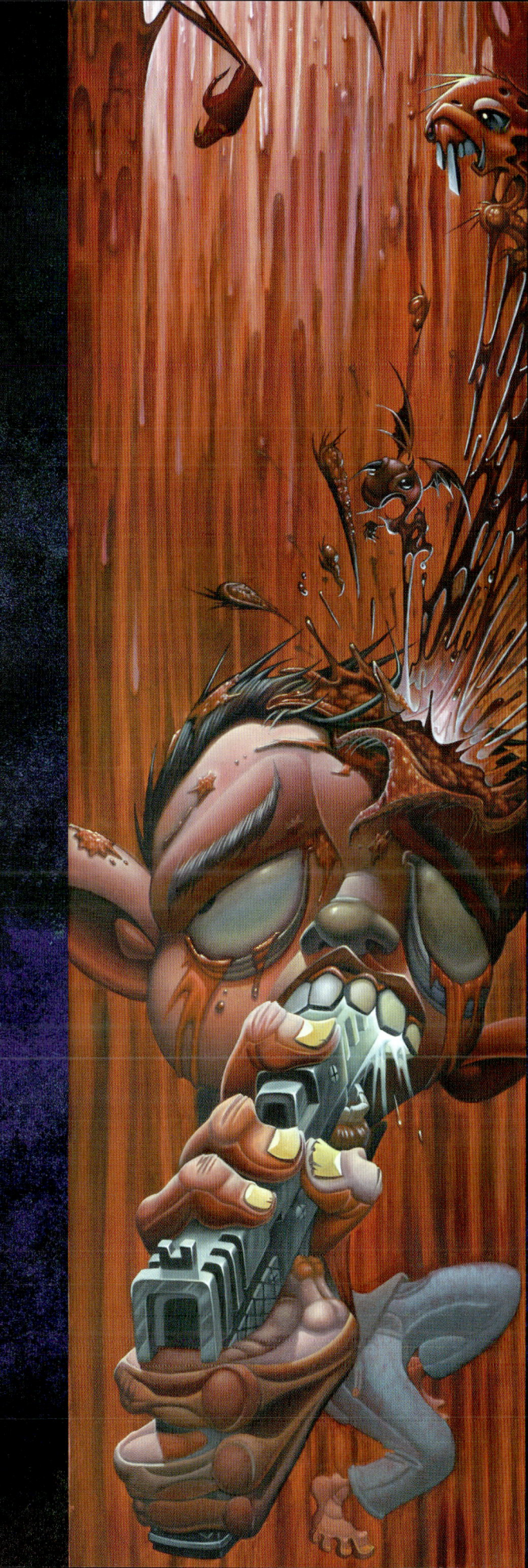

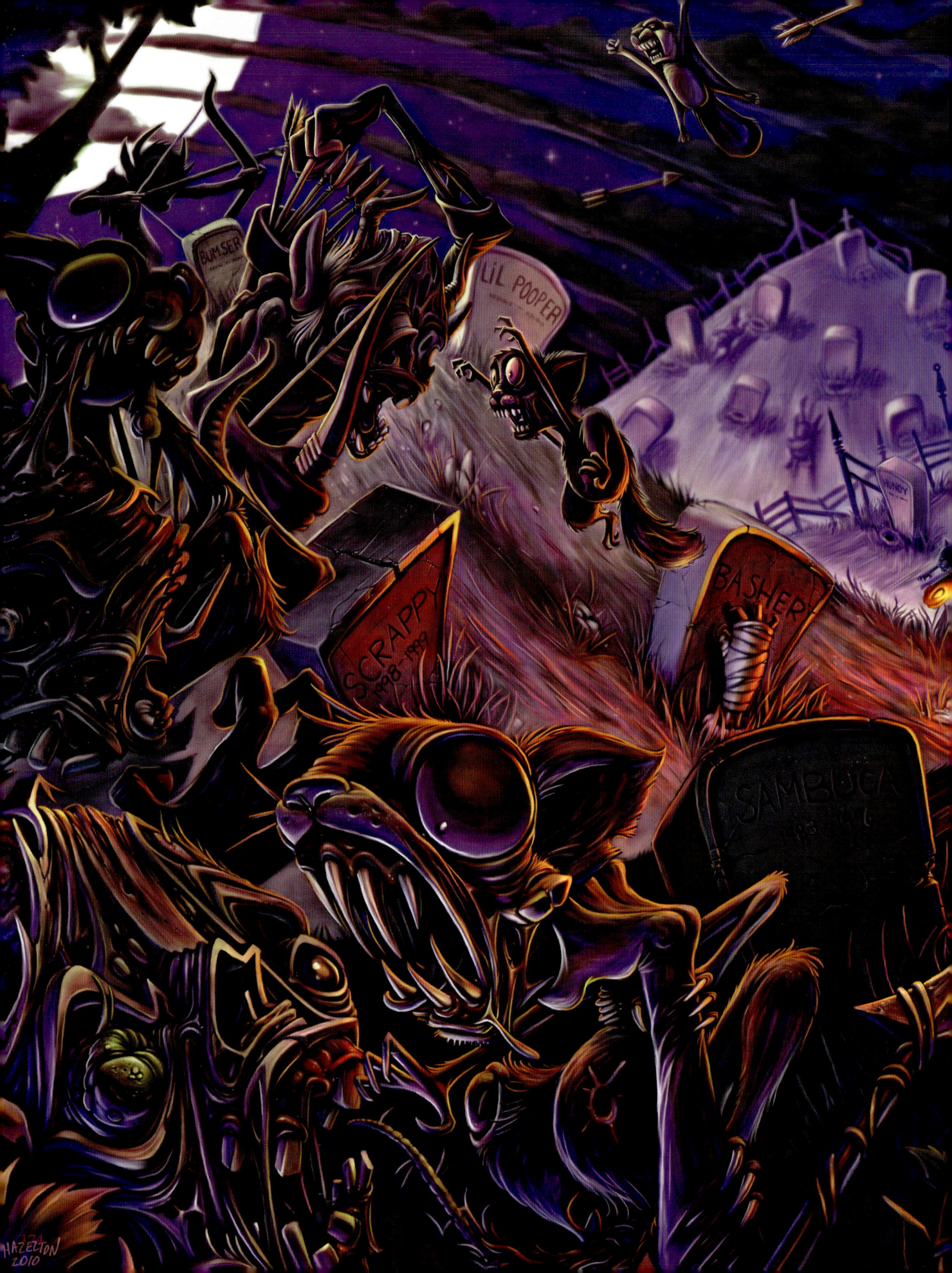

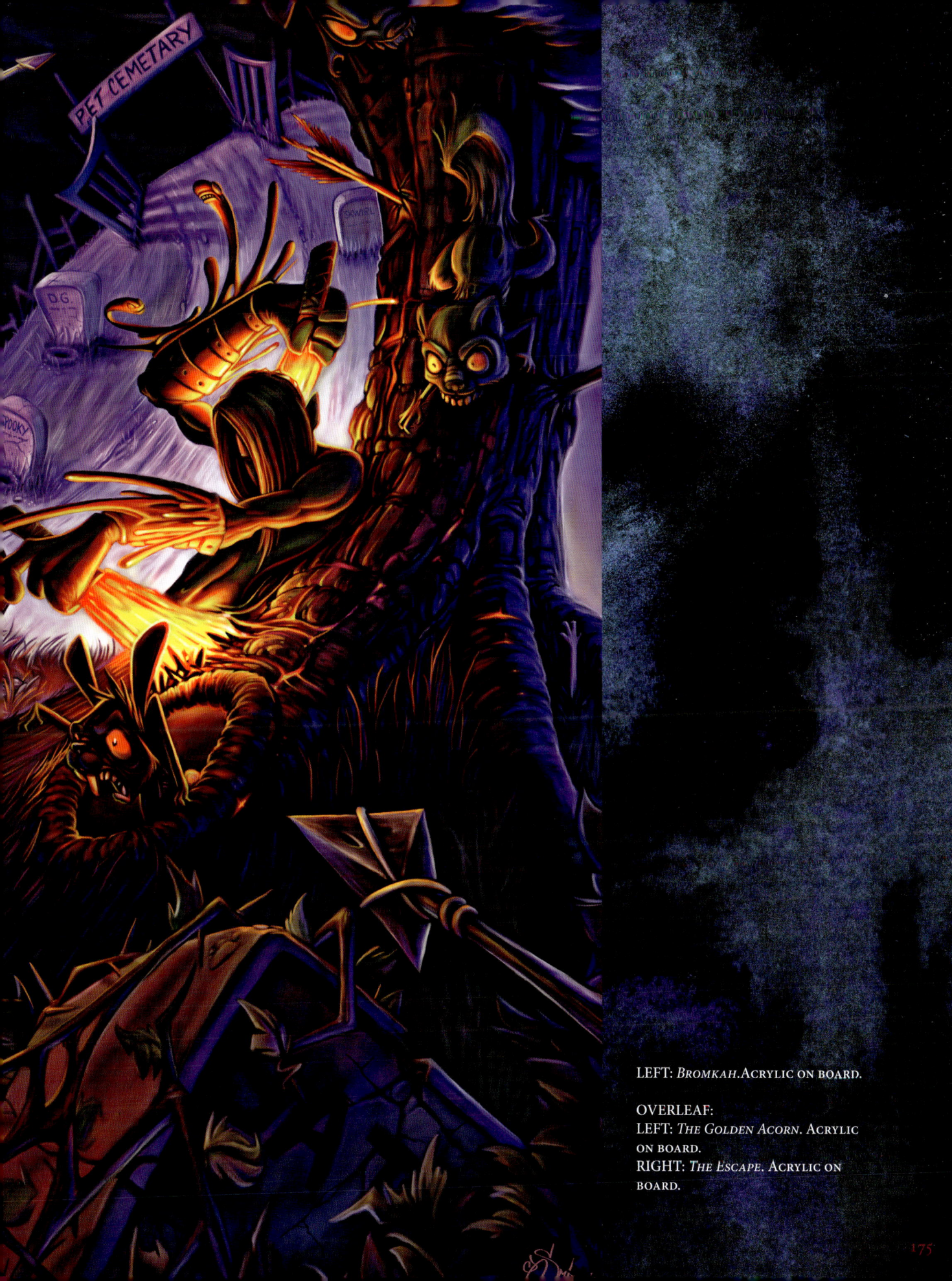

LEFT: *Bromkah*. Acrylic on board.

OVERLEAF:
LEFT: *The Golden Acorn*. Acrylic on board.
RIGHT: *The Escape*. Acrylic on board.

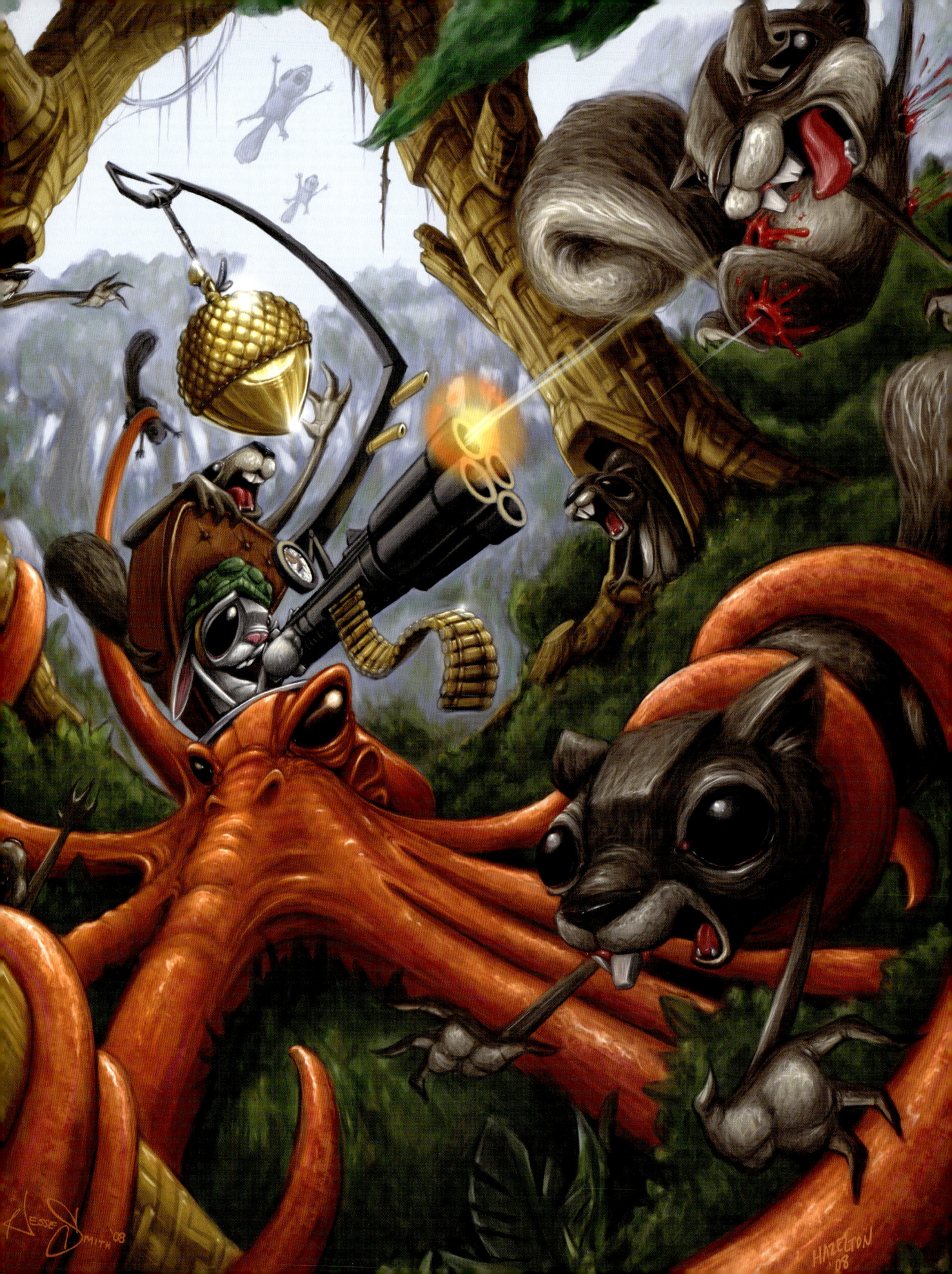

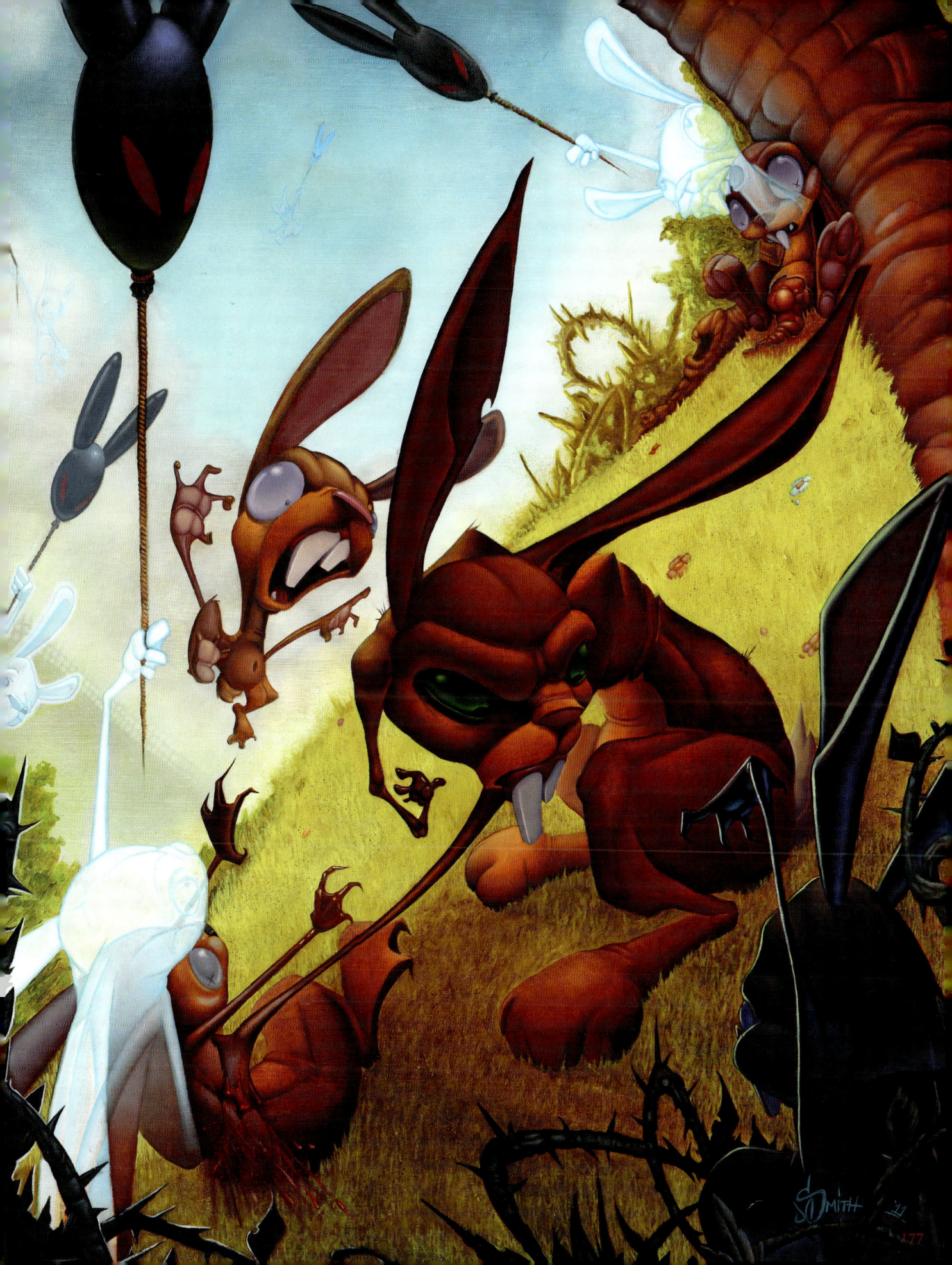

TONELLI

ITALY / LONDON, UK.

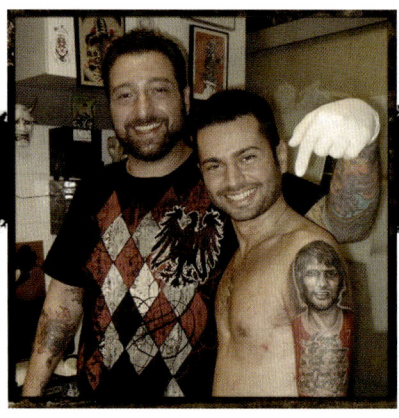

"Like most tattoo artists I liked drawing at high school, loved graffiti art. I'd do the odd t-shirt design. Some of my older friends had tattoos, really bad tattoos I realise now, so it was sort of natural that I should go to a tattoo shop to get one. After that first one, nothing happened. But after the second one something went 'boom!', and I decided I had to start doing this for myself," says Daniele Tonelli. In those days, the old school way of doing things was still the norm: "Tattooing was still a bit more 'masonic' than now. If you didn't know anyone you had to just keep knocking on doors till you got an unexpected stroke of luck." He worked for seven years at various shops in Rome, before moving to London; for the last two years he has been at the renowned The Family Business. Daniele's style is hugely influenced by Japanese iconography, and impacts most of his tattoo and artworks. "But I do want to keep trying new things, so graffiti artists, sculptors, other painters are also an influence....I tend to decide how it's going to go when I wake up in the morning." His materials are watercolours, often mixed with markers or acrylics. Inspiration comes from movies, comics, illustrations and advertising. But not from any specific movements. "I don't like to follow them. I'm not a rockabilly, skin, punk, heavy metal, or fucking whatever kind of guy. If you see me from the outside, I'm just a normal person!"

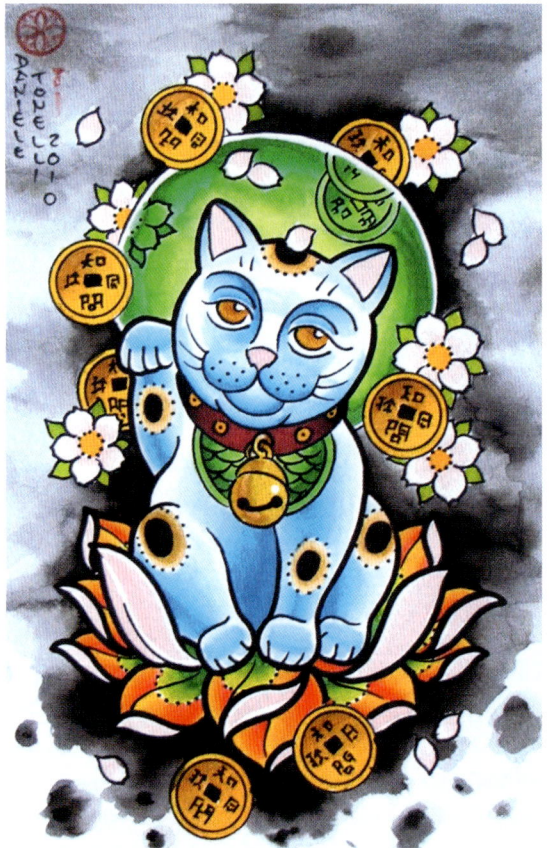

ABOVE: *Manekineko*. Watercolour and markers.

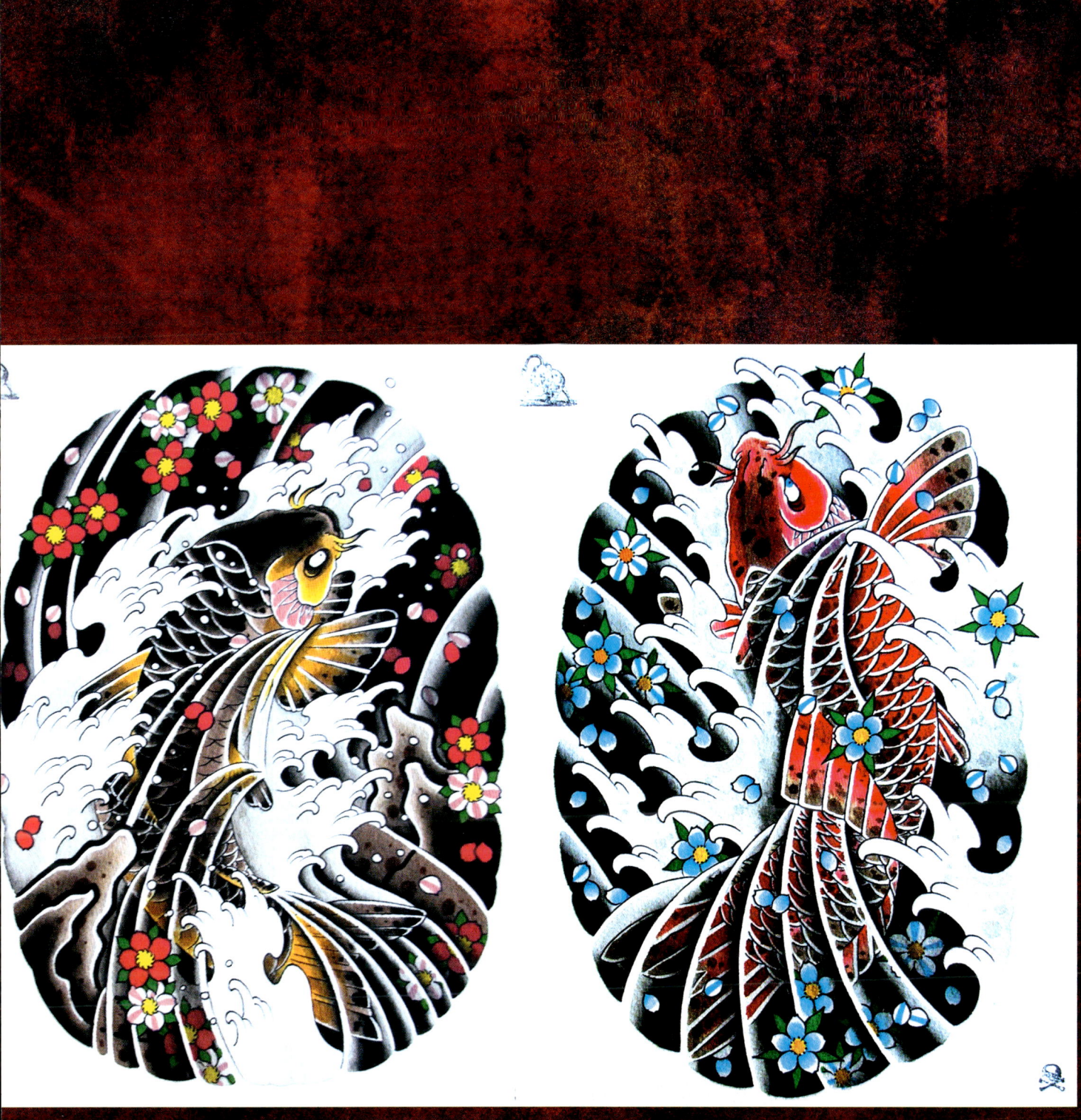

ABOVE LEFT: *Koi Carp and Cherry Blossom II*. Watercolour and markers.
ABOVE RIGHT: *Koi Carp and Cherry Blossom I*. Watercolour and markers.

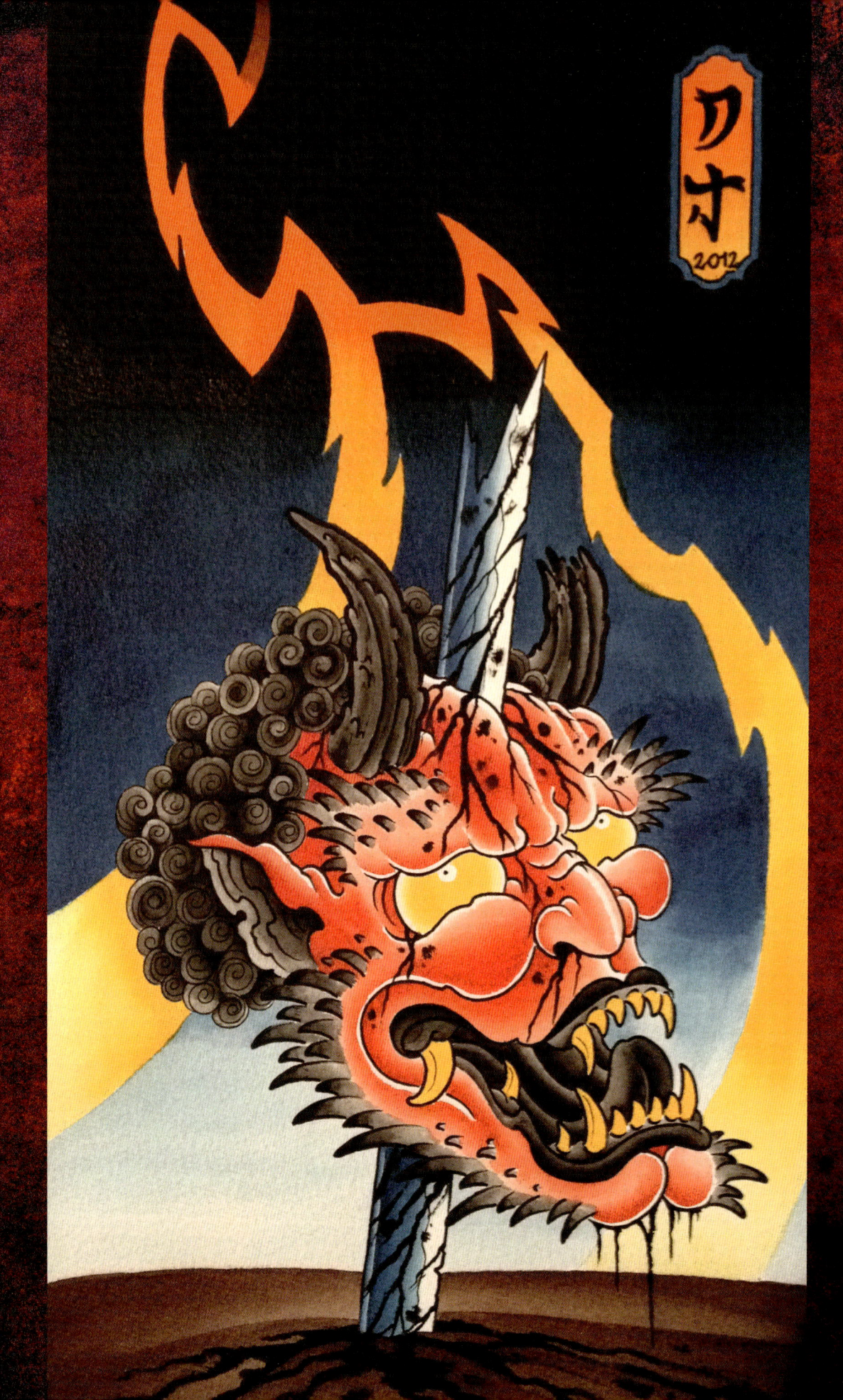

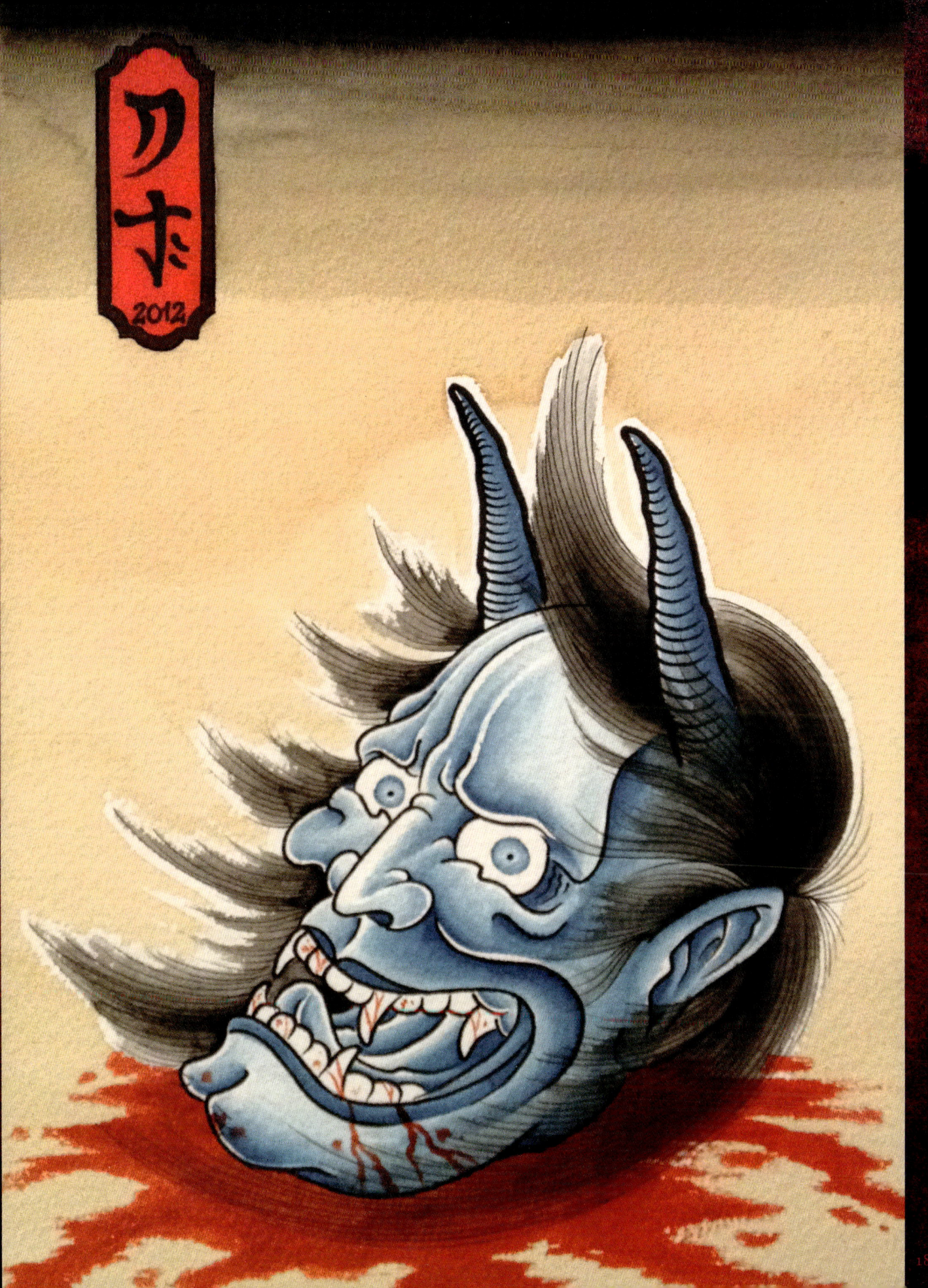

TURYANSKIY

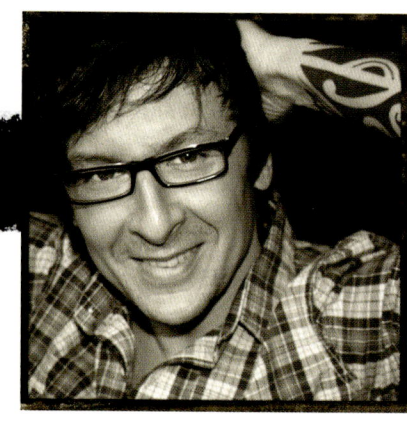

MOSCOW, RUSSIA.

"Youth, ambition, hunger to explore a new world... that's what led me into tattooing", says Oleg Turyanskiy. He started in 2001; "As all tattoo artists will tell you, the first years are tough. And some things don't stop being really tough, like drawing fine lines. Shadowing I always found quite straightforward, but the art of the fine line is a non-stop battle with different machines, needles, tattooing speeds. Even when the results look great I am still not satisfied!" Oleg is hugely inspired by the scene and the sheer talent of other artists. The latter he says "keep me motivated to do better. I try to transform the envy I feel into a positive force." When it comes to influences, the artists he cites are Shige, Jee Sayalero, Jesse Smith, Jeff Gogue, Genko and Sabado; "with all those guys you can just tell the work from the image, without having to read a caption." Tattoo has had a major impact on his painting: "Not only does it affect my vision, how I see the image, but I can't help using tattoo tricks and techniques." The only regret is that the sheer weight of work allows little time for his art. "Painting is the ultimate pleasure and I have to find a way of doing more; it's also great and challenging working to commission." Extensively published (*Skin Deep*, *Total Tattoo*, *Tattoo Fest*, *Tattoo Life*, *Tattoo Energy*, *Skin & Ink*, *International Tattoo Art*...the list goes on), Oleg is also a frequent traveller to conventions in London, Brussels, Milan, Berlin, Helsinki, Richmond VA and Pittsburgh. He reflects on the growth of the scene: "It's been exponential recently, but still keeps expanding. Tattoos are everywhere you look – not just on the street, but in movies, music videos and tv shows. It's now unquestionably one of the most vibrant art forms worldwide."

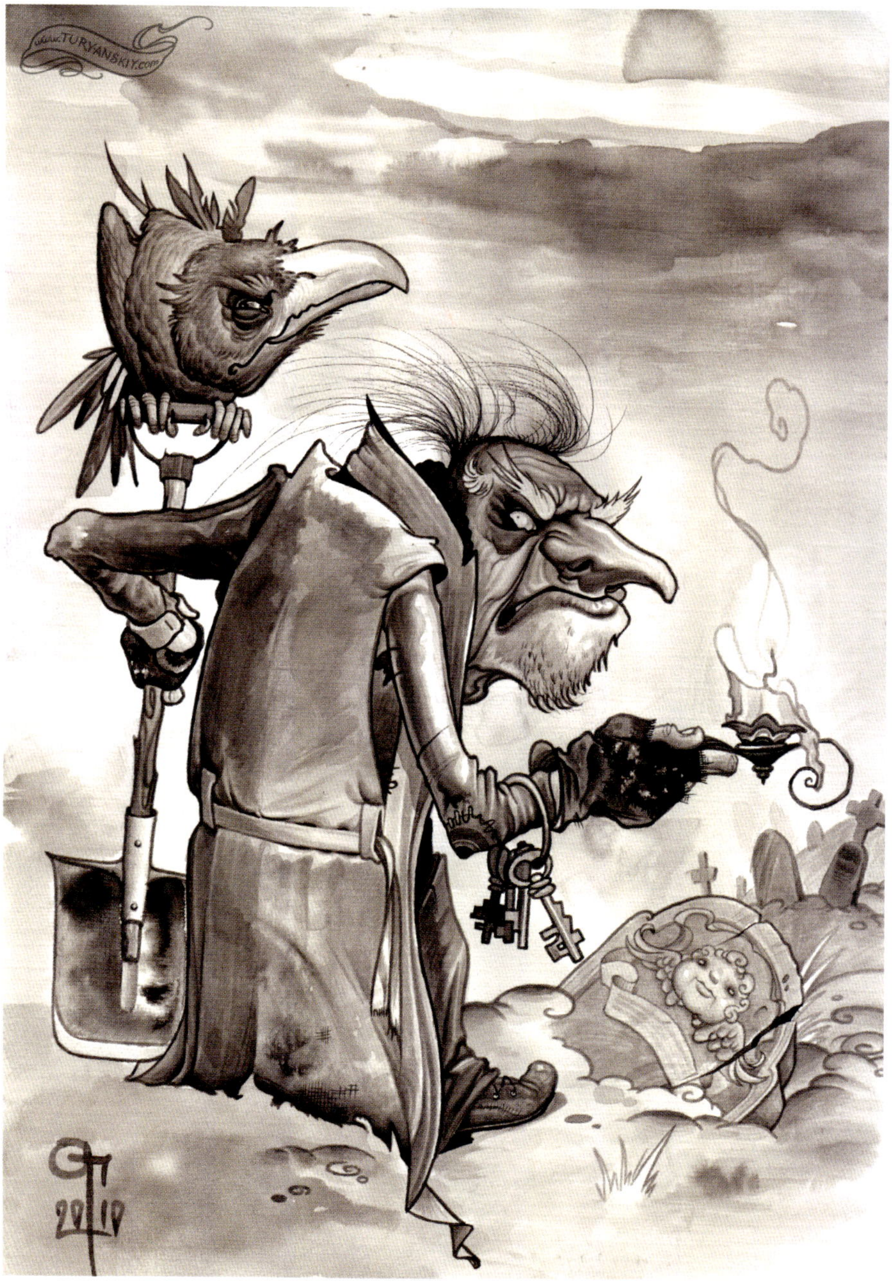

ABOVE: *Cemetery Man*. Pen and ink.
RIGHT: *Knock-knock*. Pen, ink and watercolour.

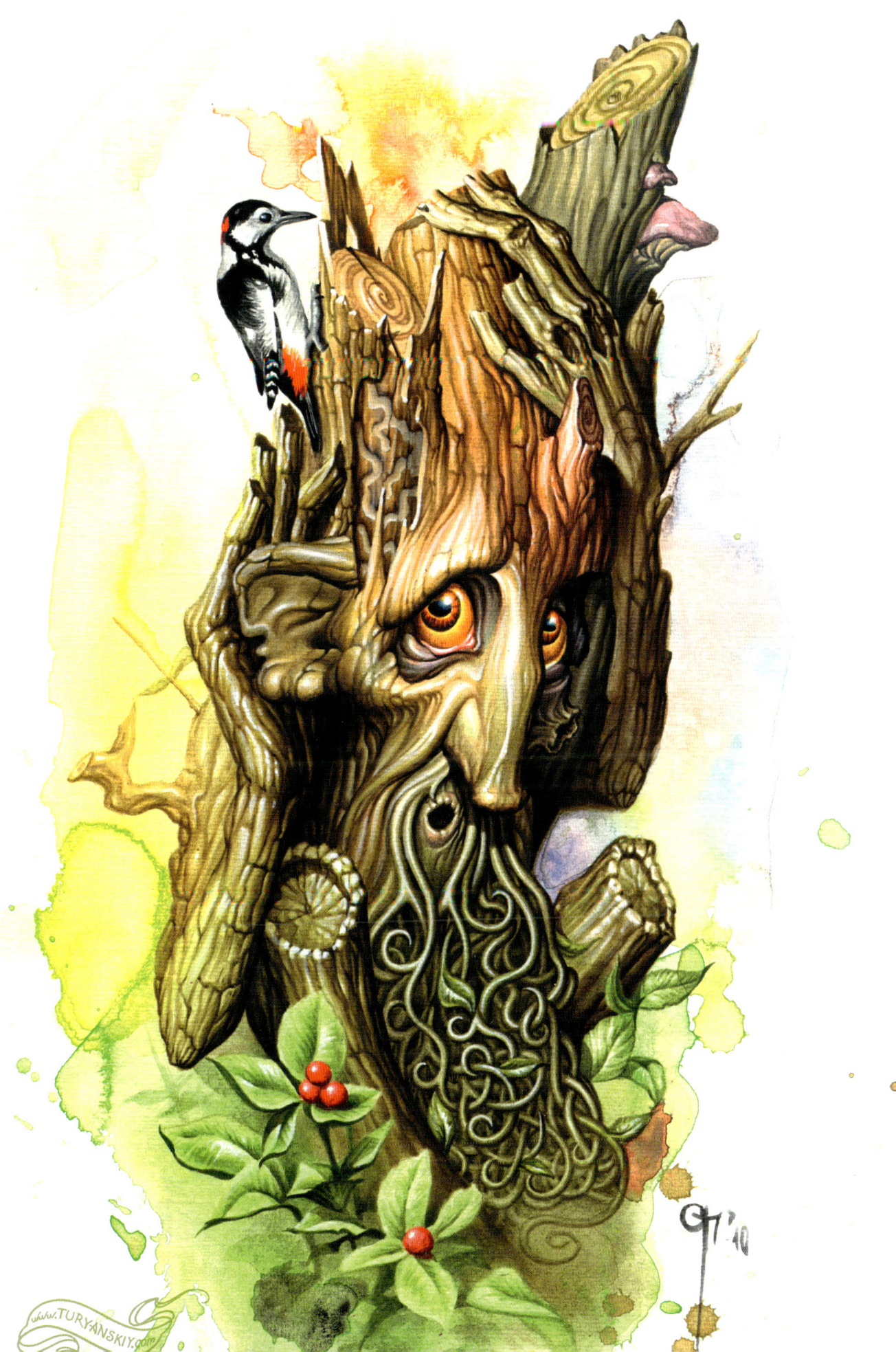

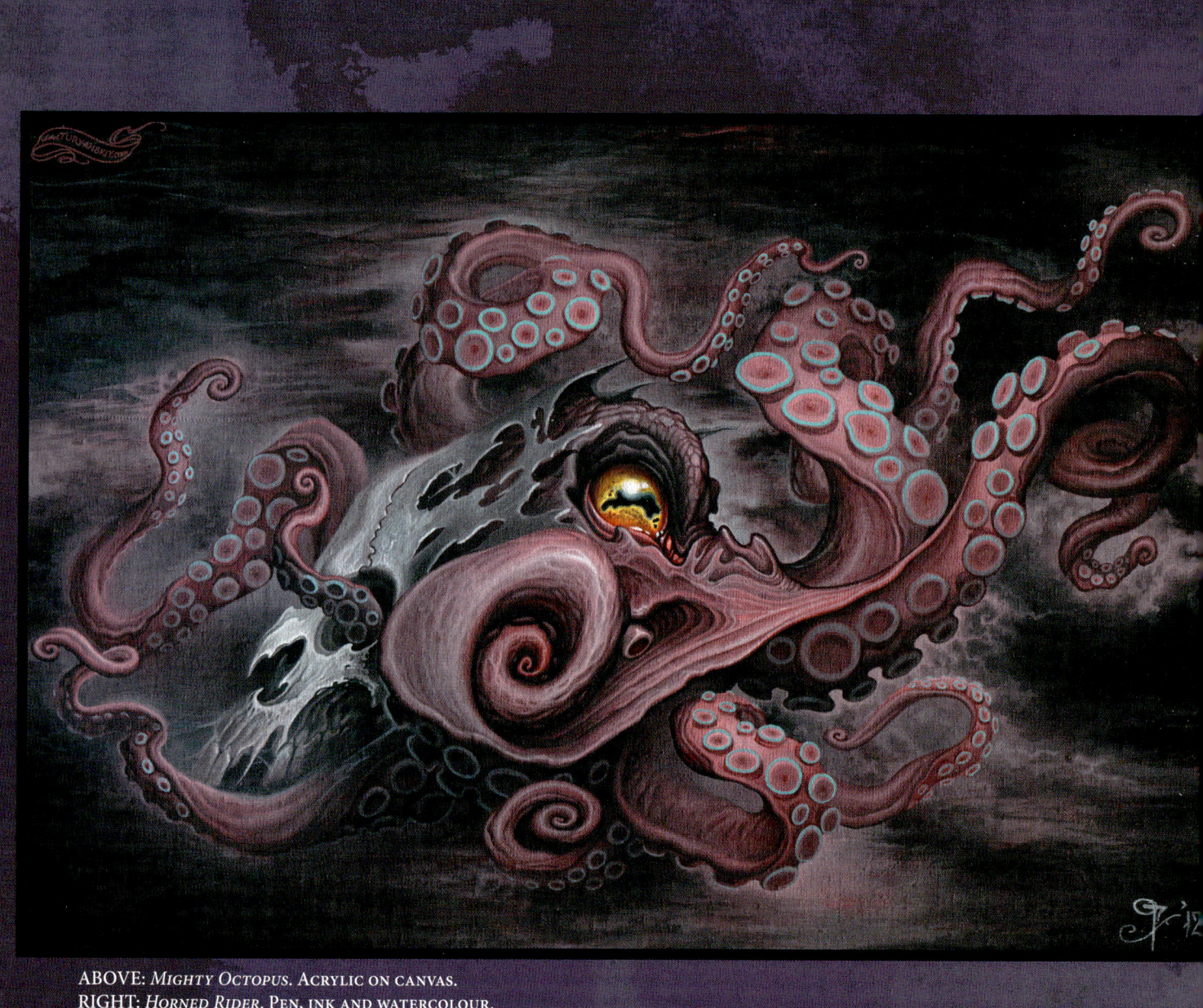

ABOVE: *Mighty Octopus*. Acrylic on canvas.
RIGHT: *Horned Rider*. Pen, ink and watercolour.

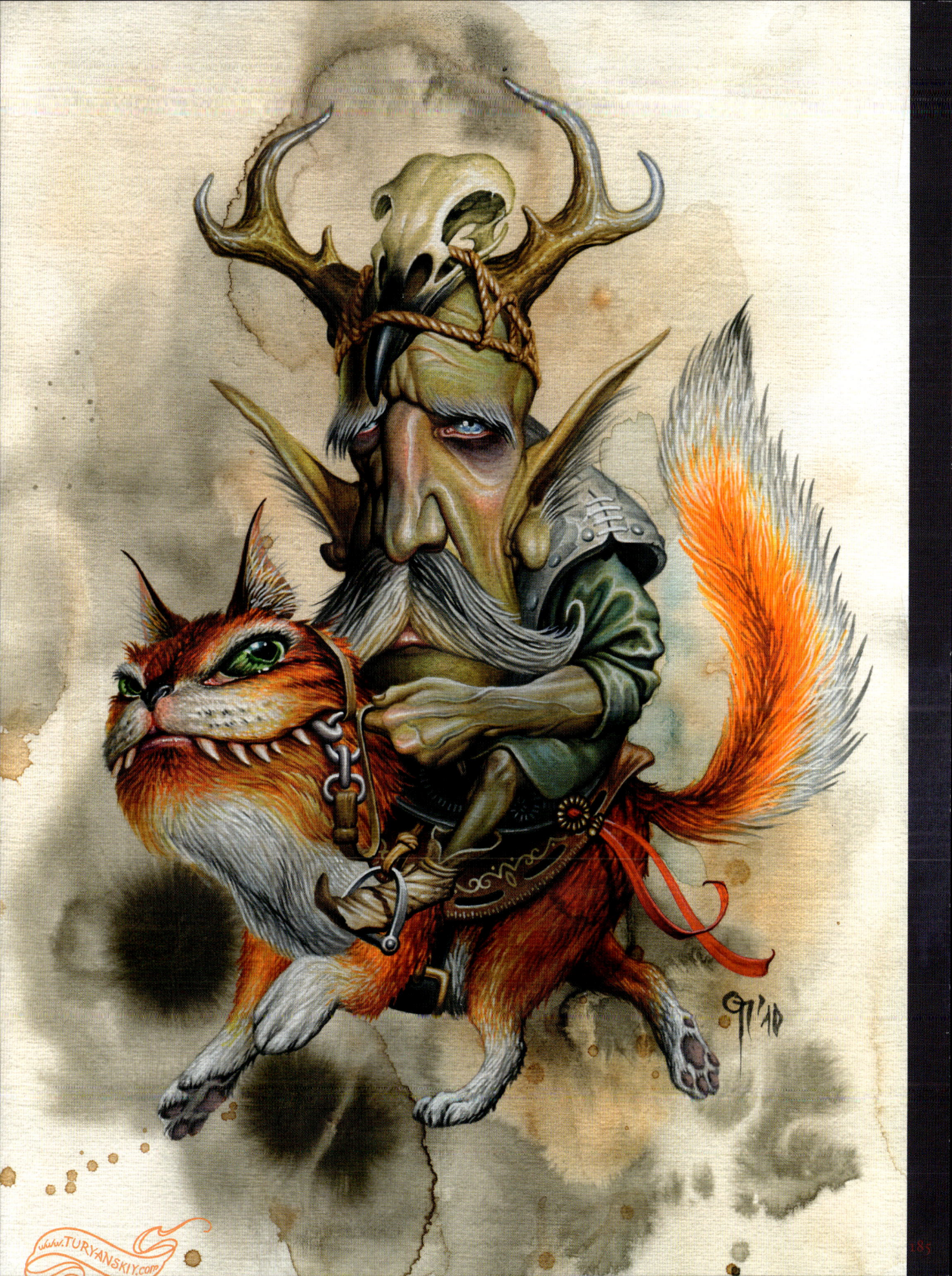

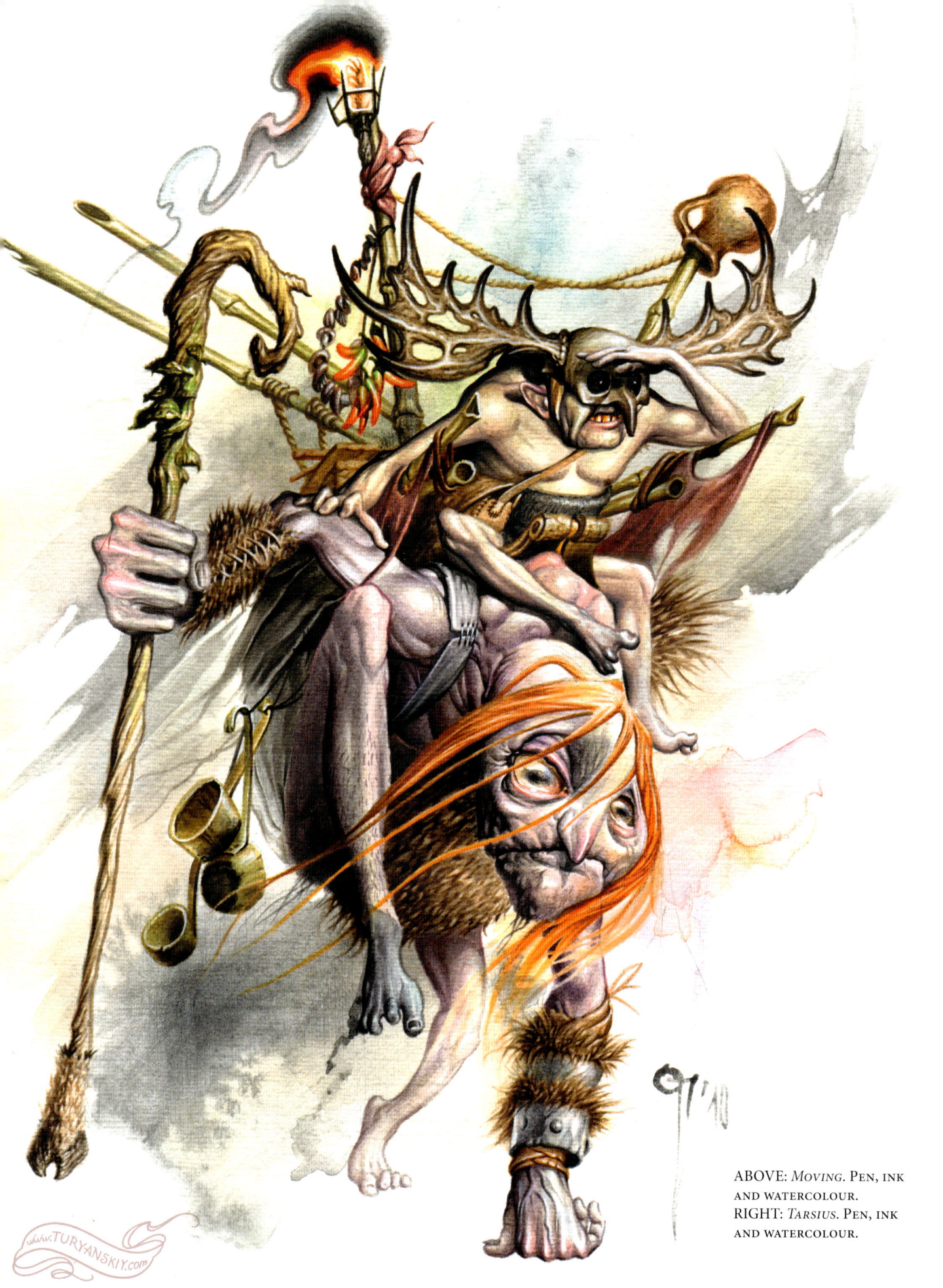

ABOVE: *Moving*. Pen, ink and watercolour.
RIGHT: *Tarsius*. Pen, ink and watercolour.

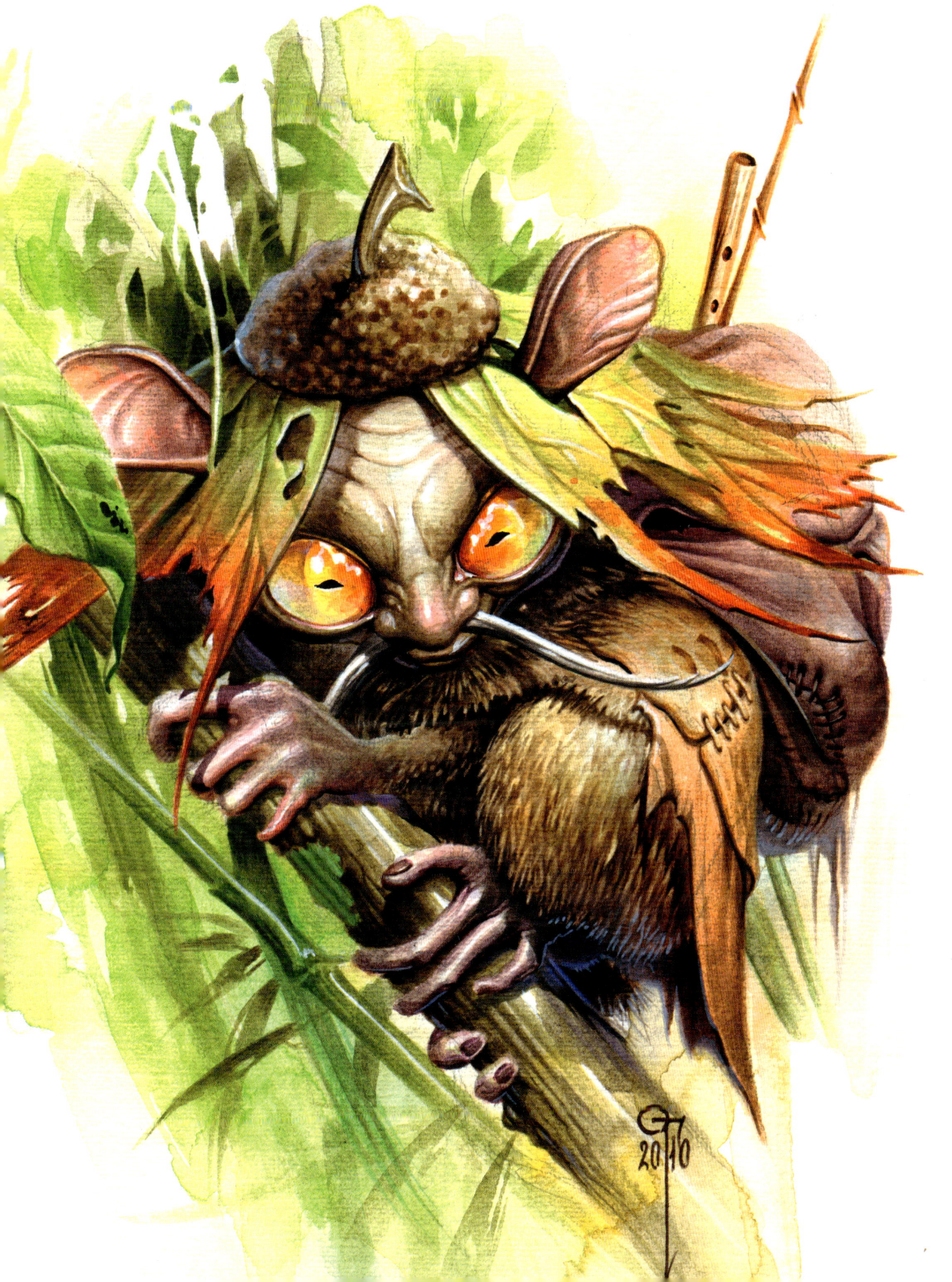

UNCLE ALLAN

DENMARK / BERLIN, GERMANY.

"At school I was into hard rock and heavy metal. The bands were often tattooed and I started drawing tattoos for my classmates, buying as many magazines for inspiration as I could find" says Uncle Allan, of his early days in Copenhagen. He was lucky with his apprenticeship at Syndicate Tattoo in the city. "I just walked in with my black book filled with drawings and pictures of my graffiti not knowing what to expect. The tattooer had a look and, after a few minutes, asked if I wanted to become his apprentice." That was a great break, but it was a tough introduction: "Learning the trade the hard way is still the best however." After a few years at Syndicate (later Copenhagen Body Extremes), Uncle Allan and another tattooer at the shop opened Tiki Lounge Tattoo (later Conspiracy). Uncle Allan was subsequently joined by Electric Pick, and finally it was Uncle Allan and his wife who owned the business, which they run to this day. When it comes to his art, Uncle Allan says: "It took me a long while to loosen the influence of tattoo – you know that straight, precise style – on my other work. I now want to explore new styles, go in different directions. I am planning a whole sequence of new work which will focus on the erotic." His influences are broad: "Other tattooists, of course, but also Alphonse Mucha in particular." Always into his music, Uncle Allan has recently been listening to black metal. "The imagery, the moods, as well as the sounds," have inspired a whole series of paintings, which he exhibited at the renowned Lionheart Gallery in Oberhausen, Germany. Of the scene he says "I hope that the hype around tattooing will die off a bit. There are some amazing new talents popping up which is great. Meanwhile I will carry on what I'm doing in peace and quiet – that's what will keep me happy."

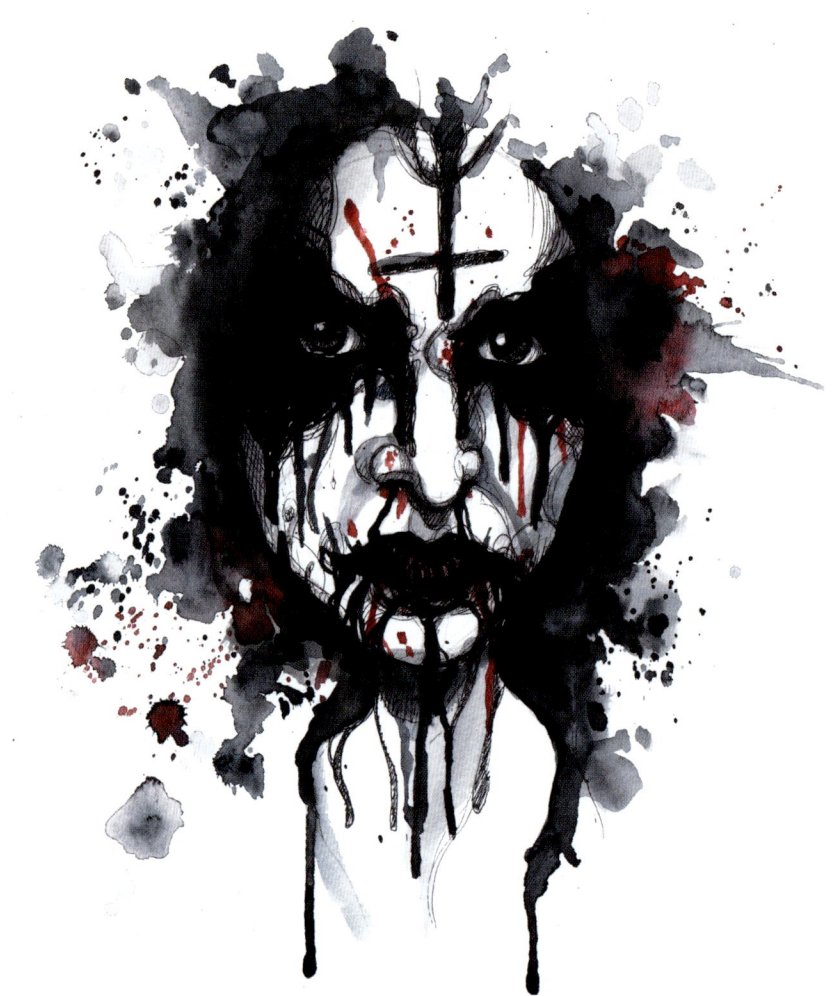

ABOVE: *Untitled*. Watercolour and marker pens.
RIGHT: *Untitled*. Watercolour, coloured pencils and marker pens.

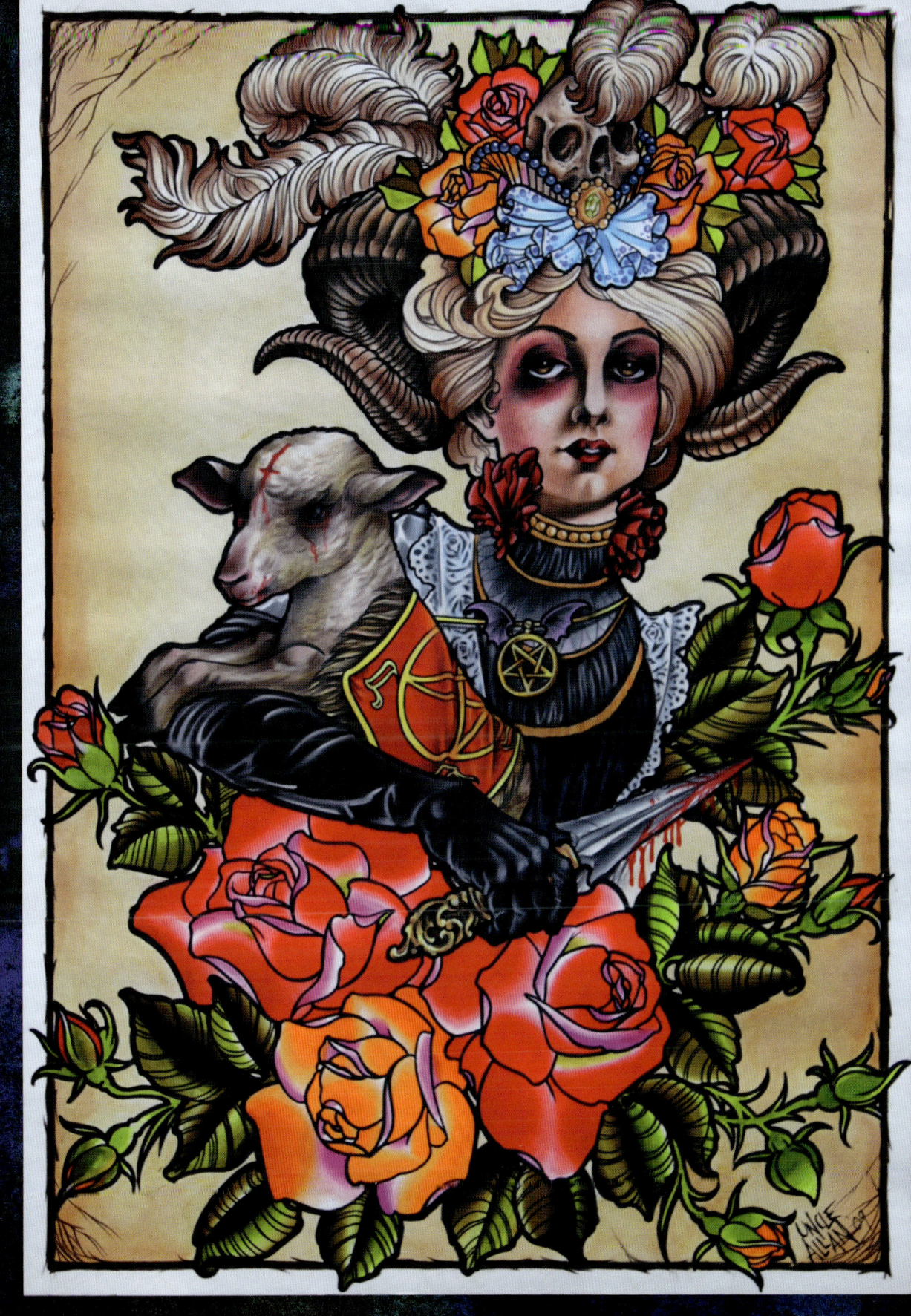

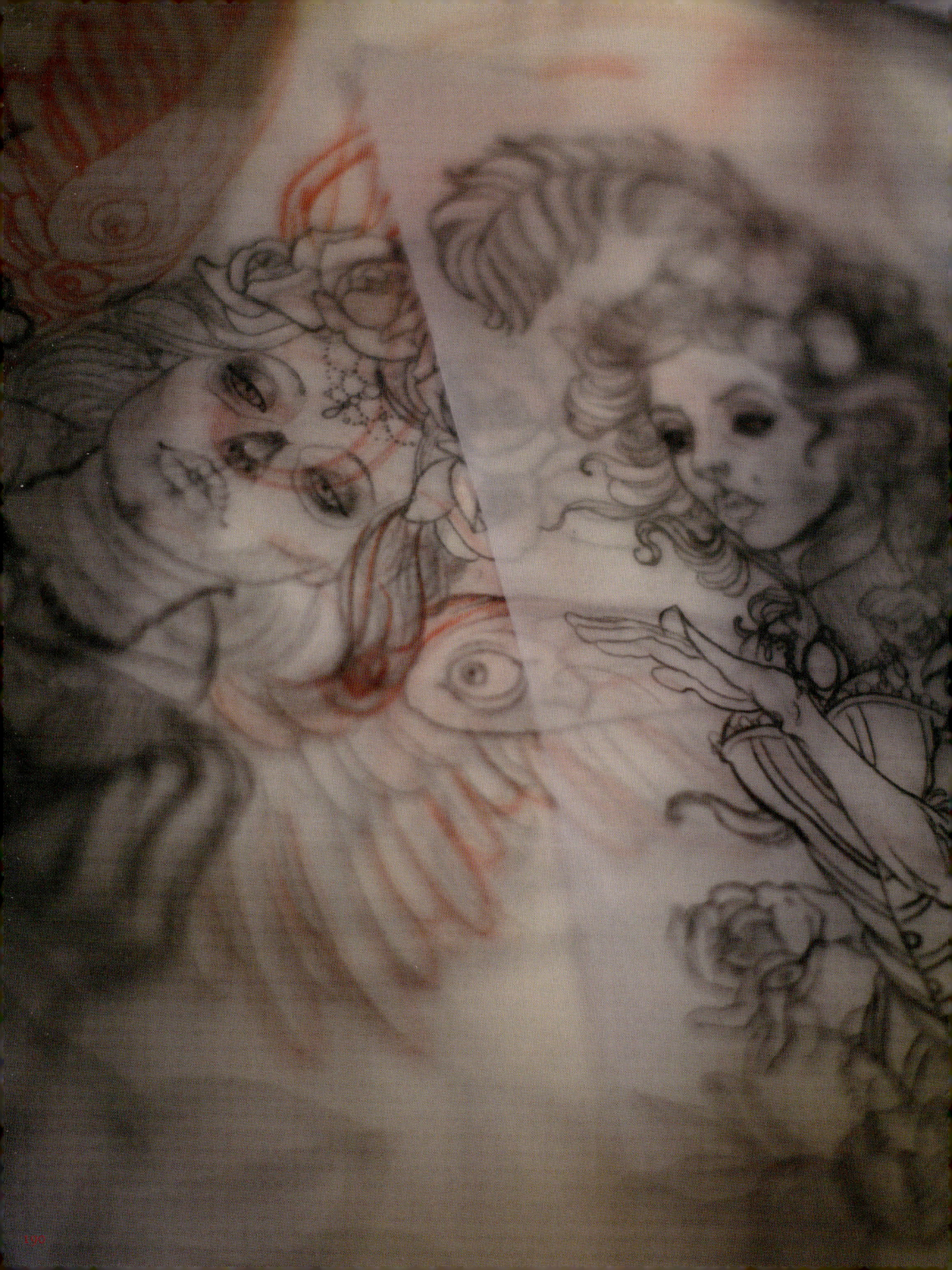

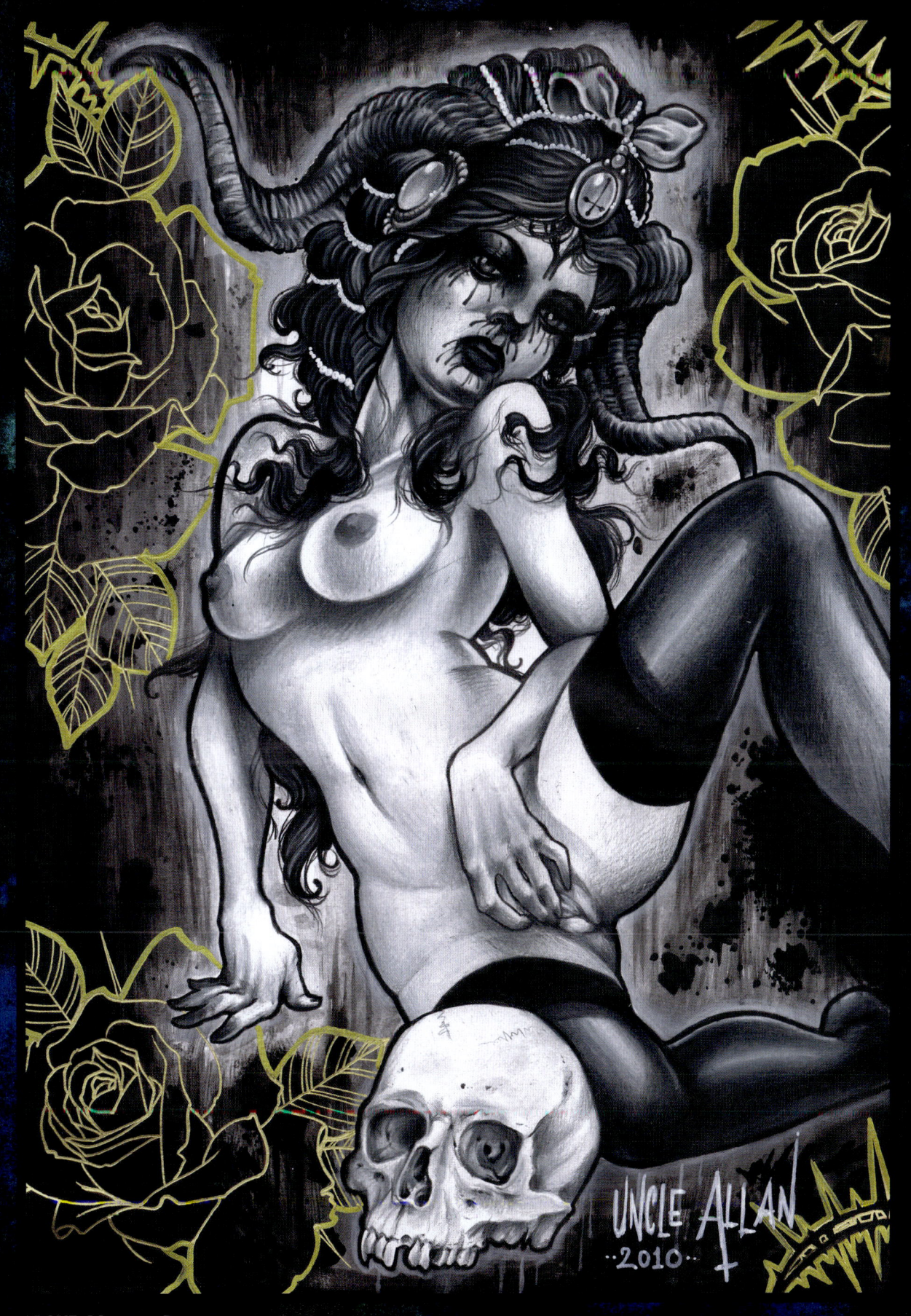

ABOVE: *I Scream*. Pen and ink, watercolour and coloured pencils.
LEFT: Tracings for future artworks. Pencil on tracing paper.

VON LUCKY

ANTWERP, BELGIUM.

"I remember, aged five, sitting at the kitchen table between my dad and a construction worker friend of his. On his forearm was a blurred tattoo, but I could still make out the form of a naked woman. With every move of his arm she seemed to dance and I was mesmerised. That's when my fascination started." Tom decided to take the plunge and become a tattooist in 1994, just after graduating from St Lucas Institute, Antwerp with a masters in illustration. He knew it would be tough, but also that he had to do it the right way, with an apprenticeship. "I knew I had to build up a portfolio. Back then I had a job working in Antwerp harbour during the day. At night I would work my ass off drawing. That lasted about a year. At the time my cousin decided he wanted a cover-up. I suggested Junkfood Johnny in Heerlen, Holland. Every three weeks I would accompany him. It was Johnny who looked at my portfolio and told me to get my ass over to Mickey B in Coventry, England. He taught me loads." Tom then worked with the renowned Daan Verbruggen at Daruma Tattoo, before opening his own shop – Lucky 1 Tattoo – in 2001. "It was a great six years, but then there was trouble with the new landlords, so I had to shut and joined Rubicon Tattoo." Today he splits his time between his private studio and Rubicon. Of his art Tom says: "The stuff I get on commission is usually for bands. I'd love to have more time to paint just for me, but any time gets swallowed by those tattoo commissions." The list of artists that have influenced him "is endless, but includes Dave Lum, Richard Stell, Freddy Corbin, Mike Giant, Dirty Donny, The Pizz and Niagara." Inspiration comes from "Everything! My six-year old son, skateboarding, punk rock, movies and friends." Of the scene he says: "Yeah, it's saturated. There's a lot of talent, but some of the magic has disappeared. Those who are in it only for fame will get weeded out. Those who give it their best shot will survive!"

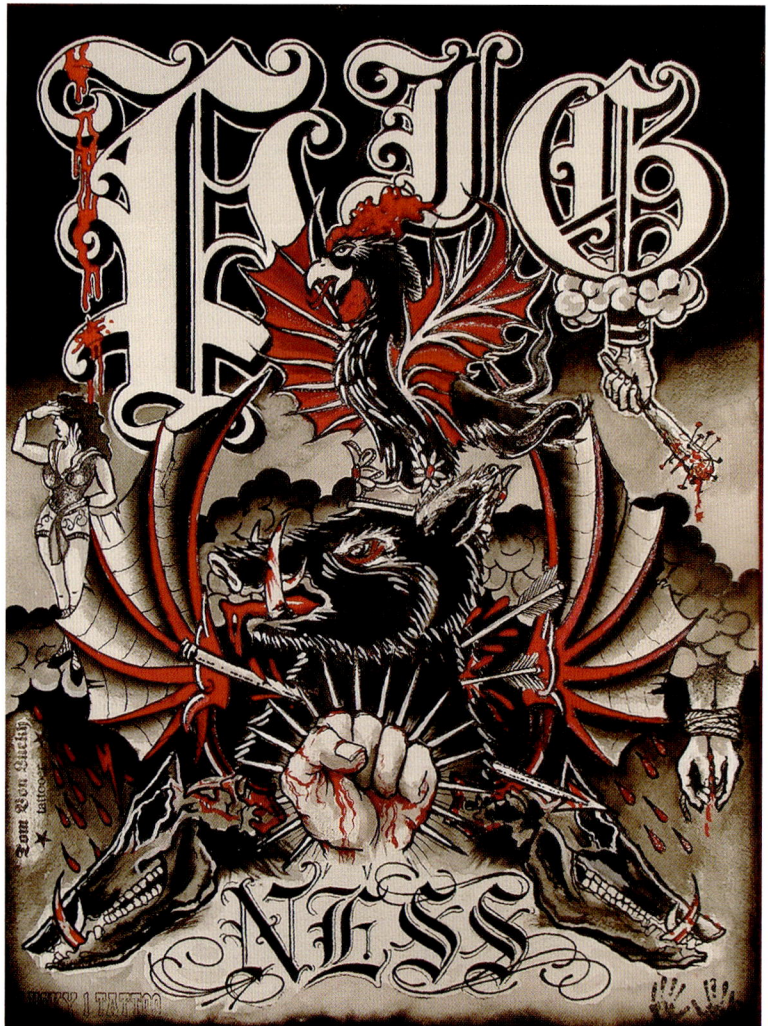

ABOVE: *Pigness*. Pen and ink.
RIGHT: *True Love*. Pen, ink and marker pens.

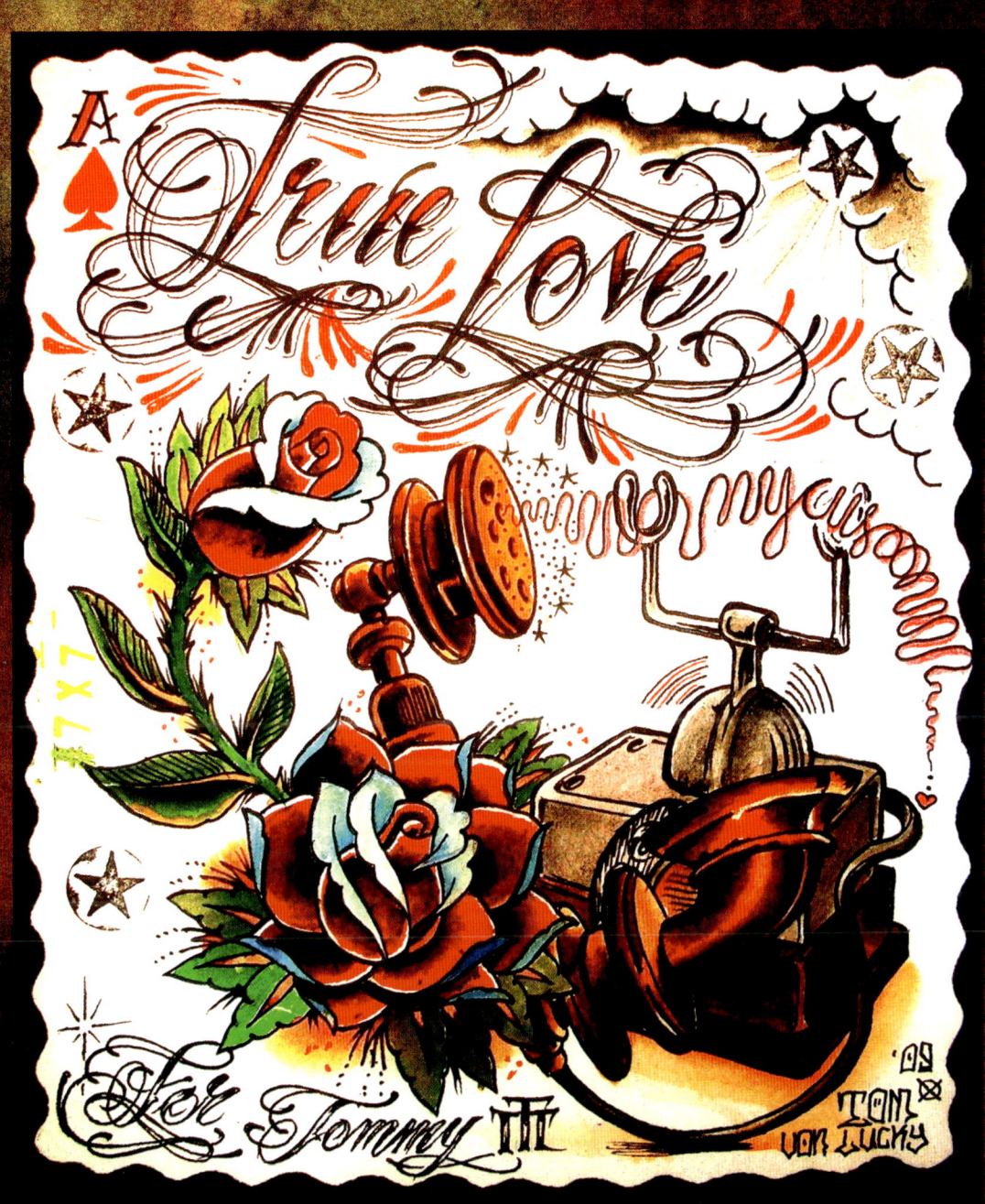

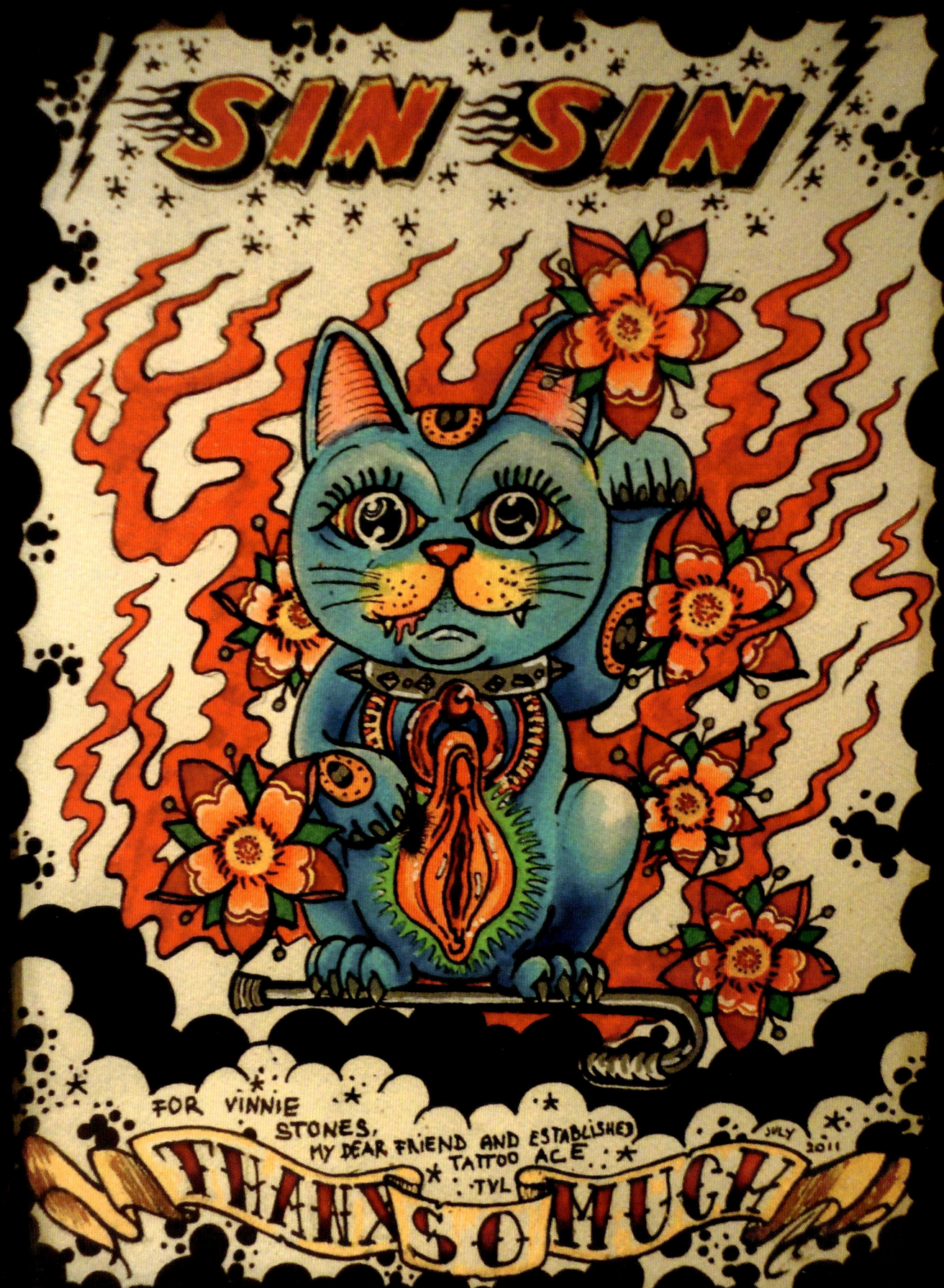

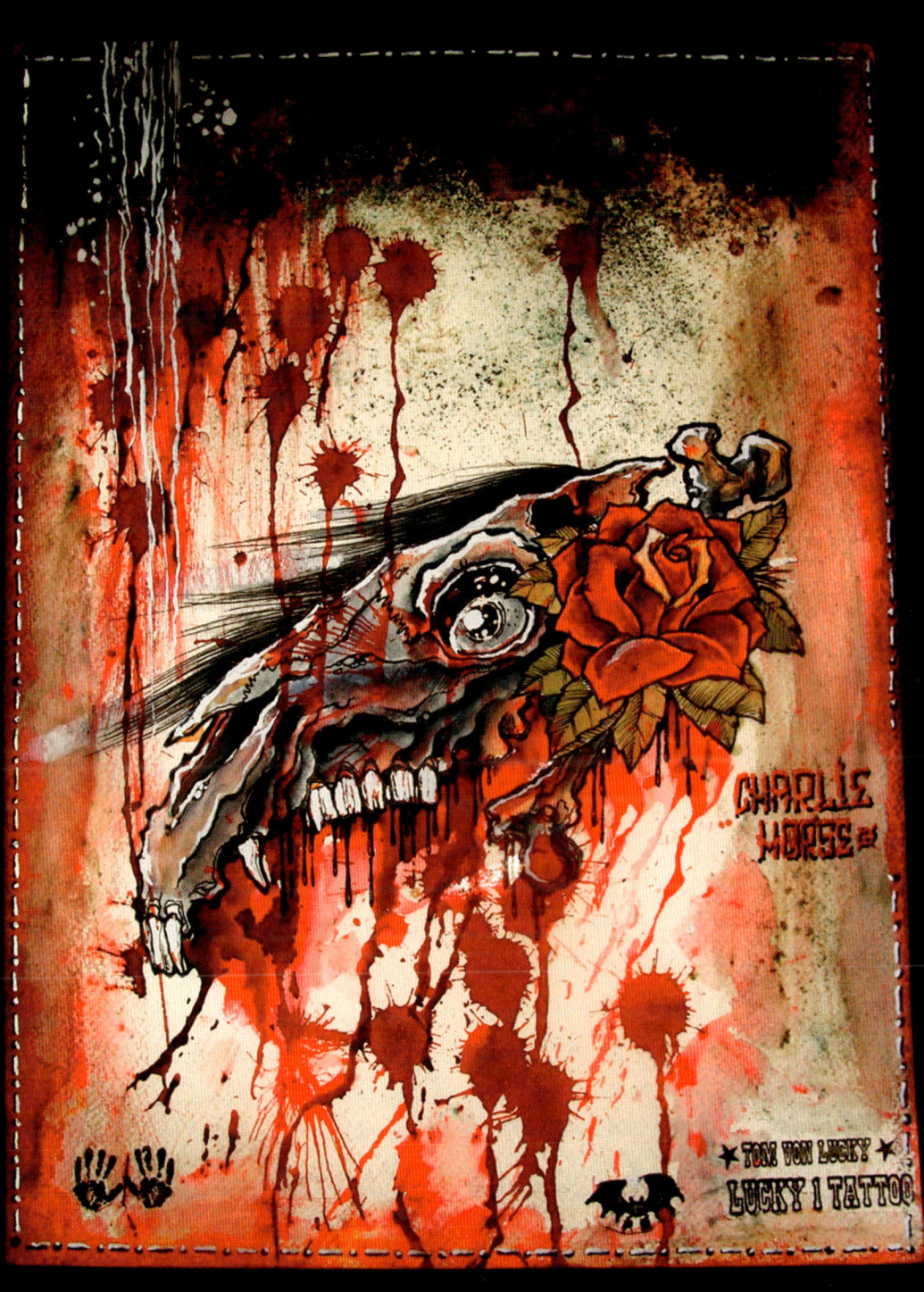

LEFT: *Thanks to Vinne Stones*. Pen, ink and watercolour.
ABOVE: *Charlie Horse*. Pen, ink and watercolour.

WALKIN

LAKE CHARLES LA, USA.

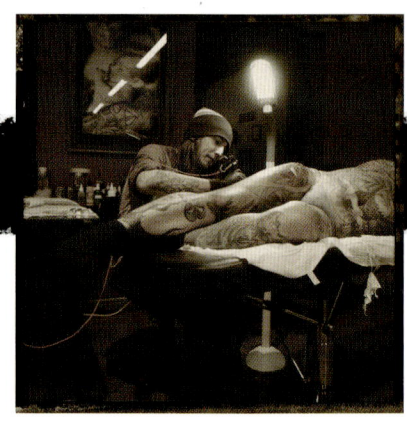

As a kid, Chris Walkin was fascinated by the whole idea of tattoos: "I just loved the concept that you would make art out of such a weird medium." As he got older, his decision to get into the trade was influenced by the fact that it was still a relatively young medium. "I still feel that way about it and love the guys who are really pushing things whilst still applying the tried rules, bending them just enough to grow the artform." He got his mentor early on, but it took a while and lot of pushing to get his apprenticeship with Rickie Ritter of Rickie's Tattoos. "It was good that it was tough…when I started I really had no idea how much there was to learn. There are so many small variable in tattooing that can change results completely…you get humbled a lot finding your way." Today he owns his own shop, with John Davis – Iron Cypress in Lake Charles. Influences are many, including the tattooers he has worked with: "Rickie Ritter of course, Denny Besnard, John Davis and Terry Ribera." Then there are the heroes: Horiyoshi, Filip Leu, Shige, Markus Lenhard, Guy Aitchison, Aaron Cain and Lars Uwe; "Those guys do things that just make me sick!" Inspiration comes from "Everything…. specifically hard music, science fiction, horrible movies, that Euro-Japanese thing that started in Switzerland and Germany and biomech all around." Chris's art influences his tattoo and vice versa. He works mostly in markers and pencil colours, working out how to make his art more tattooable. "I've been trying the digital thing in the past couple of years too, and really see why people dig it." Of the changes in the scene, Chris says: "I miss the kind of voodoo mystery that it had in the '90s, but like the fact there are more great tattooers everywhere I look and new movements all over the place. I try to ignore the silly tv game shows and soap operas. I just keep my head down and focus on what I'm doing…guess I might be getting old!"

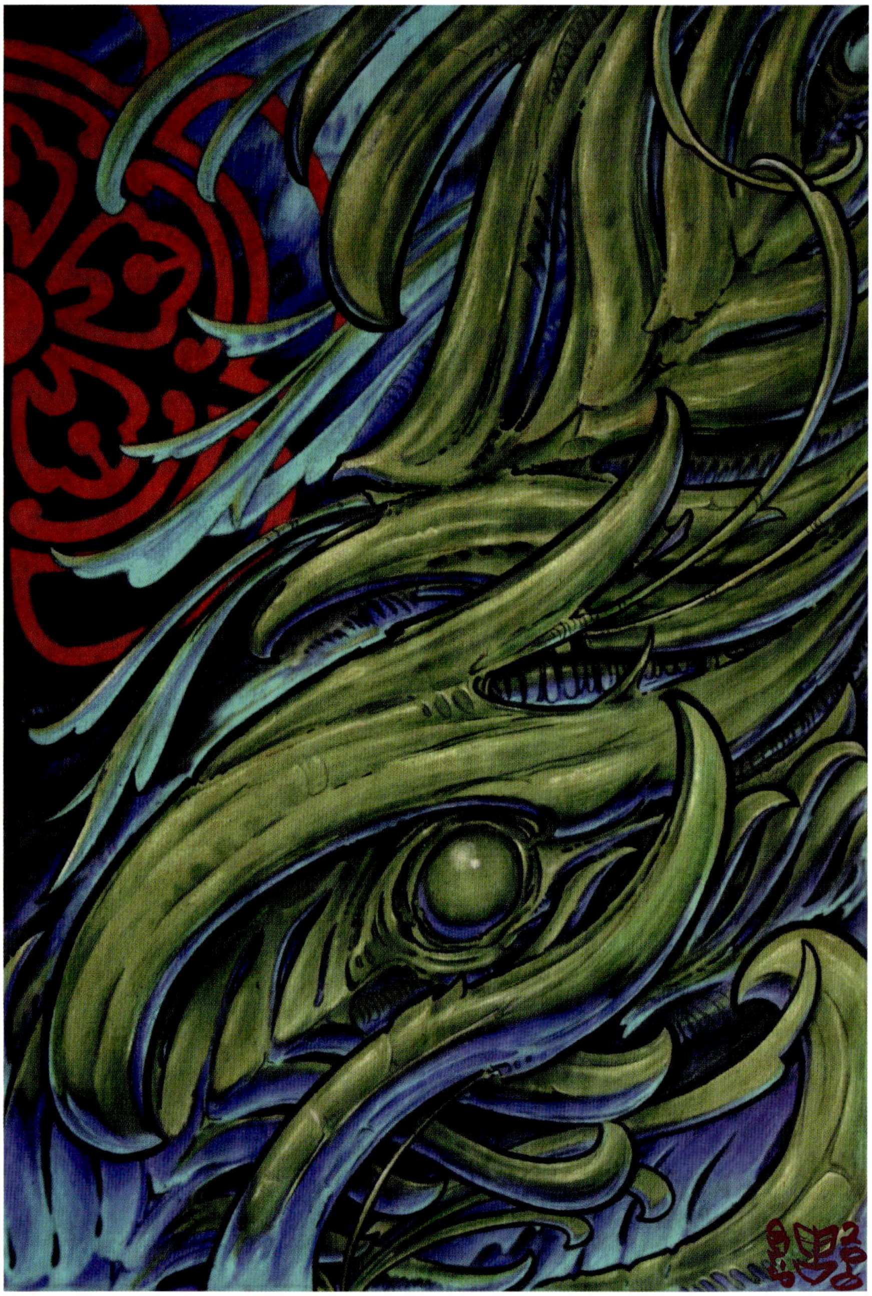

ABOVE: *Bioscape*. Prismacolor pencils on paper.
RIGHT: *Dancing Kappa*. Prismacolor pencils on paper.

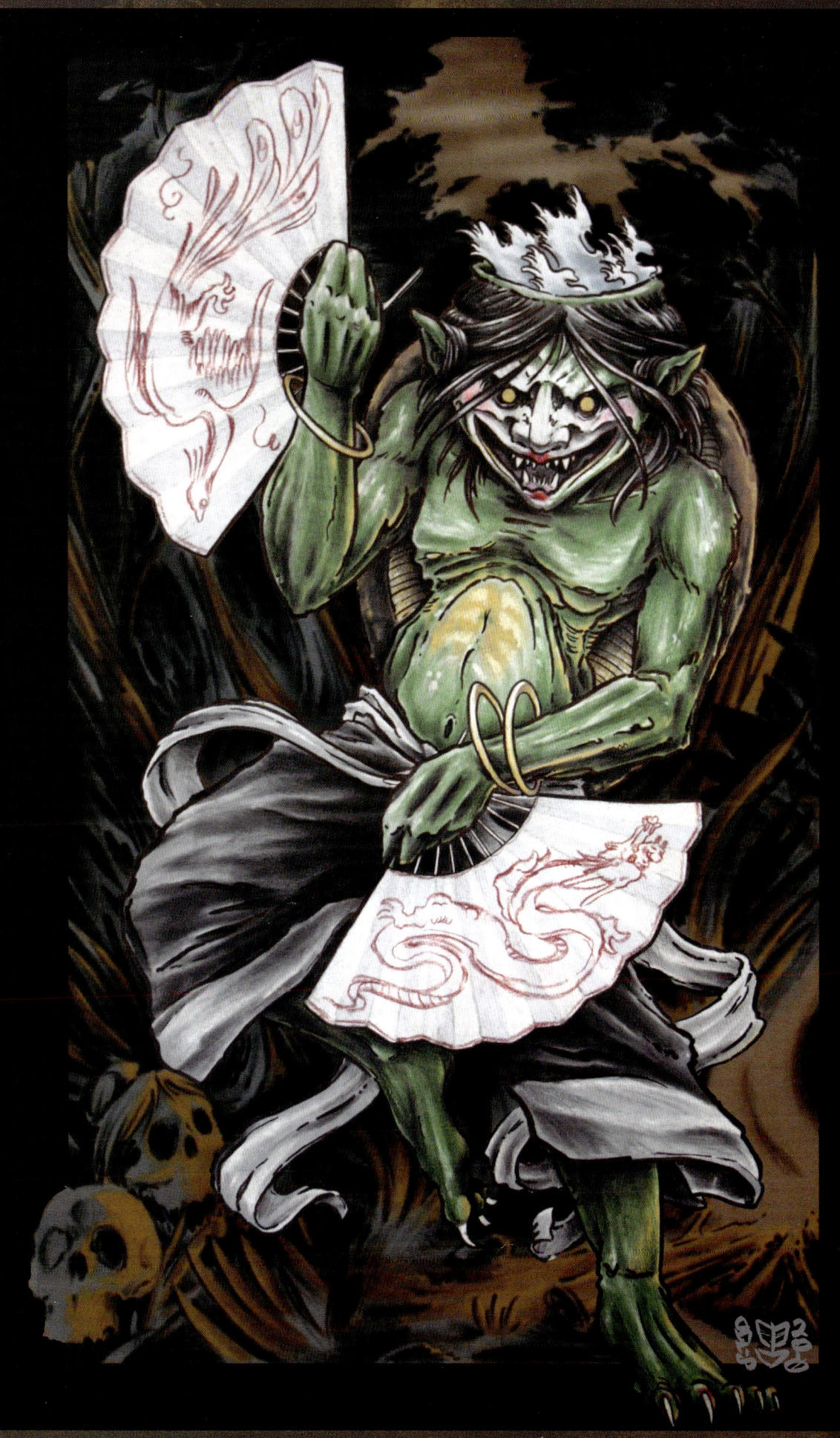

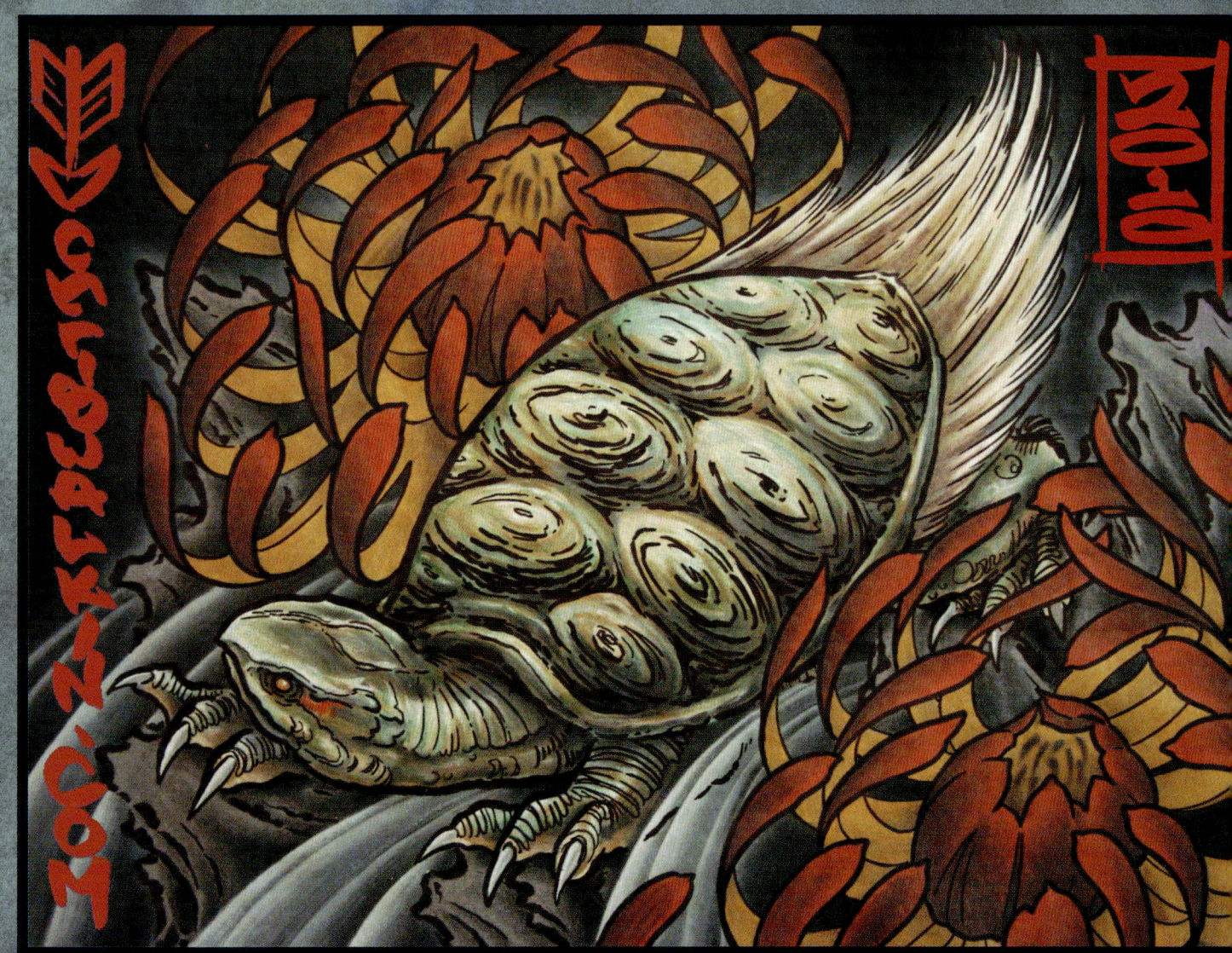

ABOVE: *Minogame*. Prismacolor pencils on paper.
RIGHT: *War Skull*. Prismacolor pencils on paper.

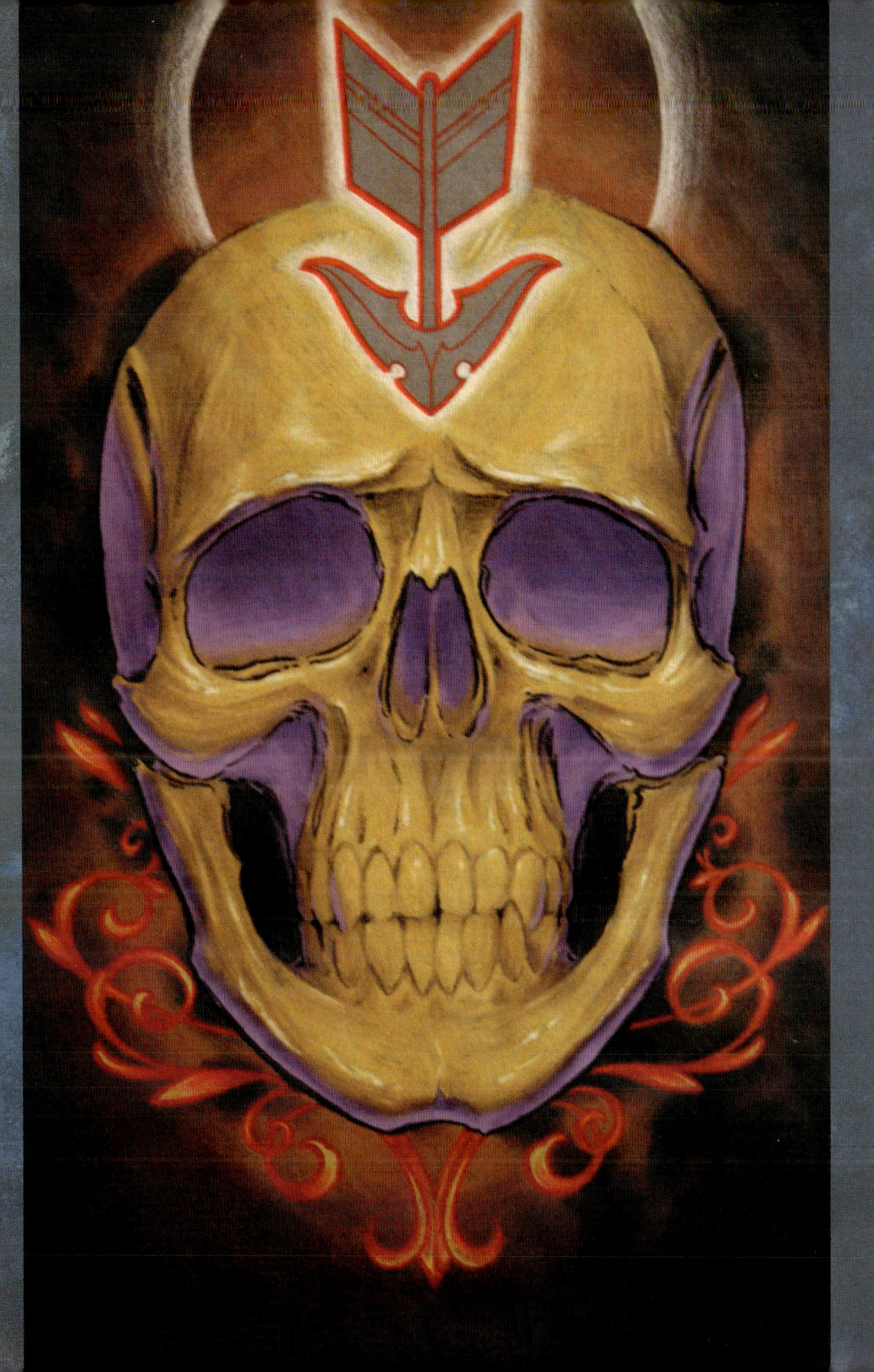

XICO

BRAZIL / LONDON, UK.

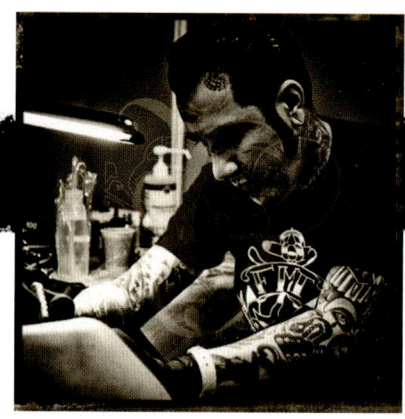

"I always preferred drawing to maths" says Xico "and used to dream of becoming a tattooist." As luck would have it, a punk tattooist came and crashed at Xico's house and a light went on. "I got a tattoo from him, which made me realise how limited his drawing skills were. So I bought his equipment and got started." That was in his native Brazil in about 2000. Xico was living in a favela in a "small wooden house with gaps in the walls that let in the wind and the rain." Equipment and information on techniques was hard to come by. There was much trial and error, practising on his brothers and friends. Xico worked in restaurants to pay the rent. Then he met the artist Sergio Terrakio, who gave him tips, helped fix his machines when they broke down and advised on buying his first 'real' tattoo machine. Six months later Xico had opened his first shop, The Subway Tattoo Bar. He sold up after six months and opened new shops, in Florianopolis and São Paulo, before moving to London where he founded Forever More Tattoo. Xico's biggest influences have been the old school tattooists, from Sailor Jerry to Percy Waters and Mike Malone. He is also fascinated by the Japanese tattoo tradition and the work of Yoshitoshi, Kuniyoshi, Hiroshige, Takashi Kobayashi and Hokusai. More broadly inspiration comes from "Rockabilly, psychobilly, country, punk, Asian movies and horror flicks." He switches techniques depending on whether he wants a traditional American or Japanese look. His art is mostly influenced by tattoo, including a recent piece, *Arm Skin* (a tattooed prosthetic limb) for the Spare Parts show in London. Xico's work has been extensively featured, including in *Tattoo Arte*, *Tattoo Life* and *Skin Deep* magazines. Of the scene he says: "In recent years it's been intense, there are some great new artists and the equipment keeps improving. However I would prefer that tattooing remained an underground art form, as the old school masters would have wished."

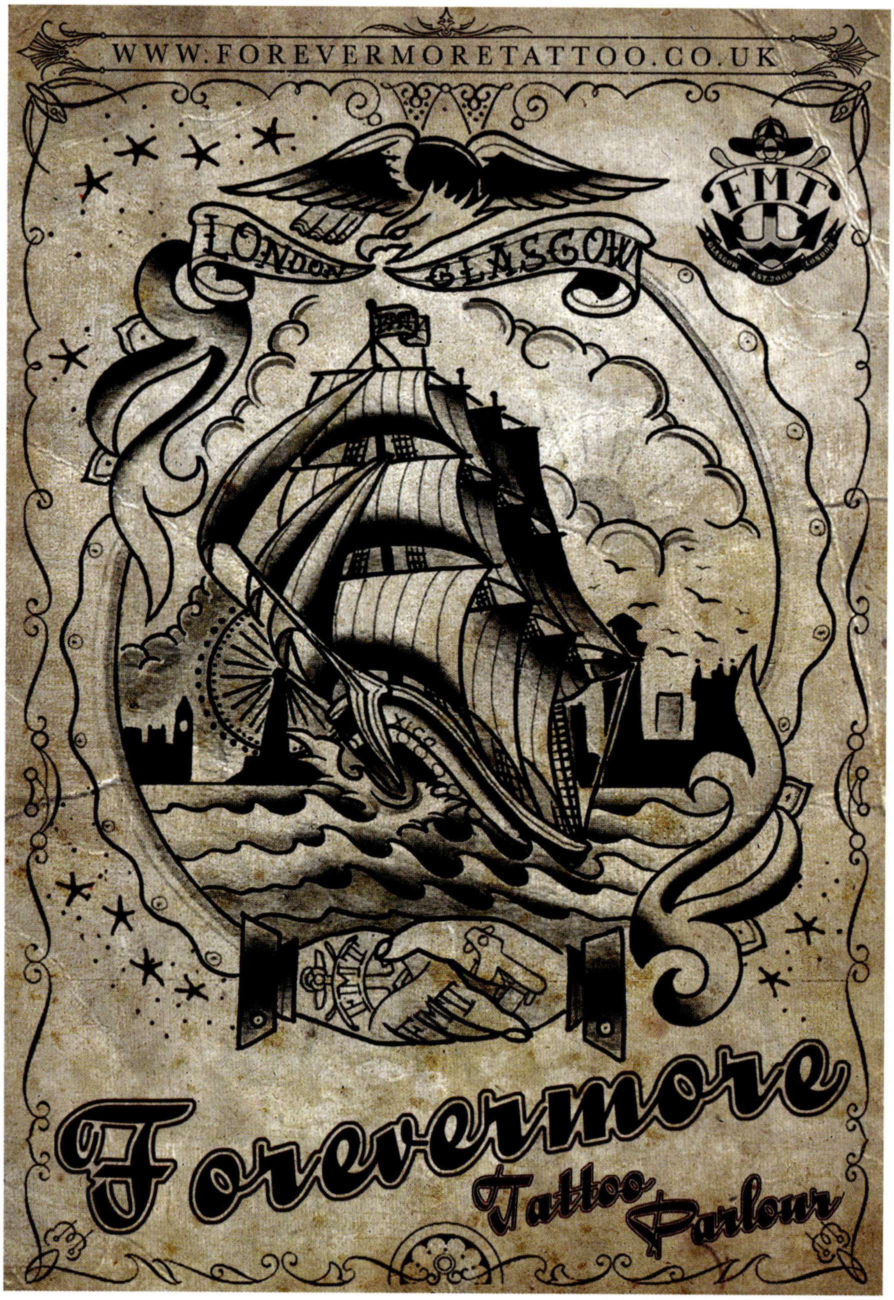

ABOVE: Design for Forevermore Tattoo. Pen and ink.
RIGHT: *Gypsy Lady*. Pen, ink, markers and watercolour.

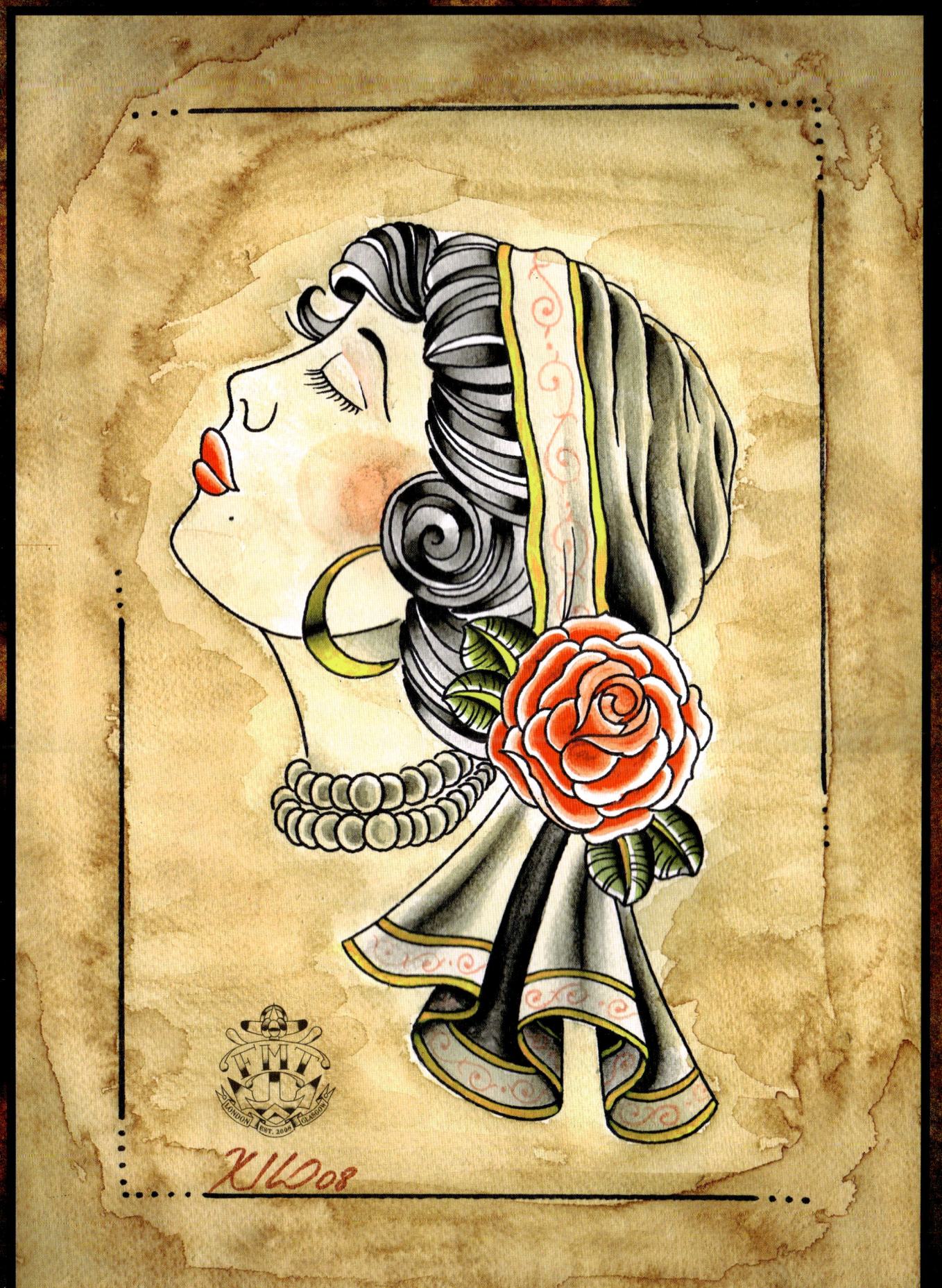

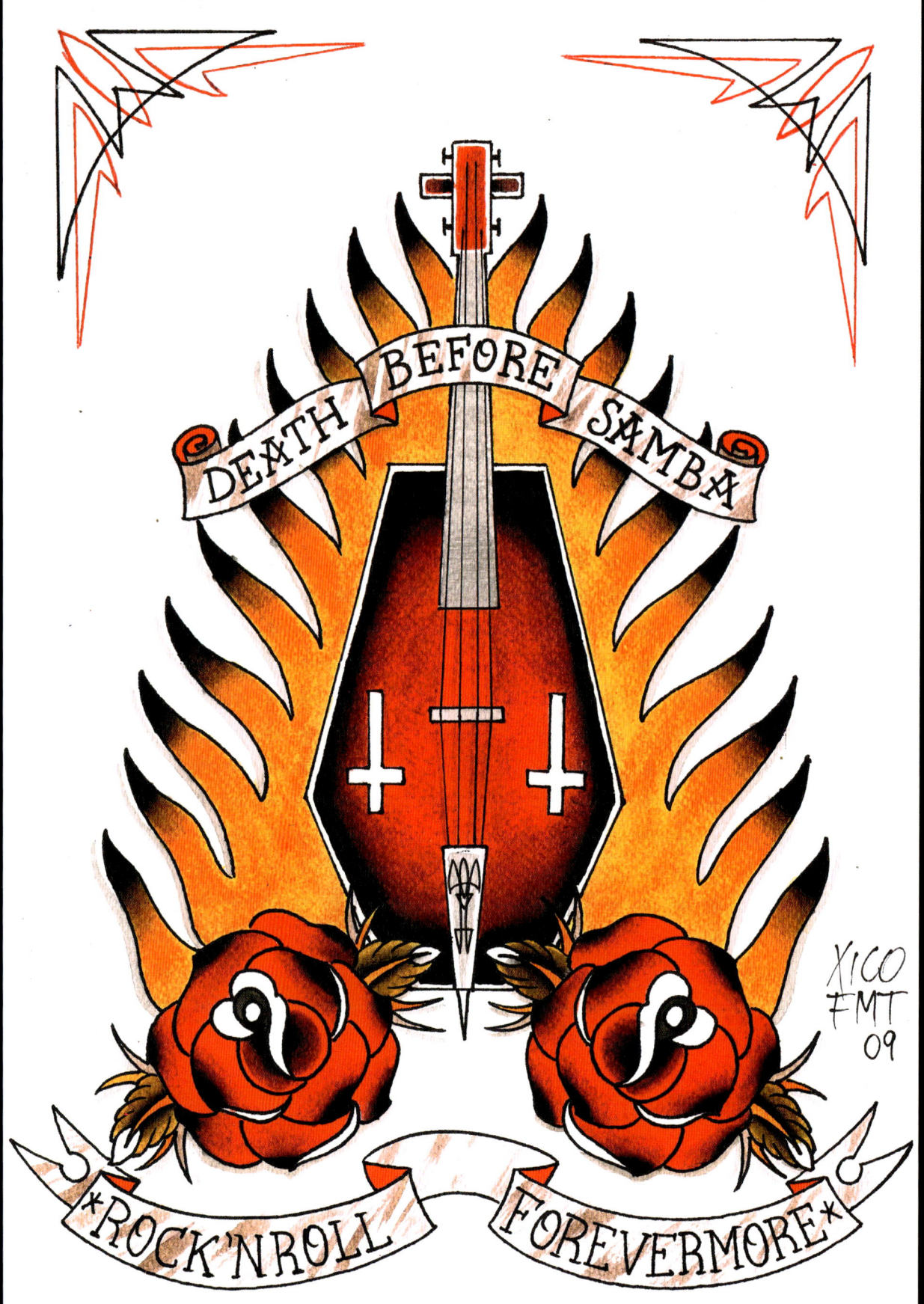

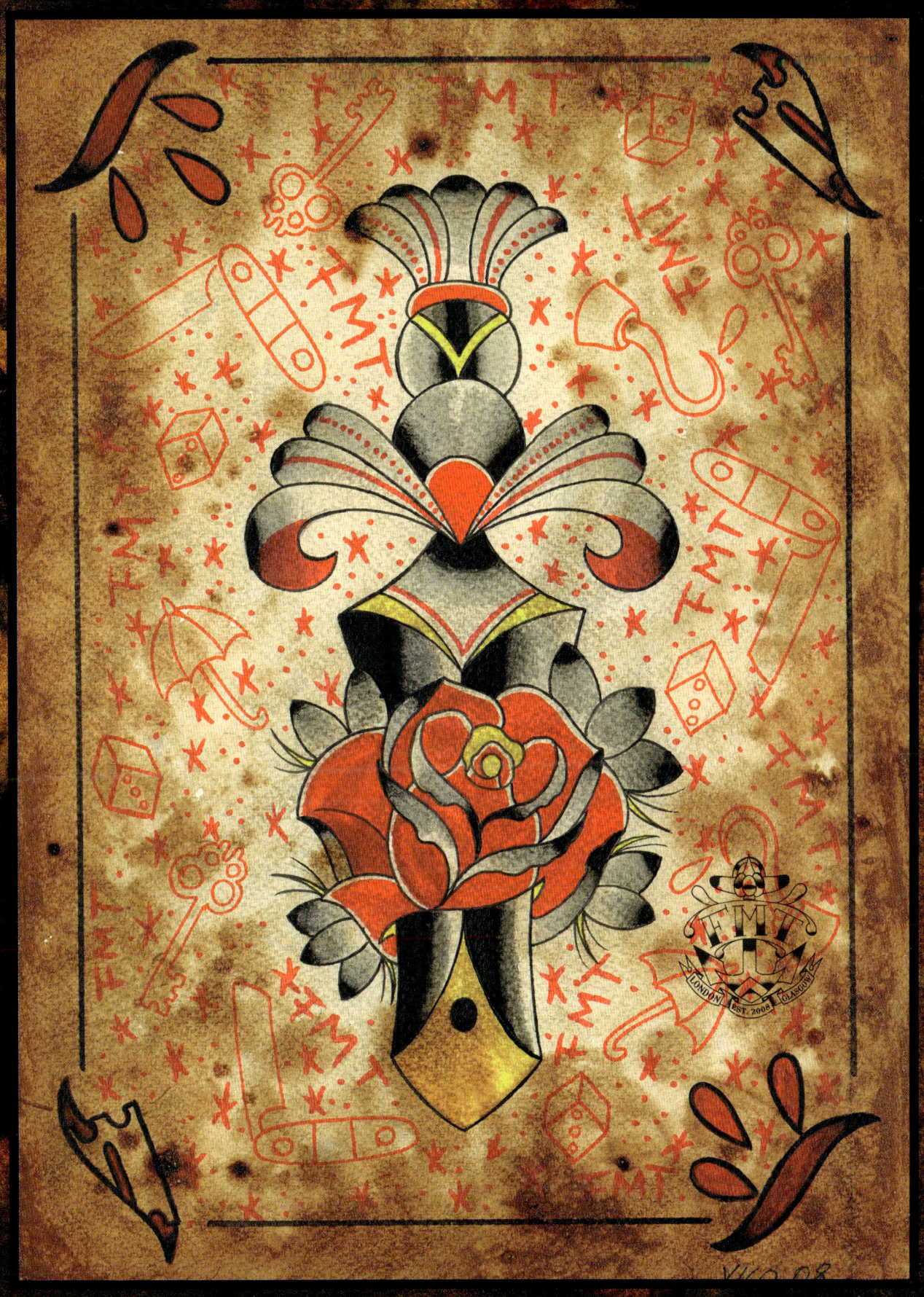

LEFT: *Death Before Samba*. Pen, ink, markers and watercolour.
ABOVE: *Dagger Rose*. Pen, ink, markers and watercolour.

APPENDIX

ARTISTS' CONTACT DETAILS

THE LISTINGS BELOW SHOW:

ARTIST'S TITLE USED IN BEYOND TATTOO

Full name | Country or us state of origin | Now working in | Web/ blog address

ALTED
Inmaculada Alted | Spain | London | inmatattooartist.com

ARIEL 7
Ariel Perez | Argentina | Madrid | tattoomagicmadrid.com

ARMOURED SOUL
Susi Armoured | Spain | Windsor (near Toronto) | armouredsoulwindsor.com

BARTHEZ
Barthez | Bulgaria | Pazardjik | facebook.com/barthez-tattoo

BURLTON
Steven Burlton | Canada | Whitby Ontario | stevenburltontattoos.com

CAMPISE
George Campise | NJ, USA | Berkeley, ca | georgecampise.com

CASTAÑO
Javi Castaño | Spain | Barcelona | barcelonaelectric.blogspot.com

CLARKE
Richie Clarke | UK | Liverpool | forevertruetattoo.co.uk

COLLINS
Adam Collins | UK | London | newwavetattoo.co.uk

CONLON
Patrick Conlon | NY, USA | New York | eastsideinktattoo.com

DAVIS
Mike Davis | OH, USA | San Francisco | everlastingtattoo.com

DE SABE
Claudia de Sabe | Italy | London | claudiadesabe.blogspot.co.uk

DIFA
Matt Difa | UK | London | jolierougestudios.blogspot.com

DU CONGO
Piet du Congo | Belgium | Antwerp | pietducongo.com

EL CARLO
El Carlo | Spain | Barcelona | elcarlotattoos.com

ENFRUNS
Sergi Enfruns | Spain | Barcelona | vilanovatattoogallery.com

GANJI
Ganji | Japan | Tokyo | threetidestattoo.com

GIANT
Mike Giant | NM, USA | San Francisco | mikegiant.com

GAFFRON
Sabine Gaffron | Germany | Zürich / Biel | sabinegaffrontattoo.de

GRAVES
Allan Graves | Transylvania | London | allangraves.net

JOÃO
João Bosco Souza Lima | Brazil | London | thefamilybusinesstattoo.com

JONDIX
Jondix | Spain | Barcelona | holytrauma.com

JØRGENSEN
Henning Jørgensen | Denmark | Helsingør | royaltattoo.com

KEZAM
Toni Kezamone | Spain | Barcelona | barcelonaelectric.blogspot.com

KYLE
Phil Kyle | USA | Brighton | magnumopustattoo.com

MONGA
El Monga Sasturain | Argentina | Barcelona | alohatattoos.com

MONTEZ
Derick Montez | NM, USA | San Francisco | derickmontez.tumblr.com

OLIVE
Scott Olive | USA | Sarasota, FL | scottolive.com

REINKE
Alex 'Kofuu' Reinke | Germany | London | holyfoxtattoos.de

RICO
Rico | Brazil | Iwate, Japan | darumagoya.com

ROBINSON
James Robinson | USA | Brighton | guildedcagetattoostudio.com

ROTOR
Rotor | Spain | Barcelona | lacobranegrashop.com

SENTO
Vicente Sento | Spain | Valencia | myspace.com/sento

SERRA
Tutti Serra | Brazil | London | blackgardentattoo.com

SINNES
Dan Sinnes | Luxembourg | Luxembourg | luxembourg-electric.com

SMITH
Jesse Smith | USA | Richmond, VA | jessesmithtattoos.com

TONELLI
Daniele Tonelli | Italy | London | thefamilybusinesstattoo.com

TURYANSKIY
Oleg Turyanskiy | Russia | Moscow | turyanskiy.com

UNCLE ALLAN
Onkel Allan | Denmark | Berlin | conspiracyinctattoo.blogspot.dk

VON LUCKY
Tom von Lucky | Belgium | Antwerp | facebook.com/lucky1tattoo

WALKIN
Chris Walkin | USA | LakeCharles, LA | chriswalkin.com

XICO
Diogo 'Xico' Melo | Brazil | London | forevermoretattoo.co.uk

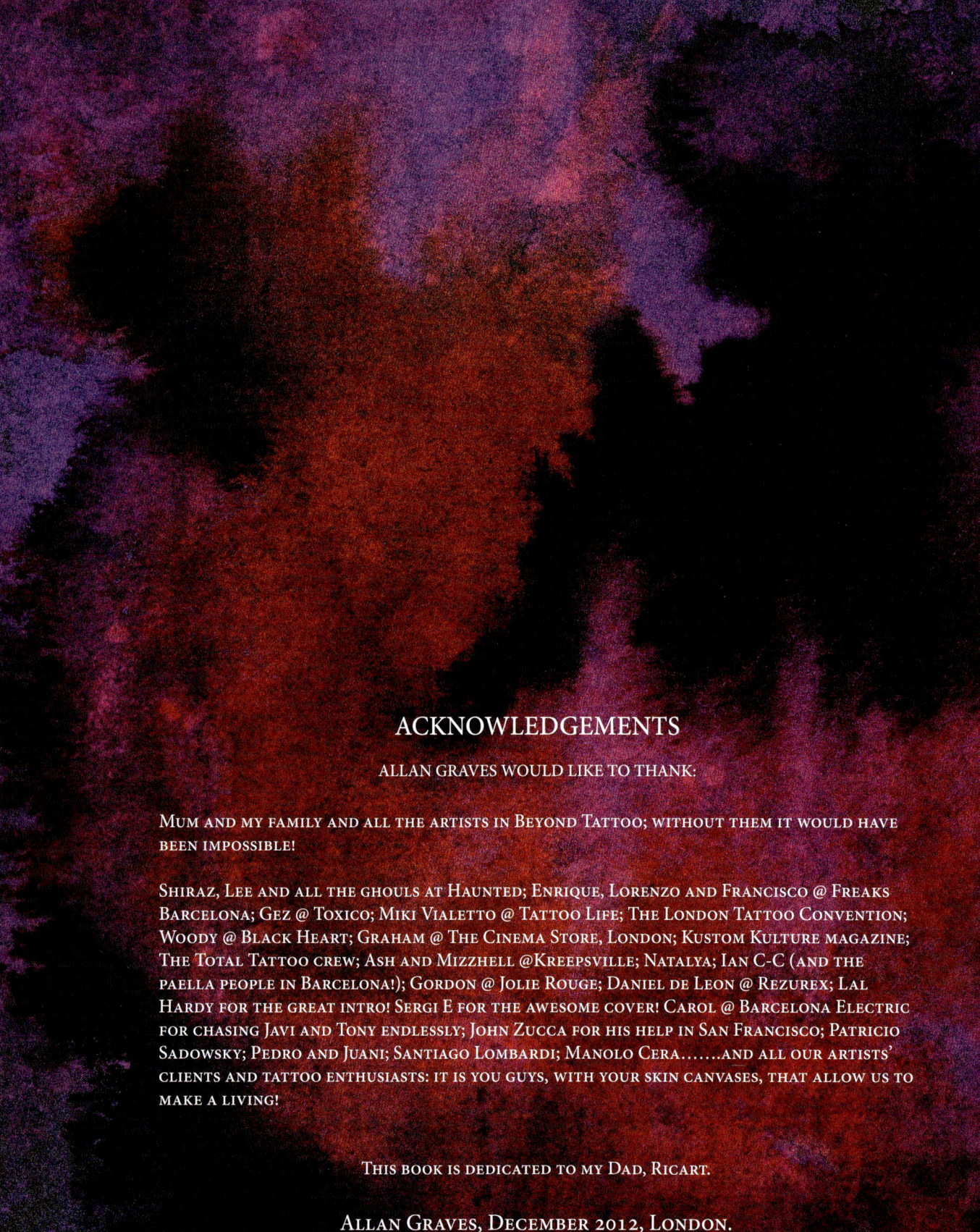

ACKNOWLEDGEMENTS

ALLAN GRAVES WOULD LIKE TO THANK:

Mum and my family and all the artists in Beyond Tattoo; without them it would have been impossible!

Shiraz, Lee and all the ghouls at Haunted; Enrique, Lorenzo and Francisco @ Freaks Barcelona; Gez @ Toxico; Miki Vialetto @ Tattoo Life; The London Tattoo Convention; Woody @ Black Heart; Graham @ The Cinema Store, London; Kustom Kulture magazine; The Total Tattoo crew; Ash and Mizzhell @Kreepsville; Natalya; Ian C-C (and the paella people in Barcelona!); Gordon @ Jolie Rouge; Daniel de Leon @ Rezurex; Lal Hardy for the great intro! Sergi E for the awesome cover! Carol @ Barcelona Electric for chasing Javi and Tony endlessly; John Zucca for his help in San Francisco; Patricio Sadowsky; Pedro and Juani; Santiago Lombardi; Manolo Cera……and all our artists' clients and tattoo enthusiasts: it is you guys, with your skin canvases, that allow us to make a living!

This book is dedicated to my Dad, Ricart.

Allan Graves, December 2012, London.